CW00937641

THE ELITE

OSPREY
PUBLISHING

THE ELITE

THE A–Z OF MODERN SPECIAL OPERATIONS FORCES

LEIGH NEVILLE

OSPREY PUBLISHING
Bloomsbury Publishing Plc
PO Box 883, Oxford, OX1 9PL, UK
1385 Broadway, 5th Floor, New York, NY 10018, USA
E-mail: info@ospreypublishing.com
www.ospreypublishing.com

OSPREY is a trademark of Osprey Publishing Ltd

First published in Great Britain in 2019

A catalogue record for this book is available from the British Library.

ISBN: HB 978 1 4728 2429 5; eBook 978 1 4728 2430 1; ePDF 978 1 4728 2431 8; XML 978 1 4728 2432 5

19 20 21 22 23   10 9 8 7 6 5 4 3 2 1

Index by Alan Rutter
Originated by PDQ Digital Media Solutions, Bungay, UK
Printed and bound in India by Replika Press Private Ltd.

Cover: A Ranger from 1st Battalion, 75th Ranger Regiment, conducts a full mission rehearsal in Afghanistan in preparation for a night combat operation, 22 April 2013. (US Army photo by Spc Ryan S. Debooy)

Title page: Members of Delta Company, 2 Commando, in Uruzgan, September 2010. (Courtesy Commonwealth of Australia, CPL Chris Moore)

Osprey Publishing supports the Woodland Trust, the UK's leading woodland conservation charity.

To find out more about our authors and books visit **www.ospreypublishing.com**. Here you will find extracts, author interviews, details of forthcoming events and the option to sign up for our newsletter.

CONTENTS

INTRODUCTION 8

UNITS 13

WEAPONS 205

INTRODUCTION

Special operations forces (SOF) have been at the forefront of operations around the world since the fateful events of 9/11. Although they trace their ancestry to the Commandos and Rangers of World War II, today's operators exist in a nebulous grey zone of 'operations other than war' with few of the clear-cut objectives (and victories) of conventional warfare.

Modern SOF entered the public imagination with the US Army Special Forces, the famous Green Berets, in Vietnam. The US Navy Sea-Air-And-Land (SEAL) Teams also began their impressive legend in the jungles of South-East Asia. The British Special Air Service (SAS), although long the acknowledged experts in reconnaissance and counter-insurgency in Malaya, Borneo and Oman, became synonymous with the new SOF role of counter-terrorism when the SAS stormed the Iranian Embassy in London in May 1980.

On the other side of the world, in the Iranian desert, an operation by the US counterparts of the SAS ended in tragedy when mechanical problems forced an abort before two of the rescue aircraft collided on a remote airstrip. Operation *Eagle Claw* was an ignominious defeat for the newly fledged Delta Force but one from which great lessons were learned. *Eagle Claw* led directly to the formation of the US Special Operations Command (SOCOM) and the secretive Joint Special Operations Command (JSOC), formed to ensure SOF had the necessary capabilities never again to suffer an *Eagle Claw*.

Throughout the 1980s, Western SOF were deployed to a bewildering number of hot-spots from Chad to Colombia and all points in between conducting counter-terrorism, counter-narcotics, foreign internal defence and special reconnaissance. The 1991 Gulf War saw the Green Berets back in their traditional role, mentoring and acting as liaison for the Arab armies committed to the fragile *Desert Storm* alliance. Delta and the SAS proved their worth against an openly sceptical General Norman Schwarzkopf, hunting Iraqi missiles and keeping Israel out of the war. A few years later, Delta and the Rangers would fight through the infamous Operation *Gothic Serpent* in Mogadishu, thankfully again learning from their experiences in a myriad of ways which would save operators' lives in the wars to come.

Following the 9/11 attacks, the Green Berets were the first soldiers on the ground in Afghanistan, preceded by paramilitaries of the Central Intelligence Agency (CIA). SOF from a huge number of nations rallied to the call and committed forces to the war against al-Qaeda, and by extension, their hosts, the Taliban. With al-Qaeda in disarray, a golden opportunity to withdraw from Afghanistan was missed in 2002.

Instead, SOF and their conventional brethren became embroiled in a 'forever war' that remains the longest campaign ever fought by American forces and one without a clear, communicable objective. What had begun as a targeted campaign against foreign terrorists and their host government became a confused and contradictory effort at nation building.

Meanwhile operations to topple Saddam Hussein's regime following the invasion of Iraq in 2003 saw SOF's political masters take their eye off Afghanistan to focus on Iraq. A stunningly successful ground war, supported and at times spearheaded by SOF, was soon followed by a bloody insurgency that saw an emergent al-Qaeda in Iraq attempt to alight a sectarian civil war. Nonetheless, SOF, and specifically JSOC, born of the *Eagle Claw* debacle, were responsible for all but destroying al-Qaeda in Iraq and a number of nationalist terror groups, including those sponsored by Iran.

The Taliban in Afghanistan had been biding their time with extensive support from elements of the Pakistani government and, in 2006, a vicious insurgency began. Fighting two insurgencies, along with all other strategic responsibilities, put significant strain on Western SOF. Once al-Qaeda in Iraq had been beaten into submission and with the increasing 'Iraq-ization' of the counter-insurgency effort, the focus for SOF returned to Afghanistan.

With a distinct lack of communications infrastructure, which had aided the 'industrial counter-terrorism' effort in Iraq, Afghanistan proved a frustrating but no less deadly campaign. Kill or capture missions to attack enemy leaders and logistical nodes were conducted alongside a counter-insurgency effort to establish local security forces and extend the influence of the central government. How successful both efforts have been is open to question.

In Iraq, the so-called Islamic State erupted, with much of the country falling under its murderous sway. Again, Western SOF returned to Iraq and later to Syria where they worked with Syrian Democratic Forces including their long-time Kurdish allies to destroy Islamic State. Elsewhere, jihadist groups gained prominence throughout Africa and parts of the Pacific. The War on Terror has truly gone global.

Along with direct action (DA), the prototypical SOF mission of striking behind enemy lines, today's operators are increasingly called upon to perform as soldier-spy-diplomats, working in often covert roles, and to train and support local forces in the world's conflict zones. Undeclared war zones like Somalia see SOF both embedding with intervention forces to hunt terrorist targets and mentoring partner units to conduct operations, along with raising local proficiency.

SOF have been the force of choice for many nations thanks to their higher skills, which reduce the number of casualties, and a public expectation that, since SOF are traditionally tasked with only the toughest missions, such casualties when they occur are inevitable. They have been the easy choice for politicians wary of body count reporting. Many SOF missions in Afghanistan and Iraq could, and arguably should, have been conducted by conventional forces. SOF are the politically sensitive choice.

Nearly two decades of constant operations have, however, taken their inevitable toll on the operators themselves. Tragically, suicides of former and serving US special operations personnel peaked in 2018. The psychological damage from the punishing operational tempo has emerged not only as post-traumatic stress but as a brutalization of operators. This has seen members of the United States' Navy storied SEAL Team 6 accused of a range of crimes, from theft and drug use to execution of prisoners and even the murder of a Green Beret in Mali.

Other units have not been left untouched by this malaise. UK Special Forces (UKSF) were the subject of a Royal Military Police investigation into alleged war crimes. Australian SOF have also been implicated in the deaths of prisoners, including the 'blooding' of new operators. The Australian Army has been the only organization to date to launch a wide-ranging inquiry which has resulted in a Federal Police criminal investigation being opened. At the time of writing, both the Army and Federal Police investigations were ongoing.

The Elite aims to be a volume on modern (predominantly post-2000) special operations units, key historical operations and the major weapons systems and vehicles used by special operators around the world. The focus of *The Elite* is to provide brief overviews of conflicts, events and equipment, as space unfortunately prohibits a full history of each and every listing. Much of the older history is covered in other works and *The Elite* is intended to be a relatively modern reference focusing in large part on the post-9/11 world.

Such an undertaking means that, inevitably and unfortunately, some units will be left out owing to space limitations or simply lack of information. Others may not be described as fully as some readers may wish because of operational security restrictions (please note for instance that this book was submitted through the UK's Defence, Press and Broadcasting Advisory Committee for comment on material relating to UKSF). Despite these restrictions, we hope that the book can provide the reader with a modern, easy-to-access, trusted source of information about special operations and their role in an ever more complex world.

A Russian Spetsnaz operator firing the indigenously produced 9x19mm PP-2000 sub machine gun during an exercise in April 2019. The PP-2000 is designed to fire extremely 'hot' 9mm armour piercing ammunition. Here it is seen coupled with an EOTech holographic sight. Note also the use of the Ops Core style helmet and Crye MultiCam copies – increasingly Russian SOF are indistinguishable from their Western counterparts, even using Heckler & Koch rifles (albeit semi-automatic civilian versions) and Glock pistols. B&T MP9 sub machine guns are another recent acquisition. (Photo by Yelena Afonina\TASS via Getty Images)

UNITS

1st New Zealand Special Air Service Regiment (1NZSAS)

Nationality: New Zealander • Branch: Army • Established: 1955

After wartime service with the original SAS and Long Range Desert Group, New Zealand's own Special Air Service (SAS), known internally simply as 'the Unit', was established two years before Australia's SAS Regiment (SASR). It served alongside the British SAS in Malaya in the 1950s and later in Borneo and Vietnam, becoming a highly regarded reconnaissance force that could creep into enemy base areas and silently snatch prisoners, conducting hasty ambushes to deter pursuit.

Unit members later operated in Bosnia providing close personal protection and also in East Timor/Timor Leste in 1999 during the United Nations International Force East Timor (INTERFET) intervention, working with 3 Squadron SASR and a troop of Special Boat Service (SBS) personnel as the multi-national Response Force or RESPFOR. INTERFET was a multinational humanitarian effort lead by the Australian Defence Force to secure the newly independent East Timor/Timor Leste from both Indonesian-supported militias and Indonesian military incursions aimed at terrorising the population. The three NZSAS patrols and 3 Squadron's Air Troop also operated as the Theatre Immediate Reaction Force supported by Australian Army Black Hawks.

The NZSAS again deployed to Timor in 2000 and was involved in several contacts with pro-Indonesian militia illegally crossing into Timor. A key part

Lance Corporal (now Corporal) Willie Apiata of the 1st New Zealand Special Air Service Regiment (seen on the right in this image) became the first recipient of the Victoria Cross for New Zealand when his patrol was attacked at night by a far larger force in Afghanistan, 2004. He saved the life of an injured comrade and took command of the situation to repel the attack. In this image he is seen supporting the Afghan Crisis Mission Unit 222 in Kabul during a Taliban offensive in 2010. Note the 5.56x45mm Colt Canada C8SFW carbines carried and the Crye MultiCam worn by both operators. Apiata's C8SFW features the once standard M4 style carrying handle and a forward mounted Aimpoint optic. The US HMMWV behind them appears to be a later model up-armoured Ground Mobility Vehicle (GMV) variant.
(© Philip Poupin)

NZSAS operators conducting direct action training with their recently issued 5.56x45mm LMT MARS-L carbines fitted with Surefire suppressors and Trijicon ACOG optics. (Courtesy New Zealand Defense Force. CC BY 4.0)

of this later deployment was tracking militias and acting as the anvil to herd them into a rapidly established blocking position manned by infantry accompanied by an SAS liaison. The success of the mission saw a dramatic dip in the number of cross-border incursions by the militia.

NZSAS was heavily committed to Afghanistan after 9/11 under Operation *Concord One* – the code name for New Zealand military deployments to Afghanistan – with squadrons rotating through for four-month tours from December 2001. As with most international units, it was assigned to the US-led Task Force K-Bar and participated in a large number of special reconnaissance missions, particularly into the mountainous east of the country, although its lack of integral vehicles proved to be a disadvantage and forced it to rely upon American helicopter support that was understandably often in short supply.

It also supported Operation *Anaconda* (see pages 320–21) with three patrols that maintained covert observation posts for ten days without compromise by the enemy. By May 2002, the unit had borrowed a number of American DMVs (desert mobility vehicles) 'Dumvees' which enabled it to conduct mounted reconnaissance patrols. These were further modified by the operators when they arrived in Kandahar.

The NZSAS mounted patrols were often spending two to three weeks in the field and conducted direct action missions with US Army Special Forces and Canada's Joint Task Force 2 (JTF2). A number of dirt bikes for route reconnaissance (a technique widely used by both the British and Australian SAS) were borrowed from the German Kommando Spezialkräfte (KSK). Having learned its lesson, NZSAS brought with it its own highly customized Pinzgauer special operations vehicles when it subsequently deployed to Afghanistan in 2005 on Operation *Concord Three*.

Between 2009 and 2012, the NZSAS deployed as Task Force 81 in half-squadron strength to mentor the Afghan 285-man Crisis Response Unit (CRU – Task Force 222) National Mission Unit (NMU) based in Kabul. Although operations were led and conducted by the CRU, 'On occasion, NZSAS personnel are also required to provide specialist enablers. Some examples of this include the British Council rescue where a specialist entry capability proved essential and, in the case of the Intercontinental Hotel, helo [helicopter] sniping was required,' explained a New Zealand Army position paper.

It was on the mission to secure the British Council in Kabul in August of 2011 that the NZSAS suffered its first casualty with an operator killed as it supported the CRU assault on the building, which had been attacked by Taliban insurgents. A month later it suffered its second casualty when an operator was shot and killed while establishing a security cordon around the CRU breaching team during the hunt for a suicide bomber cell.

The unit follows the British SAS practice and is composed of four squadrons; of these, only two are Sabre squadrons, A and B, each of four troop-strength elements. SAS squadrons have been known as Sabre squadrons since World War II, relating to their original reconnaissance role (formerly a cavalry task and named after their sabres). As in the British SAS establishment, there is no C Squadron out of respect for the original C Squadron from the Rhodesian Army SAS. D Squadron is the counter-terrorist squadron while E Squadron provides EOD (explosive ordnance disposal) support, being originally known as the 1st New Zealand Explosive Ordnance Disposal Squadron.

D Squadron was established in 2005 in emulation of the Australian Tactical Assault Groups as the Counter Terrorist Tactical Assault Group (CTTAG). It has since progressed to be its own separate command under 1st New Zealand Special Air Service Regiment (1NZSAS); it is currently known as D Squadron (Commando) and is recruited direct from across the New Zealand Army, involving passing a modified SAS selection.

The unit serves as New Zealand's principal intervention unit both domestically and overseas should New Zealand citizens be taken hostage. Counter-terrorism was formerly one of the roles of A and B Squadrons with a rotational CTT or Counter-Terrorist Team established from 1978 after extensive input from 22SAS and the German Grenzschutzgruppe 9 (GSG9).

The SAS and D and E Squadrons are today under the command of what was originally the Directorate of Special Operations but is now the New Zealand Army Special Operations Command. The SAS itself was initially called the NZSAS Group for much of its existence but was redesignated as the 1st New Zealand Special Air Service Regiment in 2013 after considerable expansion of D and E Squadrons.

Along with the MP5 series, NZSAS has replaced its earlier Diemaco (Colt Canada) C8 SFWs with the newly received New Zealand issue LMT MARS-L carbines. Its SIG-Sauer P226 pistols have been replaced with the

NZSAS soldiers at the conclusion of the siege breaking of the Intercontinental Hotel, Kabul in June 2011. Working alongside the Afghan Crisis Response Unit, NZSAS conducted a breach and clearance operation supported by NZSAS snipers in a US Black Hawk overhead. At least one NZSAS member was wounded by a terrorist detonating a suicide bomb vest at close range. Note the suppressed Diemaco (Colt Canada) C8 SFW carbines. (Pedro Ugarte/AFP/Getty Images)

Glock 17. Vehicles have also received an upgrade with the Pinzgauer giving away to the Supacat Special Operations Vehicle-Mobility Heavy (SOV-MH).

The unit has faced recent criticisms about civilian deaths during NZSAS operations in Afghanistan, particularly during the 2010 Operation *Burnham* alongside the Afghan Task Force 222 or Crisis Response Unit. The allegations relate to the alleged deaths of 21 civilians during night raids on a village, prompted by the death from an insurgent IED (improvised explosive device) of a New Zealand Army officer. Although there has been much media speculation and hyperbole, a detailed New Zealand Army report concluded that the civilian deaths were caused by fire from US helicopters falling short of the target rather than the SAS operators themselves. A further allegation of prisoner mistreatment actually pertained to the Afghan National Directorate of Security (NDS) rather than the SAS.

1st Special Forces Group (1st SFG)

Nationality: US • Branch: Army • Established: 1984

The 1st Special Forces Group (1st SFG), with the Pacific as its area of responsibility, was first activated in 1957, the second modern Special Forces Group after the 10th SFG, which had been created in 1952. Tracing its lineage back to the famous wartime First Special Service Force, 'the Group' served throughout the Vietnam War and had the sad distinction of suffering both the first and last Special Forces casualties in that conflict. Like many of the Green Beret units, it was deactivated after the Vietnam War but re-raised in 1984.

Despite its official area of responsibility, the 1st SFG was deployed in support of the NATO peacekeeping effort in Bosnia and Herzegovina. After 9/11, the Group spearheaded the largely forgotten Operation *Enduring Freedom – Philippines*, conducting foreign internal defence with Filipino SOF battling two regional jihadist groups, the Abu Sayyaf Group (ASG) and the Indonesian Jemaah Islamiyah (JI), in a conflict that continues to this day.

Sadly, the first Green Beret killed in combat in Afghanistan was from 1st Group: Sergeant First Class Nathan Chapman, attached to the CIA's Special Activities Division near Gardez, in the Paktia Province. Forward Operating Base Chapman was named after the Green Beret but unfortunately was later the site of a devastating suicide bomb attack by a double agent that killed seven CIA personnel and a Jordanian officer from their General Intelligence Directorate (see pages 300–301). One of the first casualties outside of Afghanistan in the War on Terror was also from 1st Group; a 1st SFG operator was killed by a terrorist bomb in October 2002 when he was deployed as part of Operation *Enduring Freedom – Philippines*.

A 1st Special Forces Group ODA captain confers with his Philippine Scout Rangers counterpart during foreign internal defence mentoring operations in 2002 during Operation *Enduring Freedom – Philippines*. (David Greedy/ Getty Images)

The 1st Group trained local forces in the Philippines in everything from small unit infantry tactics to in-extremis hostage rescues, a skill that was needed as Abu Sayyaf regularly kidnapped Westerners for ransom. It also conducted counter-insurgency and information operations against the insurgents, as well as running medical clinics and helping with village infrastructure issues. In 2009, two Green Berets from 1st Group were killed by an insurgent IED while providing security for a civil infrastructure project.

The Group was heavily committed to Iraq during the counter-insurgency campaign, conducting both training of Iraqi forces and direct action missions against insurgent high-value targets. The 1st SFG continues to conduct rotational deployments to Afghanistan to this day. It was instrumental in the 2018 defence of Ghazni against a massive Taliban offensive. As a gauge of the battle's ferocity, seven of the ten MRAPs (mine resistant ambush protected vehicles) from which the Operational Detachment Alphas (ODAs) operated were written off by IED, mortar and rocket strikes.

In terms of small arms, the Green Berets of all Special Forces Groups employ the M4A1 SOPMOD Block II along with the Mk17 SCAR as their principal individual weapon. Sidearms include the Glock 19 and the newly introduced M17 and M18 pistols. ODAs will often deploy with a full suite of light and medium machine guns to include the 5.56x45mm Mk46 and the 7.62x51mm Mk48 or the reduced weight 7.62x51mm M240L. Sniper and designated marksman rifles include the M110A1 Compact Semi-Automatic Sniper System and the M2010 bolt-action Enhanced Sniper Rifle.

1st Special Forces Operational Detachment – Delta
Also known as: SFOD-D, Delta Force, Combat Applications Group (CAG), Army Compartmented Element (ACE)

Nationality: US • Branch: Army • Established: 1977

In the late 1970s as Europe struggled against the scourge of international terrorism, President Jimmy Carter queried whether America's military had a similar capability to the Germans with GSG9 or the United Kingdom's SAS. In fact at the time two US Army units were competing to provide that capability – Blue Light, an ad hoc unit drawn from the Green Berets of the 5th SFG, and Delta, a unit fashioned by its hard-charging future leader, Colonel Charlie Beckwith, as a US version of the British SAS.

A third unit, the little-known Detachment A, drawn from the 10th SFG and based in Germany, was also given counter-terrorist responsibilities. Detachment A was primarily, however, a deniable stay-behind unit tasked with conducting sabotage and guerrilla warfare in the event of a Warsaw Pact invasion of Western Europe. Incidentally, many of the period images from the 1970s attributed to Delta are actually of Detachment A soldiers (their

Walther MPK sub machine guns and Walther P5 pistols are distinctive).

Along with serving in Vietnam as commander of Project Delta, a covert reconnaissance unit, Charlie Beckwith had fought in Malaya on exchange with the British SAS, returning to the United States with the goal of forming an SAS-style unit within the American military. Eventually, in 1977, Beckwith was successful and Delta was officially brought into existence with the primary mission of conducting hostage rescue operations to recover US nationals held anywhere in the world. After a six-month training programme, it became fully mission capable, with one squadron established in 1979.

The 1st Special Forces Operational Detachment – Delta (Airborne) was based in a restricted compound deep within Fort Bragg in North Carolina. It was structured, not surprisingly, along SAS lines with three Sabre squadrons (A, B and C), each composed of four 16-man troops. Selected soldiers, primarily but not exclusively from the Rangers and Special Forces, took part in a selection course that was also heavily influenced by the SAS selection process which Beckwith had completed while on exchange with 22SAS.

The 5–10 per cent who typically passed Delta selection then began the Operator Training Course (OTC), a six-month-long introduction to close quarter battle (CQB), covert reconnaissance and hostage rescue. Only at the conclusion of OTC were soldiers designated as Delta Force 'operators'.

A Squadron operators using M113 armoured personnel carriers as transport during operations in Panama, 1989. Note the lack of body armour, and the use of AWS chest rigs and plastic Pro-Tec helmets which would be replaced after Mogadishu. (Bob Pearson/AFP/Getty Images)

A Delta Force Pandur AGMS (Armored Ground Mobility System) seen in northern Syria, June 2017. The Pandurs have been extensively retrofitted and upgraded over the years; notable here is the increased vision port for the driver. Visible on this example is a TOW II anti-tank guided missile system, a field expedient solution to Islamic State suicide car bombs. (Delil Souleiman/AFP/Getty Images)

The term 'operator' has now become common shorthand for any special operations soldier but originally it referred only to Delta soldiers who had passed OTC. Beckwith was looking for a distinctive title for his soldiers and, after dismissing 'operative' as it was already used by the CIA, he settled on 'operator'. Delta itself became known simply as 'the Unit'.

The Unit's first real-world mission would sadly end in disaster. Operation *Eagle Claw* was an ambitious attempt in 1980 to rescue 52 US Embassy staff held captive by Iranian revolutionaries in Tehran. Delta's part in the mission was to conduct an assault on the Embassy to secure the hostages, along with a nearby sports stadium where Navy RH-53 helicopters would land to extract the assaulters and the hostages. Concurrently, Army Rangers would seize an Iranian air force base to allow C-141 Starlifter cargo aircraft to land. The plan called for the RH-53s to fly to the airbase where everyone would board the C-141s for the flight out of Iran. Detachment A even had a role under its own Operation *Storm Cloud*, infiltrating personnel into Tehran for advance force reconnaissance and contributing assaulters to the final mission.

The complex mission was launched but ran into difficulties when one of the RH-53s developed a serious malfunction and had to be abandoned while a second helicopter had to turn back on account of a dust storm. With too few helicopters to insert his Delta assault teams, Beckwith was reluctantly forced to abort the mission. As the helicopters attempted to refuel before exfiltration from Iran, tragedy struck when an RH-53 collided with an EC-130 refuelling aircraft at the forward base called Desert One. Eight Navy and Air Force personnel were killed in the collision and resulting explosion.

Unfortunately Delta's next operation fared little better. As part of the American invasion force to secure medical students on the tiny Caribbean island of Grenada in 1983, a B Squadron raid, supported by Rangers from 1/75, to release political prisoners saw an MH-60A Black Hawk from the then-Task Force 160 – the precursor to the 160th Special Operations Aviation Regiment (see page 53–57) – shot down with its pilot killed and some 16 Delta personnel wounded, after the mission's start time was delayed, giving the defenders advance warning. Other targets frustratingly proved to be 'dry holes'.

During much of the 1980s, Delta operators served in covert roles in Central America and Africa (including a little-known assistance mission in Sudan in 1983 to support a kidnap recovery of two American missionaries) and were forward deployed in response to several terrorist incidents including the *Achille Lauro* cruise ship hijacking in 1985; they even planned but did not execute a joint Delta–SAS mission to recover Western hostages held in Beirut.

There is a long-standing but unconfirmed rumour that the unit was responsible for the 1984 rescue of 79 hostages (including four Americans) on board a hijacked airliner in Curacao. The mission was officially credited to the Venezuelans but former Unit members have hinted to the author that the operation was conducted by Delta. Both criminal hijackers were killed in the assault and all hostages and crew were safely recovered.

The Unit was standing by to assault the hijacked TWA Flight 847 in 1985 with two full squadrons supported by SEAL Team 6 operators and Task Force 160. Frustratingly, they were never given the go-ahead and missed their best opportunity owing to a lack of dedicated air transport. The hostages were then dispersed around Beirut making a successful recovery difficult. Eventually the hostages were released after negotiation and the release of terrorist prisoners from Israeli jails. The mission did result in JSOC and consequently Delta being assigned their own designated Air Force transport aircraft, available 24 hours a day to ensure the unit could respond quickly to any global crises.

In 1987, Delta deployed domestically to Georgia under Operation *Pocket Planner* to support the FBI's Hostage Rescue Team with specialist breaching, communications and intelligence gathering during a prison siege. The siege was eventually lifted through negotiation and the operators were never called upon to support an assault.

In Panama in 1989 as part of the American invasion, A Squadron of the unit conducted a successful hostage rescue of a CIA agent held in Modelo Prison by the Panamanian authorities in Operation *Acid Gambit*. Although the mission was a success, one of the MH-6 Little Birds carrying the assault force away from the target crash-landed, wounding a number of operators and leading to them being exfiltrated by a nearby US Army armoured unit. Delta was also tasked with the capture of Panamanian ruler Manual Noriega and surrounded the fugitive outside the Vatican Embassy from where he eventually emerged after ten days.

Operation *Desert Storm* saw two squadrons deployed to Saudi Arabia to partner with 22SAS on the famous 'Scud Hunt' in the western deserts of Iraq. Delta operators in modified Pinzgauers and HMMWVs (high mobility multi-purpose wheeled vehicles) and the SAS in their 'Pinkie' Land Rovers were key to keeping Israel out of the war by drastically reducing the number of Scud missile launches against Israel and thus maintaining the fragile Arab coalition against Saddam Hussein. Three operators and four flight crew from the 160th Special Operations Aviation Regiment (SOAR) were killed during the exfiltration of a reconnaissance patrol when their MH-60 crashed.

In the 1990s Delta was busier than ever with deployments to Somalia and Colombia. Both were 'man-hunting' operations, the former to capture a Somali warlord and the latter to help track Pablo Escobar, the notorious drug kingpin (who was eventually cornered and killed by Colombian forces trained by Delta). Task Force Ranger in Somalia ended in the battle of 3 and 4 October 1993 with two 160th SOAR helicopters shot down in Mogadishu and the joint Delta and Ranger force fighting their way out of the city.

Delta also operated in the Balkans as part of an international effort to capture war criminals – known as Persons Indicted For War Crimes (PIFWC) – indicted by the International Criminal Tribunal for the former Yugoslavia under Operation *Green Light*. In addition, it worked closely with the CIA, forging a relationship that would continue in the post-9/11 years.

Delta planned a joint operation with SEAL Team 6 and the 160th SOAR to kill or capture Usama bin Laden in 1998 but the mission was cancelled. A second mission was planned the following year with covertly infiltrated Delta operators tasked with laser designating bin Laden's compound for an airstrike. Again the mission was aborted.

After the terrorist attacks on New York and the Pentagon in 2001, Delta deployed to Afghanistan on a commitment that would last for more than a decade and continues to some degree even today. It was involved in the first special operation of the war when B Squadron, reinforced by a troop from A Squadron, conducted a heliborne assault on the residence of Mullah Omar (the leader of the Taliban) outside Kandahar.

Contrary to what was reported at the time, the target was a 'dry hole' and Delta flew out after conducting a sensitive site exploitation (SSE) without a shot being fired, although one MH-47 was damaged as it clipped a wall during the infiltration (the only Delta wounded were caused by a friendly fire incident with a grenade while clearing rooms).

B Squadron conducted mounted reconnaissance patrols in its venerable Pinzgauers, often landing at remote airstrips to conduct a week-long patrol or direct action mission before returning to exfiltrate via MC-130 Combat Talons. It was supported by integral close air support from AH-6 Little Birds flown in on the same aircraft. One of these missions saw a Pinzgauer mounted troop reinforce the Green Berets shepherding future Afghan president Hamid Karzai.

At Tora Bora in December 2001, A Squadron would come frustratingly close to killing bin Laden himself. Elements of the locally recruited Afghan Militia Forces (AMF) double-crossed the Americans and, under the ruse of a cease-fire, helped by the fact

A Delta Force operator in west Baghdad, October 2003. He carries an M4A1 with EOTech optic and Knights Armament QD suppressor. Note the custom-built forward grip incorporating buttons for both his light mount and infrared laser. The 'ZE4' patch is known as a 'zap number' and can be used to identify the operator. (Patrick Baz/AFP/Getty Images)

that Delta had been denied reinforcement to close off all passes out of the mountains, allowed bin Laden and his al-Qaeda loyalists to escape. After Tora Bora, a Delta squadron continued to hunt bin Laden until mid-2002 when it rotated out of Afghanistan to focus on the upcoming invasion of Iraq.

In 2003, Delta operated in western Iraq conducting raiding and harassment operations that pinned down a substantial proportion of the Iraqi Army, stopping it from reinforcing its comrades in the south. During the following insurgency, Delta, along with the British SAS, became the lead allied SOF in the war against al-Qaeda in Iraq and sectarian terror gangs. In fact Delta was given the lead in Iraq while SEAL Team 6 took responsibility for Afghanistan (in a role that would soon see the ever-expanding Ranger Regiment rotating the overall command and control for JSOC forces under Task Force 373 in Afghanistan in 2009).

Delta fought a long and costly campaign but one that ultimately succeeded in breaking the back of al-Qaeda in Iraq and reducing the influence of the Iranian Quds Force, which, amongst other nefarious activities, was shipping deadly explosively formed projectile IEDs to the militias in the south. Sadly Delta lost a significant number of operators over the years in Iraq and suffered many more wounded as it raided multiple targets each night – and eventually in the daylight in Mosul as terrorist leaders turned off their mobile (cell) phones at night, reducing Delta's targeting efforts.

With the reduction of US forces in Iraq following the 'Anbar awakening' in 2005, which saw Sunni militias within the Anbar Province uniting to operate against al-Qaeda, and the eventual handover to Iraqi security forces, Delta along with the Rangers and SEAL Team 6 surged into Afghanistan during 2008. Its operators attempted to replicate their Iraq success but were somewhat stymied by the lack of mobile (cell) phones and other electronic communications used by their adversaries. In 2011 they deployed to Paktika Province in what developed into a two-day operation against a Haqqani Network base area. During the operation, one of the fiercest experienced by Delta in recent years, one operator was killed and a number wounded in a battle that claimed upward of 80 insurgents.

After conducting operations with local partner forces in Central Africa as part of Task Force 27, Delta returned to Iraq in 2014, establishing the Expeditionary Targeting Force (ETF) and heading up efforts to target Islamic State External Operations personnel. Officially, the ETF was created to 'conduct raids of various kinds, seizing places and people, freeing hostages and prisoners of ISIL [Islamic State], and making it such that ISIL has to fear that anywhere, anytime, it may be struck.'

In 2016 the ETF conducted an aerial vehicle interdiction on a convoy of vehicles carrying the second-in-command of Islamic State. When he exited his vehicle with an AK-47 in his hands he was shot and killed by the operators. One ETF operator from Delta has been killed in Iraq, in October 2015, during a joint operation with Kurdish SOF to rescue a large number of Kurdish and Iraqi political prisoners held by Islamic State and due to be executed the following day. A former Secretary of Defense noted in a government press release: 'We have put our Joint Special Operations Command in the lead of countering ISIL's external operations. And we have already achieved very significant results both in reducing the flow of foreign fighters and removing ISIL leaders from the battlefield.'

There is still a small Delta presence in Afghanistan dedicated largely to combating Islamic State – Khorasan (ISIS-K), a branch of the militant Islamic State group which is active in the east of the country, although most special operations are conducted by Rangers and Green Beret ODAs partnered with Afghan special units. Delta has also maintained a small task force in Libya.

This team famously captured an al-Qaeda linked high-value target in a covert snatch in October 2013. The next year it also captured one of the leaders of the militia responsible for the attack on the Benghazi Consulate and CIA outstation (in which two Delta operators from Task Force 27 had actually led a small rescue force to evacuate the remaining Americans) in Operation *Greenbrier River*.

Somewhere in the region of 200 personnel including a Delta squadron have been operating in Syria since 2015. This number is in addition to those operators assigned to the ETF which is believed to be based in northern Iraq with a forward location in Jordan and to conduct kill or capture missions in both Syria and Iraq.

One of its better-known recent operations was the defence of a forward operating base at Deir al-Zour, Syria in February 2018. A small contingent of operators and Rangers was faced with a night-time attack by Russian mercenaries and Iranian-backed Syrian jihadists supported by T72 tanks

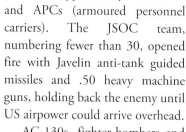

and APCs (armoured personnel carriers). The JSOC team, numbering fewer than 30, opened fire with Javelin anti-tank guided missiles and .50 heavy machine guns, holding back the enemy until US airpower could arrive overhead.

AC-130s, fighter-bombers and armed UAVs (unmanned aerial vehicles) all engaged the Russians and their jihadist allies for a number of hours, targeting both infantry and armoured vehicles. Some 200–300 enemy including a large contingent of Russians from the Wagner private military company

Delta Force operators in Baghdad, April 2004, soon after the building they were raiding was demolished by a suspected BBIED (building-borne IED). Four HMMWVs from National Guard and Army Reserve units parked outside as part of the blocking force were destroyed killing two US servicemen. Note the wounded operator being loaded into an Iraqi ambulance. Although just out of shot, the operator to the left carries the venerable .45ACP Caspian M1911 pistol, which was later replaced by the .40S&W Glock 22. (Marwan Naamani/AFP/Getty Images)

were killed. Incredibly not a single operator or Ranger was wounded despite coming under prolonged mortar and artillery fire.

Delta has expanded greatly over the years and now operates four Sabre squadrons – A, B, C and D – along with Echo Squadron which flies low-signature or deniable aircraft for the unit and G Squadron, formerly the Operational Support Troop, which employs both male and female operators to conduct undercover reconnaissance and advanced force operations. Each Sabre squadron also has its own complement of four combat assault dogs with specially trained handlers. It is equipped with low-light video cameras and body armour that are drawn from the Combat Support Squadron, which also maintains the unit's capabilities in heavy breaching, EOD and counter-WMD (weapons of mass destruction).

2nd Commando Regiment (2 Commando)

Nationality: Australian • Branch: Army • Established: 1997

The 2nd Commando Regiment (2 Commando) was initially raised as 4RAR or the 4th Battalion of the Royal Australian Regiment, transitioning from an infantry battalion to the commando role in 1997 as an expansion of Australia's SOF, which up until that point were provided solely by the SASR.

The unit would begin life as an elite raiding unit with similar capabilities to the US Army Rangers, along with providing a second counter-terrorist intervention unit for the Australian Army, Tactical Assault Group – East (the first such unit was based with and manned by SASR on the west coast in Perth). The then-4RAR deployed in support of operations in East Timor in 1999 and members were amongst the first on the ground to secure Dili Airport with the SASR.

2 Commando is currently composed of four commando companies, an operational support company and headquarters and training companies. It is part of Australian Special Operations Command (SOCOMD), first raised in 2002, which comprises the SASR, two light infantry battalions – 1st (Reserve) and 2nd Commando Regiments – and the Special Operations Engineer Regiment (SOER).

The regiment deployed along with SASR to Iraq in 2003 as part of the Australian Special Forces Task Group (SFTG) or Task Force 64, providing a Quick Reaction Force known as Alert Force for the SASR, along with a combat search and rescue capability in the western desert. Its first deployment to Afghanistan was in 2005 under Australia's contribution, Operation *Falconer*, in another joint SFTG with SASR. The Commandos, 56 strong, were involved in numerous special reconnaissance and direct action missions although rivalries developed with SASR as the Commandos felt they sometimes 'played second fiddle' to the operators.

A 2 Commando soldier mentoring the Philippines Joint Special Operations Group conducts CQB training in September 2017. The soldier carries a Heckler & Koch HK416A5, which were initially purchased for the 2 Commando-based Tactical Assault Group – East but were withdrawn because of difficulties procuring new barrels. (Courtesy US Army photo by Staff Sgt Kwadwo Frimpong)

In Afghanistan, each SASR squadron and Commando platoon or company would deploy for six months with a similarly rotating complement of Royal Australian Air Force personnel flying two CH-47 Chinooks in support. During its second rotation in January 2006 the mortar platoon often accompanied SASR patrols to provide an organic fires capability. By April, the Commandos had finally had their first major contact with the enemy in a village called Kakarak where the insurgents were less than 30 metres away. It also included a memorable duel between a Taliban RPG gunner and a young Commando with a Carl Gustav M2 84mm.

The unit's third rotation was composed of two platoons from D Company with 3 Squadron of SASR. While the Commandos worked closely with the Dutch Task Group Viper from the Korps Commandotroepen (KCT), they later also partnered up with Canada's JTF2 and the Afghan Commandos they were mentoring to capture or kill a Taliban leader known as Objective Nile who was believed to have a six-man bodyguard team with him at all times. Unfortunately, the intelligence failed to register that he was in the area to conduct a Shura (meeting) and around 200 insurgents surrounded the target area.

Landed in the two Australian Chinooks, the JTF2 assaulters used an explosive charge to breach the compound and a close quarter firefight developed. The targeted Taliban leader was killed with an RPG in his hands. As they cleared the compound, enemy reinforcements began closing in and JTF2 snipers took to the compound roof to hold them off. An Afghan Commando was killed and three other friendlies wounded including an attached CIA Special Activities Division (SAD) operator.

While an AC-130 was vectored in to thin the ranks of the insurgents converging on the objective, the Australian Commandos, who had been standing by with their vehicles as an Immediate Reaction Force, raced toward the firefight. In four SRVs (surveillance and reconnaissance vehicles), unarmoured Land Rovers bristling with machine guns, and three Bushmaster protected mobility vehicles, the Commandos managed to fight their way into the compound and linked up with the JTF2 operators.

ABOVE Force Element Bravo
drawn from Alpha Company
of 2 Commando conducting
a mounted patrol in Land
Rover 110-based SRVs
in Uruzgan Province,
Afghanistan, 2007. (Courtesy
Commonwealth of Australia,
Leading Aircraftman Rodney
Welch)

LEFT Tactical Assault Group
– East operators storm a
terrorist stronghold during
a 2006 exercise. Note the
Aimpoint-equipped Heckler
& Koch MP5A3s which have
since been largely replaced
by M4A1s and, for a brief
time, the HK416. The vehicle
is a heavily modified Toyota
Land Cruiser. (Courtesy
Commonwealth of Australia,
Leading Aircraftman Rodney
Welch)

The Canadians, Australians and Afghan Commandos attempted to suppress enemy firing points as the two lumbering Australian Chinooks returned and landed under fire to extract the Canadians and their Afghan charges. Two RPGs barely missed the helicopters as they took to the sky, doorguns blazing. The Australian Commandos now had to contend with the insurgents on their own. With enemy fire from all directions, the platoon grimly fought its way out, dealing with a bogged SRV and a Bushmaster that was so damaged it eventually had to be towed. But incredibly all of the Commandos got out in one piece. In the wake of the battle, some of the open hostility from SASR perhaps thawed.

Members of Delta Company, 2 Commando, in Uruzgan, September 2010. Note the now-outlawed 'Punisher' patches. The soldiers carry an assortment of M4A1 carbines and a Minimi Para (F89) and one carries a slung Javelin anti-tank guided missile. In the background is a Bushmaster protected mobility vehicle sporting a Kongsberg remote weapon station. (Courtesy Commonwealth of Australia, CPL Chris Moore)

The Commandos again deployed to Afghanistan as part of the Special Operations Task Group (SOTG) in 2007. With an Australian Army Reconstruction Task Force (RTF) also deployed in Uruzgan Province, the SOTG conducted shaping and force protection missions in support of the RTF, clearing the immediate area around the base at Tarin Kowt of insurgents to allow the RTF to do its job.

The SOTG was also committed to an increasing number of missions for both the American Operation *Enduring Freedom – Afghanistan* and NATO's International Security Assistance Force (ISAF), seeing the Australian Commandos operating widely across southern Afghanistan. Most of its missions, however, were tasked directly by ISAF Regional Command South.

The 2007 deployment was also different in that there was a much smaller SASR element and a company-sized Commando element, divided into two separate Force Elements, Alpha (SASR) and Bravo (Commandos). Increasingly Force Element Bravo was conducting independent operations, often mounted patrols lasting weeks to deny the enemy freedom of movement around Uruzgan.

In June 2010, the Commandos launched on Operation *Tevara Sin VII*, a reconnaissance in force into the Shah Wali Kot Valley, a known insurgent sanctuary. After infiltration by American helicopters, the Australians were immediately in contact with large numbers of enemy and remained so for hours, fighting off numerous enemy attempts to encircle them.

Meanwhile SASR struck a Taliban high-value target in the village of Tizak, also in the Shah Wali Kot. Unknown to SASR, the village was now a staging area for insurgents preparing to attack the Commandos in the valley with a resulting battle that entered the history books. In 2013, the Commandos and SASR both received the distinction of a battle honour for the Eastern Shah Wali Kot in recognition of the offensive operations conducted in the Shah Wali Kot Valley.

On further deployments, the IED threat increased substantially until it became difficult to launch vehicle-mounted patrols and the Commandos began to rely more upon aviation support, both from the overworked Australian Chinooks and from a range of American aviation units. This ended in tragedy not once but twice for the Commandos, first when three Commandos were killed in a US Army Black Hawk crash in June 2010 and again in August 2012 when two Commandos were killed in a second helicopter crash involving a Marine Corps CH-53.

Increasingly 2 Commando was employed in kill or capture missions. Until recently beaten by Canada's JTF2 in Iraq, two snipers from 2 Commando held the world record for the longest range sniper kill during such an operation in Kajaki, Helmand Province in 2012. Using .50 Barrett M82A1 anti-materiel rifles, both men engaged and killed an insurgent commander at a distance of 2,815 metres.

The last 2 Commando and SOTG rotation to Afghanistan ended in December 2013. Twelve had lost their lives and several hundred were wounded over the nine years of deployments. The unit's experiences in Afghanistan had seen it develop from a raiding and blocking force for SASR to an outstanding SOF that equals SASR in many areas.

Its sister unit, 1 Commando, was also involved in compound clearances and, in February 2009, a firefight erupted in a village in the Sorkh Morghab region. Taking AK-47 fire from inside a building, fire was returned and two fragmentation grenades lobbed through the window. Along with the gunman, five children were unfortunately killed. Incredibly, the Australian Director of Military Prosecutions subsequently charged the two Commandos with manslaughter along with lesser charges for those in their chain of command. Thankfully the charges were later dismissed.

2 Commando has since returned to Iraq making up most of the original 200-man SOTG rotation in 2014, which has worked closely with the Iraqi

1st SOF Brigade. The SOTG has since been reduced to around eight operators but the Commandos have accompanied Iraqi Special Operations Forces (ISOF) into the field on a number of occasions to act as combat air controllers to manage close air support for the Iraqi operators, including during the battle for Mosul in 2004.

The Commandos are armed principally with Colt M4A1 carbines known in Australian service as the M4A5. A number of HK417s are also used, both as marksman/sniper weapons and for building clearance. Sidearms are the Heckler & Koch USP (universal self-loading pistol) and the regular Australian Army issue Browning. Commando sniper teams use the HK417, the SR-25, the Blaser R93 Tactical 2 and the Barrett M82A1. For the counter-terrorist role, both the MP5 series and the M4A5 are employed. Some 130 HK416s were purchased but have since been largely retired as acquiring replacement parts including barrels proved increasingly problematic.

3rd Special Forces Group (3rd SFG)

Nationality: US • Branch: Army • Established: 1990

The 3rd Special Forces Group (3rd SFG), based at Fort Bragg, North Carolina, was first raised during the early 1960s and served in Vietnam. Although it was originally intended for service in the Middle East and Africa – something reflected in its language and cultural training focus that was to be of little use in South-East Asia. It did however conduct numerous training team deployments and was influential on the eventual structure of the Jordanian and Iraqi Special Forces.

'The Group' was disbanded in the post-Vietnam drawdowns only to be reactivated in 1990 as the frail new post-Cold War world demanded ever more Green Berets, specifically to conduct foreign internal defence with allied nations, a key tasking which continues today. ODAs deployed under Operation *Desert Storm* to conduct special reconnaissance missions along the Kuwaiti border. ODAs from 1st Battalion were the first to secure the US Embassy in Kuwait along with a contingent of SEALs in fast attack vehicles.

The Group was also instrumental in creating the African Crisis Response Initiative, which trained African armies for regional peacekeeping operations, an experience that would give 3rd Group an advantage later in Afghanistan and Iraq. 3rd Group also ran one of the earliest military assistance missions to Sierra Leone in 1997 under Operation *Noble Obelisk*.

The 1st Battalion of the 3rd SFG deployed to Afghanistan as part of Task Force K-Bar in 2001 and later to Iraq with the 3rd Battalion as part of Operation *Viking Hammer* in 2003 working with the 10th Group and the Kurdish Peshmerga. A number of 3rd Group ODAs were instrumental in the

battle of Debecka Pass in 2003 where the Green Berets successfully stopped an Iraqi armoured attack using their newly acquired Javelin anti-tank missiles.

The Group continued to rotate through both Afghanistan and Iraq for much of the 2000s, focused principally on foreign internal defence with local forces. Later in Afghanistan, it was heavily involved, as were virtually all SFGs, in the village stability operations (VSO) initiative (see pages 322–23), attempting to implement the 'inkblot' counter-insurgency strategy. The 'inkblot' strategy aims to develop small 'inkblots' of security providing increased infrastructure and economic advantage. The theory aims for these 'inkblots' to grow and eventually link up like inkblots on a page as the influence of the insurgents is blotted out. The Group also conducted direct action missions including a famous 2008 attempt to kill or capture Gulbuddin Hekmatyar in Operation *Commando Wrath*. Although ultimately unsuccessful, ten operators from the Group were awarded Silver Stars for bravery in face of heavy and sustained enemy fire, with the combat medic Staff Sergeant Ronald J. Shurer's subsequently upgraded to a Medal of Honor.

Recently, 3rd Group has been heavily committed to Africa, leading training teams across the region. In October 2017, four 3rd Group soldiers were ambushed and killed during a partnered reconnaissance mission in Niger (see pages 344–45). Just over a year later, 3rd Group ODAs were back in Afghanistan, losing two members and several critically wounded in an IED attack on their RG-33 MRAP (mine resistant ambush protected vehicle).

Operators from 3rd Special Forces Group practise a direct action assault from a USAF CV-22 Osprey tilt-rotor. The lead soldier carries an M4A1 with 261mm (10.3 inch) barrel and Aimpoint optic. (Courtesy USAF by Staff Sgt Clayton Cupit)

5th Special Forces Group (5th SFG)

Nationality: US • Branch: Army • Established: 1961

The 5th Special Forces Group (5th SFG) is perhaps the most storied Green Beret unit in post-9/11, modern history. Today its operators are known as the 'Horse Soldiers' from their early efforts in Afghanistan to topple the Taliban while riding Afghan ponies. However, the unit has a long and distinguished history of duty in almost every modern theatre of war. After serving with distinction in Vietnam, and providing many of the operators for the covert MACV-SOG (Military Assistance Command Vietnam – Studies & Observations Group, otherwise known as Special Operations Group: a covert SOF task force that conducted a wide range of reconnaissance and direct action missions during the Vietnam War and the predecessor to SOCOM and JSOC), the 5th was also instrumental in the Coalition victory over Saddam Hussein's forces in Operation *Desert Storm* in 1991.

With an area of responsibility of the Middle East and thus already possessing the necessary language skills, the 5th Group was assigned a number of vital roles. It established the Coalition Warfare Support Team (CWST) concept, a variant on the traditional Special Forces role of foreign internal

5th Special Forces Group operators pictured in a commercial non-standard vehicle in Deir Ezzor, Syria in September 2018. They carry suppressed SOPMOD Block II M4A1 carbines. (Delil Souleiman/AFP/Getty Images)

defence, and embedded operators across Coalition armies from the likes of Egypt, Kuwait and Saudi Arabia.

A total of 106 of these CWSTs from 5th Group were attached to every Arab battalion in the Coalition, acting as the vital glue to keep the fragile alliance together. ODAs were also tasked with the reconstitution of the Kuwaiti Army as a viable fighting force and eventually led them into Kuwait City.

Along with the foreign internal defence mission, the 5th SFG was tasked with both mounted and dismounted special reconnaissance. For the mounted role, the operators utilized their DMVs (desert mobility vehicles), which were desert specification HMMWVs. Indeed 5th Group was the only SFG to have such a fleet of organic vehicles that had been modified for its specific needs. It was, at the time, also the only SFG to have conducted specific desert mobility training.

Following *Desert Storm*, 5th Group ODAs deployed to Somalia in a rural counter-insurgency role and later conducted operations in Bosnia and Kosovo. Their ODAs were the first Special Forces 'boots on the ground' in Afghanistan and provided guidance for Coalition airstrikes while serving as advisers to the Northern Alliance, one of the largest anti-Taliban groups. 'The Group' was deployed to Iraq in 2003 as part of Task Force Dagger (Combined Joint Special Operations Task Force – West) where it conducted special reconnaissance missions and hunted mobile Scud launchers.

The 5th SFG has been a constant presence in both Afghanistan and Iraq conducting mentoring and carrying out direct action missions. It also provided much of the manpower for Task Force 17 in Iraq, the dedicated counter-Iranian influence unit working for JSOC. Today, the 5th Group is again heavily committed to Iraq and Syria and was among the first of the American forces on the ground in northern Syria.

5th Special Forces Regiment (5th SFR)

Nationality: Slovakian • Branch: Army • Established: 1994

The 5th Special Forces Regiment (5th SFR) is Slovakia's primary special operations and counter-terrorist force. Its roles include reconnaissance and observation (direct action), foreign internal defence such as strike action and military assistance, support to law enforcement in terrorist cases, provision of specialists (supporting conventional units with technical skills) and anti-terrorist operations. It reports directly to the General Staff as an equal to Land Forces and Air Force command.

The regiment is composed of four platoon-strength operational elements along with a specialist support company, which provides the unit's combat divers, snipers and anti-tank capability. The operational platoons, known as

A soldier from the 5th Special Forces Regiment's Slovak Special Operations Advisory Team fires his 7.62x39mm Vz.58 at a range in Afghanistan, 2014. Unusually the Vz.58 has not been modernized with Picatinny rails as is a standard feature of Slovak weapons. Note what appears to be a SIG-Sauer P226 pistol, also an unusual choice as soldiers typically carry Glocks or the issue CZ P-09. The grip has been replaced with a Crimson Trace CTC featuring an integral laser. (Courtesy NATO, US Army Master Sgt Felix Figueroa)

the combat element, are composed of four 12-man detachments modelled on the American ODA principle. The unit also maintains a training platoon, signal platoon and medical section.

The unit had been confirmed as certified to serve as part of the special operations component of the NATO Very High Readiness Joint Task Force. The unit deployed three 20-man Special Operations Task Units in both 2011 and 2012 to Afghanistan as part of Task Force 10 to mentor Afghan Provincial Response Companies and later deployed a larger Special Operations Task Group in 2014. Under Operation *Resolute Support*, Slovak Special Operations Advisory Teams (SOATs) have deployed to train the Afghan Commandos, including helping to run the Afghan Commando Qualification Course.

On the domestic side, the Lynx Commando, the Unit of Special Assignment or UOU, raised in 1996 with the motto 'Impossible does not exist', conducts high-risk raids and counter-terrorist interventions for the Ministry of the Interior. Along with intervention, UOU provides close personal protection and has deployed to the Slovakian Embassy in Baghdad.

Weapons used by the 5th SFR include railed versions of the issue Vz.58, which were standard issue; HK416s, which were subsequently purchased and were issued for the Afghanistan deployments; suppressed Heckler & Koch UMP sub machine guns; Accuracy International AW sniper rifles; and Glock pistols. Lynx employs the MP5 series, G36K carbines, Steyr SSG 3000 sniper rifles and Glock sidearms. Lynx operators are distinctive as they wear the Ulbricht helmet with ballistic visor pioneered by Germany's GSG9.

7th Special Forces Group (7th SFG)

Nationality: US • Branch: Army • Established: 1960

The 7th Special Forces Group (7th SFG) has the geographic area of responsibility for Central and Southern America. After service in Vietnam, 'the Group' was responsible for the training of many SOF groups in countries such as El Salvador and Colombia which still show the influence of ODA organization. During the 1980s, the 7th SFG was at the forefront of assisting numerous countries in Central America battling insurgencies, including the FARC (Revolutionary Armed Forces of Colombia – People's Army) in Colombia.

As the nexus of 'narco' gangs and insurgents became increasingly obvious (the first of what would later be termed 'Dark Networks'), 7th SFG established training teams with police and military counter-narcotics units, for instance with the Colombian Special Anti-Drug Brigade, often accompanying its charges into the fields during raids on cocaine-processing sites. The 3rd Battalion also operated as Task Force Black in Operation *Just Cause* in Panama in 1989.

The unit first deployed to Afghanistan in 2002 and operated for a number of years in rotational deployments with the 7th SFG as the core element of Combined Joint Special Operations Task Force – Afghanistan. It was further deployed during the village stability operations (VSO) initiative (see pages 322–23). It also acted as liaison and advisers for the El Salvadorian deployment to Iraq while continuing deployments to Afghanistan and Central America.

The Group was the lead SOF component for Operation *Willing Spirit*, the effort to secure the release of three American contractors held by the FARC since 2003; this resulted in the Colombian-led Operation *Jaque* (Checkmate), which

A 7th Special Forces Group soldier overcomes adversity using his bionic prosthesis to grip his SODMOD Block II M4A1 fitted with Aimpoint NCOS-N optic. (Courtesy US Army by Staff Sgt Christopher Schmiett)

successfully secured the release of the Americans as well as 15 other hostages. It continues to conduct training team missions with a large number of Central American nations. In a recent US government press release, a Colombian officer noted the positive operational impact: 'Every time we do an operation we do better with the training and the assistance that the detachments give us.'

10th Special Forces Group (10th SFG)

Nationality: US • Branch: Army • Established: 1952

The 10th Special Forces Group (10th SFG) is the oldest continually serving SFG in the US Army. Originally tasked with Europe as its area of responsibility, 10th Group has operated in all corners of the globe. In the 1960s, while 5th Group was heavily committed to Vietnam, 10th SFG began training SOFs in the Middle East, beginning long relationships with units in Jordan, Iraq and Turkey and with Kurdish irregulars in Iran, a relationship that would pay dividends over 40 years later.

During the 1970s it prepared for conventional war with the Warsaw Pact countries in Europe. Drawn mainly from the 10th was Detachment A, a classified unit with a secret mission to fight behind enemy lines should the unthinkable occur. 10th Group was also responsible for caching weapons and

10th Special Forces Group operators assigned to Task Force Viking in northern Iraq in April 2003. Note the GMV mounting Browning M2 .50 with day/night optic and M224 60mm lightweight mortar. (Patrick Barth/Getty Images)

equipment for use by Detachment A and other friendly forces who were tasked to stay behind after a Warsaw Pact offensive. The 10th also trained in the use of the fabled 'backpack nuke', in fact the SADM or special atomic demolition munition, which was intended as the final option to slow a Warsaw Pact advance.

In 2003 it was the main force for the invasion of Iraq from the north with Combined Joint Special Operations Task Force – North, or Task Force Viking. With Turkey refusing to cooperate, the 10th Group flew directly into the Kurdish-controlled north from their staging area in Romania. With no Turkish basing, close air support was up to 90 minutes away. Viking, planned as a supporting effort to a massive conventional airborne operation, suddenly became the main effort.

Task Force Viking managed to briefly unite two rival Kurdish factions to assist them. At the same time, the ODAs had to ensure that the Kurds did not advance too far, too quickly, as Turkey was fearful of the declaration of an independent Kurdish state post hostilities. The 'warrior-diplomats' of the Green Berets had their work cut out for them. Along with contending with Iraqi forces, 10th Group conducted an assault on an Ansar al-Islam encampment complete with crude chemical warfare laboratory.

It was reinforced by the 173rd Airborne, who parachuted into the Kurdish zone and managed to tie up the majority of Iraqi forces to the north, ensuring they could not move to reinforce units in the south fighting against the three-pronged Coalition assault. By mid-April, Viking had recaptured Kirkuk and Mosul.

The 10th Group, despite its European language and cultural training, has become the key special operations force supporting Operation *Enduring Freedom – Trans Sahara* (now called Operation *Juniper Shield*), conducting advise and assist activities with countries including Chad, Mali, Niger, Nigeria and Senegal.

22nd Special Air Service Regiment (22SAS)

Nationality: UK • Branch: Army • Established: 1941

The Special Air Service (SAS), known within the unit simply as 'the Regiment', is the world's most well-known and emulated special operations unit. Conceived in the western desert in World War II, the unit has come to epitomize the very concept of special forces. The SAS was actually disbanded at the end of the war (in common with many other SOF units) but was re-raised in 1952 after the Territorial 21SAS was first established in 1947, and would go on to conduct formative operations in Malaya during the Emergency (1948–60; a counter-insurgency campaign against the communist insurgency of the Malayan National Liberation Army. The Emergency was also one of the first counter-insurgency campaigns to be widely considered a success).

UK Special Forces, likely 22SAS, seen at Borough Market, London, following the June 2017 terrorist attack. They had very publicly arrived via an unmarked AS365N3 Dolphin helicopter which landed directly on the nearby London Bridge. This soldier's night vision goggles appear to be the PVS-15 and his helmet features what seems to be an FX Simunitions mask which protects his identity whilst also guarding against flying debris. UKSF breachers have also been seen wearing the Ops-Core Special Operations Tactical Respirator filtration mask which filters out almost 100 per cent of airborne particles caused by the likes of explosive breaches. (Chris J Ratcliffe/AFP/Getty Images)

The modern 22nd Special Air Service Regiment (22SAS) came to mass public recognition in May 1980 during Operation *Nimrod* at the Iranian Embassy siege in London. The Regiment was back in action a mere two years later, however, as part of Operation *Corporate*, the British Task Force to retake the Falkland Islands from the Argentines. The SAS conducted a range of activities and was instrumental, along with its sister unit the SBS, in the successful recapture of the islands. D Squadron conducted a dismounted attack on an Argentine airstrip in clear echoes of its wartime forefathers, destroying 11 aircraft and decimating the Argentine Air Force and Naval Aviation's small fleet of ground attack aircraft. The Regiment also suffered its greatest losses since World War II during the Falklands campaign when 20 operators from D and G Squadrons died while cross-decking in a Sea King helicopter from HMS *Hermes* to HMS *Intrepid*.

The unit had been given responsibility for counter-terrorism since 1972 and served for decades conducting counter-terrorist operations in Northern Ireland. The SAS typically deployed 'the Ulster Troop' which provided a special forces capability for both the British Army and the security services. Over the years, particularly in the late 1970s and late 1980s, the Regiment was involved in numerous operations against the Provisional Irish Republican Army (PIRA), sometimes interdicting terrorist plots in motion, at others staking out terrorist arms caches.

In 1988, the unit was involved in its most controversial incident, Operation *Flavius* in Gibraltar. Called in to assist the Security Service (MI5) with the apprehension of a PIRA cell planning a terrorist bombing, the team, deployed from the stand-by counter-terrorist Pagoda Team, was deployed to trail the terrorists. When one appeared to make a suspicious movement, the operators opened fire with their concealed Browning pistols, quickly and efficiently killing all three in seconds. Although all three were in fact unarmed, a number of AK-47s and 60 kilograms of plastic explosive were later recovered.

The Regiment famously deployed on Operation *Granby* in 1991 and was the first SOF unit to cross into Iraq in the pursuit of Iraqi Scud ballistic missiles. The SAS operators drove in columns of 'Pinkies', their nickname for the desert patrol vehicle (DPV) variant of the Land Rover 110 developed by the unit's mobility troop members. Others were infiltrated by RAF Chinook to establish covert observation posts to monitor Iraqi troop movements.

It was during one such mission that a half-troop-strength patrol from B Squadron, callsign Bravo Two Zero, was compromised and forced to escape and evade Iraqi forces. Three operators died, two from hypothermia and one killed by enemy fire. Four others, including the patrol commander, were captured and tortured. Only one operator managed to escape, walking almost 300 kilometres to cross the border into Syria where he was promptly arrested but later released.

The SAS played an instrumental role in the Balkans in the 1990s, including rescuing a Sea Harrier pilot in Gorazde and conducting special reconnaissance missions to vector in NATO airstrikes. On one operation, an SAS operator was tragically killed in a firefight with Serbian forces. The SAS was also an integral component of the Allied SOF elements tracking war criminals for the International Criminal Tribunal and conducted the first successful snatch mission, Operation *Tango* in 1997, although it ended in the target's death when he drew a sidearm and fired on the operators, who understandably returned fire.

The next major operation concerning the Regiment was Operation *Barras* in 2002, a hostage rescue in Sierra Leone where members of D Squadron supported by 1 Para (the future basis for the Special Forces Support Group) conducted a heliborne assault on two villages where five British servicemen and a Sierra Leonean liaison were being held hostage by a rebel faction. The mission was a success; however, one operator was lost in the close quarter battle. D Squadron was also involved in an advisory capacity, along with a pair

A UK Special Forces Bushmaster mounting a Kongsberg remote weapons station seen in Deir Ezzor, Syria in December 2018 following a 5th Special Forces Group M-ATV. Bushmasters had been earlier seen operating with both Green Beret M-ATVs and Delta Force Pandurs outside the Islamic State 'capital' of Raqqah. (Delil Souleiman/AFP/Getty Images)

of RAF CH-47 Chinooks, in the Indian Army's largely forgotten Operation *Khukri*, to successfully rescue a number of United Nations observers who had been taken hostage by the militia.

Following 9/11, the SAS was, along with the SBS, amongst the first Western SOF to infiltrate Afghanistan. The early days for the Regiment were largely disappointing with American JSOC units assigned the choicest missions, leaving the SAS to conduct low-level reconnaissance taskings and one memorable but strategically of little value mission to destroy a Taliban drug processing site.

In 2003, however, 22SAS became an integral part of the Coalition SOF campaign during the invasion of Iraq. Both B and D Squadrons were committed and operated in western Iraq conducting mounted raids and patrols. The Regiment was known initially as Task Force 14 in Iraq, a name it took into the initial stages of its campaign against the insurgency. Post invasion, the Regiment became a key partner in the 'industrial counter-terrorism' campaign against the burgeoning insurgency.

It was, however, hard pressed for manpower as one squadron was responsible for both Iraq and Afghanistan (where only a troop-strength element was typically deployed), one for Special Projects or counter-terrorist duty in the United Kingdom, and one for training tasks and block leave. This ended when the SBS was given primacy in Afghanistan and full SAS squadrons could be deployed to Iraq.

The need for a protected mobility vehicle during these gruelling raids saw the Regiment adopt the Australian Bushmaster fitted with a remote weapon station. This replaced the motley collection of HMMWVs that the unit had begged and borrowed from American Special Forces. It had also begun to employ combat assault dogs from 2005 following the practice of Delta, who had even taken their dogs with them into the western desert during the invasion, in special air-conditioned kennels.

At one point in the campaign, as Delta Force was taking significant casualties in its operations against insurgent base areas in al-Qaim on the Syrian border, JSOC requested that a British SAS squadron be detached direct to Delta to help make up for the losses. With the British government uneasy about the conditions under which insurgent prisoners were being held, the SAS was forced to demur and a second Delta squadron was flown in instead. The SAS had, however, cemented its relationship with Delta during this brutal campaign, a relationship that continues today with joint operations conducted in Syria and Northern Iraq, with Delta Pandurs and SAS Bushmasters seen side by side.

The Regiment was instrumental in hammering al-Qaeda in Iraq and literally halving the number of terrorist car bombs after a concerted campaign targeting the bombers under the fittingly named Operation *Fly* and Operation *Spider*. In the five years of core operations in Iraq post the invasion, the Regiment lost four

operators killed in action, an additional two in a Puma helicopter crash, and a great number of wounded. These included one SAS NCO (non-commissioned officer), who had already been wounded by gunfire in a particularly hazardous raid against an al-Qaeda cell in Yusufiyah before being wounded a second time as a terrorist he was chasing detonated his suicide bomb vest, blowing the operator down a staircase.

The SAS also conducted at least one successful hostage rescue in Iraq under Operation *Ney 3*, recovering three hostages from a Christian peace group. In the hunt for the hostages, B Squadron had conducted an incredible 44 house assaults, with Delta and the Rangers conducting a further six. Operations in Iraq began to wind down in 2008 and much of the SAS focus was transferred to Afghanistan and Operation *Kindle* (the codename for UK Special Forces operations in Afghanistan).

In Afghanistan, the SAS operated as part of Task Force 42 along with rotational elements from the SBS and Special Reconnaissance Regiment (SRR), the UK Special Forces Task Group that carried out operations for both the British-led Task Force Helmand and the American JSOC. Its main role was to ramp up an existing kill or capture campaign known to the Afghans as 'night raids', following its Iraq success in targeting insurgent high-value targets.

An SAS strike team from Task Force Spartan in Basra, 2007. Note that they are using a lightly armoured Snatch 2 Land Rover, though it is fitted with an electronic countermeasures system to protect against improvised explosive devices. The operator in the centre wears what appears to be an American MICH helmet with a desert DPM cover, and a Paraclete plate carrier; his weapon is an ACOG-equipped L119A1. (Author's Collection)

One example of such an operation was Operation *Holmes* in July 2009 to 'kill or capture Kajaki Taliban Commander Abdul'; seven insurgents were captured along with an AK-74, AK-47s, AK-47 ammo, M16 ammo, field binoculars and a pistol. Another operation was described in an after-action report as follows: 'TF42 conducted kinetic operations ISO [in support of] Op Bers Simi in order to disrupt EF [enemy forces] IED facilitation and supply lines. Area was secured and searched leading to the discovery of weapons and IED components. IED manufacturing facility was discovered, searched, exploited and destroyed.'

Such operations continued until 2014 when British forces largely withdrew from Afghanistan. Although it still sometimes deployed to Afghanistan for specific missions and to mentor Afghan National Mission Units, the SAS was being kept busy elsewhere. Members of D Squadron for instance first deployed to eastern Libya in 2012 to guide NATO airstrikes and mentor National Transitional Council elements where they worked alongside operators from Qatari Special Forces Company.

Informed rumours also suggest that there is a rotational presence of one Sabre squadron based in Jordan and Syria. In 2016, unidentified operators, allegedly SAS, were seen on the Jordanian border using Jankel Al-Thalab (Fox) long range patrol vehicles, possibly borrowed from Jordanian SOF.

As the SAS has been seen operating Bushmasters and civilian Toyota Hiluxes in Syria, it is surprising to see its operators in Jordanian vehicles; however, the .50 Brownings on the vehicles mounted a Trijicon advanced combat optical gunsight (ACOG), a minor but normally telltale sign of an SAS presence. This, together with the presence of a Heckler & Koch GMG, which does not appear to be in service with the Jordanians, is telling.

An image of poor quality but considerable historical interest; it shows the then-commander of the American JSOC, Lieutenant General Stanley McChrystal (second right), alongside the then-CO of 22 SAS, accompanying a Task Force Black assault team in Iraq. Of A Squadron's tour in 2007 General McChrystal subsequently noted that in a six-month rotation of 180 days they did an astonishing 175 operations – a combat assault virtually every night. (Author's Collection)

In November 2018, video footage appeared of two tan-painted UKSF Bushmasters complete with rolled-up camouflage nets near Hajin, the last bastion held by Islamic State in eastern Syria, confirming that 22SAS are still operating in the region.

The latest public SAS deployment was in the United Kingdom itself with operators photographed in London following the London Bridge terrorist attack (after arriving in one of their unmarked Dauphin helicopters nicknamed 'Blue Thunder' by the tabloids) and in Manchester after the bombing of a pop concert – both in 2017. In the former incident it appeared the operators were part of an advance party deployed to support the Counter Terrorist Specialist Firearms Officers (CTSFOs) of SCO19, the London Metropolitan Police's firearms unit (see pages 184–86).

The high tempo of operations has seen an expansion of manpower, with the Pagoda or Special Projects Team recently being increased by the addition of another troop of operators bringing the stand-by counter-terrorist unit to around 80 soldiers. The counter-terrorist stand-by capacity is now shared among the SAS, SBS and Special Forces Support Group (SFSG).

The four Sabre squadrons remain A, B, D and G (C was used by the Rhodesian SAS and so in a mark of respect 22SAS do not deploy a C Squadron). There has long been rumour of a fifth squadron, E Squadron, established in 2007. Like the alleged 4 Squadron of the Australian SASR or G Squadron of Delta, E Squadron is responsible for low-visibility operations in non-permissive environments, meaning going undercover into bad places. Rumours suggest the squadron is tasked both by Director Special Forces and by the Secret Intelligence Service (SIS) and is composed of operators from all three core UKSF units – 22SAS, SBS and SRR (Special Reconnaissance Regiment).

The only known operation by E Squadron was covert support for the Libyan National Transitional Council (NTC) during the uprising to topple the regime. In March 2011, a team of six E Squadron operators accompanied a number of SIS officers into Libya to meet with representatives of the NTC. Their arrival in a Chinook helicopter raised much suspicion and they were promptly arrested but later released. There is also a rumour that the unit was preparing to conduct a hostage rescue attempt to recover a British hostage held in Mali by al-Qaeda in the Islamic Maghreb (AQIM) in 2009 but the hostage was beheaded before an agreement could be made with Mali to deploy British operators.

22SAS maintains its own range of specialist small arms. It has replaced the venerable SIG-Sauer P226 with the Glock 19 as its primary pistol and now uses the Colt Canada L119A2 carbine as its principal shoulder weapon, including in the counter-terrorist mission. The integrally suppressed variant of the SIG-Sauer MCX has also been adopted in .300 Blackout to replace the Regiment's well-worn collection of MP5SD3s. The LWRC M6A2 Ultra Compact Individual Weapon was also procured for the unit's dog handlers and signallers.

24th Special Tactics Squadron (STS)

Nationality: US • Branch: Air Force • Established: 1992

Command Chief Master Sergeant Ramon Colon-Lopez, a pararescue jumper with the 24th Special Tactics Squadron, pictured here in Afghanistan, 2004. Colon-Lopez led the 24th's Advance Force Operations unit. Note the combination of civilian outdoors and Afghan clothing and compact Glock tucked into his body armour, either a Glock 26 in 9x19mm or a Glock 27 in .40 Smith & Wesson. (Courtesy US Department of Defense)

Originally known by the cover name of Brand X, the 24th Special Tactics Squadron (24th STS) was formed to support Operation *Eagle Claw* and the subsequent contingency planning for a second operation. It was later renamed as Det 1 MACOS (Military Airlift Command Operating Staff) and Det 4 NAFCOS (Numbered Air Force Combat Operations Staff) until the 1724th Special Tactics Squadron was formally established in 1985.

The unit was tasked to provide specialist support to Delta Force and SEAL Team 6, initially for their counter-terrorist role. Within the squadron are combat controllers (CCTs) trained to manage close air support and aeromedical evacuations, pararescue jumpers (PJs), who are highly trained combat rescue medics often assigned to combat search and rescue (CSAR), and special operations weather technicians who conduct environmental reconnaissance missions and advise on meteorological conditions for joint SOF task forces.

The first operational deployment of the 1724th was in support of the planned mission to recapture the *Achille Lauro* cruise liner in 1985. Unfortunately the mission never went ahead and the terrorists were allowed to escape by Italian authorities. Operators also deployed to Panama during the American invasion in 1989–90 in support of Ranger, Delta and SEAL operations. In 1990 Air Force Special Operations Command (AFSOC) was stood up as the US Air Force component of SOCOM. The 1724th STS became the Air Force component of JSOC and deployed along with other JSOC units on Operation *Desert Storm*; it was renamed the 24th STS in 1992.

CCTs and PJs were assigned to Task Force Ranger in Mogadishu in 1993 and were heavily involved in the 3 and 4 October battle. The 24th deployed operators to Afghanistan alongside Task Force Sword and were permanent attachments to all Delta, Ranger and SEAL missions. They were also on the ground in Iraq during the invasion in 2003. A 24th STS CCT was tragically killed in a fratricide incident when the Ranger Reconnaissance Detachment GMV (ground mobility vehicle) he was travelling in was engaged by an M1A1 Abrams from Team Tank, the small armoured element attached to Task Force Wolverine in western Iraq.

AFSOC maintains a number of other Special Tactics Squadrons based both in the US and overseas, including in the UK. They are either given a geographical responsibility or attached to specific units from SOCOM. Special Tactics airmen are all parachute trained and many are qualified in HALO (high altitude low opening) and HAHO (high altitude high opening). Others are SCUBA certified and are trained in small boat operations.

They are also trained in close combat skills as their role requires them to fight alongside the special operators they are supporting.

The 24th mirrors the JSOC units it works with and issues Glock pistols and HK416 carbines. Other Special Tactics units use the M4A1, the Mk16 and Mk17 SCAR and the Mk14 Enhanced Battle Rifle. AFSOC deploys a range of dirt bikes, quads and specialist vehicles such as the Flyer 60 and Flyer 72 for ground operations along with both the GMV-STS and now the ground mobility vehicle GMV 1.1.

25th Commando Brigade

Nationality: Kuwaiti • Branch: Army • Established: 1973

Kuwait maintains a small SOF capability in the form of the 25th Commando Brigade. The brigade is composed of two battalions trained in emulation of the US Army Special Forces. The unit was involved in close protection duties at Kuwait's Beirut Embassy in the 1980s and later deployed a small element to Somalia in 1993. Rumour also abounds that the 25th Commando Brigade was deployed during the opening stages of Operation *Iraqi Freedom*.

Kuwaiti operators from the 25th Commando Brigade pictured in 2017 during Exercise Eagle Resolve, an annual SOF exercise including US and Gulf Cooperation Council nations. Note the unusually forward mounted Trijicon ACOG on the central operator's Bushmaster M4 (most units have transitioned to so-called 'flat-top' M4s that feature a Picatinny rail in place of the carrying handle). (Courtesy US Army, Master Sgt Timothy Lawn)

A Kuwaiti special operator, likely from the 25th Commando Brigade, seen in 2010 whilst conducting cross-training with US SOCOM units. His weapon is the .338 Lapua Magnum Accuracy International Arctic Warfare Super Magnum. (Courtesy US Army, Master Sgt David Largent)

It has been active along with the Kuwait Police Special Force in disrupting Islamic State cells within the country, although Kuwaiti authorities are criticized for using both military and police special units to crack down on internal political dissent. The most well-known of these units is the Kuwait Police Special Weapons and Tactics (SWAT) Team established in 1978. The Kuwaiti Navy also maintains its own Commando Marine units.

The operators of the 25th use the MP5 series in the counter-terrorism mission while the standard rifle is the Bushmaster M4. They also employ French VBL Mk2 armoured cars fitted with remote weapon systems, painted in a garish grey and blue urban camouflage pattern. The police SWAT Team use the Glock, the MP5 and Blaser sniper rifles.

64th Special Forces Brigade

Nationality: Saudi Arabian • Branch: Army • Established: 1960

The principal SOF units in the Saudi Kingdom are the Army's 64th Special Forces Brigade, equivalent to US Army Special Forces, and the 1st Airborne Commando Brigade, equivalent to the US Army Rangers, along with two Navy Special Security Groups to conduct maritime and littoral operations.

Saudi special operations units have been deployed to Yemen since 2015 under Operation *Decisive Storm*. The 64th has been instrumental in developing the nascent Yemen National Army (YNA) along with training and advising local militia. Controversially, US Army Green Berets have also deployed to support them in 2017, providing much-needed expertise in calling in airstrikes. In March 2019, it was reported that five members of the UK's SBS were also operating alongside the 64th Brigade in Yemen.

The Saudi Ministry of the Interior also maintains the Special Security Forces (SSF), which officially are tasked with special and emergency operations

to preserve internal security and are the nation's primary counter-terrorism intervention force. Owing to the risk of coups, military special operations are relegated to external operations overseas only.

The SSF are equipped with Heckler & Koch G36K assault rifles and the MP5 series of sub machine guns along with the Heckler & Koch MSG90 sniper rifle. The 64th Special Forces Brigade issues the AK-103 as its principal individual weapon and a range of Canadian PGW bolt action sniper rifles to its snipers, with the Glock 17 issued as the sidearm.

A Saudi Special Forces soldier pictured during 2017 exercises in Jordan aiming a 7.62x39mm AK-103 fitted with vertical foregrip and unidentified optic. (Courtesy US Army, Sergeant 1st Class Suzanne Ringle)

75th Ranger Regiment

Nationality: US • Branch: Army • Established: 1974

With a storied and illustrious history dating back to the French–Indian War of the 1750s, the Rangers are regarded as the elite light infantry raiding force of the US Army. The 1st Ranger Battalion, established in 1942 and trained by British Commandos, operated in North Africa, the Pacific, Italy and Europe, with the defining battle at Pointe du Hoc on the Normandy coast embedding them in the public imagination.

Although the battalion was disbanded after World War II, independent Ranger companies fought with distinction in Korea and Vietnam where they became synonymous with the fabled Long Range Reconnaissance Patrol companies. A Ranger battalion was eventually raised in 1974 with a second following later that year. A third battalion was added in 1984.

A partnered kill or capture mission in Helmand Province, Afghanistan, 2012, with a Ranger on the left conducting a 'manual breach' and an Afghan Special Forces soldier to the right. (Courtesy Department of Defense, US Army Spc Justin Young)

Today the Ranger Regiment is still composed of those core three battalions; however, a Ranger Special Troops Battalion (RSTB) has been added to their establishment. The RSTB is composed of four company-strength elements: the Ranger Military Intelligence Company, the Regimental Reconnaissance Company (RRC), the Ranger Communications Company and the Ranger Selection and Training Company. The RRC was formerly known as the Ranger Reconnaissance Detachment but was renamed after being assigned direct to JSOC. The specialist 28th EOD Company supports 'the Regiment' on all operations.

A Ranger pictured during a kill or capture mission in Afghanistan, 2012. He carries the Mk17 SCAR-H chambered for 7.62x51mm. Note the PVS-15 night vision goggles and the combat applications tourniquet worn on his magazine pouches. (Courtesy Department of Defense, US Army Spc Justin Young)

Ranger companies consist of three rifle platoons and a weapons platoon that includes three anti-tank teams and two 60mm mortar teams. Each rifle platoon has a three-man headquarters, three nine-man rifle squads and a weapons platoon with three two-man medium machine gun teams and a squad leader. They are

supported by sniper teams from the Battalion Sniper Platoon and reconnaissance teams from the Battalion Reconnaissance Platoon (raised in 2007 to replace the Ranger Reconnaissance Detachment that was shifted to direct JSOC command).

In the modern era, the Rangers have deployed on Operation *Urgent Fury* to Grenada in 1983, Operation *Just Cause* to Panama in 1989 and Operation *Desert Storm* in 1991 under Operation *Elusive Concept*, an unfortunately fitting codename. In the case of the two former operations, the Regiment conducted a traditional Ranger role, making opposed combat drops to seize enemy-held airfields. In *Desert Storm*, the unit was conspicuously largely left out of proceedings, nominally down to General Norman Schwarzkopf's dislike for special operations, which also initially hampered Delta's efforts to join the fray. Eventually B Company of 1st Battalion was assigned Operation *Ranger Run 1* to destroy an Iraqi microwave relay tower. Although the operation was successful, rumours continue that the site was in fact long abandoned.

The most famous Ranger mission was Operation *Gothic Serpent* in Mogadishu, Somalia. Hunting a renegade warlord, the Rangers conducted six missions with varying degrees of success until October 3, 1993 when a mission to capture two of the warlord's top lieutenants ended in two MH-60 Black Hawks being shot down by RPG fire over the city. The Rangers and Delta

A 2nd Battalion Ranger machine-gunner from Task Force Red/North providing overwatch for an assault element during a kill or capture operation in Iraq, 2006. He is armed with the Mk46 light machine gun in 5.56x45mm, a special operations variant of the Minimi or M249 SAW. He wears a PCU (Protective Combat Uniform) soft-shell jacket and uses the older PVS 14 monocular night vision goggle. (Courtesy USASOC)

assaulters were surrounded in the city and fought a pitched battle until the next morning when the body of one of the trapped pilots was finally recovered and a relief column managed to fight its way through.

Afghanistan and Iraq had the greatest influence on the development of the 75th Rangers. During the invasion of Iraq in 2003, the Rangers deployed several companies from all three battalions which were assigned to JSOC's Task Force 20. The unit conducted a large number of operations including the capture of the Haditha Dam complex and the later destruction of a foreign fighter camp in Anbar Province known as Objective Reindeer.

During the Anbar operation, which took place in June 2003, two Ranger platoons from B Company, 2/75 conducted a night-time heliborne infiltration into the target after preparatory airstrikes. A third platoon arrived in GMVs (ground mobility vehicles) to provide mortar fire support and establish blocking positions. Despite the preparatory bombing, and with an AC-130 in the air above them, the Rangers were soon engaged in a massive firefight that ended with upwards of 70 dead insurgents. Incredibly, only one Ranger was seriously wounded, his leg cleaved off by an RPG.

During the insurgency, company-sized elements deployed in support of Army Special Forces, SEAL Team 6 or Delta deployments, but soon the Rangers graduated to leading their own task forces. In Iraq, Task Force Red, as the Rangers were known (the title was first used during Operation *Just Cause* in 1989), was given responsibility for the northern area of operations under the umbrella JSOC Task Force commanded by former Ranger General Stanley McChrystal.

A Ranger-modified M1126 Stryker pictured on the Syrian border with Turkey in April 2017. The Rangers were given the unusual mission of acting as very visible deterrents to stop clashes between Turkey and the YPG Kurds working with US forces. Note the Pandur style driver's compartment in particular – an effort to increase the situational awareness. (Delil Souleiman/ AFP/Getty Images)

The Regiment fought a protracted and brutal counter-terrorist campaign in Iraq. The Regiment suffered casualties from small arms fire and multiple incidents where its Stryker ICVs (infantry carrier vehicles) were ambushed by IEDs. One of the more harrowing deaths occurred in November 2007 when a Ranger sergeant fell from an MH-60 and plunged 40 feet to his death during a Task Force Red operation near Balad. Telling of the high operational tempo, the young Ranger had served in four Iraq rotations and one to Afghanistan in his four years in the Army (special operations rotations are typically shorter than for conventional troops with three to four months being common, owing to the unforgiving nature of their work).

When their al-Qaeda targets became wise to the fact that their mobile (cell) phones were being tracked, they turned them off at night so the Rangers began to raid during daylight hours, increasing the danger a hundred-fold. The unit had many notable successes including killing the second-in-command of al-Qaeda in Iraq, who was shot as he attempted to detonate a suicide bomb vest.

In 2008, as part of Task Force Red, Rangers from 2/75th Ranger Regiment found themselves under fire near Mosul during a night-time helicopter infiltration targeting al-Qaeda in Iraq. One of the Rangers actually stepped upon a hidden insurgent in chest-high grass and ended up in a brutal hand-to-hand battle with the Iraqi, who was attempting to trigger his suicide bomb vest. Eventually the young Ranger stunned the insurgent sufficiently to employ his M4 to kill him.

In Afghanistan, McChrystal gave the Rangers a shot at managing the JSOC Task Force deployed to that country on a rotational basis with SEAL

Rangers provide top cover for a Stryker near the Syrian city of Manbij in March 2017, which was at the time held by Islamic State. A year later, after the city had fallen, a Delta operator and a British SAS soldier were killed by an IED whilst hunting Islamic State remnants. Note the shortened M240L 7.62x51mm medium machine gun which is in use with the Rangers, along with the special operations Mk48, a 7.62x51mm variant of the Minimi. (Delil Souleiman/AFP/ Getty Images)

Team 6. Eventually the Rangers took solo command in 2009 as the SEALs were spread thin across Africa, the Middle East and Afghanistan. Although also conducting kill or capture missions and helping to train the Afghan National Mission Units, the Rangers were responsible for Team Darby, later renamed Team Merrill.

The Darby/Merrill operations were undoubtedly audacious. Insert a Ranger force into a named area of interest (NAO: an insurgent safe area), establish strongpoints in compounds rented from Afghans and wait until the insurgents attacked. Once baited, the Rangers could call upon massive amounts of firepower from both GPS-guided G-MLRS multiple rocket launchers and airpower to destroy concentrations of the enemy. The Rangers would stay in the field until the insurgents were killed or withdrew. Although wildly successfully at culling the numbers of rank and file insurgents, Darby/Merrill resulted in the combat deaths of 16 Rangers in less than one year of operations, giving a grim indication of the ferocity of the deployment.

The Rangers continue to operate in Afghanistan, where they command the JSOC Task Force. Many of their operations are conducted with the assistance of Army ODAs against the so-called Islamic State – Khorasan (ISIS-K), the Afghan splinter group operating to the north and east of the country and openly at war with the Afghan Taliban (it principally recruits from members of the rival Pakistani Taliban).

A reinforced platoon of Rangers from 3rd Battalion infiltrated into the Mohmand Valley alongside a platoon from an Afghan National Mission Unit in an attempt to kill the leader of ISIS-K. As it closed in on target compounds, a firefight erupted which would last three hours. Two Rangers were shot and killed early in the engagement. A Department of Defense spokesperson explained that the mission was ultimately regarded as successful: 'US Special Operations Forces killed several senior ISIS-K leaders along with about 35 ISIS operatives, which should significantly degrade ISIS-K operations and help to destroy the ISIS-K affiliate that's there.'

Two other Rangers killed in Afghanistan the following year were probably assigned to the shadowy ANSOF or Afghan National Special Operations Force, a new name for an old organization, the CIA Special Activities Division's Counter Terrorist Pursuit Teams, also known as Omega Teams. A Ranger from the 1st Battalion attached to ANSOF was deployed on a 2018 mission to intercept an al-Qaeda courier in Helmand Province, when he was killed, possibly from friendly fire by a member of their Afghan partner unit.

The Rangers have also deployed to Syria with operators spotted crewing modified M1126 Strykers near the Turkish border in March 2017. Displaying prominent American flags, the trio of Strykers represented an effort to deconflict the Turks and America's Kurdish allies. Rangers were also part of the Delta-led element at the Conoco gas plant, near Deir al-Zour, in February 2018 where hundreds of jihadists and Russian mercenaries were killed.

The Rangers use SOPMOD (Special Operations Peculiar Modifications) Block 2 M4A1 carbines as their primary weapon with the Glock 17 (including suppressed examples) and the new SIG-Sauer M17 as their standard sidearms, although, for the Regimental Reconnaissance Company (RRC), pistols such as the sub-compact Glock 26 are also available for undercover operations. Additionally both standard and suppressed MP5s are available, although these are likely to be replaced by the MCX low visibility assault weapon. SAW gunners carry both Para SAWs and the Mk46, a special operations variant of the M249.

Sniper and marksman rifles include the Mk13 and M2010 in .300 Winchester Magnum; the M110, the Mk17 SCAR-H and the new M110A1, all in 7.62x51mm (although both of the later rifles are likely to be rechambered to 6.5mm Creedmoor). Machine gunners operate both the titanium-based M240L and the Mk48, a 7.62x51mm variant of the Minimi (M249).

160th Special Operations Aviation Regiment (Airborne) (SOAR)

Nationality: US • Branch: Army • Established: 1980

The US Army 160th Special Operations Aviation Regiment (160th SOAR) grew from an ad hoc aviation unit established in the wake of the failed Operation *Eagle Claw* in 1980. As planners developed options for a second attempt to rescue the American hostages held in Iran, a detachment of aviators from the 101st Airborne Division was reassigned to the Joint Task Force and christened Task Force 160 or TF160, a title that even today is still used by members of the unit.

The United States' JSOC was established in November 1980 and Task Force 160, along with the Army and Navy special mission units, Delta Force and SEAL Team 6 respectively, was assigned to the new command. In the following year it was designated as the 160th Aviation Battalion and in 1986 as the 160th Special Operations Aviation Group (Airborne). In 1990, the unit became the 160th Special Operations Aviation Regiment (SOAR) (Airborne).

The 160th is composed of four operational battalions (the fourth being added only in 2006 following the demands of concurrent operations in Iraq and Afghanistan) along with a regimental headquarters and training element. Each battalion specializes in certain helicopter types.

1st Battalion has a company of AH-6M armed Little Birds, a company of MH-6M transport Little Birds fitted with detachable people pods to enable operators to be carried externally, and three companies of the MH-60M Black Hawk. 2nd Battalion is equipped solely with the heavy lift element of

MH-60M Black Hawks of the 160th Special Operations Aviation Regiment hover over a mock village located within the grounds of Fort Bragg, North Carolina while US Army Rangers prepare to fast-rope onto the buildings. (Courtesy Michael Bottoms, US SOCOM Office of Communications)

MH-47G Chinooks, while 3rd and 4th Battalions each man two companies of MH-47Gs and one company of MH-60M Black Hawks.

The 160th has been integrally involved in virtually every modern special operation conducted by US forces since 1980. It flew Black Hawks and Little Birds in support of Delta and SEAL Team 6 operations in Grenada in 1983, operated helicopters from the decks of Navy ships in the Persian Gulf under Operation *Prime Chance* in the late 1980s – a mission to keep the Persian Gulf clear of Iranian interference using both SEALs and helicopters from the 160th – and again flew missions for Delta and the SEALs during Operation *Just Cause* in Panama in 1989, including Operation *Acid Gambit*, the Modelo Prison rescue that saw one MH-6 crash-land in the street under enemy fire.

The unit also served in *Desert Storm*, ferrying Delta and Special Forces reconnaissance teams deep into Iraqi territory, losing one MH-60 that crashed, killing the crew and three Delta operators. In 1993, the unit deployed as part of Task Force Ranger to Mogadishu, Somalia where two MH-60s were shot down by RPG (rocket-propelled grenade) fire and another two barely limped back to base with serious damage.

Elements were deployed to the Balkans in support of the Persons Indicted For War Crimes (PIFWC) hunt in the former Yugoslavia during the late 1990s and in 2001 to Afghanistan. The 160th flew some of the first Special Forces ODAs into the country from Uzbekistan, often contending with terrible flying conditions to do so. After the invasion, a small detachment was based at Bagram to support Task Force Sword/Task Force 5 in the continuing pursuit of al-Qaeda high-value targets.

Afghanistan proved something of a challenge for the airframes of the 160th, particularly in the mountainous east. The Little Birds had difficulty operating at extreme altitudes and the MH-47 soon became the favoured platform for infiltrating operators into the border region. The 160th fired the first shots during the invasion of Iraq in 2003 with 'Black Swarm' flights engaging Iraqi observation posts along Iraq's western and southern borders.

Each 'Black Swarm' flight consisted of a pair of AH-6 armed Little Birds and an MH-60L direct action penetrator (DAP) from the 160th guided onto their targets by an MH-6 equipped with a forward-looking infrared (FLIR) laser. For tougher targets, a flight of two A-10A Warthogs was assigned to each 'Black Swarm'. Their operations opened up air corridors for Coalition SOF who flew into Iraq from their staging area in Jordan.

The 160th conducted literally thousands of missions during the invasion and the later insurgency in Iraq. An airstrip was established in Baghdad at Mission Support Site Fernandez (named after a fallen Delta operator), at the rear of a number of Saddam Hussein's former palaces that housed the Delta, Ranger and 22SAS contingents of the JSOC task force.

Normally flying at night to make full use of its technological advantages in night vision, the 160th would skim across Iraqi rooftops, depositing elements of operators and re-running to retrieve them and their prisoners once the objective was secure. In 2006, during the height of JSOC's war against al-Qaeda in Iraq, an AH-6 was shot down while supporting an aerial vehicle interdiction north-west of Baghdad, forcing the remaining AH-6 to hold back waves of insurgents racing toward the crash site until Delta Force could secure the area and rescue the pilots.

Another AH-6 was shot down in the notorious Yusufiyah area, home to a number of al-Qaeda car-bomb cells. Following a rare daylight infiltration by MH-60, members of Delta's B Squadron were engaged in a heavy firefight as they left the helicopters. The situation was so intense that the doorgunners on the MH-60s were forced to fire their miniguns from the air. An AH-6 sent to relieve the pair of Little Birds at the objective was shot down and both aviators from the 1st Battalion were tragically killed in the crash.

As Iraq wound down, the 160th increasingly turned its attentions to Afghanistan, although the unit had never really left. In 2005, it suffered

A 1st Special Forces Group soldier free-fall parachutes from an MH-47G Chinook of the 160th Special Operations Aviation Regiment. (Courtesy US Army, Sgt Joseph Parrish)

its worst day in terms of casualties when an MH-47 was downed by RPG fire during the infamous Operation *Red Wings II*, the personnel recovery effort launched after a four-man SEAL reconnaissance element were ambushed whilst hunting for signs of a Taliban high value target. (Operation *Red Wings II* was later made famous by the book and film *Lone Survivor*). The Chinook was carrying an eight-man crew from the 160th and eight SEALs from both SEAL Team 10 and SEAL Delivery Vehicle Team One. All were killed in the crash. A year after the shoot-down another MH-47 was hit by an RPG in Afghanistan but managed to land safely and was secured by a mixed element of Rangers and SEALs until the crew could be safely evacuated.

In Afghanistan, the 160th again conducted nightly missions across the country infiltrating SOF teams conducting capture or kill operations against the Taliban. The AH-6s and MH-60 DAPs again proved their worth time and again in providing close air support for the operators on the ground. In 2017, the 4th Battalion lost an aviator in Logar Province when an MH-47G crashed, killing the pilot and injuring six other members of the unit.

Known as 'the Nightstalkers', the 160th sports the official motto 'Night Stalkers Don't Quit', a phrase famously repeated by the wife of captured 160th aviator Mike Durant after Durant was captured in Mogadishu (she was making a coded reference to various notes Mike had encrypted in a Red Cross letter to his family). The unofficial credo of the 160th however is to deliver their 'customers', as they call the operators, at their objective 'plus or minus 30 seconds time on target'.

SOAR trains extensively to reduce the noise signature of its helicopters to maximize the effect of surprise. Every second is an advantage if operators are being infiltrated directly onto the objective ('landing on the X'). If an off-set LZ (landing zone) is required (a landing zone located some distance from the target to avoid losing the element of surprise), minimizing noise maximizes the possibility of the operators remaining uncompromised while they approach the objective on foot or on light vehicles. This was one of the key drivers for perhaps SOAR's most intriguing airframe, the 'stealthy' Silent Hawk used for the raid on bin Laden's compound in Abbottabad in 2011 (see pages 338–40) and probably for at least one Delta raid into Syria.

The 160th continues to quietly support JSOC missions into northern Iraq and Syria. In August 2018, an MH-60 returning from one such mission crashed near Sinjar, Ninevah Province, and a pilot from the 1st Battalion was killed. A number of the ten operators being transported in the MH-60 were injured in the crash. Occasionally amateur video recordings emerge of mixed flights of MH-60s and MH-47s skimming low across the Iraqi desert in the pre-dawn light, reinforcing that the 160th are still very much in the fight.

Afghan National Army Special Operations Command (ANASOC)

Nationality: Afghan • Branch: Army • Established: 2007

The Afghan National Army (ANA) Commandos are the Afghan Army's Ranger equivalents, trained to conduct direct action raids and special operations. The units are established into 650-man Afghan battalions or kandaks called Special Operations Kandaks (SOKs) attached to Afghan Army Corps drawn from across Pashto, Tajik, Hazara, Uzbek and Turkmen ethnic groups to avoid tribal allegiances and corruption.

The SOKs each comprise three Commando companies and an Afghan National Army Special Forces (ANASF) or Qeta-ye Khas company. The commando role is to 'conduct elite, light-infantry operations against threat networks in support of the regional corps' counter-insurgency operations and provide a strategic response capability against strategic targets,' as explained by an Operation *Enduring Freedom* status report. Each SOK includes organic support from a military intelligence company, an engineer company and training, support and headquarters companies.

Soldiers from the Afghan 7th Special Operations Kandak (SOK) Commandos release a prisoner held by the Taliban in Helmand Province, July 2018. (Courtesy NATO, US Army, Pfc Joshua Belser)

The ANASF were created and trained in the image of the US Army Special Forces and have a similar role with emphasis placed on both direct action and the skills of liaison, foreign internal defence and counter-insurgency. These have now been subsumed into the SOKs but organized into a 'special company' of eight Qeta-ye Khas ODA teams alongside the standard three companies which make up a Commando kandak. The Qeta-ye Khas conduct special reconnaissance and covert operations while the Commandos, officially at least, do the raiding.

Prior to 2007, only two ANA kandaks were considered SOF capable to any degree, one of these being the sole original Commando kandak. There are currently ten active SOKs, organized under two brigade commands under the ANA Special Operations Command (ANASOC), along with the Special Mission Wing (SMW) that provides organic helicopter support with a range of Mi-17s and PC-12 fixed-wing ISR (intelligence, surveillance and reconnaissance) aircraft.

Officially the SMW is the only Afghan National Defense Security Forces (ANDSF) organization with night-vision, rotary-wing air assault, and fixed-wing ISR capabilities. It is composed of four squadrons with two based in the capital, one in Kandahar and one in Mazar-e-Sharif. The Afghan Air Force additionally fields UH-60s and MD-530 Little Bird attack helicopters that can support ANASOC units in the field.

In 2018 it was announced by the Afghan government that it hoped to double the number of Commando kandaks by 2020 with all Afghan SOFs to be placed under the ANASOC. This would include three newly raised SOKs and the addition of a fourth Commando company in each kandak.

Their first official Commando operation was in September 2007 after initial training by the 5th SFG. The Commandos are mentored by a rotational team of Army Green Berets, Marine Raiders and Navy SEALs with each kandak hosting two ODAs, a Marine Special Operations Team or a SEAL platoon. Even amongst the best ANA SOKs, they are still often accompanied by a full Special Forces ODA and require significant direction and mentoring unlike the National Mission Units (NMUs) or ANASF.

After the withdrawal of NATO ground combat forces, the Commandos have been increasingly squandered by conducting conventional operations as they are the best troops available to ANA Command. An astonishing 70 per cent of ANA offensive operations are conducted by the Commandos or NMUs.

They are supported by regular ANA Mobile Strike Force Vehicle (MSFV) brigades, who operate independently but are increasingly receiving commando training and have bolstered the numbers in the Commando Corps. The long-term plan is to attach one of the Commando-trained MSFV brigades, in US supplied HMMWVs and MRAPs (mine resistant ambush protected vehicles), to partner with every two Commando kandaks.

The Ministry of the Interior's General Command of Police Special Units (GCPSU) is another entity that provides a Special Weapons and Tactics (SWAT)-like function to the Afghan National Police (ANP); its members, according to the Pentagon, 'execute high-risk arrests, and respond to high-profile attacks. The GCPSU also provides rapid response to critical situations such as emergencies or hostage scenarios.' There are currently 33 Police Special Units.

Most Afghan Commando and PSU units now use Colt M4 carbines, M249 SAWs and PKM medium machine guns, although US-supplied M240s are gradually replacing the tried and true PKM. Beretta M9s are the standard sidearm. Both Dragunov SVD and M24 sniper rifles are used.

Agrupación de Fuerzas Especiales Antiterroristas Urbanas (AFEAU)

Nationality: Colombian • Branch: Army • Established: 1985

The Agrupación de Fuerzas Especiales Antiterroristas Urbanas (AFEAU or Special Forces Urban Counter Terrorism Group) is the Colombian Army's key counter-terrorist and direct action unit and is modelled heavily on Delta Force, although more recently the unit has received mentoring from both the US Army Rangers and 22SAS. Formed in 1985 after insurgents seized the Palace of Justice in the Colombian capital Bogota, the AFEAU consists of just four 15-man assault teams and is justifiably considered the elite of Colombian SOF.

The Army maintains the Brigada de Fuerzas Especiales Commando (Special Forces Commando Brigade), which consists of four battalions and is closely modelled on the US Army Special Forces with key responsibilities for special operations and counter-insurgency. A fifth battalion was raised in 2017 as the Urban Special Forces Battalion.

All of the Brigada de Fuerzas Especiales Commando are trained and mentored by the 7th SFG, the Green Berets with Spanish language skills assigned to Latin America. These units, and the Brigade Command, are under the command of the Army's Special Forces Division, also newly established in 2017. Amongst the Commandos, the Commando Battalion No.1 'Ambrosio Almeyda' is considered the best trained and equipped.

The 7th SFG's Combatant Commanders In-Extremis Force (CIF) was also involved in raising and training a number of new units during the 1980s and 1990s, among them La Fuerza de Despliegue Rápido (FUDRA or the Rapid Deployment Force), a unit based on the Rangers as elite light infantry;

A Colombian sniper from AFEAU competing in a competitive event in Paraguay, July 2017. His rifle is the 7.62x51mm Remington R11 RSASS (Remington Semi-Automatic Sniper System). (Courtesy US Army, Sgt 1st Class James Brown)

and the Brigada Aviación (BA or Aviation Brigade), a dedicated helicopter unit to support the operators. Other units such as the Comando Especial del Ejército (EEC or Army Special Command), a direct action counter-terrorism force, were trained and organized by the SEALs.

Today these units, along with AFEAU, are organized under the Commando Conjunto de Operaciones Especiales (CCOES or Colombian Joint Special Operations Command) although command of individual units still lies with the relevant service. The Navy maintains the Batallón Fuerza Especial de Infantería de Marina (BFEIM or Naval Infantry Special Forces Brigade), for instance, a battalion-strength unit trained by the US Navy SEALs that is available for tasking by CCOES.

One of the most famous and successful Colombian AFEAU operations was Operation *Jaque* (Checkmate) in July 2008 with Colombian operators disguised as a humanitarian group securing the release of US contractors seized as hostages in 2003 during a counter-narcotics operation. A squadron from Delta stood by with 160th Special Operations Aviation Regiment (160th SOAR) helicopters in case the mission went awry but the Colombian operators managed to rescue the hostages in a high-stakes game of deception.

The AFEAU is armed with a range of M4A1 carbines, often fitted with suppressors, with Glock pistols, while the Commando Brigade is principally armed with Tavor TAR-21 and the MP5 series with Beretta M9 sidearms. The Army units use a range of sniper platforms including the SR-25, the Remington R11 and the Barrett M82A1.

The Colombian National Police maintain the Commando de Operaciones Especiales (COPES or Special Operations Command), which acts as a tactical response unit in support of the police. The counter-terrorist Grupos de Acción Unificada Libertad Personal (GAULA or Unified Action Groups for Personal

Liberty), a unit which has a presence in each province of the country, is the principal police counter-terrorism and hostage recovery unit although it is primarily involved in kidnapping cases which are sadly endemic in Colombia. Unusually, the GAULA units include units drawn from Army and Navy personnel as well as police.

Brigada 6 Operaţii Speciale

Nationality: Romanian • Branch: Army • Established: 2011

Formerly known as the 1st Special Operations Regiment, Brigada 6 Operaţii Speciale or the 6th Special Operations Brigade was established in 2011 to command two Special Forces battalions: the 610th and 602nd Special Operations Battalions, the latter comprising the 630th Paratrooper Battalion and the 640th Logistics Battalion. The 610th is the oldest SOF in the Romanian Land Forces, trained by both US Army Special Forces and Turkish Special Forces Brigades. Not surprisingly, the Romanians follow US Green Beret doctrine and organize their Special Forces battalions into ODAs. They have also subsumed the counter-terrorist intervention function formerly conducted by the Rapid Intervention Detachment.

A Romanian SOF soldier from the 610th Special Operations Battalion conducts multi-national training. Note his British temperate pattern DPM fatigues and borrowed carbine; the Romanian units typically use the G36 series. (Courtesy US Army, Sgt Daniel Carter)

Members of the 610th deployed to Afghanistan in 2007 to mentor the Afghan security forces. They also participated in combat operations with the Green Berets. By 2012, there were four Romanian ODAs deployed. Since 2015, the Romanians have formalized their participation with the Special Operations Advisory Group (SOAG) under International Security Assistance Force (ISAF) command.

One operator, an officer from Romanian Special Forces Operational Detachment Alpha 012, was killed in Afghanistan during operations partnered with the US 10th SFG in 2009. In 2016, two further members of the 610th were killed in a green-on-blue shooting by a member of the Afghan Police Special Unit they were mentoring.

The Independent Special Interventions and Actions Service or SIIAS is the Romanian Ministry of the Interior police unit with domestic counter-terrorism intervention responsibilities. Divided into two 30-man detachments, the Special Battalion of Anti-terrorist Intervention and Special Actions and the Special Battalion of Intervention, they can be air-transported to the site of an incident by the Police Special Aviation Unit.

The SIIAS is supported by local police Detaşamentul de Intervenţii şi Acţiuni Speciale (DIAS or Special Intervention and Action Detachments) who will provide the initial response and cordon until SIIAS is deployed. The Romanian intelligence service, the Serviciul Român de Informaţii (SRI or Romanian Intelligence Service), also have a counter-terrorist and special operations unit called the Brigada Antiteroristă (BAT or Anti-Terrorism Brigade.)

The Romanian Land Forces units use the G36K and C along with a limited number of the SIG 551, the UMP sub machine gun, and Glock pistols. In Afghanistan they typically wore British desert DPM camouflage and in Europe temperate pattern DPM but they have more recently been seen in MultiCam. The SIIAS uses MP5A3s and MP5SD3, SIG-Sauer P226 pistols and SIG 552 assault rifles.

Canadian Special Operations Regiment (CSOR)

Nationality: Canadian • Branch: Army • Established: 2006

The Canadian Special Operations Regiment (CSOR) defines itself as a 'battalion-sized, high-readiness special operations unit capable of conducting and enabling a broad range of missions, including direct action (DA), defence, diplomacy and military assistance (DDMA) and special reconnaissance (SR).' It is one of a handful of modern units that can trace its lineage back to the famous joint US/Canadian First Special Service Force but was in fact established only in 2006.

Prior to this, JTF2 had been the sole Canadian SOF unit. The Canadian Airborne Regiment, which provided something of a Ranger-like capability, had been disbanded under controversial circumstances after the torture and death of a civilian during a deployment to Somalia in 1992. There remains a parachute capability within one infantry battalion.

CSOR and JTF2 fall under the command and control of Canadian Armed Forces Special Operations Forces Command (CANSOFCOM) along with the Canadian Joint Incident Response Unit (CJIRU), a CBRN (chemical, biological, radiological and nuclear) response team with its own organic EOD; the 427th Special Operations Aviation Squadron (427 SOAS) flying the CH-146 Griffon helicopter in direct support; and the Canadian Special Operations Training Centre (CSOTC).

CSOR is a battalion-strength unit created initially to support JTF2 in a similar manner to the British Special Forces Support Group. It was ground breaking in terms of female inclusion with one, now sadly deceased, female operator passing all selection criteria and serving with the unit for a number of years.

The unit deployed to Afghanistan in 2007 and suffered its first casualty that year when an operator was killed in a fall. In 2011, it lost a second operator in a non-combat-related incident in Kandahar. CSOR was heavily committed to mentoring the ANA (Afghan National Army) Commando kandaks and in particular the ANA Special Forces under Task Force 58, with CSOR termed the 'Green Team' conducting the advise and assist mission and JTF2 the 'Black Team' conducting direct action and mentoring Afghan National Mission Units (NMUs).

In 2011, while mentoring the Afghan Provincial Response Company – Kandahar (PRC-K), CSOR elements became involved in the response to a Taliban attack on the Governor's Palace in Kandahar City, one of dozens of coordinated terrorist incidents in the Taliban's efforts to retake the city. Later they accompanied their Afghan charges in a highly complex building clearance of a shopping mall.

With over 100 rooms to clear with only the 25-man CSOR detachment and 55 PRC-K operators, it was a daunting task. Additionally a US MRAP (mine resistant ambush protected vehicle) had just been struck by an IED as the Canadians and Afghans approached their objective. CSOR established overwatch in a nearby building with its snipers and JTACs (joint terminal attack controllers).

The combined force managed to clear most of the mall, rescuing a number of Afghan civilians, until it ran into a number of barricaded insurgents. Despite the force's use of 40mm grenades, heavy machine gun and sniper fire against them, the insurgents remained in place and opened fire whenever an assault was launched. Eventually around midnight, a JTF2 element arrived and began planning a new assault. Soon after the insurgents detonated a pre-positioned VBIED (vehicle-borne IED) or car bomb, almost demolishing the building housing the CSOR snipers and command element.

A volley of LAW (light anti-armour weapon) rockets and 40mm rounds from an Mk47 automatic grenade launcher 'mouse-holed' the walls surrounding the insurgent position, allowing the snipers to engage targets. The ordnance also started a fire. When the flames had died down, the JTF2 'Black Team' led the way in the final assault, discovering a number of charred insurgent corpses in their strongpoint.

Canada's contribution to the International Security Assistance Force (ISAF) was wound down in 2014; however, numbers of CSOR personnel provide a mentoring capability to Afghan Commando kandaks. The unit

A CSOR soldier pictured in 2012 during an exercise. Note the Canadian Disruptive Pattern – Terrain Woodland (CADPAT TW) and US MICH helmet. He carries a Colt Canada C8 carbine; unusually it has the standard carrying handle attached and an EOTech optic forward mounted. (Luis Acosta/AFP/Getty Images)

deployed to Iraq under Operation *Impact* in late 2014 with a 70-member task force including members of both JTF2 and CSOR. A minor controversy erupted when CSOR operators were photographed wearing Kurdish flag patches near Erbil where they were training the Peshmerga. Little precise detail of their accomplishments is available although one operator was sadly killed in a fratricide incident in 2015.

A statement by the Canadian government noted: 'Sergeant Doiron was killed while conducting advise and assist operations in Iraq when he and other members of the Special Operations Forces were mistakenly engaged by Iraqi Kurdish forces following their return to an observation post behind the front lines.' Along with Iraq and Afghanistan, CSOR elements have deployed on advise and assist missions to Jordan, Kenya, Mali and Niger, highlighting the importance of Africa as the next battlefield in the War on Terror.

The unit uses the SIG-Sauer P226 sidearm often fitted with weapon light and the Colt Canada C8A3 carbine as its principal small arms. The C9A2, a Minimi Para variant, is issued as the unit's light machine gun, while the Colt Canada M203A1 is the issue underslung grenade launcher. Unit snipers employ the .338 Lapua Magnum C14 Timberwolf MRSWS (Medium Range Sniper Weapon System).

Comando Conjunto de Operaciones Especiales de las Ff.Aa. de Filipinas (AFPSOCOM)
Nationality: Filipino • Branch: Joint • Established: 2018

The AFP (Armed Forces of the Philippines) Special Operations Command (AFPSOCOM), or Comando Conjunto de Operaciones Especiales de las Ff.Aa. de Filipinas, was established in 2018 to oversee all AFP special operations units. It replaced the Army's Special Operations Command and brings all the service's units under one roof including the Naval Special Operations Group; the Air Force 710th Special Operations Wing; the Army's Light Reaction Regiment, Special Forces Regiment and Scout Ranger Regiment and the counter-terrorist Joint Special Operations Group.

The Scout Rangers, light infantry who enjoy a lineage that dates to back the late 1940s counter-insurgency (the Huk insurgency saw alleged communist insurgents fighting firstly Japanese occupation forces and later Philippine government forces), are one of the oldest special operations forces in the AFP. They are regionally based to support AFP area commands. The Army's Special Forces Regiment was established in 1962 and follows Green Beret doctrine in both role and structure with a focus on unconventional warfare. The Light Reaction Regiment is the AFP's principal

counter-terrorist intervention unit with three companies of operators drawn from both the Special Forces and Scout Rangers.

The Navy's Special Operations Group is SEAL trained and carries out similar maritime special operations tasks, and operational units are even termed SEAL Team Companies. These SEAL Team Companies provide the maritime counter-terrorist element to the Joint Special Operations Group which also includes elements of the Light Reaction Regiment, the 723rd Special Operations Squadron and organic EOD and canine units.

Elements from these units are formed into three individual Joint Special Operations Units. The Philippine Marine Corps also maintains the Marine Special Operations Group (formerly the Force Recon Battalion) which provides an amphibious SOF capability.

In 2013, the AFP carried out complex warfighting in the city of Zamboanga, the capital of Mindanao, against the Rogue Moro National Liberation Front with the insurgents taking many hostages. Both the AFP and the Philippine National Police Special Action Force (PNP-SAF) were deployed with the Light Reaction Regiment which was reinforced by some 45 SEALs.

The 2017 battle of Marawi saw AFP special operators conducting urban warfare in another protracted offensive against jihadists who had overrun the city of Marawi, hoisting the Islamic State flag above the city. Marine units operated alongside Joint Special Operations Units in task groups eventually to retake the city with American and Australian technical support including Australian P-3 surveillance aircraft which contributed to intelligence, surveillance and reconnaissance (ISR), a capability still lacking in AFP special operations forces. Just under one thousand jihadists and 168 members of the AFP and police units were killed by the time the city was retaken.

Operators from the Navy's Special Operations Group, part of the Armed Forces of the Philippines (AFP), pictured in 2007. Note the Vietnam style 'tiger stripe' camouflage fatigues and 5.56x45mm M4 mounting a C-More optic. (Courtesy US Defense Department, Tech Sgt Jerry Morrison)

Although US Joint Special Operations Task Force – Philippines (JSOTF-P; established in the wake of 9/11 to support regional counter-terrorism and counter-insurgency operations in the Philippines) was deactivated in 2015, US special operators still rotate on training and technical assistance missions in support of the AFP, including deployment of assets to provide the AFP with ISR from US UAVs (unmanned aerial vehicles). The US has provided both ScanEagle and RQ-11 Raven UAVs along with dedicated ISR propeller aircraft under the provisions of the US Counterterrorism Partnerships Fund. Rumours of a US Predator strike against a Jemaah Islamiyah leader in Mindanao in 2006 have never been confirmed.

The Philippine National Police Special Action Force is the primary law enforcement counter-terrorist unit although it deploys alongside AFPSOCOM units for large and complex operations such as Marawi. The unit is divided into six battalions along with a Rapid Deployment Battalion with several more being established. These are composed of Special Action Companies, a number of which are dedicated to maritime operations and are known as Special Operations Companies (Seaborne). The PNP-SAF has received training from the French Recherche, Assistance, Intervention, Dissuasion (RAID) and Israel's Yamam along with the American 1st SFG.

The unit suffered its heaviest losses during an operation in Mamasapano in 2015, aimed at capturing a jihadist bomb-maker. Instead the unit was embroiled in a prolonged battle after one of the high-value targets was killed, leading to the deaths of an unbelievable 44 members of the unit (some of whom were wounded and executed). From 55th Special Action Company, 35 operators were killed leaving only one alive.

All of the AFP units use predominantly US small arms with the M4 being the most common individual weapon along with the M249 SAW and M203 grenade launcher. Both Russian RPG-7Vs and the US-produced Airtronic RPG-7 provide bunker-busting capability. The SAF use the Glock 17, compact Glock 30 in .45ACP, the X-95 Tavor and various M4 carbines along with older M16A1s and M14s. Pakistani-licensed MP5 copies are also in use.

Comando de Operações Especiais

Nationality: Brazilian • Branch: Joint • Established: 2002

Despite a long history of incorporating SOF into its establishment, Brazil maintains its special units under each service command. When an operation is planned, a Joint Special Operations Task Force (JSOTF or Forcas Tarefa Conjuntas de Operacoes Especiais) is established that will command and control all units assigned to the particular mission or campaign. The elements of the JSOTF may be drawn from the Army, Navy, Marines and the Military Police.

A Brazilian soldier firing the 7.62x51mm Remington R11 RSASS (Remington Semi-Automatic Sniper System) in 2017. He wears indigenously produced 'Lizard' pattern camouflage based on a post-war French and later Portuguese pattern. (Courtesy US Army, Sgt Alexis K. Washburn-Jasinski)

The Brazilian Army's Comando de Operações Especiais (Special Operations Command) brings together the Army's units under a Special Operations Brigade that comprises the 1st Special Forces Battalion, the 1st Commando Actions Battalion, the Special Operations Support Battalion, the 3rd Special Forces Company, the 1st Chemical, Biological and Nuclear Defense Platoon, and the 6th Army Police Platoon.

The 1st Special Forces Battalion is modelled closely on US Army Special Forces and is composed of two special forces companies, a command and support company and the Destacamento de Contraterrorismo or Counterterrorism Detachment. Each of these companies (Force 1 and Force 2) is composed of a command element and four special forces operational detachments or SFODs. Each SFOD includes 12 special forces officers and senior NCOs, all specialists in core areas in the same fashion as the Green Berets. The independent 3rd Special Forces Company is similarly organized but based in the Amazon and its members are specialists in jungle warfare.

Additional Army units are attached as required from SOCOM such as the Chemical Counterterrorism Team which operates a counter-CBRN (chemical, biological, radiological and nuclear) capability and is deployed alongside the 1st Special Forces Battalion's counter-terrorism detachment. SFODs can be reinforced with detachments from the 1st Commandos Action Battalion. These joint elements are known as Immediate Action Detachments.

The Commandos Action Battalion is an elite light infantry force trained in unconventional warfare. The battalion includes a command and support company, three commando companies and a reconnaissance and sniper detachment. Each commando company is composed of a headquarters function and three commando detachments, each comprising 42 operators supported by members of the reconnaissance and sniper detachment as needed.

The Navy maintains GRUMEC, Grupamento de Mergulhadores da Marinha do Brasil or the Navy Combat Divers Group, established in 1998, which is comparable to the US Navy SEALs and conducts all maritime special operations including maritime counter-terrorism. GRUMEC includes three special operations teams (Alpha, Bravo and Charlie Teams) and the maritime counter-terrorist (MCT) unit, the Rescue and Recovery Special Group.

The Brazilian Marines have their own Marine Corps Special Operations Battalion composed of a command and support company, and three Marine special operations companies, each with a specialist role: special reconnaissance; commando and raiding; and counter-terrorist intervention, which is the responsibility of the Rescue and Retaking Special Group.

The Military Police, a separate police force in Brazil, has a Special Police Operations Battalion within each regional district including the infamous BOPE (Batalhão de Operações Policiais Especiais of the State of Rio de Janeiro Military Police. The civilian police also has its own SWAT-style intervention teams such as the Special Resources Coordination unit of the Rio Police.

Both military and police units have long been employed in the war in the favelas against Brazil's notorious drug gangs who are often armed with military-grade small arms. Prior to the 2016 Olympic Games in Rio, an Islamic State-inspired plot to commit terrorist attacks at the games was uncovered and successfully foiled. The 1st Special Forces Battalion and the 1st Commandos Action Battalion were also both committed to a successful joint operation in 1991 with Colombian forces against insurgents from the Revolutionary Armed Forces of Colombia – People's Army (FARC) who had crossed the border and attacked a Brazilian Army outpost.

Brazilian special operators commonly use Colt M4 carbines and G36 variants along with the MP5SD series (intriguingly GRUMEC divers deploy the Israeli Mini-UZI). Glock 17 pistols are standard for the military units while BOPE use an indigenously produced Beretta M92 copy, the Taurus PT-92 (also used by GRUMEC). Remington M24 and Barrett M82A1 sniper rifles are favoured.

Comando Interforze per le Operazioni delle Forze Speciali (COFS)

Nationality: Italian • Branch: Joint • Established: 2004

The Italian Comando Interforze per le Operazioni delle Forze Speciali (COFS or Joint Special Operations Command) is based on the experiences of Task Force Nibbio, the Italian Joint Task Force that served in Afghanistan under International Security Assistance Force (ISAF) command. The COFS brings together all Italian military and Carabinieri SOF units under a single unified command and control structure although some units are maintained by their respective services.

These units under direct COFS tasking include the Army's famous Col Moschin or the 9º Reggimento d'Assalto Incursori Paracadutisti (9th Paratrooper Assault Regiment); the Air Force's 17º Stormo Incursori (17th Assault Regiment); the Navy's Gruppo Operativo Incursori (GOI or Operational Raider Group); and the Carabinieri's Gruppo Intervento Speciale (GIS or Special Intervention Group).

Units available to COFS for specific operations or to support its core units include the Army's 185 Ricognizione Acquisizione Obiettivi (185th Reconnaissance and Target Acquisition Paratrooper Regiment), a special reconnaissance unit; the 4 Reggimento Alpini Paracadutisti (4th Alpine Paratrooper Regiment) akin to the US Army Rangers; the 11 Reggimento del Segnale (11th Communication Regiment); and the 3 Reggimento di Elicotteri per Operazioni Speciali (3rd Special Operations Helicopter Regiment); along with the Air Force's 9 Reggimento di Elicotteri (9th Helicopter Regiment). COFS can also draw upon a number of other units, principally Army reconnaissance and engineers, should the mission dictate.

Col Moschin, commonly known as simply 'the 9th', is named in veneration of the unit (the 9th Arditi Battalion) that participated in the battle for

Operators from the Carabinieri's GIS or Special Intervention Group (Gruppo Intervento Speciale) including both assaulters and snipers clad in Ghillie Suits. Note the accessorized MP5s including one mounting a B&T stock designed for use with ballistic face masks. (Fabrizio Villa/ Getty Images)

Col Moschin during World War I between the Italian Army and the Austro-Hungarian Army (not to some mythical Colonel Moschin as even this writer once assumed!). The unit has served as the Italian Army's principal SOF and unconventional warfare unit since 1975. Counter-terrorism was added to its taskings in 1977.

Today Col Moschin comprises the 1st Assault Battalion supported by communications, training and logistics companies. The Assault Battalion is structured around four operational companies (Special Operations Task Units), each of three detachments of eight *Incursore* or operators. The 9th deployed to Iraq under Operation *Ancient Babylon* where in 2004 it conducted the successful hostage recovery of a British citizen.

It has also deployed numerous times to Afghanistan and launched a joint operation with the British SBS in 2007 to rescue a pair of Italian intelligence agents. The SBS provided the cut-off force including aerial snipers while Col Moschin crept up on the target building to conduct the assault, an American Predator UAV (unmanned aerial vehicle) in the skies above. The Italian operators' plans were thwarted when the hostage takers brought the two hostages out to a number of SUVs (sport utility vehicles) and drove off with them. The SBS was forced to intervene and in the resulting gun battle both hostages were badly wounded with one later dying of his wounds.

The other key intervention capability for COFS is provided by the GIS. Raised in 1978, GIS has responsibility for the domestic counter-terrorist intervention capability. Although since 2004 its role has expanded to include special reconnaissance and counter-WMD (weapons of mass destruction) tasks. The GIS has three troop-strength detachments of operators trained in HALO and HAHO (high altitude low opening and high altitude high opening), composed of four teams of four. These teams include integral EOD support and a breacher. The assault teams are supported by the Intelligence-gathering, Reconnaissance and Target Acquisition Section which houses the unit's snipers.

GIS also deployed to Iraq in 2006 as part of the Italian contingent to Operation *Iraqi Freedom* and to Afghanistan since 2008 where it operated as part of Task Force 45 and was instrumental in resolving a 2011 Taliban hostage taking in Herat in a combined operation with the GOI. It has also successfully concluded several hundred armed criminal and terrorist sieges.

The 17° Stormo Incursori provides the equivalent capabilities of US Air Force Special Tactics, primarily in combat control of airstrikes, medical evacuations and helicopter insertions; and in combat search and rescue. The Navy GOI are one element of the larger Comando Raggruppamento Subacquei e Incursori (COMSUBIN or Combat Swimmers and Commandos Command), the other being Gruppo Operativo Subacqueo or GOS, specialist combat divers trained to conduct underwater EOD tasks and carry out beach reconnaissance along with mining enemy harbours. The GOI is the rough equivalent of the British SBS and is composed of six 25-man detachments although they typically operate in small units of between six and ten operators.

Italian SOF units use the Glock series of pistols, the MP5 and MP7 series, Benelli M4 shotguns, the HK416 which is replacing a range of Bushmaster and Colt M4s and G36 variants (Col Moschin also issue the 7.62x51mm Fabrique Nationale SCAR as a marksman rifle), and the Heckler & Koch MSG90 sniper rifle and Sako TRG-42 along with Accuracy International sniper rifles in a number of calibres.

Combined Joint Special Operations Task Force (CJSOTF)

Nationality: US • Branch: Joint/Army • Established: date unknown

Combined or Joint Special Operations Task Forces (CJSOTFs) are organizations, usually US-led, which temporarily bring together a number of special operations units to deploy to a particular theatre or purpose under one command. The term Joint Special Operations Task Forces denotes that the grouping may include services other than the Army while Combined Joint Special Operations Task Forces may include allied special operations units.

An example of a Joint Special Operations Task Force was Joint Special Operations Task Force – North (JSOTF-N) in Afghanistan, the famous 'Task Force Dagger' deployed in late 2001 and largely responsible for the successful overthrow of the Taliban government (both JSOC task forces, in Afghanistan and later Iraq, originally operated under the Task Force Dagger – and later Sword – title before they became numbered task forces such as Task Force 11 and Task Force 20). It was built around a core of the 5th SFG as the ground component and supported by a range of other Army and Air Force assets including the 2nd Battalion of the 160th Special Operations Aviation Regiment (160th SOAR) and Air Force Special Tactics combat controllers (CCTs) and pararescue jumpers (PJs).

A Combined Joint Special Operations Task Force would be best exemplified by the Combined Joint Special Operations Task Force – Arabian Peninsula (CJSOTF-AP) which replaced the various JSOTFs deployed during the invasion of Iraq. All special operations units, including allied units like the Polish GROM, operated under the auspices of CJSOTF-AP, including Navy SEAL, Air Force Special Tactics and Army Special Forces.

Classified task forces such as those commanded by the JSOC are simply denoted as a 'Task Force' with no further explanation. They may be joint or combined or, rarely, based on only one unit. The use of the 'Task Force' designation is an operational security measure which limits the amount of information that can be surmised purely from the organization's title.

US Army Special Forces soldiers assigned to Combined Joint Special Operations Task Force – Afghanistan in contact with the enemy in Nangarhar Province in 2014. The Green Beret fires the stand-alone version of the 40mm M320 grenade launcher – note the holster. (Courtesy US Army, Spc Connor Mendez)

As a modern example, Task Force 27 operates in Iraq and Syria and is structured around a Delta squadron supported by a Ranger company and assets from the 160th SOAR. It also houses Special Tactics operators and often works with a rotational component drawn from the British 22SAS. Thus it is in reality a Combined Joint Special Operations Task Force as it includes both multi-service and allied units.

The sub task force, Task Force 27.2, is responsible for JSOC missions in East Africa and appears to be a solely US effort headed up by SEAL Team 6 with aviation support from the 160th; thus it would be termed a Joint Special Operations Task Force as no allied or Coalition forces are permanently attached to the command.

Commandement des Opérations Spéciales (COS)

Nationality: French • Branch: Joint • Established: 1992

The French Commandement des Opérations Spéciales (COS or Special Operations Command) is roughly equivalent to the US SOCOM or JSOC and was established in 1992 to bring together operational control of all French military special operations units. These include the Navy's Force Maritime des Fusiliers Marins et Commandos (FORFUSCO or Maritime Force Fusilier Marines and Commandos), the Air Force's Commando Parachutiste de l'Air no10 (CPA-10 or Parachute Commandos no. 10) and Division des Opérations Spéciales (Special Operations Division), which provide integral air transport, and the Army's own Groupement Spécial Autonome (Special Forces Command).

The Groupement Spécial Autonome includes the specialist reconnaissance unit, the 13e Régiment de Dragons Parachutistes (13e RDP or 13th Parachute Dragoon Regiment); the 4e Régiment d'Hélicoptères des Forces Spéciales (4eRHFS or 4th Special Forces Helicopter Regiment), which provides organic helicopter support in a similar manner to the 160th Special Operations Aviation Regiment (160th SOAR), with a range of transport and attack helicopters; and the 1er Régiment de Parachutistes d'Infanterie de Marine (1er RPIMa or 1st Marine Infantry Parachute Regiment).

The 13e RDP is composed of seven squadrons, each with a specialist role. 1st Squadron conducts unit training; 2nd is a maritime unit including combat divers; 3rd is dedicated to mountain and arctic warfare; 4th Squadron contains the desert mobility specialists; 5th comprises the regiment's parachutists, trained in both HALO and HAHO (high altitude low opening and high altitude high opening); 6th is responsible for communications, including signals intelligence; and the 7th and final squadron comprises the regiment's integral human intelligence gatherers and often operates in advance force operations.

HK416-armed French COS soldiers, unknown but likely drawn from 1er RPIMa, prepare to assault a hotel besieged by al-Shabaab terrorists in Burkina Faso, January 2016. Two US JSOC operators, likely from Delta Force, can be seen immediately above the hood of the SUV in the olive trousers and black tee-shirt – both carry HK416A5s. (Ahmed Ouoba/AFP/Getty Images)

The 1er RPIMa is the direct descendant of the wartime French SAS and maintains many of its traditions, including the use of 'Who Dares Wins' as its unit motto. The unit is composed of four companies, each with its own speciality: one is centred on counter-terrorism (including close protection) as well as housing the unit's parachuting specialists; another is focused on infiltrating and operating in extreme environments; the third focuses on mobility operations; while the fourth is the reconnaissance and surveillance company, whose responsibilities include the deployment of UAVs (unmanned aerial vehicles).

All four companies are trained in counter-terrorism intervention and close quarter battle along with core SOF skills. In this way, the unit as a whole is similar to the British 22SAS or the Australian SASR in many respects. The companies are even known as SAS for Stick Action Spéciale (Special Action Stick). The unit saw some success during the PIFWC (Persons Indicted For War Crimes) hunt in the Balkans during the 1990s and early 2000s and later deployed to Afghanistan, operating between 2003 and 2006 as Task Group Ares (see page 321). Seven COS personnel were killed during this period. It was later deployed to Libya in 2011 where it worked alongside a mixed team of British operators from 22SAS and the Special Reconnaissance Regiment (SRR).

In 2016, three unidentified French special operators were killed when their helicopter, a deniable Mi-17, crashed (or was shot down) south of Benghazi, Libya. The then-French president was forced to acknowledge: 'Special forces are there, of course, to help and to make sure France is present everywhere in the struggle against terrorists.'

The maritime element of COS consists of seven commandos of naval special operators, each comprising around 90 operators, under the command of the Force Maritime des Fusiliers Marins et Commandos (FORFUSCO), analogous to the US Navy's Special Warfare Command. The best known of these units, Commando Hubert, consists of combat divers with two companies; the first includes four sections with one designated for counter-terrorism, one operating submersibles, one operating small boats and one command element. Each operational section consists of between 15 and 20 parachute qualified operators. The second company is responsible for technical support and logistics.

Commandos Jaubert and Trepek are counter-terrorism specialists; they provide France's maritime counter-terrorist (MCT) capability and are equivalent to Britain's SBS. Commando Penfentenyo is the special reconnaissance unit while Commando Kieffer is focused on intelligence gathering including the deployment of unmanned aerial vehicles (UAVs), along with an CBRN (chemical, biological, radiological and nuclear) role. Commando Monfort provides heavy weapon and sniper support. All of the Commandos are supported by Commando Ponchardier, a research and logistic unit.

COS units have been heavily committed to Central and Eastern Africa with the command heading up a long-term counter-terrorist mission in Burkina Faso called Operation *Sabre*. They were also at the forefront of operations into Mali with a 4eRHFS Gazelle being shot down during initial operations. A combined force of only 40 operators from 1er RPIMa and 13e RDP managed to seize a vital airport in a surprise heliborne assault. COS operators were also embedded as liaisons with Malian and Chadian forces. Most recently, Commando Hubert conducted a successful hostage rescue in Burkina Fasa in May 2019, recovering four Western hostages and killing four terrorists. Sadly two Marine Commandos lost their lives during the assault.

1er RPIMa typically carries out operations for both the military and France's Direction Générale de la Sécurité Extérieure (DGSE or General Directorate for External Security) although the intelligence agency has its own paramilitary force akin to the CIA's Special Activities Division. Variously known as the Special Operations Service, Le Service Action (The Action Service) or sometimes Action Division, the unit is composed of three principal elements: a clandestine operations command responsible for special reconnaissance and surveillance, a combat diver unit for maritime operations, and the Close Quarter Battle Group, which conducts special operations. It is supported by a unit similar to SAD's Air Branch or Delta's

Echo Squadron: the 56e Groupe Aérien Combiné (56th Combined Air Group), which operates both transport aircraft and helicopters.

One of their most recent operations was the failed hostage rescue in Somalia to recover a captured DGSE agent, a former Special Forces operator. After infiltrating by helicopter to an off-set LZ (landing zone) to avoid warning the al-Shabaab hostage takers, the 50-man unit proceeded on foot to surround the target compound. At that point, as they prepared to breach, they were compromised by an al-Shabaab sentry and a vicious firefight broke out.

One operator was killed and another, the unit's leader, was severely wounded along with another five Action Division operators before they broke contact and headed for their emergency pick-up. Under the cover of supporting Tigre attack helicopters, the team managed to board its Caracal transport helicopters and escape. Tragically the hostage was executed by al-Shabaab and the wounded DGSE captain died en route to a Navy ship off the coast. The French Defence Ministry acknowledged the mission: 'The DGSE commando force encountered strong resistance and in the course of the attack, which saw heavy combat in places, two soldiers lost their lives.'

The French Air Force also has its own special operations unit in the form of the famed Commando Parachutiste de l'Air no10 (Air Parachute Commando Number 10 or CPA-10), rather uniquely once an Air Commando unit charged with protecting France's nuclear arsenal. It forms, along with special operations helicopter units, the Air Force element of COS. Broadly similar in role to the US Air Force's Special Tactics Squadrons, CPA-10 members are parachute qualified and provide both combat search and rescue and terminal guidance for airstrikes along with conducting UAV operations. They deploy in ten-man teams.

French naval commandos of the Navy's Force Maritime des Fusiliers Marins et Commandos (FORFUSCO), likely of Commando Montfort, display their uniforms and equipment. (Frank Perry/AFP/Getty Images)

They are also trained in conducting special reconnaissance and surveillance and can be infiltrated into a conflict area to conduct covert advanced force operations for follow-on COS elements. CPA-10, like all French SOF units, is also trained to conduct in-extremis hostage rescues. In fact, elements from CPA-10 were involved in a hostage rescue mission to retake the Radisson Blu hotel in Bamako, Mali, in November 2015 along with a small contingent from GIGN and a handful of Delta operators who were in the country on another tasking.

French special operators have been conducting mentoring and training with partner forces in Iraq as Task Force Hydra. An operator from COS' specialist reconnaissance unit, the 13e Régiment de Dragons Parachutistes (13e RDP or 13th Parachute Dragoon Regiment), was shot and killed by insurgents in Iraq in September 2017. Two CPA-10 operators working with the Kurdish Peshmerga were wounded in Iraq in 2016 by an Islamic State UAV equipped with a small explosive charge, probably a mortar bomb or grenade. COS units supported Kurdish forces during the bloody Mosul offensive.

French special operators have also long been rumoured to be operational in Syria, a fact that was publicly confirmed in 2018 when images of unidentified French special operators were seen patrolling with US Army Special Forces in Manbij. Elements from 1er RPIMa have been operating alongside US SOCOM and JSOC units based at Kobani with reports indicating a detachment of 70 operators have been in action. COS also make up the French SOF contingent in Yemen.

French special operators have used a wide variety of small arms including the SIG 551 series of assault rifles and the Mk17 and Mk18 SCAR along with the venerable M4A1 carbine. Increasingly, all are being replaced by the HK416 and HK417. Suppressed MP5SDs are still in the inventory (and are favoured by the likes of Commando Hubert) although MP7A1s have largely replaced them in COS service. Both Glock and Heckler & Koch USP pistols are in use, often suppressed (Commando Hubert also employs suppressed .45ACP Glock 21s).

Counter Terrorist Service (CTS)

Nationality: Iraqi • Branch: Army • Established: 2004

Originally trained and organized in 2004 by US Army Green Berets in Iraq and Jordanian instructors in Jordan, the Iraqi Counter Terrorist Service (CTS) was known initially as the Iraqi Counter Terrorism Force (ICTF). The three-month training programme for prospective recruits was called the Operator Training Course, in obvious homage to Delta Force's OTC.

A second Iraqi unit, the 36th Iraqi Civil Defense Corps (ICDC) Battalion, was raised by US Special Forces as a full-spectrum SOF unit – more akin to the US Army Rangers – rather than focusing purely on counter-terrorism

Iraqi Counter Terrorist Service (CTS) operators mentored by Australian Special Forces conduct an urban warfare exercise. Both wear the distinctive black uniforms of the CTS and carry EOTech-equipped M4 carbines. (Courtesy Commonwealth of Australia, LSIS Jake Badior)

skills. Both units were later amalgamated into the Iraqi Special Operations Brigade. A third unit, officially the Mobile Legion Security Company but known as the Recce Company, was added to provide specialist reconnaissance and surveillance capabilities.

By 2008, the CTS was operating almost as an additional special operations task force – now organized as two Iraqi Special Operations Forces (ISOF) Brigades – alongside US JSOC and SOCOM units deployed to Iraq. Green Berets were still attached as advisers and accompanied their units into the field on operations. ISOF by this stage were conducting multiple raids per night, hunting down al-Qaeda in Iraq and Iranian Quds Force elements.

A success story for both US Army Special Forces and the Iraqi security forces, the CTS soon gained the reputation as perhaps the finest SOF unit in the Middle East (with the honourable exception of the Israelis and perhaps the Jordanians). This was evidenced by the 2010 operation in Tikrit, which saw ISOF assault a terrorist safehouse in a joint operation with Task Force Red Rangers providing heliborne quick reaction and combat search and rescue support. Both the leader of the nascent Islamic State and a key deputy were killed in the assault.

After the expiration of the Status of Force Agreement (SOFA), which governed the deployment of US forces in Iraq, Green Berets shifted CTS training to Jordan in order to comply with Iraqi requirements and continued to train the Iraqi commandos as they fought against Islamic State. The CTS was at the forefront of attempts to recapture cities seized by the emerging Islamic State in late 2013 and into 2014.

With relatively few special operators, the CTS was forced to hand over defence of recaptured territory to regular Army and Ministry of the Interior units who suffered from poor morale and training and who often withdrew under concerted Islamic State attacks. The CTS was also fighting an increasingly conventional war, one it had not trained for, but it represented the best Iraq could offer and was deployed as the spearhead for most offensives. After it suffered heavy losses, an agreement was reached to again allow US Army Green Berets, primarily drawn from 3rd SFG, to train and mentor the CTS on Iraqi soil.

While conducting largely conventional urban warfare operations, the CTS still maintained its counter-terrorism skills, evidenced by the 2014 large-scale hostage rescue at the University of Anbar, freeing almost 1,000 hostages held by Islamic State elements. The 2017 battle for Mosul was perhaps the most brutal the CTS has yet faced, combining counter-terrorist raids and urban warfighting in a heavily IED infested city. According to US military reports, the CTS suffered 40 per cent casualty rates retaking Mosul.

The CTS, and in particular its 1st Brigade, the 'Golden Brigade', were very visible in their black uniforms (with many wearing skull masks) and black-painted up-armoured M1123 HMMWVs during the retaking of Mosul. Along with contending with IEDs, mines and street-by-street clearance of Islamic State cells, the CTS faced wave after wave of suicide vehicle-borne IEDs. Many of these were crudely armoured to protect the driver until he could detonate the device.

Today the CTS incorporates the Counter Terrorist Command and three ISOF Brigades, each with geographic responsibilities. It is supported by the 15th Special Operations Squadron flying armed Mi-17 helicopters. The Ministry of the Interior also maintains its own counter-terrorism unit, the Emergency Response Brigade.

ISOF employ M4-style carbines (the Rock River Arms LAR-15, North Eastern Arms PDW-CCS and SIG-Sauer M400 predominantly) along with a far smaller number of Korean S&T Motiv K2C carbines. Sniper platforms include US-donated M24s and Russian Orsis T-5000s, both in 7.62x51mm, while marksmen carry the Mk14 EBR (Enhanced Battle Rifle). Both the M249 SAW and its special operations variant, the Mk46, are carried, as are US M240 medium machine guns.

Directorate of Special Units (Intervention Unit) (DSU)

Nationality: Belgian • Branch: Army • Established: 2003

The Belgian Federal Police maintains a special operations capability in the form of the renowned Directorate of Special Units (DSU) Intervention Unit, formerly known as Groupe Diane (named after the Greek goddess of the hunt) and Escadron Spécial d'Intervention (ESI or Special Intervention Squadron). DSU are one of the oldest counter-terrorist units in Europe and a founding member of the ATLAS Network, a European-wide counter-terrorism network which innovates and shares tactics and techniques. Along with the German GSG9 and French GIGN, it has helped train dozens of counter-terrorist units across Europe.

As Diane and later ESI, the unit had much experience combating extreme leftist terrorist groups in the 1980s along with a notable success against the Provisional IRA in a plot that left unchecked might have led to a bombing attack on the Princess of Wales during a state visit. One of its other most high-profile operations was against members of the Algerian Groupe Islamique Armé (GIA or Armed Islamic Group) who had managed to slip from the grasp of a 1996 operation by the French RAID to capture them. One terrorist was killed in a shootout with local police after they crossed the border into Belgium before the surviving terrorist took hostages in a nearby residence. ESI, as it was known at the time, breached into the building, throwing flashbang grenades, and overpowered the hostage taker before a shot could be fired.

As DSU, it has operated both in support of the Federal Police as a kind of 'super SWAT' and as the principal counter-terrorist intervention response, including a number of high-profile actions against Islamic State-inspired terrorists. Following the Islamic State suicide bombing at Brussels International Airport in 2016, DSU deployed against a number of terrorist suspects in the town of Forest. After opening fire on a DSU entry team, one terrorist was shot dead by a DSU sniper.

The unit currently employs around 60 full-time operators, including a 12-man sniper cell. It is supported by the Observation Service, which provides both physical and technical surveillance and tracking and will conduct pre-raid reconnaissance for the assaulters.

The DSU in its earlier guise as the ESI was instrumental in developing canine programmes that would later be recognized as combat assault dogs.

Belgian operators from the Directorate of Special Units (DSU) Intervention Unit, formerly known as Groupe Diane, with one of their iconic Malinois combat assault dogs. Note the FN SCAR carried by the operator to the left with its stock folded. DSU has moved to Arc'teryx grey uniforms partly for reasons of urban camouflage and for identification as many jihadist terrorists today dress in black with hoods. (Olivier Matthys/ Getty Images)

With combat assault dogs trained to accompany assault teams since 1984, DSU popularized the now famous Belgian Malinois as the breed of choice for SOFs including SEAL Team 6. The unit's Dog Service currently houses eight explosive detection dogs and a pair of combat assault dogs.

It was also instrumental in developing a motorcycle-equipped Quick Reaction Force that can support local police until a full DSU team can be deployed. DSU not surprisingly employs a majority of Fabrique Nationale small arms including the SCAR (Special Operations Forces Combat Assault Rifle) and P90, often suppressed, along with modified Heckler & Koch G3s as its short range sniper rifle, the British AXMC as its long range sniper platform and the Austrian Glock family as its sidearm.

Echo Squadron/Seaspray

Nationality: US • Branch: Army/CIA • Established: 1981

Echo Squadron, which is today the 'covered' or undercover flight unit nestled within Delta Force, began life in 1981 as a joint US Army/CIA endeavour called Seaspray (later renamed Quasar Talent). The unit, like many that would later become part of JSOC, was created in the aftermath of the failure of Operation *Eagle Claw* in Iran. One of the key lessons learnt was that Delta needed its own integral air transport, which would train with and understand its specialist requirements rather than drafting in a composite force of Air Force and Marine aviators as had occurred in *Eagle Claw*.

Seaspray flew in both unmarked Hughes MD-500 series Little Birds and civilian registered light aircraft. The mission of this new unit was either to support CIA clandestine actions such as the recovery of agents or assets from conflict zones or to infiltrate/exfiltrate Delta operators into targets in 'non-permissive' environments. Seaspray and its aircraft were also employed by another newly formed unit – the Field Operations Group (also known as the Foreign Operating Group), which had morphed into the Intelligence Support Activity (ISA) – who used them for aerial signals intelligence missions in Central America.

After operating predominantly in Central America supporting CIA operations into Nicaragua along with the occasional mission to the Middle East, Seaspray was broken up. Most of the helicopter component was assigned directly to Delta as E or Echo Squadron in 1989. From that point, new aviators, primarily drawn from the then-Task Force 160, would complete a selection programme run by Delta. Their light aircraft appear to have gone to another covert JSOC element called Flight Concepts Division mainly to support ISA.

The unit expanded under Delta and provided an essential capability by mounting video cameras in a range of airframes which could transmit real-time footage to the on-scene Delta commander in an early foreshadowing of the huge capability increase provided by latter-day Predator and Reaper UAVs (unmanned aerial response vehicles). In the 1990s, Echo operated extensively during the PIFWC (Persons Indicted For War Crimes) hunt in the Balkans and deployed with ISA operators to Colombia in the hunt for the Colombian drug lord and narcoterrorist Pablo Escobar. Two of its highly modified civilian MD530F Little Birds were seen supporting Task Force Ranger in Somalia. An unmarked Little

A rare image, taken by a friend of the author, of an Echo Squadron Little Bird in Western Iraq at the end of March 2003. The unmarked helicopter, which mounted 2.75-inch rocket pods, landed to recover an Iraqi general who had been captured by 5th Special Forces Group. (Author's Collection)

Bird from Echo even picked up an Iraqi general captured by 5th SFG in the early stages of the invasion of Iraq.

During the JSOC counter-terrorism campaign in Iraq, Echo both flew aerial reconnaissance with Wescam Ball video cameras (known by the fitting callsign 'Birdseye'), allowing the aerial tracking of terrorist vehicles, and contributed to the airborne signals intelligence campaign along with aircraft from the ISA and an Air Force surveillance unit. Echo has now been involved in thousands of missions around the world, providing organic intelligence, surveillance, targeting and reconnaissance (ISTAR) support for JSOC, and occasionally the CIA (which now has its own covert air unit, Air Branch, nestled within the Special Activities Division), along with conducting operations in denied areas.

At some point during the War on Terror, its specialized Little Birds were gradually replaced with Bell 407s, probably owing to their superior ability to blend in, particularly when wearing civilian markings, across virtually any conflict zone (and the fact that the Little Birds were suffering from the thousands of hours flown in the harshest environments). Echo (sometimes referred to as the Aviation Squadron in Pentagon reports) and the equally secretive Flight Concepts Division, now known as the Aviation Technology Office, also flies a range of Russian-made helicopters and commercial S-92 Sikorskys which have appeared on operations in Afghanistan, Djibouti, Iraq, Syria and Yemen.

Einsatzkommando Cobra

Nationality: Austrian • Branch: Ministry of the Interior • Established: 1978

Originally known as GEK (Gendarmerieeinsatzkommando) Cobra, the Austrian counter-terrorist intervention unit was established with the assistance of both Germany's GSG9 and Israel's Sayeret Matkal and Yamam, units which themselves maintain especially close links. The GEK Cobra was in fact developed from an earlier unit used to protect Jewish immigrants from the Soviet Union from Palestinian terrorism. GEK Cobra was structured into four elements, each commanding a platoon (*Zug*) of two intervention groups.

The unit was renamed as EKO Cobra in 2002 when a major restructure occurred. This brought the majority of local and regional police special units, including the Mobile Einsatzkommandos (MEKs or Federal Police Mobile Task Forces) and the Sondereinsatzgruppen (SEGs or Special Task Forces) of the former Provincial Gendarmerie, into EKO Cobra to provide a national response capability across the country, with four operational sub-units (Graz, Linz, Vienna and Innsbruck) and three operational field offices (Klagenfurt, Salzburg and Bregenz) in addition to its headquarters at Wiener Neustadt.

Austrian EKO Cobra operators pictured during an operation in 2017. Note the Steyr AUG A2 and B&T APC9. Their iconic Ulbrichts AM-95 ballistic helmet with visor with German Flecktarn pattern cover are also visible. (Hans Punz/AFP/Getty Images)

Four detachments are based at each sub-unit (each staffed by between ten and 25 operators) and two at each field office. In 2013, a further restructure saw EKO Cobra incorporated with other specialist elements under the Directorate for Special Forces bringing together disparate surveillance and EOD resources. The unit now numbers some 450 personnel in total.

Thankfully Austria has been spared the onslaught of international terrorism; however, EKO Cobra has deployed to thousands of criminal sieges and arrests of armed suspects along with providing close personal protection for Austrian diplomatic staff in conflict zones such as Iraq. It has also deployed at least once to Germany in 2016 to support GSG9 after a mass shooting. One EKO Cobra operator was killed during a police operation in 2013.

Originally armed with the four-inch barrel Manurhin MR73 .357 Magnum revolver, EKO Cobra now uses the Glock series with Glock weapon lights as its primary sidearm. Its original sub machine gun was the Israeli 9x19mm UZI, since replaced with the MP5 series (particularly the MP5SD3) and small numbers of the MP7A1 (principally for close personal protection duties), before these were in turn recently replaced with the Swiss B&T APC9 developed in close coordination with the unit.

Since EOK Cobra's formation, its primary assault rifle has been the Steyr AUG; the latest variant in use is the A2 featuring LLM01 laser and light illuminators. Its standard sniper rifle is the Steyr SSG08, another platform developed with input from the unit, along with the .50 French PGM Hecate.

Its operators often wear the distinctive Ulbrichts AM-95 ballistic helmet with visor with a German Flecktarn pattern camouflage cover, reminiscent of Germany's GSG9 in the 1980s and '90s.

Emergency Response Unit (ERU)

Nationality: Irish • Branch: Police • Established: 1977

Originally created as the Special Task Force of the Irish Garda Síochána or simply Garda, this unit was tasked with domestic counter-terrorist intervention before being renamed the Anti-Terrorist Unit in 1984. The role later expanded to include a wide range of police tactical responsibilities including dealing with armed criminals and sieges and the unit was again renamed the Emergency Response Unit (ERU) in 1987.

Local Garda Armed Support Units were introduced in 2012 to provide an immediate response to both armed criminal and terrorist incidents in a similar manner to the Armed Response Vehicles of the Metropolitan Police's SCO19. In 2017 the ERU, today some 100 officers strong, and the Armed Support Units were placed under the command of the Special Tactics and Operational Command. The ERU is operationally structured into 12-man teams with two teams immediately available – one on stand-by and another conducting training.

The Irish Army maintains the Army Ranger Wing (ARW), originally established in 1980 as a counter-terrorist unit to manage incidents involving hostage taking of Irish nationals overseas. Its predecessor was the Special Assault Groups, which were based largely on the US Army Ranger concept and could provide a rudimentary military counter-terrorist response. The ARW has since expanded its mission set dramatically and now serves as a full-spectrum SOF unit, with counter-terrorism only one responsibility.

Soldiers from the Irish Defence Forces' Army Ranger Wing in full counter-terrorist kit in 2010. Note the extended magazine and light mount on the centre operator's SIG-Sauer P226, the MP5 with twin magazines and the ballistic face shields. (Julien Behal/PA Images)

The ARW is organized in six-man assault teams, several of which make up a task unit. The unit maintains a number of specialist task units including maritime (combat diving and small boats), military free-fall and a reconnaissance/sniper cell. The ARW has deployed operationally to Chad, East Timor/Timor Leste, Liberia, Mali and Somalia. A handful of operators conducted two tours in Afghanistan under International Security Assistance Force (ISAF) Special Operations command from October 2006 to March 2007 and again from September 2014 to March 2015, although these were staff roles for the unit to gain experience in multi-national task forces. The unit has recently been announced as a core component of the EU Special Operations Task Group.

The Garda ERU is well equipped with 9x19mm SIG-Sauer P226 sidearms, 4.6x30mm MP7A1 sub machine guns and 5.56x45mm HK416 carbines. The ARW also employs the P226 and the HK416A5, along with suppressed USPs, railed MP5s and the HK417. Both units use the Accuracy International series of sniper rifles.

Fuerza Especial de Reacción (FER)

Nationality: Mexican • Branch: Army • Established: 1987

The Fuerza Especial de Reacción (FER or Special Reaction Force) is the Mexican Army's counter-terrorist and direct action unit.

Originally known as FERIAM or Fuerza Especial de Reacción Inmediata del Alto Mando (the High Command Immediate Reaction Special Force), the force was trained by France's GIGN and later by Delta. It has also since worked extensively with the Israeli Sayeret Matkal. Little is known about the structure of the unit. All members are qualified in HALO/HAHO (high altitude low opening/high altitude high opening) parachute jumping and receive extensive close quarter battle training.

The FER has lost a number of operators to the war against the cartels, notably including the 2015 downing of a Mexican Air Force EC725 Super Cougar helicopter by an RPG, killing the five FER operators that were on board. The unit has been prominent in the captures of numerous high-ranking cartel leaders, its operators often wearing MultiCam uniforms and Ops Core helmets, their faces concealed behind masks.

Within the Mexican Army there are currently six Special Forces battalions with an additional battalion acting as a rapid deployment force. All train with the US Army's 7th SFG. The Paratrooper Brigade and Military Police Brigade also have their own independent Special Forces battalions that do not come under the command of the Cuerpo de Fuerzas Especiales (CFE or Special Forces Corps), a US SOCOM-like organization that controls the regular Special Forces battalions and the FER.

The Mexican Navy maintains its own Fuerzas Especiales (FES or Special Forces) under the command of the Unidad de Operaciones Especiales (UNOPES or Special Operations Unit). The FES is for all intents and purposes the Mexican SEALs – trained in special reconnaissance and opposed visit-board-search-seizure missions and parachute and SCUBA qualified, they are split into three sub-units with geographical responsibilities.

These are Fuerzas Especiales del Pacifico (FESPA or Special Forces Pacific), Fuerzas Especiales del Centro (FESCENT or Special Forces Center) and Fuerzas Especiales del Golfo (FESGO or Special Forces Gulf), each structured in a similar manner to a US Navy SEAL Team. A similar unit to SEAL Team 6 exists, nestled within the FES headquarters and known as the High Impact Group or Navy High Command Special Forces. The FES operators are supported by two battalions of the Comandos de Infantería de Marina or Marine Commandos, which is roughly the equivalent of the USMC's Force Recon or the British Royal Marine Brigade Reconnaissance Force (both of which conduct reconnaissance for their parent organisations and are trained to infiltrate target areas by land, sea and air).

Along with their warfighting role, the FES and Marine Commandos have been deployed in the war against the drug cartels, probably as they are seen as less susceptible to corruption. One former Army Special Forces officer infamously ended up selling out to one of the cartels, taking a platoon of operators with him. They later formed their own cartel, Los Zetas. He was eventually shot dead by his former Special Forces comrades, allegedly members of the FER.

Mexican Army Special Forces employ the newly issued, Mexican-designed and produced FX-05 Xiuhcoatl assault rifle, the Para Minimi squad automatic

A Mexican soldier from the Cuerpo de Fuerzas Especiales (Special Forces Corps) fires his 5.56x45mm Fabrique Nationale F2000 bullpup rifle fitted with EOTech sight. (Courtesy US Army, Cpl Joanna Bradshaw)

weapon, and Accuracy International sniper platforms. The Fabrique Nationale F2000 bullpup has also been seen in use. FER issues Colt LE6945 carbines, SIG 716 rifles and SIG-Sauer P2022 pistols. The Naval FES teams and Marine Commandos employ the M4A1 for general issue and the Fabrique Nationale P90, often equipped with suppressors, for boarding actions.

The Mexican Federal Police had its own tactical unit, Grupo de Operaciones Especiales (GOPES or Special Operations Group), which received training from RAID and the Spanish Grupos de Operaciones Especiales (GEO) and was organized into eight- to 12-man teams. They were heavily armed with Tavor assault rifles including the MTAR-21, SIG-Sauer 3000 sniper rifles and M60E4 medium machine guns. As of July 2018, the unit was disbanded owing to corruption allegations. It is unknown at the time of writing what new unit will be established to replace its capabilities.

Grenzschutzgruppe 9 (GSG9)

Nationality: German • Branch: Federal Police • Established: 1972

Formed as part of the then-West German Federal Border Guard Service, in part because of German concerns about military special units stemming from World War II, Grenzschutzgruppe 9 (GSG9) is Germany's primary domestic counter-terrorist intervention unit. Since 2005, the unit has become part of the Federal Police; it has maintained its former name but is officially now GSG9 der Bundespolizei.

GSG9 was established on 1 October 1972 after the Munich massacre, when 11 Israeli Olympic athletes were taken hostage and killed by the Black September terrorist organization. It was formally activated the following year, on 30 April 1973. Its first leader, the late then-Colonel Ulrich 'Ricky' Wegener, received assistance from both the British SAS and Israel's Sayeret Matkal (which had been training for a contingency operation to rescue the athletes in Munich before the debacle by German Federal Police). Intriguingly the East Germans also created a similar unit, Diensteinheit IX (Service 9), although it appears to have been largely employed against Soviet deserters.

GSG9's original mandate, according to the German governent planning document which brought it into existence, called for the unit to:

... [undertake] the liberation of hostages; to put especially dangerous and active criminals out of action, such as plane hijackers; the warding off of terrorist acts, carried out with firearms, explosives, or incendiaries; protecting criminal court procedures with a high grade of danger and interference attached; other criminal acts which necessitate a forcible elimination of delinquents, groups of criminals,

or the clearing out of hiding places; concrete security measures on the personnel and material side.

A modern reader does wonder about the 'forcible elimination of delinquents'…

The unit is composed of four components, each with a specialization. GSG9/1 is the hostage rescue intervention unit and contains the unit's snipers, GSG9/2 comprises the unit's maritime specialists working with small boats and SCUBA infiltrations, and GSG9/3 contains the parachutists, skilled in MFF (military free-fall), HAHO (high altitude high opening) and HALO (high altitude low opening). A new contingent trained in CBRN (chemical, biological, radiological and nuclear), presumably GSG9/4, was established in 2017 and is based in Berlin. Each unit is believed to number about 45 personnel, although the size of each is currently being increased following the wave of Islamic State-inspired terrorist attacks across Europe.

TOP LEFT A 2017 image of a GSG9 operator carrying a 7.62x51mm HK417A2 in RAL8000 finish. He wears an olive-drab Crye uniform and Lindner Taktik plate carrier. (Michele Tantussi/Getty Images)

TOP RIGHT A GSG9 operator pictured in 2007 wearing the unit's iconic Ulbrichts AM-95 ballistic helmet with visor. He carries the 5.56x45mm Heckler & Koch G36C with EOTech optic. (Juergen Schwarz/Getty Images)

One unit of 30 operators is on rotational one-hour notice to move, while all four GSG9 elements are able to deploy to anywhere within Germany within a maximum of four hours, facilitated by their integral helicopter component. They are supported by regional and municipality-based police Spezial Einsatzkommandos (SEKs, who changed their name from Sonder Einsatzkommando in 2013 owing to negative wartime connotations), and Mobile Einsatzkommandos (MEKs – plainclothes units roughly equivalent to France's Brigade de Recherche et d'Intervention, the BRI or Research and Intervention Brigade), which conduct frequent exercises with GSG9, are often called upon to conduct counter-terrorist arrests and are the first response to any domestic terrorist incident.

Another unit, the BFE+ (Beweissicherungs- und Festnahmeeinheit plus or Evidence Collection and Arrest Unit Plus), was established in Berlin but now has five operational locations across Germany, each employing a 50-man team. In the event of a terrorist incident, BFE+ would assist GSG9 and the relevant SEK/MEK in providing manpower for cordons, searches and roadblocks along with the ability to raid suspect addresses. In contrast, standard BFEs are local police arrest teams who target violent criminals and may also support SEKs and MEKs in counter-terrorist operations.

The unit first came to the world's attention when it successfully stormed the hijacked Air Lufthansa Flight 181 that had landed at Mogadishu Airport in an operation codenamed *Fire Magic*. Apart from with *Fire Magic*, GSG9 has been involved in thousands of operations targeting both terrorists and armed criminals. In 1993 it conducted a second successful counter-hijack mission, recapturing a hijacked Dutch KLM aircraft at Düsseldorf. GSG9 has suffered three casualties since its inception; two operators were killed in Fallujah, Iraq conducting close personal protection duties while the third was shot and killed while attempting to capture a pair of Red Army Faction leaders in 1993.

GSG9's establishment called rather quaintly for 'hand fire-arms; machine guns; special rifles with telescope-sight and infrared equipment; silencers; anaesthetic additives' according to the briefing document calling for their establishment, but today GSG9 employs a wide range of small arms. It pioneered the use of the MP5 series of sub machine guns, which are still employed, along with the MP7A1 and A2. In terms of sidearms, the unit began life using both .38 Special and .357 Magnum revolvers, along with 9mm Heckler & Koch P9S automatics. These were later replaced by the 9mm P7 and P7M13. Current issue is the 9mm Glock in a number of variants and the underwater P11 is still issued for GSG9/2 specialist tasks.

For many years, versions of the G36 but typically the G36C have been the principal shoulder weapon but these have been supplemented by recently issued Heckler & Koch HK416s. The unit's principal light sniper rifle is the HK417 while longer range tasks are handled by the French PGM Mini Hecate in .338 Lapua Magnum and its .50 cousin.

Groupe d'Intervention de la Gendarmerie nationale (GIGN)

Nationality: French • Branch: Gendarmerie • Established: 1974

Groupe d'Intervention de la Gendarmerie nationale (GIGN or National Police Intervention Group), along with Germany's GSG9, is perhaps the most recognized of the European counter-terrorist units. Its missions have been recognized in celluloid (*L'Assaut* in 2010) and it has been at the forefront of the battle against Islamic State cells in France. The unit was first established in 1974 as the Commando Régionale d'intervention (Regional Intervention Commando) in the wake of the 1972 Munich massacre (see page 88) and developed strong bonds with both the Germans and the British SAS.

The basic structure of the unit has remained largely unchanged in the decades since; GIGN's assaulters are organized into four self-contained intervention groups (Force Intervention: FI or Intervention Force) of 25 operators. At any one time, one group is on stand-by and one is training at GIGN's headquarters in Versailles-Satory, available to reinforce the first.

A French GIGN operator pictured in 2011 with 5.56x45mm HK416 assault rifle. After the events at the Bataclan siege, GIGN has supplemented its HK416s with the Czech 7.62x39mm CZ806 Bren 2 fitted with suppressor to take advantage of the larger calibre, with an increase in both the 'barrier blindness' and terminal effects. (Fred Dufour/AFP/ Getty Images)

A GIGN dog handler with his Malinois combat assault dog (CAD) flanked by two operators armed with 9x19mm Glock 17 pistols. Another of their CADs, Diesel, a seven-year old Malinois, was killed during an operation to capture terrorists responsible for the November 2015 Paris attacks. (Baptiste Giroudon/Paris Match via Getty Images)

The Force Intervention is supported by the Force Observation/Recherche (FOR or Observation and Research Force), which provides the unit's reconnaissance and surveillance capability, and the Force Appui Opérationnel (FAO or Operational Support Force), which houses the unit's organic EOD, canine element and heavy breachers.

A GIGN operator prepared to operate in hazardous environments in Avon respirator with its own air supply. He is armed with the Fabrique Nationale P90 equipped with weapon light and Aimpoint optic. (Xavier Rossi/Gamma-Rapho via Getty Images)

In 2016, the unit was expanded by the inclusion of what are termed GIGN Antenna units, regional tactical units known as PI2G (Pelotons d'intervention interrégionaux de la Gendarmerie or Inter-regional Police Intervention Squads, aka GIGN branches). GIGN along with RAID is supported by the Puma helicopters from the 4th and 5th Squadrons of the 4e Régiment d'Hélicoptères des Forces Spéciales (4eRHFS or 4th Special Forces Helicopter Regiment), operating as the Groupe Interarmées d'Hélicoptères or Joint Helicopter Group.

Although renowned for its involvement in a 1976 hostage taking in Djibouti, when a busload of 30 French school children was taken hostage, and for the textbook counter-hijacking operation to retake Air France Flight 8969 in 1994, GIGN has been involved in hundreds of operations against both al-Qaeda- and Islamic State-inspired terrorists within France in the past decade. Most well-known would be its successful neutralization of the terrorists responsible for the *Charlie Hebdo* murders in 2015, although it carried out extensive raids in the wake of the November 2015 Paris attacks, including a rare cross-border operation supporting the Belgian Directorate of Special Units (DSU).

GIGN deployed to Mali in response to the terrorist siege of the Radisson Blu hotel in 2015 although operators from the French Army's 1er Régiment de Parachutistes d'Infanteriede Marine (1er RPIMa or 1st Marine Infantry Parachute Regiment) and a pair of Delta Force operators had managed to retake the hotel alongside the Malian commandos before GIGN arrived.

In March 2018, an Islamic State terrorist murdered three civilians, fired upon local police and seized a supermarket in Trèbes, southern France. The Toulouse-based GIGN Antenna responded and, while negotiations were under way, a senior Gendarmerie officer traded places with the last hostage. After three hours, the officer saw his opportunity and attempted to disarm the terrorist, shouting 'Assault! Assault!' into his mobile (cell) phone which he had left on an open call with the GIGN Antenna. The operators immediately assaulted and the terrorist was shot dead but not before he managed to shoot and fatally stab the Gendarmerie officer.

Today GIGN carries the Glock 17 in preference to its traditional sidearm, the .357 Magnum Manurhin MR73 revolver. The MP5 is still widely used, equipped with rails and a specialist stock to enable its use with ballistic visors (the Antenna units employ the UMP). The HK416 and HK417 have largely replaced the G36KA3 and SIG 552.

Following the Paris attacks, the unit also adopted the Czech Bren 2 in 7.62x39mm to improve penetration against terrorists wearing body armour (as the terrorist who seized the kosher hypermarket immediately following and in support of the *Charlie Hebdo* massacre did). Sniper platforms include the Accuracy International AWM, Tikka Tactical T3 and the PGM Hecate anti-materiel rifle. The unit's members wear the MSA Gallet helmet with trademark ballistic visor.

Groupement d'Intervention Spécialise (GIS)

Nationality: Algerian • Branch: Army • Established: 1955

Groupement d'Intervention Spécialise (GIS or Special Operations Group) was established in 1986 as a counter-terrorist intervention and close personal protection unit within the Algerian security service's Direction Générale de Surêté Nationale (DGSN or National Security General Directorate). The unit conducted training with the likes of Italy's Col Moschin, the French GIGN and the Russian Spetsgruppy-A.

The unit saw significant combat against the jihadists of the Groupe Islamique Armé (GIA or Armed Islamic Group) during the Algerian Civil War from 1991 to 2000, known as 'La Sale Guerre' or the 'The Dirty War', owing to the number of atrocities carried out by both sides. A GIS operator was responsible for the assassination of the acting Algerian president in 1992, gunning him down with his MP5. After this incident, the GIS was understandably removed from close personal protection duties.

The Groupe Salafiste pour la Prédication et le Combat (GSPC or Salafist Group for Preaching and Combat) remained in conflict with the Algerian government after most of the GIA and other insurgent groups had been eliminated or surrendered under an amnesty programme. The GSPC pledged allegiance to al-Qaeda and eventually became the nucleus of al-Qaeda in the Islamic Maghreb (AQIM), spreading its campaign of terror to Mali.

In May 2003, the GIS conducted a hostage rescue operation to recover 17 hostages from a larger group of 32 European tourists who had been captured by GSPC in southern Algeria. The remaining hostages were freed after a ransom payment was made. GIS also conducted a covert non-combatant evacuation from Libya in 2014. The unit was disbanded the following year.

Algeria also has the Détachement Spécial d'Intervention (DSI or Special Intervention Detachment), established in 1989 as part of the National Gendarmerie. The DSI was modelled upon and trained by GIGN. Indeed on domestic operations, the black-clad DSI operators resemble the French GIGN or RAID, using ballistic shields and helmets with distinctive ballistic visors.

Officially DSI are tasked with 'The neutralization of rabid criminals; the participation in the judicial police operations; escorting and transporting dangerous prisoners; close protection and escort of VIPs; fighting banditry and terrorism,' according to the Algerian government. The Gendarmerie also fields a number of other special units including the Groupe d'Intervention et de Recherche (GIR or Intervention and Reconnaissance Group), a regionally based counter-terrorist intervention unit similar in concept to the older GIGN Antenna units.

The Ministry of the Interior maintains the Brigade de Recherche et d'Intervention (BRI or Research and Intervention Brigade), better known as

Brigade 127, which is primarily a tactical unit to respond to public order and armed criminals. The Ministry has established its own counter-terrorist unit, the Groupement des Opérations Spéciales de la Police (GOSP or Police Special Operations Group) based on the French RAID. The Algerian Army also currently has two special operations regiments, the 104th and the 112th, composed of Army commandos and former members of the GIS.

A final unit which is shrouded in secrecy is the formerly named Service de Coordination Opérationnelle et de Renseignement Antiterroriste (SCORAT or Service for Operational Coordination and Antiterrorist Intelligence), originally created and commanded by the nation's intelligence service, the Département du Renseignement et de la Sécurité (DRS). SCORAT tracks jihadists and has been key in the fight against AQIM; it has been described by intelligence professionals as a cross between 'AMAN and the Institute' meaning Israeli military intelligence and the Mossad. SCORAT has its own clandestine direct action unit, which operates both within and outside Algerian borders. It is thought to be responsible for the killing of the leader of the jihadist group Southern Children's Movement for Justice in Libya in 2018.

The SCORAT is now known as the SCAAT, or Service Central Algérien pour Antiterroriste (Algerian Central Service for Anti-Terrorism), after political reshuffling which saw the unit moved from the DRS to the Ministry

A 1993 image of Algeria's GIS, 'the Ninjas', with AK-pattern rifles. AKs are still used today by GIS but upgraded with reflex optics. (Pool Merillon/Turpin/ Gamma-Rapho via Getty Images)

of National Defence (MND). GIS was also a victim of Machiavellian politics as the military and DGSN fought over resources and influence.

In January 2013, a BP natural gas complex facility in Amenas was seized by more than 30 members of the Signed with Blood Battalion of AQIM. Some 800 hostages were captured. The terrorists were heavily armed with ordnance pilfered or purchased in Libya including light mortars, RPGs and anti-personnel mines. Offers of assistance from France, the United States and the United Kingdom, including provision of their special operations units to conduct a hostage rescue, were refused by the Algerians. GIS led the operations, although DSI deployed a platoon-strength element of snipers.

Three separate attempts were made by GIS and DSI to retake the facility, each resulting in some hostages rescued but also ending in the deaths of multiple hostages, some caused by Algerian attack helicopters that supported the assaults. Twenty-seven of the AQIM terrorists were eventually killed although at least 37 hostages were also killed both by the terrorists and in the government assaults. The Algerians operated with a mindset that prioritized the killing of the terrorists over the rescue of the hostages, a residual effect of 'the Dirty War' and probably the impact of Russian training.

The AQIM terrorists conducted themselves brutally with hostages being strapped to a car bomb, which was then detonated in an effort to ignite the gas pipes. Other hostages had IEDs strapped around their necks and set off. During the final Algerian assault, the terrorists executed a number of hostages as the security forces closed in until DSI snipers could eliminate them. In a fitting postscript, in 2015 the United States' JSOC orchestrated an airstrike in Libya which killed the head of AQIM at the time of the Amenas incident, Mokhtar Belmokhtar.

Algerian special operators have been deployed to southern Libya since 2014, including on joint operations with the Egyptians, French and Chadians to eradicate AQIM and related terrorists who have taken up Libya as a safe haven, many dispersed by French operations in Mali. Elements from the Army's 104th and 112th also conducted operations in Mali itself in 2012 and rumours of other operations in Niger abound. Algeria walks a very fine line in these operations alongside units from France and the United States, both of which are viewed as pariahs by much of the Algerian population.

The former GIS and current DSI and GOSP use Glock sidearms. Steyr AUG bullpups, AK variants fitted with reflex sights and MP5s are standard (DSI also bizarrely seems to use crossbows for silent killing). The Russian SVD Dragunov, the Remington MSR and the bolt action Remington 700 (the basis for the US Army's M24) are the principal sniping platforms for Algerian forces. The 12.7x108mm Zastava M93 anti-materiel rifle has also been seen in service with DSI snipers.

Grupa Reagowania Operacyjno Manewrowego (GROM)

Nationality: Polish • Branch: Army • Established: 1990

Grupa Reagowania Operacyjno Manewrowego (Operational Mobile Reaction Group) or GROM (an acronym as well as meaning 'thunderbolt' in Polish), otherwise known as Unit 2305, is the Polish Army's 'full-spectrum' special operations force. Originally created as a counter-terrorist unit, GROM has since expanded into the full range of special operations including reconnaissance, advance force operations and foreign internal defence.

The Polish military describes GROM's taskings as 'special and reconnaissance tasks in the territory of the country and outside, including for participation in actions concerning prevention of terrorist acts or their effects outside the country; tasks within the Special Operations Forces of the North Atlantic Treaty Organization; rescue and protection tasks.'

Nicknamed 'the Surgeons', the unit is divided into three Assault Groups, each comprising five land assault teams and three maritime assault teams, each typically of three six-man elements. The land assault teams are trained in both 'black tactics' (counter-terrorism) and 'green tactics' (warfighting) while the maritime teams receive the same counter-terrorist training along with 'blue tactics' (maritime operations including maritime counter-terrorism).

It has a particularly strong-relationship with Delta Force, which was instrumental in its initial training and development as a unit, and the two units are now visually virtually indistinguishable. One of its first missions was Operation *Simoom* where it assisted in retrieving a number of US CIA and Defense Intelligence Agency (DIA) operatives trapped in Iraq when Saddam Hussein invaded Kuwait, and smuggling them out of the country.

Polish special operators from the Commando Unit (Unit 4101 or the Jednostka Wojskowa Komandosów), identified by their distinctive patches. Both carry Bushmaster M4s which are being replaced by the HK416. Instead of MultiCam, they wear A-TACS FG (Foliage Green) camouflage. (Courtesy US Army, Staff Sgt Marcus Butler)

The unit deployed a small team on close personal protection duties in Haiti in 1994. GROM also conducted a number of operations hunting war criminals in both Croatia and later Kosovo. It operated as the Polish Special Police Group and later as simply the Polish Special Group. GROM captured the first war criminal indicted by the International Criminal Tribunal for the former Yugoslavia in a daring undercover operation in 1996.

It first deployed to Afghanistan in 2001. Since then, GROM has been a near-constant presence in the country, codenamed Task Force 49. In 2003, GROM also participated in Operation *Iraqi Freedom* as part of the Naval Special Operations Task Group, seizing the Khor al Amaya Oil Terminal in southern Iraq during the initial invasion. GROM also conducted a joint operation with SEAL Team 5 to capture the Mukarayin Dam in a heliborne operation. GROM deployed again to Iraq in 2007, operating alongside the US 5th SFG.

In Afghanistan the unit, along with the Polish Commando Unit (then known as the 1st Special Commando Regiment), deployed again in 2007. It was particularly valued by US planners as the Polish imposed no national caveats which could limit when and where the GROM operators were employed, apart from one restriction forbidding cross-border operations into Pakistan. Consequently it was employed against targets on the Joint Prioritised Effects List (the JSOC kill or capture list of insurgent targets) along with taskings for International Security Assistance Force (ISAF) Special Operations.

Polish SOF units have been under the control of the Polish Special Operations Center – Special Troops Component Command since 2007. The Special Troops Component Command has direct command of GROM, the Commando Unit, the Agat Unit, the Formoza Unit, the Nil Unit and the Polish Air Force's 7th Special Operations Squadron.

The Commando Unit is also referred to as Unit 4101 or the Jednostka Wojskowa Komandosów and is a raiding and special reconnaissance unit with similarities to the British Special Forces Support Group (SFSG) or the US Rangers. The unit is composed of four Combat Groups with an emphasis on 'green tactics' of conducting unconventional warfare within a conventional conflict.

In 2010, the Commando Unit joined GROM in Afghanistan and was assigned as Task Force 50.

In 2011, Task Force 50 took responsibility for mentoring the Afghan Provincial Response Company (PRC) in Paktika Province. In January of the following year, the unit conducted a textbook hostage rescue mission after a failed suicide bomber attack on an Afghan government meeting. The five terrorists were holed up with hostages in a building when the PRC and Task Force 50 arrived.

Two assaults by a mixed force of Afghan National Police (ANP) and National Directorate of Security (NDS) agents were repulsed with the loss of one ANP officer, although a pair of hostages managed to make good their

escape. Task Force 50 convinced the Afghans to allow the PRC along with the Poles to conduct the next assault.

The Polish Commandos established two sniper posts with operators armed with 7.62x51mm TRG-22 sniper rifles to provide overwatch. The remainder of the detachment split into two even assault groups of four Commandos and 12 PRC and commenced their approach. Using a Heckler & Koch AG36 grenade launcher, the Poles blew in a side door to the building and stormed inside. They were immediately taken under fire by an insurgent. Using a flashbang grenade to stun the insurgent, they quickly killed him, allowing the teams to flood into the building.

Two terrorists wearing suicide bomb vests were engaged and killed before they could detonate their devices and the last two terrorists were found dead, killed in the earlier assaults. Both hostages were safely recovered. The Poles discovered that the suicide vests were equipped with a secondary detonator

The famous shot of Polish GROM soldiers at Umm Qasr, southern Iraq in 2003. The unit conducted both unilateral and joint operations with SEAL Team 5. This was the first time that Polish operators had openly worked alongside American forces. Note the soldiers in both black counter-terrorism gear and wz. 93 Pantera, a camouflage pattern originally developed for GROM. (Courtesy US Navy, Photographer's Mate 1st Class Arlo K. Abrahamson)

triggered by mobile (cell) phones; one terrorist had managed to arm his vest before he died and the device detonated the following day as an American EOD team secured the site, unfortunately wounding two of the bomb technicians.

The Agat Unit (Unit 3940 or Jednostka Wojskowa Agat) was raised in 2011 as a clandestine, behind enemy lines sabotage and reconnaissance unit. It has additional counter-terrorist responsibilities and could be employed in extremis if GROM were not available. The Formoza Unit (Unit 4026 or Jednostka Wojskowa Formoza) was first established as a combat diving unit in 1975 before it was reassigned to the Special Troops Component Command. Formoza provides maritime capabilities but has expanded into land warfare in a similar fashion to the US Navy SEALs.

The Nil Unit (Unit 4724 or Jednostka Wojskowa Nil) provides all logistical support, research and procurement along with medical services to Special Troops Component Command personnel. It also has an important intelligence gathering and analysis function and maintains a fleet of FlyEye and ScanEagle UAVs (unmanned aerial vehicles). The 7th Special Operations Squadron provides organic helicopter transport in modified Mi-17s.

GROM carries the HK416 as its primary assault rifle; this replaced Colt and Bushmaster M4s with Glock sidearms and Minimi Para light machine guns. Unit snipers use an array of platforms including the Knight's Armament Company SR-25, the Accuracy International AWM, the bolt action CheyTac M200 Intervention in the proprietary .408 CheyTac and the semi-automatic .50 Barrett M82A1. Formoza operators carry the G36C and G36KV3 assault rifle, MP5s and the Accuracy International AW sniper rifle.

GROM used GMV HMMWVs borrowed from US Army Special Forces for most of its time in Iraq although it now has a dedicated complement of Land Rover Defenders outfitted as assault trucks for counter-terrorism missions alongside armoured SUVs (sport utility vehicles), while Agat is equipped with American Oshkosh M-ATV MRAPs (mine resistant ambush protected all-terrain vehicles). Formoza has a number of DPDs (diver propulsion devices) along with a range of Zodiac raiding craft.

The Biuro Operacji Antyterrorystycznych (BOA or Office of Anti-Terrorist Operations) is the National Police counter-terrorist response unit. It includes eight assault teams and two sniper teams along with the Operational Support Division, which supplies negotiators, surveillance and EOD teams. Regionally, the BOA is supported by the Samodzielny Pododdział Antyterrorystyczny Policji (SPAP or Police Anti-Terrorist Unit) which conducts tactical operations and can act as the first response to terrorist incidents. The BOA and SPAP were heavily involved in security for the 2012 UEFA European Championship and were reinforced by two squadrons from GROM and two from Formoza.

Grupo de Operações Especiais (GOE)

Nationality: Portuguese • Branch: Police • Established: 1982

Although efforts to create a counter-terrorist capability began in 1978, it was not until 1982 that Portugal's Grupo de Operações Especiais (GOE or Special Operations Group) was officially established within the Public Security Police to, according to the Portuguese government, 'combat situations of violence that go beyond normal security' with the assistance of Britain's 22SAS. The unit assaulters are organized under the Special Intervention Unit of the GOE, which comprises three self-contained operational Assault Groups of around 20 operators each, and a Technical Operational Group, which provides canine and surveillance support.

GOE has conducted a number of non-combatant evacuations from Africa, Bosnia and Egypt.

In the early 1990s, GOE's mission was expanded to include close personal protection of diplomats and Portuguese embassies in conflict zones. Their one major counter-terrorist operation occurred in 1983 when Armenian terrorists seized the Turkish ambassador's residence. As GOE prepared for an assault as negotiations worsened, one of the terrorists inadvertently detonated explosive charges they had distributed around the building, killing two hostages and all five terrorists.

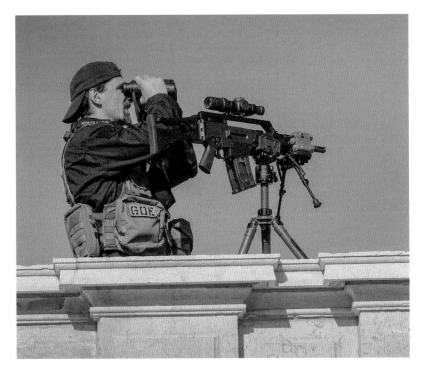

A Portuguese GOE soldier manning a counter-sniper post during close protection duties in 2018. He is armed with what appears to be a scoped 5.56x45mm Heckler & Koch G36K. (Horacio Villalobos – Corbis/Corbis via Getty Images)

The Portuguese Army has a commando battalion, a unit of elite light infantry and part of the Brigada de Reaccao Rapida (Rapid Reaction Brigade) with three commando companies supported by a training company. Additionally there is the Força de Operações Especiais (FOE or Special Operations Force, also known as the Rangers), which conducts special reconnaissance, direct action and counter-terrorism missions. The Navy maintains the Destacamento de Acoes Especials (DAE or Special Actions Detachment), a Navy SEAL equivalent composed of four ten-man elements.

The GOE uses Glock 17s and SIG-Sauer P226s, the MP5 family of sub machine guns and G36C assault rifles while the FOE uses the P226 and the suppressed Heckler & Koch USP along with HK416s, HK417s and the Fabarm STF 12 compact shotgun. Both units deploy Accuracy International sniper rifles (the AW and the AXMC); the FOE additionally uses the Barret M107A1. Heckler & Koch HK269 grenade launchers have also been recently procured.

Grupos de Operaciones Especiales (GEO)

Nationality: Spanish • Branch: Army • Established: 1979

The Grupos de Operaciones Especiales (GEO or Special Operations Group) is the Spanish National Police's counter-terrorist intervention force. Although raised in 1977, it was not officially operational until two years later after extensive support from Germany's GSG9. The GEO was the first unit of its type in Spain and there was no textbook to follow.

The unit operators are divided into two Operational Action Groups; OAG 40 and OAG 50. Each OAG comprises two sets of three five-man teams, giving each OAG 30 operators. Each of these operational teams is trained in a specialist area – breaching, combat medicine, diving and small boats, sniping or surveillance – but all are trained in close quarter battle.

In March 2004, the unit suffered its single casualty from enemy action, when a senior GEO officer was killed in an explosion triggered by the terrorists responsible for the Madrid railway bombing. GEO is supported by Grupos Operativos Especiales de Seguridad (GEOS); these are regional police tactical units somewhat in the vein of the French Brigade de Recherche et d'Intervention – Brigade Anticommando (BRI-BAC or Research and Intervention Brigade – Anti-Commando Brigade) and typically deal with armed criminals and organized crime raids but will likely be amongst the first responders to a terrorist incident on Spanish soil.

A second counter-terrorist unit exists within the Guardia Civil, the Unidad Especial de Intervención (UEI or Special Intervention Unit), distinctive in its bottle-green Nomex coveralls. The UEI was established in 1978; it has

responsibility for federal government buildings and installations, airports and ports and is the lead intervention unit against the Basque ETA terrorist group. The Catalan Police also has its own special unit, the GEI (Grup Especial d'Intervenció or Special Intervention Group). Although only a 35-man-strong team, it faces over 100 call-outs a year.

The standard GEO sidearm is the SIG-Sauer P226 with the USP Compact available. Both MP5s (including the Navy variant with three-round burst) and P90s are employed, as are SIG 551 and 552 assault rifles. They have recently acquired a number of short barrelled HK417s to deal with terrorists wearing body armour. GEO (along with GEI) is one of the few units equipped with the exquisite DSR-1, a phenomenally expensive bullpup sniper rifle from Germany. It also employs a range of Sako models including the 7.62x51mm TRG-21, the TRG 41 in .338 Lapua Magnum and the integrally suppressed AAII in 7.62x51mm.

The UEI also uses the P90 and MP5 family but has adopted both the HK416 and HK417. It is also equipped with Accuracy International AW sniper rifles. Like RAID, each GEI operator carries two pistols, the Heckler & Koch P30L pistol along with his older USP – one typically in a drop holster and the other mounted on his body armour. The unit's principal shoulder weapon is the MP5A3 and the Mk16 SCAR-L while the unit's snipers use the HK417, the TRG-22 and the DSR-1.

Operators of the Guardia Civil's Unidad Especial de Intervención or UEI (Special Intervention Unit), distinctive in their bottle-green uniforms, prepare to breach from the ladder ramp of their assault vehicle. They carry a mix of MP5s and an HK417. (Pablo Cuadra/Getty Images)

Hostage Rescue Team (HRT)

Nationality: US • Branch: FBI • Established: 1982

Along with the foundation of Delta Force in the late 1970s, there was a move within federal law enforcement to give the Federal Bureau of Investigation (FBI) a similar domestic capability should 'another Munich' occur in the American homeland (see page 88 for the Munich massacre of 1972). The first Hostage Rescue Team (HRT) members completed an abbreviated version of Delta's Operator Training Course (now formalized as the New Operator Training School) and 50 initial operators were selected to be trained by Delta in core close quarter battle skills.

The HRT is supported by its own organic air component called the Tactical Helicopter Unit (THU), which flies a fleet of Black Hawks, Bell 407s and MD-530 Little Birds. They have their own canine unit with two dogs available for deployment. The unit rotates its teams in a similar fashion to Delta, with one on stand-by or operations, one on long-term training/exercises and one readying for operations.

The unit has deployed on a large number of incidents against far-right and/or religious extremists in the United States; these include controversial operations at Ruby Ridge in 1992 where an HRT sniper killed an unarmed women and the Waco siege of 1993 where the HRT made the fatal call to introduce CS gas into the cult's compound, which may have caused the fires which subsequently engulfed the compound. It has also successfully resolved hundreds of criminal hostage takings and sieges, in the vast majority of cases without a shot being fired.

The FBI's Hostage Rescue Team conducting a breaching exercise in 2006. Note the M4A1 carbines and flight suits. They have since transitioned to the HK416 and wear Crye MultiCam uniforms. (Courtesy Federal Bureau of Investigation)

The HRT has maintained a very close relationship with Delta and the 160th Special Operations Aviation Regiment (160th SOAR) since its earliest days when Delta helped train the first HRT operators. Numerous former Delta and 160th personnel have joined the HRT or the THU after leaving the Army. The relationship has also seen FBI operators deploy with JSOC task forces around the world including in Afghanistan, Iraq and Libya. The addition of HRT personnel allows high-value terrorist targets to be arrested and tried in US courts (before these deployments, JSOC would detain the individual until he could be formally arrested by an FBI agent).

During a deployment alongside the Rangers, an HRT operator was seriously wounded by a suicide bomber during a night raid. HRT operators were also present during two JSOC operations in 2013, including the successful capture by Delta of a Libyan terrorist and the unsuccessful SEAL Team 6 operation in Somalia to capture an al-Shabaab high-value target.

The HRT still maintains custom .45 pistols after issuing the then-standard .40 Smith & Wesson Glock 22 for a number of years (its first issue pistol was the Browning Hi-Power in emulation of the British SAS). Along with its Springfield Custom Professional 1911A1s, the HRT follows Delta's lead and carries the HK416. The MP5 series is still in the armoury but is seldom used today.

Intelligence Support Activity (ISA)

Nationality: US • Branch: Army • Established: 1980

Known originally as the Foreign Operating Group or FOG in July 1980, the unit was established as a covert reconnaissance and intelligence gathering entity with the express purpose of ensuring the Department of Defense would never again have to rely upon the CIA for actionable intelligence. The Army in particular had found the CIA's efforts during preparation for Operation *Eagle Claw* to be wanting, with little understanding of the kinds of intelligence required for counter-terrorist missions.

The FOG, consisting of both Army intelligence and Special Forces operators, would be able to travel into denied areas such as Iran and conduct intelligence gathering, procure safehouses, rent vehicles or conduct any other support tasks needed to enable a Delta or SEAL Team 6 package to conduct a mission although its remit was Army wide and was not confined to the newly formed JSOC. The FOG was renamed the Intelligence Support Activity (ISA) in 1981.

Its early operations were focused on supporting the mujahideen in Afghanistan, countering the Nicaraguan regime and attempting to locate hostages held in Beirut. It was also controversially involved in a private sector effort to locate American prisoners of war still held in Laos, all the while as JSOC and Delta alongside the CIA, under Operation *Pocket Change*, planned

The MC-12W Liberty provides signals and visual intelligence over the battlefield for both conventional and SOF units. This one is pictured at Bagram, Afghanistan in 2012. Based on the King Air 350, the Intelligence Support Activity often operates in unmarked civilian versions. (Courtesy US Air Force, Staff Sgt Jeffrey Nevison)

their own operation to free any identified prisoners held at the jungle camp. Both the ISA and JSOC effort resulted in a 'dry hole' as reconnaissance revealed no prisoners of war still to be held at the site. It also assisted in the successful hostage rescue by the Italian Nucleo Operativo Centrale di Sicurezza (NOCS or Central Security Operations Service) of American General James Dozier from the Italian Red Brigades.

Working with the covert air unit Seaspray, ISA added a new capability – aerial signals intelligence and tracking, the idea being that targeted high-value targets could be located from the air to allow a Delta element to close in on them on the ground. Their most famous operation was Operation *Heavy Shadow*, the JSOC mission supporting the hunt for Pablo Escobar in Colombia in the 1990s, where the unit was known as Centra Spike, one of dozens of designations which change every few months. It was also on the ground in Mogadishu in 1993 supporting Task Force Ranger under yet another cover identity, the US Army Office of Military Support or simply OMS.

In 2002, ISA was formally reassigned to JSOC. In the meantime, Delta had developed its own rival signals intelligence capability and had expanded its Operational Support Troop (eventually into G Squadron) which specialized in covert advanced force operations. Despite this, ISA, now called Grey Fox, supported a number of crucial operations in Afghanistan (for instance there was a Grey Fox operator on the MH-47 that attempted to land on Takur Ghar during Operation *Anaconda* in 2002 – see pages 320–21), and later Iraq, including the eventual capture of Saddam Hussein.

ISA procured its own fleet of light aircraft which it outfitted with signals intelligence equipment that allowed the JSOC task force in Iraq to pinpoint and vector in on mobile (cell) phone transmissions (the ISA signals intelligence capability was officially known as the Special Intelligence Squadron). Once a target was confirmed in a locality by the presence of his phone, an assault team would infiltrate to kill or capture him. They are also supported by the Aviation Tactics Evaluation Group, another JSOC unit which flies deniable and low-signature aircraft primarily in signals intelligence missions.

It has also long performed undercover activities under non-official cover, including conducting forays into Syria during the Iraq insurgency and accompanying Ethiopian forces into Somalia. Unlike Delta and SEAL Team 6, which have reasonably defined geographic areas of responsibility, ISA deploys anywhere it is needed, conducting tasks for JSOC and for other agencies such as the National Security Agency. For many years it monitored al-Qaeda in the Arabic Peninsula, identifying targets for USN drone strikes.

More recently, the unit has been renamed the Mission Support Activity after cycling through such names as Torn Victor and Intrepid Spear. Most still refer to it as Task Force Orange, its colour coding shorthand in JSOC (Rangers are Red, Delta is Green, the 160th is Brown, SEAL Team 6 is Blue etc.) It has become one of the most vital components of JSOC.

ISA has recently operated in Africa, Afghanistan and Iraq, often conducting unilateral reconnaissance operations or supporting allied special operations. In Niger, the blended unit tasked with the tracking of Islamic State aligned insurgents, in the incident that led to the deaths of four Special Forces soldiers in October 2017, was drawn from Task Force Orange along with SEAL shooters.

Jægerkorpset (Jaeger Corps) (JGK)

Nationality: Danish • Branch: Joint • Established: 1961

The Jægerkorpset (JGK or Hunter Corps) is the Danish Army's only SOF unit. Specialoperationskommandoen (SOKOM or Special Operations Command) now commands both the core Danish units, the Army's Jægerkorpset and the Navy's Frømandskorpset (FKP or Frogman Corps). The Særlig Støtte-og Rekognosceringskompagni (Special Support and Reconnaissance Company) provides the Army with a long range reconnaissance capability that may also be utilized on certain SOKOM missions.

In the modern era, the Jægerkorpset deployed to Sarajevo in 1995 in a politically controversial counter-sniper deployment but their first deployment to a counter-insurgency war was as Task Group Ferret, deployed as a force element with the larger Task Force K-Bar. The Danes conducted numerous reconnaissance missions and provided a number of teams to support Operation *Anaconda* in 2002 (see pages 320–21). The JGK was later awarded the US Presidential Unit Citation for its efforts including the capture of a Taliban high-value target in a joint operation with the US Navy SEALs.

The Danish Army deployed in 2006 under International Security Assistance Force (ISAF) command and was assigned the troublesome Helmand Province as part of the British-led Task Force Helmand. In Musa Qala in 2006, eight snipers from the Jægerkorpset reinforced Danish soldiers holding the district centre against repeated Taliban onslaughts. The JGK also

Members of the Danish FKP conduct a VBSS boarding exercise with US Navy SEALs in June 2018. They use a boarding/caving ladder fired from a compressed air grapnel launcher or delivered by a telescoping pole. The hook, trailing the ladder, is affixed onto the superstructure, allowing rapid climbing. Powered ascenders are also used which can quickly haul an operator to the deck. (Courtesy US Special Operations Command Europe)

conducted numerous direct action missions including covert infiltrations dressed in Afghan clothing.

The JGK again deployed to Afghanistan from 2011 firstly under Task Force 10 and later as Task Force 7 mentoring Afghan police special units. In January 2013, the JGK lost its first operator in Afghanistan to an IED in Helmand Province while deployed in the advise and assist role. Members of both the JGK and FKP have been deployed to Iraq since 2016 to train Iraqi Special Forces (ISOF) until the Danes were withdrawn in late 2018. They also deployed to Mali in 2016 within the Dutch-led Special Operations Task Group in northern Mali.

Domestic counter-terrorism is the province of the Politiets Aktionsstyrke or AKS (commonly referred to as the Action Force), which is responsible for hostage rescue, counter-terrorist efforts, high-risk arrests and complex intervention assignments. The unit has been in existence since 1972, one consequence of the Munich massacre (see page 88), and today numbers around 100 operators, although in recent years it has struggled with recruitment. The AKS shot dead an Islamic State-inspired terrorist in 2015 after he murdered a Danish film-maker.

JGK and FKP operators use the Heckler & Koch USP, the MP5 and MP7 series and the Colt Canada C8SFW, which is being replaced by the M/10, a variant of the C8IUR. The HK417 has been adopted as a marksman weapon while the units' snipers are equipped with the Sako TRG-42.

Japanese Special Forces Group (JSFG)

Nationality: Japanese • Branch: Ground Self Defence Force • Established: 2003

Japan was one of the latest nations to establish a formal SOF unit. Trained by members of Delta Force, the Special Forces Group is a unit created solely as Japan's national counter-terrorism response. Initially titled the Special Operations Group, it was later retitled as the Special Forces Group and merged into a new Central Readiness Force, which brought together Japanese Ground Self Defence Force (JGSDF) crisis response units including dedicated helicopter support.

Along with overseas counter-terrorism, direct action and special reconnaissance for the JGSDF, the Central Readiness Force provides close protection teams from JSFG for Japanese diplomats in high-risk environments and is charged with the evacuation of Japanese citizens from conflict or disaster zones internationally.

US 1st Special Forces Group and Japanese Navy Special Boarding Unit conduct a joint exercise in 2018. The flat-top M4A1 carbines carried are purely for force on force 'Simunition' training. (Courtesy US Navy, Chief Mass Communication Specialist William Tonacchio)

At roughly battalion strength, the unit's companies follow the Delta and British SAS model of being based around their insertion method although all members are parachute qualified and undertake specialist close quarter battle training. Intriguingly, personal security is taken to an extreme with operators mandated to wear masks whenever they might be seen by other JGSDF service personnel.

Influenced by Delta, the JSFG uses the HK416 as its primary weapon along with both MP5SD3 and suppressed MP7A1s. Its issue sidearm also appears to be a Heckler & Koch model, the USP also used by Australian Special Forces with which the JSFG often cross-trains. Eight Australian Bushmaster protected mobility vehicles have been purchased to aid the Central Readiness Force and the JSFG in non-combatant evacuation missions.

The JSFG has a naval sister unit with maritime counter-terrorism responsibilities called the Special Boarding Unit, created with the assistance of both the US Naval Special Warfare and the British SBS. Regional police SWAT units known as Special Units or Special Assault Teams have domestic counter-terrorist responsibility supported by Counter-terrorism Unit-Japan, a multi-agency group that develops intelligence on potential threats.

Joint Special Operations Command (JSOC)

Nationality: US • Branch: Department of Defense • Established: 1980

Established in October 1980 in direct response to the tragedy at Desert One during Operation *Eagle Claw*, the Joint Special Operations Command or JSOC was originally known as the Counterterrorist Joint Task Force. The driving force behind the establishment of a specialist counter-terrorist command was to integrate all the units necessary for a successful hostage rescue under a single unified command,

Since its establishment, JSOC and its component units have expanded both in terms of numbers and in capability. No longer solely focused on hostage rescue, JSOC now supports a full range of special operations activities with an emphasis on advanced force operations, including undercover missions, direct action strikes against terrorist leaders and facilitators, and operations alongside partner forces in conflict zones where there is no overt American presence.

The domestic counter-terrorism role is still a priority, with elements from all three core units on rotational stand-by to respond in support of the FBI's Hostage Rescue Team (HRT): Aztec (Delta), Trident (SEAL Team 6) and Silver Bullet (160th Special Operations Aviation Regiment or 160th SOAR). The stand-by units are also the first to get the call should a special mission force be required at short notice overseas for a developing operation such as American citizens being seized or attacked.

A likely JSOC operator or USASOC instructor pictured during the Fuerzas Comando 2016 competition in Peru which sees SOF units from across South and Central America compete for honours. The long slide Glock 34 and the HK416 mounting what appears to be a Schmidt & Bender Short Dot would usually indicate a member of Delta Force. (Courtesy US Army, Cpl Joanna Bradshaw)

It also maintains the national counter-WMD (weapons of mass destruction) mission, now known as counter-proliferation and headed up by SEAL Team 6, along with the Department of Energy's Nuclear Emergency Search Teams (NESTs). Another little-known role of JSOC is to provide a troop of operators whenever the American President visits a high-risk country. The JSOC operators work in direct support of the Secret Service and their Counter Assault Teams.

JSOC currently commands the two national mission units, Delta Force and SEAL Team 6; the Intelligence Support Activity; the Joint Communications Unit (which maintains all signals support); the Regimental Reconnaissance Company; and the 24th Special Tactics Squadron. A number of other supporting units fall under JSOC including their Joint Medical Augmentation Unit which accompanies every major deployment with a full trauma team; the JSOC Intelligence Brigade which houses both analysts and targeting staff along with running its own human intelligence networks in theatre; and a number of Air Force units which provide 'covered' transport and intelligence, surveillance, targeting and reconnaissance (ISTAR) support. Units which often operate under JSOC command include both the Ranger Regiment and the 160th SOAR.

Joint Task Force 2 (JTF2)

Nationality: Canadian • Branch: Army • Established: 1993

Joint Task Force 2 (JTF2) is the Canadian Forces' direct action and counter-terrorist intervention unit. The unit was formed to replace a Royal Canadian Mounted Police unit known as the Special Emergency Response Team, which was roughly equivalent to the FBI's Hostage Rescue Team (HRT). JTF2 is under the command of Canadian Armed Forces Special Operations Forces Command (CANSOFCOM), itself established in 2006 with a number of component commands including JTF2, the Canadian Special Operations Regiment (CSOR), the Canadian Joint Incident Response Unit (CJIRU), and their dedicated helicopter capability in 427 Special Operations Aviation Squadron (427 SOAS).

JTF2 has a dedicated maritime counter-terrorist element that, according to official doctrine, 'operate the unit's various boats and Special Operations Crafts (SOC). SO Cox'ns are expected to operate small high performance boats in open ocean environments under adverse conditions' but can also be supported by the Canadian Navy's Maritime Tactical Operations Group, which provides an enhanced naval boarding party capability and would be employed to conduct opposed visit-board-search-seizure missions.

Under the unit motto of '*Facta, non verba*' or 'Deeds, not words', the Canadian unit has established itself to be the equal of other Western 'tier one' SOF units. Although notoriously secretive, it is understood that JTF2 first deployed in Bosnia where it operated on the ground in contested areas to designated targets for NATO strike aircraft.

An unidentified Canadian SOF sniper team pictured during the annual Warrior Competition in 2014 in Amman, Jordan. The Warrior competition is an invite-only event that pits many of the world's finest SOF against each other in a series of gruelling scenarios. The sniper appears to be carrying the Canadian manufactured .338 Lapua Magnum PGW Timberwolf. (Tom Stoddart/ Getty Images)

JTF2 also routinely provides close personal protection teams for senior Canadian diplomats and officers in a similar fashion to Germany's GSG9. During one such 1996 mission to protect a Canadian general supporting the United Nations in Rwanda, the JTF2 team was ambushed and had to shoot its way out.

One of its still-classified operations was the hostage rescue of a number of non-government organization hostages held by the Revolutionary Armed Forces of Columbia – People's Army (FARC). It was also allegedly involved in the 1996 operation to rescue hostages held at the Japanese Embassy in Lima, Peru, although probably in an advisory and observation role, as were members of the British 22SAS and the United States' Delta.

In 2001 JTF2 secretly deployed to Afghanistan under Task Force K-Bar (although by some accounts, it had deployed previously to Afghanistan in 1998 on an intelligence gathering mission). The 2001 deployment was not announced publicly and few in the Canadian government were even aware of the deployment until an image of obviously Canadian operators escorting a hooded detainee reached the press.

JTF2 was tasked with both special reconnaissance and direct action roles. Both the New Zealand Special Air Service (NZSAS) and Australian Commandos worked closely together with JTF2 on a number of high-value target raids. A Canadian senior officer noted its efficiency in kill or capture operations in support of the Canadian units deployed to Kandahar Province: 'We've removed seven commanders who have been responsible for the deaths of 27 soldiers.'*

JTF2 was also active during the NATO air campaign in Libya in 2011, conducting a non-combatant evacuation of Canadian nationals and later contributing to the targeting of regime elements. It deployed to Iraq under the Canadian Operation *Impact* in 2014, mentoring both Yekîneyên Antî Teror (YAT) Kurdish special operators and the Iraqi Counter Terrorist Service. Their sniper teams provided force protection for the Canadian operators when accompanying their charges into the field. One sniper team from JTF2, operating alongside two from CSOR, made a record-breaking shot in 2017 against an Islamic State target.

Canadian Forces were unusually frank in admitting the record shot but refrained from releasing any further details of the engagement: 'The Canadian Special Operations Command can confirm that a member of Joint Task Force 2 successfully hit a target at 3,540 metres. For operational security reasons and to preserve the safety of our personnel and our Coalition partners we will not discuss precise details on when and how this incident took place.'

* https://www.theglobeandmail.com/news/national/silent-killers-secrecy-security-and-jtf2/article1319588/

JTF2 issues suppressed C8IURs which are very similar to the L119A2 carbines carried by UKSF. The MP5 series along with small numbers of the Fabrique Nationale P90 are available although the C8IUR is now used in the counter-terrorist as well as conventional warfighting role. Snipers employ the Accuracy International AW and AWM and famously the bolt action C15 LRSW (Long Range Sniper Weapon based on the McMillan TAC-50 anti-materiel rifle), which was used to effect the record-beating 3,540-metre shot in Iraq.

Jordanian Joint Special Operations Command (JSOC)

Nationality: Jordanian • Branch: Army • Established: 2016

Jordan's Army 101st Special Forces Battalion was for many years the key component of Jordanian special operations. Within the 101st, its first counter-terrorist unit, the Special Operations Unit, was formed and saw action in a 1978 hostage taking by Palestinian terrorists in Amman which ended in the deaths of all but one of the four terrorists but also saw two operators killed during the assault. Seven hostages had been killed prior to the intervention.

JORSOCOM or Jordanian Special Operations Command was formed in 1996 with three Army brigade groupings – the 37th Special Force Brigade, which included the 101st SFB, the 71st SFB and the 81st Special Airborne Battalion; the 28th Royal Ranger Brigade; and the 5th Special Operations Aviation Brigade, which operates both UH-60L Black Hawks and Hughes MD-530F Little Bird variants, roughly mirroring the United States' SOCOM.

In 2016, JORSOCOM was disbanded and the new Jordanian Joint Special Operations Command or JSOC was raised. The Ranger Brigade was re-tasked as a rapid response light infantry unit and the Aviation Brigade was placed under Jordanian Air Force command. JSOC now consists of two Special Units – Special Unit 1 devoted to full-spectrum special operations and based around the 101st Special Forces Battalion and Special Unit 2 focusing on counter-terrorism, based around the 71st Special Forces Battalion (now Counter-terrorism) Battalion, along with a third smaller unit which conducts close personal protection.

There is also the 61st Special Reconnaissance Regiment, which works alongside the JSOC elements in a similar fashion to Britain's Special Reconnaissance Regiment (SRR) but also includes a CBRN (chemical, biological, radiological and nuclear) resource, the Chemical Support Unit. Additionally the Navy contributes the 77th Marine Reconnaissance Battalion while the Interior Ministry provides two police tactical units – Special Unit 14 (Special Intervention) and the all-female Special Unit 30 (Support).

During the opening stages of Operation *Iraqi Freedom*, it has long been rumoured that Jordanian special operators conducted missions in western Iraq in support of both Task Force 20 and Task Force Dagger, the Combined Special Operations Task Force – West. They were also involved in joint training missions with US JSOC units to Yemen in 2002. Additionally they contributed SOF to Afghanistan in support of the International Security Assistance Force (ISAF) in 2007 and again in 2009. Jordanian intelligence elements were also employed in Afghanistan, notably a Jordanian military intelligence officer who was killed in the infamous Camp Chapman bombing by a Jordanian double agent (see pages 300–301).

Jordan is a key ally in the campaign against Islamic State and rumours abound of Jordanian operators conducting joint operations with British and US forces in Syria. Units have also deployed into Iraq itself with the tacit but secret agreement of the Iraqi government, dressed in Iraqi and Kurdish Peshmerga uniforms. As another sign of the strengthening ties to Israel, Israeli UAVs (unmanned aerial vehicles) including the Heron were supplied to the Jordanian operators for use against Islamic State.

Jordan is a crucial partner in the US-led Operation *Gallant Phoenix*, which tracks foreign fighters in the region. Jordanian operators were present during the Delta Force raid in May 2015 to kill an Islamic State high-value target in Al-Amr, Syria and it is likely they have been involved in other partnered missions with Delta, including a rumoured April 2017 operation to exfiltrate a Jordanian intelligence asset who had penetrated Islamic State.

A 2014 capabilities demonstration by Jordanian 71st Special Forces (now Counter-terrorism) Battalion in Amman, Jordan. Note the multiple breaching points and use of the HARAS (Height Adjustable Rescue Assault System) mobile assault ladder. (Salah Malkawi/Anadolu Agency/Getty Images)

They were also alleged to have been present during a Delta operation to attempt the rescue of kidnapped American journalist James Foley in July 2014, during which one Jordanian operator was wounded in a firefight with insurgents. Reports indicate that the unit launched an operation on 1 January 2015 to attempt to rescue a downed Jordanian pilot, who was later horrifically burnt to death by Islamic State. The night-time operation into the former insurgent capital of Raqqah failed when 5th Special Operations Aviation Brigade helicopters came under heavy fire during their approach and the operation was aborted. The Jordanian pilot was murdered several days later.

Jordanian JSOC has a significant internal jihadist presence to contend with. In 2016, the commander of the 71st was killed during an assault on a terrorist safehouse in Irbid in which seven terrorists perished. It has also operated in partnered operations with the UK's 22SAS against Islamic State in Libya during 2016 and with UKSF in Somalia in the same year.

It maintains an especially close relationship with Delta (former members of which instruct at the King Abdullah II Special Operations Training Centre), 22SAS, JTF2, the Canadian Special Operations Regiment, US Army Special Forces and the 160th Special Operations Aviation Regiment (160th SOAR). The relationship with the US prospered after the 1994 treaty with Israel and may now even include intelligence sharing with Israel.

Not surprisingly the Jordanians follow Delta in terms of armament, with both HK416s and SIG-Sauer MCXs in use and apparently replacing a mix of G36Cs, M4A1s and SIG 550/551s. Both Glock and Heckler & Koch USP pistols appear to be issued. Snipers have been seen using both Accuracy International and Sako TRG platforms. Mobility is provided by both armoured Al-Jawad response vehicles with HARAS (Height Adjustable Rescue Assault System) assault ladders and the Jankel Al-Thalab or Fox Long Range Patrol Vehicle along with the Polaris MRZR.

Komando Pasukan Khusus (Kopassus)

Nationality: Indonesian • Branch: Army • Established: 1952

The Komando Pasukan Khusus (Kopassus) is composed of five sub-commands under the Indonesian Army Special Forces Command; the 1st and 2nd Para Commando Groups, the counter-terrorist Detasemen Khusus 81 (SAT-81), the Sandhi Yudha counter-insurgency unit and the Special Forces Training and Education Centre. The Para Commandos conduct full-spectrum SOF tasks and are akin to US Army Special Forces while SAT-81 specializes in counter-terrorism tactics and Sandhi Yudha conducts special reconnaissance and raiding.

SAT-81 is also a component command of the Indonesian National Agency for Combating Terrorism or National Counter-terrorism Agency. The organization includes the Den Gegana of the Korps Brigade Mobil of the National Police, which provides local SWAT, EOD and counter-terrorism capabilities and is based regionally in small detachments; and Densus 88 (Detachment 88) which is the National Police's domestic counter-terrorist unit and akin to the FBI's Hostage Rescue Unit (HRT).

Providing maritime and air elements are the Navy's Detasemen Jala Mangkara or Denjaka which are the Indonesian equivalent of the US Navy SEALs and are trained in counter-terrorism along with maritime reconnaissance and raiding; and the Indonesian Air Force's Bravo Detachment 90 which provides similar capabilities to the French Commando Parachutiste de l'Air no10 (CPA-10) and has primacy in counter-hijack operations.

SAT-81 was established in 1982 with the assistance of Germany's GSG9 after a hijacking attempt on an Indonesian aircraft in Bangkok the preceding year. Its operators are distinctive in their black uniforms and red berets. Although originally trained purely as a hostage rescue force, its role has expanded to include close personal protection and intelligence gathering along with a fledgling cyber warfare capability. In 2018, SAT-81 was attached to a police task force after a wave of terrorist suicide bombings against Christian churches.

Kopassus has been plagued by accusations of human rights abuses. Its Sandhi Yudha unit has been accused of conducting targeted killings of dissidents and was almost certainly involved in supporting anti-independence militias in East Timor/Timor Leste who opened fire on Australian and New Zealand forces on a number of occasions during the 1999 United Nations International Force East Timor (INTERFET) intervention into East Timor/Timor Leste (see page 13).

In 2013, four Kopassus operators were found guilty of breaking into a prison and murdering four criminals who had been responsible for the killing of a former Kopassus operator in an off-duty nightclub dispute. They were part of a 12-man Kopassus team which swore revenge for the murder of their comrade and stormed the prison carrying deniable AK-47s.

The Kopassus maintains a relationship with Australia's SASR, which conducts joint training and exercises after a three-year period following

A Kopassus soldier (left) pictured with an Australian SASR soldier (right) in 2006 during joint counter-terrorism exercises. Note the modified MP5A3 carried by the Australian – an SASR armoury-fitted forward grip and MP5K end cap with no stock. The Kopassus soldier appears to carry a rigid stocked MP5A3. The chemical lights carried by the SASR soldier are for indicating cleared rooms, wounded or suspected IEDs. (Courtesy Australian Department of Defence)

INTERFET, which saw the relationship essentially frozen owing to Indonesian political constraints. According to SASR sources, however, the training given to Kopassus is limited to core special operations skills in acknowledgment of the possibility, however remote, of a future conflict with Indonesia. Until 2010 the US maintained a ban on conducting training with Kopassus due to their involvement in human rights abuses in East Timor/Timor Leste.

Komandovanie sil spetsial'nalnykh operatsii (KSSO)

Nationality: Russian • Branch: Army • Established: 2012

The Komandovanie sil spetsial'nalnykh operatsii (KSSO or Special Operations Forces Command) is roughly the equivalent of the United States' JSOC in both organisation and roles. Raised only in 2012, the KSSO was originally built around the 346th Spetsnaz Brigade (Prokhladny), which was initially a Military Police unit. Intriguingly it appears to deploy in small units of comparable size to British SAS or US Delta Force troops; 16-man teams are often mentioned, with three such troops in each KSSO 'department', which looks similar to a squadron in Western terms. These operators are referred to as sily spetsial'nykh operatsii or SSO, roughly equivalent to the Western term 'SOF', to denote they are a separate entity to Spetsnaz.

Probable Russian KSSO operators provide security during a visit by Russian President Putin in Crimea, 2018. (Mikhail Metzel/TASS via Getty Images)

KSSO units seem to follow a similar pattern of specialization with troops dedicated to mountaineering, military free-fall and specialist parachuting, close personal protection, urban combat and sniping, and combat diving. With a third of the Russian military composed of conscripts, KSSO instead employs contract soldiers who sign up for longer terms and recruits from Army Spetsnaz detachments.

The KSSO is central to the Russian 'new generation warfare' doctrine (often referred to as 'hybrid warfare' in the West), using a mix of deception/information warfare, offensive cyber and deniable special operations assets. The KSSO SSO operators and Spetsnaz in general (including contractors who may or may not be officially employed) have become known as the 'Polite People' in Russia because of their appearance in Crimea and Ukraine, where they rejected any queries about their identity politely but firmly (in the West, these deployments saw them nicknamed the 'Little Green Men').

The KSSO has deployed SSO teams in support of the Winter Games in 2014 and to Crimea, where they were tasked with seizing the Crimean Parliament. Since 2015, SSO units have been deployed to Syria, conducting a wide range of tasks including target designation for airstrikes. Indeed, a Russian staff officer noted, in a rare admission of KSSO's existence in a Russian Army press statement, that its role involved 'reconnoitring targets for Russian airstrikes, providing targeting information for the bombers, and conducting other special missions.'

On such missions, two of its members qualified as JTACs (joint terminal attack controllers) have been killed in action. One SSO member operating as a JTAC even called in a fire mission upon his own position when surrounded by insurgents, an act that saw him awarded a posthumous Hero of Russia.

There have also been unverified reports that the unit hunted down those responsible for the downing of a Russian airliner in 2015 by Egyptian Islamic State terrorists. During the Aleppo offensive in Syria, a troop-strength SSO element was credited with killing upwards of 300 insurgents in a pitched firefight in May 2017. It has also conducted mentoring with both pro-Assad regular and irregular forces and Iranian-backed Hezbollah militias, with one SSO operator even spotted sporting a Hezbollah shoulder patch.

SSO units use a range of both Western and domestic small arms. Their primary rifle is the AK-74M fitted with rails and sound suppressors, although the AK-12 is scheduled to replace the AK-74M. The civilian version of the HK417, the MR762, has been identified being employed by SSO snipers who also appear to have sourced the bolt action SIG-Sauer SSG08 and the Accuracy International AW. They have also deployed the Russian ASVK bolt action anti-materiel rifle in 12.7x108mm (.50).

SSO employs the PKP Pecheneg medium machine gun with the 'Predator'-style Scorpion ammunition backpack and is currently being issued with the recently developed RPK-16 light machine gun. Sidearms include Glock 17s and the compact Glock 26 for low-profile operations (a mixed batch of 318 Glocks were purchased by KSSO in 2014 at the exorbitant rate of $6,000 USD per pistol, leading to a corruption investigation).

KSSO units also make use of UGVs (unmanned ground vehicles) including the heavy tracked BAS-01G Soratnik which mounts a 12.7mm NSV heavy machine gun, an AGS-17 automatic grenade launcher or Kornet ATGMs (anti-tank guided missiles). Like their Western counterparts, SSO operators have employed ATGMs against jihadist armoured suicide car bombs in Syria.

The unit has deployed a range of vehicles in Syria from the Chaborz M-6 (a distant relative of the American Polaris MRZR) to the Tigr-M patrol vehicle to the six-wheeled Kamaz Typhoon MRAP (mine resistant ambush protected vehicle) and the eight-wheeled BTR-82A armoured personnel carrier. It has also widely employed 'Non-Tac' commercial SUVs (sport utility vehicles) such as the Toyota Hilux and the Russian-built Patriot pick-up.

Kommando Spezialkräfte (KSK)

Nationality: German • Branch: Army • Established: 1996

The Kommando Spezialkräfte (KSK or Special Forces Command) is the German Army's battalion-strength special operations unit. It was created initially with the assistance of the British SAS, Germany's own GSG9 and Delta Force as a response to the requirement for long range non-combatant evacuations from combat zones such as that which occurred in Rwanda in 1994, when Belgian and French special operators had to evacuate German nationals as the Bundeswehr had no capacity to do so.

Although this was the impetus for its creation, KSK is a 'full-spectrum' special operations unit, capable of conducting special reconnaissance and surveillance, direct action to include hostage rescue, foreign internal defence and operations in support of conventional forces. In the field of counter-terrorism, KSK has the remit for operations outside Germany's borders and in conflict zones, while GSG9 operates domestically; however, there is still some ambiguity as members of GSG9 have deployed overseas on a number of occasions to Iraq and Afghanistan, although typically in a close personal protection role.

KSK is organized into four commando companies, each of four platoons of four detachments or patrols, along with a Special Commando Company responsible for electronic warfare. The companies are supported by KSK's own specialist communications company. The unit follows typical practice by assigning specialities to each of the five platoons within its four companies – arctic warfare, mountaineering, vehicle-mounted, military free-fall parachuting and amphibious operations, although all members are HALO/HAHO (high altitude low opening/high altitude high opening) and SCUBA qualified. Each company also maintains its own sniper cell. The platoons are further divided into four groups of four operators, again based on the SAS principle.

The first real combat deployment for KSK to Afghanistan was also the first for Germany since 1945, although a small detachment of KSK operators had deployed to Kosovo in 1999 as a close protection party for German commanders (where they had also assisted in the Persons Indicted For War Crimes or PIFWC hunt in Bosnia). In December 2001, a company of KSK operators arrived in Kandahar for a secretive deployment (it was not publically acknowledged until March the following year) in support of the American-led Operation *Enduring Freedom* and was assigned to the multi-national special operations task force, Task Force K-Bar.

During 2001 and 2002, KSK conducted numerous reconnaissance and sensitive site exploitations (SSEs), often operating with US Navy SEAL Team 3. It also deployed several teams in covert observation posts during Operation *Anaconda* (see pages 320–21) to assist in blocking the escape of foreign fighters. One challenge was that KSK did not deploy with its own vehicles and was forced to borrow American HMMWVs from the 3rd SFG. It also had to rely upon American helicopter support.

This malady was finally solved in 2011 with the raising of the DSK or Division Schnelle Kräfte (Rapid Reaction Division), which brought a number of German Army Aviation units under its command along with KSK. In 2013, some 15 Airbus H145M helicopters were purchased for KSK as designated helicopter support, particularly for its counter-terrorist role.

The German unit was well regarded by the Americans and their NATO peers although, like almost all non-US units at the time, it experienced the allocation of direct action missions to US units, while more prosaic reconnaissance and SSEs were left to the multi-nationals. Despite this, KSK received a US Presidential Unit Citation for its efforts on Task Force K-Bar.

A classic early image of the German KSK taken in 2000 during counter-terrorist training. Along with the G36K, the soldiers are equipped with the 9x19mm Heckler & Koch MP5K PDW with side folding stock. (German Federal Defence Ministry/Getty Images)

A German KSK operator with 5.56x45mm Heckler & Koch G36K equipped with EOTech optic. The G36 series has been recently replaced in KSK service with the HK416A7 to be known as the G95. (Thomas Trutschel/ Photothek via Getty Images)

Like the Australian Special Operations Task Group (SOTG), part of KSK's role was to conduct shaping operations to establish an outer cordon of protection around the German International Security Assistance Force (ISAF) contingent. It also operated under the direct command of NATO Special Operations Component Command, carrying out capture operations against senior insurgent leaders, the training and mentoring of Afghan forces, and reconnaissance tasks.

In one of its better-known operations in Kabul in 2006, KSK captured a safehouse used by transiting Pakistani suicide bombers. Another operation in 2012 saw the unit capture Mullah Abdul Rahman in Kunduz Province, where he was responsible for ambushes on NATO supply convoys. One KSK operator has lost his life during operations in Afghanistan. He was killed during a partnered operation in Baghlan in May 2013. One of his comrades escaped death in the same firefight, only because his ballistic helmet stopped an insurgent bullet.

More recently the unit has been deployed to northern Iraq, Mali, Senegal and Nigeria in a mentoring capacity to train local forces. There are unconfirmed reports that KSK operators are also conducting mentoring tasks in Syria alongside British, French and US SOF contingents but this has been strenuously denied by the German government.

Maritime operations are conducted by the Kommando Spezialkräfte Marine or KSM established in 2014. Composed of combat divers, the KSM includes three combat diving groups of 16 personnel along with three specialist detachments, which are responsible for the provision of ground vehicles, submersibles and raider craft, and rotary air support.

KSK has adopted the Heckler & Koch HK416A7 to be known as the G95 in KSK service. Prior to the HK416, KSK employed the G36K and G36C. It continues to use suppressed MP7A1s and both the Heckler & Koch P8, a variant of the 9mm USP, and the suppressed P12, a .45ACP model of the USP Tactical (the .45ACP is chosen as the ammunition is subsonic). Today the unit also has its own fleet of Mercedes G-Wagen-based AGF Serval Special Operations Vehicles.

Korps Commandotroepen (KCT)

Nationality: Dutch • Branch: Army • Established: 1950

The Dutch Korps Commandotroepen (KCT or Army Commando Corps) has a long and storied history; it drew its lineage to wartime commando units but served as the Commando Waarnemer-Verkenner or Commando Force Reconnaissance for much of the post-war period, training for special reconnaissance and raiding tasks in support of conventional forces. As of December 2018, it is under the command of the newly established Netherlands Special Operations Command (NLD SOCOM).

In the aftermath of the 9/11 attacks, the KCT was re-tasked as Commando Speciale Operaties (Commando Special Operations), widening its responsibility to include full-spectrum counter-terrorism and special operations. These are defined in the Dutch context by NLD SOCOM themselves as 'Special Reconnaissance: special reconnaissance missions to acquire information about a hostile or semi-hostile area, about a threat or about the effects of an attack; Direct Action: offensive actions, such as ambushes, sabotage and target designation; Military Assistance: military assistance with the aim of training or advising allies or groups.'

The KCT is composed of three commando companies, each comprising eight commando detachments of eight operators. It served in the former Yugoslavia between 1994 and 2000 before deploying to Afghanistan in 2002 under International Security Assistance Force (ISAF) Special Operations command. It participated in Operation *Anaconda* (see pages 320–21), providing teams to establish covert observation posts and calling in Coalition air support. It also deployed to Iraq in 2003 as part of the Multi-National Force – Iraq in Al Muthanna Province and conducted a non-combatant evacuation from the Ivory Coast under Operation *Golden Eagle* in 2004.

The KCT redeployed to Afghanistan in 2005 and 2006 under US command as Task Group Orange (no relation to the American JSOC unit). In 2006 and 2007 it again deployed under ISAF Special Operations command as Task Group Viper, a particularly large commitment of 165 personnel and four CH-47 helicopters in support of Task Force Uruzgan, working with the Australian Special Operations Task Group and Dutch regular forces who were the lead nation in Uruzgan. It returned to Afghanistan in 2009, operating under ISAF as Task Force 55.

A Dutch KCT soldier in Mali. His weapon is the HK416 with an Aimpoint CompM red dot optic and x3 Aimpoint magnifier. (Courtesy Dutch Ministry of Defence, CC0)

In 2014 the unit deployed to Mali as Task Group Scorpion as part of the United Nations Multidimensional Integrated Stabilization Mission in Mali (MINUSMA). Since 2015, KCT has been in northern Iraq advising and assisting the Kurdish Peshmerga but has recently relocated to Baghdad to train and mentor Iraqi units.

KCT carries the Glock 17 and the HK416 carbine or Fabrique Nationale P90 as standard. The Minimi Para provides heavier firepower and snipers are armed with the 7.62x51mm Accuracy International AW and .338 Lapua Magnum AWM although the .50 Barrett M82A1 is also in the armoury. The KCT has recently taken possession of a number of new patrol vehicles, the Defenture ATTV Vector, which will replace the Mercedes-Benz 290GDs which served them so well in Uruzgan Province.

Lietuvos Specialiųjų Operacijų Pajėgos (SOP)

Nationality: Lithuanian • Branch: Army • Established: 2002

The Lietuvos Specialiųjų Operacijų Pajėgos (SOP or Special Operations Forces) is a command similar to the United States' SOCOM established to command and control all Lithuanian Special Operations Forces (LITHSOF). There are four units under the SOP: the Specialiosios misijos skyrius (Special Mission Unit – formerly the Ypatingosios paskirties tarnyba or Special Purpose Service but often referred to as Specialiųjų Operacijų Junginys 'Aitvaras' or Special Operations Squadron Aitvaras); Kovinių narų tarnyba (KNT or Combat Divers Service); Vytauto Didžiojo jėgerių batalionas (Vytautas, the Great Jaeger Battalion); and the Mokymo ir kovinės paramos centras (Combat Support and Training Centre). In 2008, the SOP became the fourth branch of the Lithuanian military.

The Specialiosios misijos skyrius, whose operators are known as 'Žaliukas' or 'Forest Brothers' in honour of the resistance fighters against Soviet occupation, is officially responsible for 'counterterrorism, hostage release operations, close protection, special operations across water, air and land domains' while the naval component, the KNT, conducts 'maritime and underwater special operations, boat infiltration and exfiltration, as well as to support hostage release operations'. The Vytauto Didžiojo jėgerių batalionas is the LITHSOF equivalent of the Rangers or the UK's Special Forces Support Group (SFSG) in that it conducts 'special reconnaissance, raids, ambushes and indirect fire support to other Lithuanian SOF units', according to LITHSOF itself.

The Specialiųjų Operacijų Junginys 'Aitvaras' deployed to Afghanistan under US command in 2002 including a mission to recover a crashed US Predator UAV (unmanned aerial vehicle) before completing its tour in 2004. It returned as part of SOP in 2007 and served until 2015 in southern

Afghanistan. A mentoring element was again dispatched in 2015. LITHSOF also contributes to the Multi-national Training Group – Ukraine and under the Joint Special Operations Task Force – Iraq.

The Lithuanian domestic counter-terrorist unit is known as ARAS (Anti-terrorist Operations Unit) and is composed of three regionally based 30-man detachments and the 'Special Team', an equivalent of SCO19's CTSFOs (Counter Terrorist Specialist Firearms Officers) or the FBI's Hostage Rescue Team (HRT).

LITHSOF issues the Glock 17; the MP5 series; and G36K and C models including some with underslung HK269 grenade launchers, and has recently purchased Accuracy International AXMX sniper rifles to supplement and in some cases replace the Fabrique Nationale SCAR-H PR (Precision Rifle) that operators employed in Afghanistan. ARAS uses the Glock 17 and 19, the MP5A3, the G36C, the recently acquired SIG-Sauer MCX Virtus, which is believed to be replacing the G36C, and the French PGM Ultima Ratio sniper rifle.

Lithuania's Special Mission Unit/Special Purpose Service exfiltrates the target area by US Army Black Hawk during a joint exercise in 2016. Note the flight suits, assault ladders and at least one Heckler & Koch G36C visible. (Courtesy US Army)

Marine Special Operations Command (MARSOC)

Nationality: US • Branch: United States Marine Corps • Established: 2006

For many years, the Marine Corps resisted efforts to provide elements to the multi-service US Special Operations Command (SOCOM), believing that its own special operations requirements were met by its Force Recon and Marine Fleet Anti-terrorism Security Team (FAST) units (indeed Marines claim the first US SOF to see action in World War II were the Raider Battalions in the Pacific).

A MARSOC Marine in Helmand Province, Afghanistan, 2012. The operator is assigned to a mentoring task with an Afghan Special Operations Kandak; note the Afghan Commando patch. (Courtesy US Marine Corps, Cpl Kyle McNally)

Marine Commandants were equally wary of relinquishing control of their best Marines to SOCOM.

Following several years of SOCOM-led operations in Afghanistan and Iraq, the Marines raised the Marine Special Operations Command or MARSOC in 2006 after the successful trial of a small Marine SOF element known as Detachment One, which served under SEAL command in Iraq in 2004. Originally, MARSOC was only composed of a small Foreign Military Training Unit which was later renamed the Marine Special Operations Advisor Group (MSOAG).

Two Marine Special Operations Battalions (MSOBs) were soon raised based on the 1st and 2nd Force Reconnaissance (Force Recon) Companies with a third added in 2009 when the MSOAG was stood up as the 3rd MSOB. Fox Company of 2nd MSOB was the first MARSOC element to deploy to Afghanistan in 2007.

Their deployment abruptly ended in controversy when the unit was accused of civilian deaths following a complex ambush and a SOCOM officer ordered the unit to return to the United States with both the commanding officer and his second-in-command relieved of duty. All operators were eventually cleared after multiple investigations but the incident left a stain on MARSOC that took many years to redress.

SOCOM pushed the newly established MARSOC into foreign internal defence in Afghanistan, taking up much of the slack in the village stability operations (VSO; see pages 322–23). The foreign internal defence/village stability operations (FID/VSO) role was widely considered the most onerous

SOF tasking as units had increasingly gravitated toward more kinetic direct action (DA). MARSOC, however, took the opportunities given and became masters of the FID space, in many ways comparable to the Green Berets who were the traditional exponents of that domain.

Today, MARSOC consists of three Raider Battalions (MARSOC operators are now known as Raiders in homage to their World War II predecessors and the former Marine Special Operations Regiment, is now the Raider Regiment), each with a geographic focus. Each Raider Battalion comprises four Marine Special Operations Companies (MSOCs); each of these includes four 14-man Marine Special Operations Teams (MSOTs), each of which is an ODA-style team in both organization and capability which can be split into a pair of Tactical Elements, each consisting of an NCO (non-commissioned officer), four critical skills operators (CSOs) and a Navy Special Amphibious Reconnaissance Corpsman (SARC).

MARSOC has operated in Iraq, Afghanistan and across Africa deploying in the advise and assist role. It has also deployed with Kurdish forces to Syria. In one incident in 2016, a MARSOC SARC was pinned down by enemy fire and responded by deploying smoke grenades to mask his movement, allowing him to retrieve an Mk13 .300 Winchester Magnum sniper rifle which he used to engage multiple Islamic State firing positions.

MARSOC issues the Block 2 SOPMOD M4A1, typically suppressed and some with 10.3-inch uppers, and the Glock 19 as standard (its once distinctive .45ACP M45A1 pistols were replaced by the Glock). MP5A3s and MP5SD3s are also available for specialist tasks. The M249 SAW and Mk48 light machine gun are also employed as is the 7.62x51mm Mk17 SCAR as a designated marksman rifle, along with the M110. MARSOC, like the Green Berets, increasingly uses the stand-alone M320 grenade launcher although the multi-shot M32A1 is often carried in vehicles because of its increased firepower.

National Mission Units (NMUs)

Nationality: Afghan • Branch: Ministry of the Interior • Established: 2002

The National Mission Units of the Afghan General Command of Police Special Units are the most highly trained and experienced special operators within the Afghan security forces. They were originally developed as partner forces for US and UK special operations units with some of the oldest, for example the Crisis Response Unit (CRU), dating their origins back to 2002.

Today operators all complete a National Unit Operators Course, which is modelled in part on the British SAS and the United States' Delta selection processes and trains all members in close quarter battle, breaching methodology, heliborne operations and post-raid sensitive site exploitation.

There are three NMUs: Task Force 222, also known as the Crisis Response Unit (CRU) or CRU 22, based in Kabul and previously mentored by the British SBS, the New Zealand Special Air Service (NZSAS) and the Norwegian Forsvarets Spesialkommando (FSK); the Logar-based Task Force 333 mentored by the British Special Forces Support Group (SFSG); and the Afghan Territorial Force 444 (also known as Task Force 444) in Helmand, again with UKSF advisers. All of these units now belong to a National Mission Brigade.

The NMUs are also organized along SAS and Delta lines with units composed of three squadrons, each made up of several troops of around 16 operators. While the CRU is the primary counter-terrorist intervention force, Task Forces 333 and 444 are special reconnaissance and direct action focused. Additionally, a fourth NMU was established within the Afghan National Army from the 6th Special Operations Kandak in 2017 and is based in Kabul.

When the rules governing night raids changed in 2009 (see page 292), it was the NMUs who would conduct the 'call-out' for the international units, giving any insurgents a chance to surrender before entry was made (although how often this happened in reality is open to question as it ceded the element of surprise to the enemy). CRU is perhaps best known for its March 2017 assault against Islamic State – Khorasan terrorists at a Kabul hospital – where it conducted multiple explosive breaches, clearing the eight-floor building and rescuing the remaining hostages. It also worked with the SBS in April 2012 to eliminate a Taliban cell that seized a building in central Kabul.

Its operators are armed and equipped by their mentors with M4 carbines, M249 squad automatic weapons and PKM medium machine guns, along with MICH helmets and Ghostex Kilo-1 camouflage. In appearance they

An Afghan National Mission Unit trains with US Army Special Forces in Logar Province, Afghanistan, in September 2018. He is firing an ACOG-equipped M4A1 with a Beretta M9 pistol in a drop holster at his side. Note the GMV 1.1 parked in the centre background.
(Courtesy US Air Force, Staff Sgt Nicholas Byers)

Afghan Crisis Response Unit 222, one of the Afghan National Mission Units, training in 2018. The National Mission Units are increasingly wearing Western clothing and equipment such as the Crye MultiCam and the M4A1 carbines seen here. (Courtesy US Army, Sgt 1st Class Sun Vega, NSOCC-A)

resemble US Army Special Forces and at a distance could easily be mistaken for such. The unit is one of the few Afghan formations with night vision and infrared illuminators issued at the rate of one set per man, giving its members a formidable advantage in the night.

Western SOF teams are assigned to each squadron although on operations typically only a small element of three to five operators will accompany the assault. Increasingly the NMUs are conducting unilateral operations with no direct field input from their mentors, although Western SOF will frequently infiltrate an overwatch element, often snipers, to provide extra insurance while the Afghans conduct the core of the mission.

Supporting the NMUs are the Provincial Response Units or PRUs (formerly known as Provincial Response Companies). There are currently 19 PRUs spread across Afghanistan. They function as a local special operations capability for the Afghan National Police (ANP) and work closely with Coalition forces. Each PRU has three platoons each with three eight-man sections (squads) along with integral sniper, EOD and sensitive site exploitation (SSE) teams.

Each PRU is mentored by a NATO special operations unit and often partners with these units on operations, although intelligence, surveillance and reconnaissance (ISR) data is commonly not shared with the PRUs as in the words of one adviser, noted in a SOCOM report: 'If they get addicted to that, then they would never cross the wadi'. They are typically equipped with a mixture of Afghan National Army (ANA) issue and Western SOF weapons and equipment. For instance, the Uruzgan PRU uses the Hungarian AMD-65 while others are equipped with M16A2s.

Afghan Crisis Response Unit 222 conducting counter-terrorist training, likely a demonstration based on the inclusion of the Afghan flag. Again they wear a mixture of MICH helmets fitted with side rails, Blackhawk packs and Crye uniforms. (Courtesy US Army, Sgt 1st Class Sun Vega, NSOCC-A)

The Ktah Khas is an Afghan unit trained and mentored by JSOC units, primarily the Rangers, since 2009 and is known as the Afghan Partner Unit. It is, along with the three publicly recognized NMUs, the most well trained and experienced Afghan SOF unit. It also employs a Female Tactical Platoon to gather intelligence from female civilians on raids.

Former head of JSOC, Admiral Bill McRaven, described them as follows: 'These were the Afghans that went on target with the JSOC forces forward to ensure that we had an Afghan that was, if you will, going through the door first.'* The US government describes them as 'accomplished in conducting intelligence-driven counterterrorism raids, particularly against high-value individuals, and vehicle interdictions utilizing both ground and air mobility platforms.'

The Ktah Khas includes three operational companies supported by the standard SOK complement of an engineer company, a military intelligence company and support, training and headquarters companies. The Ktah Khas support company, however, includes specialist components such as an integral EOD element and the aforementioned Female Tactical Platoon.

A final Afghan force is the secretive Afghan National Special Operations Force (ANSOF), once known as Omega Teams. These were established by JSOC and the CIA's Special Activities Division (SAD) from 2002 as Counter Terrorist Pursuit Teams or CTPTs (although the first was originally christened the Afghan Combat Applications Group). Another such unit was called the Khost Protection Force.

Secondments from SEAL Team 6, the Ranger Regiment and occasionally Delta were assigned to the CTPTs to coordinate air support and medical

---

* https://www.thedrive.com/the-war-zone/10114/this-shadowy-afghan-unit-fights-alongside-americas-most-elite-forces evacuations along with access to JSOC intelligence for operations along the border with and into Pakistan. The Afghans recruited for these covert units were from local militias; they were trained by the CIA and JSOC and did not come under the command of the Afghan military. The first Delta operator killed in Afghanistan died during an operation with the first CTPT unit while working as a contractor to the CIA.

National Security Guard (NSG)

Nationality: Indian • Branch: Ministry of Home Affairs • Established: 1984

The National Security Guard (NSG) was created in 1984 with the aid of Germany's GSG9 to act as India's primary armed counter-terrorist response. It sits under the Indian Ministry of Home Affairs and curiously employs both Army and police personnel. Its core intervention capability is the Special Action Group (SAG), whose operators are all Indian Army personnel.

The SAG includes a dedicated counter-hijack capability in 52 Special Action Group and two general counter-terrorism elements in 51 Special Action Group and 11 SRG (Special Ranger Group). Other SRGs provide support to the SAG elements in counter-terrorist operations and they also have a close personal protection capability.

Indian National Security Guard 'Black Cat' operators fast-rope from an Mi-17 transport helicopter as the unit storms the Nariman House at Colaba Market during the multiple terrorist incidents in Mumbai, November 2008. (Pedro Ugarte/AFP/Getty Images)

Its best-known operations were in 1988 when the Golden Temple, a religious pilgrimage site in Amritsar, was captured by domestic Sikh terrorists. After a three-day battle, the temple was recaptured with some 40 militant deaths. The SAGs have also been responsible for a number of successful counter-hijack operations, combating terrorists who attacked an air force base in 2016 and, most famously, the response to the 2008 Mumbai attacks when Pakistani terrorists conducted multiple marauding terrorist firearms attacks (MTFAs) in the city in an eerie foreshadow of the later Paris attacks.

SAG was responsible for breaching into the seized locations and clearing hotels and a Jewish centre, rescuing hostages and ultimately killing nine terrorists. Two SAG operators were killed during the operation. The government, NSG and the SAGs were criticized for their slow response and the length of time it took to kill or capture the ten terrorists responsible. More than 160 people were killed in the multiple bomb and shooting attacks.

However, a senior GSG9 officer commented: 'It is not professional for one to comment in an operation that we have not be [sic] involved in. But the NSG did a highly professional job and we hold the highest regard for NSG and the Mumbai police for the way they handled the situation. It was an unprecedented and complex situation.'*

The NSG now also has five regional units known as Special Composite Groups that can provide an immediate counter-terrorist response and contain an incident until the arrival of an SAG, another example of a similar system to that of the French and Germans and a move taken after criticism of the ten hours it took for SAGs to deploy to the objectives.

After Mumbai, GSG9 was involved in assisting the expansion of the NSG into six regional hubs (similar to the French model) and provided support in improving its communications systems and training. A Mumbai Police SWAT unit was also created with GSG9's assistance to assist the Mumbai Anti-terrorist Squad. US Army Special Forces have also begun joint training with the SAGs with the first such exercise held in 2015.

The NSG and SAG pre-Mumbai were relatively poorly equipped but budgets have since been made available. Operators carry Glock sidearms, SIG 553 assault rifles and the MP5 family and employ Heckler & Koch MSG90 and PSG1 sniper rifles. They also have a number of Israeli Glock Corner Shot devices. The SAGs acquired unidentified but likely Switchblade 'kamikaze' UAVs (unmanned aerial vehicles) in 2018 along with more standard surveillance models. They have also acquired vehicle-mounted HARAS (Height Adjustable Rescue Assault System) assault ladder systems and French Renault Sherpa 2 armoured vehicles.

---

* https://indianexpress.com/article/news-archive/web/german-counterterror-force-to-help-set-up-mumbai-swat-team/

Naval Special Warfare Development Group (NSWDG or SEAL Team 6)

Nationality: US • Branch: Navy • Established: 1980

The fabled SEAL Team 6 (ST6) began life as a maritime component to the fledgling JSOC. Legend has it that its first commander, the controversial Richard Marcinko, altered a briefing paper calling for a naval SEAL counter-terrorist element to work with Delta Force, changing the wording to indicate that a larger command was needed. He even named the unit to confuse the Russians, as at the time only two SEAL Teams existed.

Drawing from the other SEAL Teams for recruits, ST6 gained an early reputation for cowboy behaviour with much centred on a culture of hard drinking and hard partying. Despite this, the unit was certified as mission capable in 1980 and became the national special mission unit, initially for any terrorist incidents on the seas or in coastal regions. This soon expanded as the unit pressed to engage in the full spectrum of counter-terrorist missions such as counter-hijacking. With this expansion of mission came an amplification of the intense rivalry between Delta and ST6.

The first real-world ST6 operation was unfortunately somewhat less than successful. Team 6 operators were assigned several missions during the US invasion of Grenada in 1983, including securing the governor-general of the island state who had been placed under house arrest. Operating as part of the JSOC Task Force 123, the SEALs quickly secured the governor-general and his family; however one of the MH-60s inserting the team was engaged by ground fire and had to abort with a wounded pilot.

SEALs from SEAL Team 6 providing close personal protection (CPP) for former Afghan president Hamid Karzai in August 2002. The following month, the SEALs foiled a claimed assassination attempt but tragically also engaged and killed a bystander and an Afghan government bodyguard attempting to disarm the gunman. DynCorp, a private security company, took over CPP duties for Karzai later that month. (Atta Kenare/AFP/Getty Images)

The SEALs' radio equipment was left behind in the second helicopter as the operators fast-roped to the ground. The operators found themselves in a brief firefight at the mansion before Grenadian People's Revolutionary Army in APCs (armoured personnel carriers) arrived. The SEALs' single radio ran out of battery power and they were forced to use the governor-general's telephone to call for fire support. The SEALs were eventually relieved by a force of US Marines, but not before two Marine Cobra attack helicopters were shot down while supporting the operation, holding back PRA reinforcements.

Another element was assigned a job perhaps better suited for the regular SEAL Teams, covertly infiltrating the island to act as pathfinders for a Ranger parachute drop at Point Salinas airfield. After a low altitude 'wet jump', four of the 12 Team 6 operators tragically drowned. Another mission saw ST6 operators capture Radio Grenada, only to be forced to withdraw when a Grenadian Quick Reaction Force in APCs arrived, although they managed to destroy the radio transmitter before breaking contact.

Grenada was a largely unsuccessful operation for all of the assigned SOF including ST6 and Delta. Poor planning, accelerated start times that saw operations launched in daylight, and a general lack of command understanding of exactly what SOF could bring to the table resulted in a number of dead and wounded and the failure of the majority of the SOF missions on the island.

Along with Delta's rotational Aztec squadron, which was on call to deal with any and all international terrorist incidents globally, ST6 stood up Trident, a similar rotational tasking which could and did compete with Delta for deployments. On particularly large missions, including the preparations for the aborted recapture of the hijacked *Achille Lauro* cruise liner in 1985, both units would be deployed, although in that instance, ST6 would take the lead thanks to its greater training and experience in visit-board-search-seizure operations against ships under way. In a curious twist of fate, ST6 operators would eventually capture the leader of the *Achille Lauro* terrorists in Baghdad in 2003.

ST6 also conducted a number of missions in support of Operation *Just Cause* in 1989, principally working alongside Delta to hunt Manuel Noriega – the deposed military leader of Panama. High Speed Boat Teams assigned to ST6 were deployed to the Gulf for *Desert Storm* in 1991 but, as far as it is known, no full squadrons deployed. Four SEAL snipers and a command element did deploy with Task Force Ranger to Mogadishu in 1993, with only one escaping injury during the battle of the 'Lost Convoy' as the Rangers attempted to fight their way back to their base.

For ST6, the 1990s ended with operations in the Balkans hunting war criminals. Here they were very successful and conducted one of the earliest snatch missions against a Serbian war criminal who called himself the 'Serb Adolf'. ST6 also snatched Radislav Krstić, one of the architects of the genocide. Most of the capture operations ended successfully without a shot fired.

The initial SOF deployment to Afghanistan in 2001 was Army dominated with only a handful of ST6 operators working with Delta on advanced force operations (AFO). In January 2002, ST6's Red Squadron replaced a Delta squadron in a move that was viewed by many as politically motivated to 'get the SEALs into the fight' but was explained by JSOC as an effort to ensure that Delta was not burnt out early in what many were predicting would be a long war.

Elements from the recce/sniper troop of Red Squadron were deployed into the Shahikot Valley in eastern Afghanistan in support of Operation *Anaconda* (see pages 320–21) by JSOC leadership against the wishes of the Delta leader of the AFO cell, who wanted to ensure that the SEALs were properly prepared for the operation.

One element, Mako 30, was ordered to land on Takur Ghar, an imposing mountain with strategic views across the valley. Delayed by helicopter malfunctions, the infiltration of the eight-man SEAL element was finally accomplished by landing directly upon the peak, the planned site of its covert observation post, a cardinal sin in reconnaissance work. Unfortunately, apart from Mako 30, there were other armed men on the mountaintop, and as its MH-47 prepared to land, it was engaged by machine gun and RPG fire. As the pilots desperately tried to evade, a SEAL fell from the open ramp into the snow below.

The MH-47, already hit by two RPGs, managed to limp away and crash-land at the northern end of the Shahikot. Another MH-47 arrived and took the team to the peak, managing to land the team, who were immediately locked into a firefight with the al-Qaeda-aligned Islamic Movement of Uzbekistan defenders. Two of the operators were wounded, with one losing a foot to an RPG, and the team's attached Air Force combat controller was shot and presumed dead.

The SEALs withdrew from the peak with their wounded. The JSOC command, Task Force 11, had launched the Ranger Quick Reaction Force (QRF) from Bagram. Owing to the chaos on the ground and communications problems, neither the Rangers nor the pilots of their MH-47s were warned that the peak was still held by the insurgents. As the first MH-47, Razor 04, touched down, the helicopter was struck by a withering barrage of heavy machine gun and RPG fire. A crewmember and one of the Rangers were killed and both pilots badly wounded. More Rangers were killed as they ran down the ramp.

It was the beginning of a protracted firefight with the team's attached combat controller calling in numerous 'danger close' airstrikes, including the first ever use of the Predator UAV (unmanned aerial vehicle) in a close air support mission. The second half of the QRF had landed at an off-set landing zone and climbed to the peak as quickly as it could, its members even shedding their body armour plates to make the best possible speed. Eventually the two

Ranger squads were reunited and launched a further assault on the peak, killing the last defenders.

The Rangers fought off numerous attempts by the insurgents to re-take the peak, with the assistance of Coalition SOF teams stationed on surrounding mountains calling in airstrikes. After darkness fell, the Rangers were finally exfiltrated. The fate of the SEALs' attached combat controller, Technical Sergeant John Chapman, has always sat uneasily with many of the Rangers and Delta operators. Was he in fact still alive when the SEALs withdrew from the peak?

AC-130 and Predator footage showed a figure engaged in a vicious close quarter firefight, capturing an enemy bunker and killing several insurgents before he fell from his wounds. Was this evidence of Islamic Movement of Uzbekistan (IMU) insurgents firing at each other in the chaos or was it evidence of Chapman surviving and fighting on?

The author was told by a Delta veteran that it was an open secret within JSOC that Chapman had still been alive and was killed moments before rescue. It did nothing to endear ST6 to the Army or Air Force Special Tactics units. Apparent contradictions in accounts provided by the SEAL leader and his operators, who refused to sign their statements, only added to the enmity.

Rubbing salt on the wound, the leader of the Mako 30 was awarded the Medal of Honor in 2018 for his actions on Takur Ghar. Soon after, news of a posthumous Medal of Honor for Chapman was announced along with the results of an Air Force investigation into the events surrounding his death.

Overhead footage examined during Air Force investigations conclusively proved that Chapman had indeed survived his initial gunshot wound. He had fought a brave rearguard action but was finally gunned down literally seconds away from the arrival of Razor 04 and the Ranger QRF. Some surmise he may have heard the rotors of the Chinook and was desperately trying to suppress the enemy and save the helicopter.

ST6 rotated through Afghanistan, which in the early 2000s was very much a secondary front with the Taliban in disarray and most al-Qaeda dead or in Pakistan. The unit was involved in the Delta-led 'industrial counter-terrorism' in Iraq with troop-strength elements operating as Task Force West working alongside a Ranger platoon. Others were attached to Delta's Task Force Central and Task Force North.

The unit was placed in rotational command with the Rangers of the small JSOC element in Afghanistan while Delta took responsibility for Iraq. After the 'Surge' and the incredible success of the kill or capture campaign in Iraq, along with the 'Anbar awakening' of 2005 which brought former enemies back into the fold to battle al-Qaeda in Iraq, SOF began to withdraw slowly from Iraq. Afghanistan was the new priority as another surge was announced to try and replicate the Iraq success.

ST6 was at the forefront of the kill and capture campaign in Afghanistan, conducting as many as five raids a night. Their efforts eliminated much of the Taliban's infrastructure in terms of bomb-makers and junior to mid-level leadership although the resilient insurgents continued to recover. ST6 and the Rangers formed an unlikely but successful partnership during these years, with both units rotating the 'assault' and 'security' elements on raids.

The unit suffered its most costly loss with the 2011 downing of Extortion 17, an Army CH-47 Chinook. The aircraft was carrying 15 members of Gold Squadron, seven Naval Special Warfare personnel including two members of another SEAL Team and various support personnel, three Air Force Special Tactics operators, seven Afghan special operators, an interpreter and a SEAL combat assault dog, along with the helicopter's five-man crew. All were lost when the Chinook was struck by an RPG, which destroyed the rear rotor assembly.

The SEALs had been acting as the Immediate Reaction Force (IRF) for a joint Ranger and Afghan assault force that had inserted onto a target compound hunting a Taliban high-value target in the Tangi Valley. A number of insurgents managed to evade the assault force and the SEAL IRF was called in to head them off before they could escape. As Extortion 17 flared to land, a hidden RPG team fired at least two rockets at the helicopters, one of which struck with devastating consequences.

In May 2012, ST6 and Britain's 22SAS conducted a coordinated hostage rescue in Afghanistan labelled Operation *Jubilee*. Both units were infiltrated by the 160th SOAR and struck two caves that drone surveillance indicated were inhabited by insurgents. The SEALs killed seven insurgents but with no sign of the hostages, two British and Kenyan aid workers. Moments later the SAS team reported in that four insurgents had been killed at their target and all of the hostages safely recovered.

In December of the same year, ST6 carried out the successful rescue of a kidnapped American doctor in eastern Afghanistan, tragically losing one of its

The burnt-out remains of Razor 01, a 160th Special Operations Aviation Regiment MH-47E shot down by Uzbek insurgents on Takur Ghar in March 2002. After the Rangers were exfiltrated, the Chinook was destroyed by an airstrike to deny any sensitive equipment to the enemy. (Joe Raedle/Getty Images)

own during the operation. Other hostage rescues had been less successful, including the mission to recover Linda Norgrove, a British aid worker and alleged MI6 asset, which ended in tragedy when a SEAL posted a fragmentation grenade which killed both an insurgent and, unintentionally, the hostage. An operation in August 2016 to rescue an American academic and an Australian academic narrowly missed catching the hostage takers, who had recently moved locations.

One of their most famous successes was not in Afghanistan but off the coast of Somalia in April 2009 following the hijacking of the *Maersk Alabama* cargo ship by Somali pirates. The captain of the ship, Richard Phillips, had been kidnapped by a number of pirates who had attempted to escape in a lifeboat. ST6 conducted a parachute drop into the water near a US Navy warship and set up their sniper teams. When the frustrated and increasingly erratic pirates began firing on the warship and threatening Phillips, the snipers engaged their targets simultaneously, killing all three.

Another successful hostage rescue mission in January 2012 was conducted in Somalia itself after an American and several Danish relief workers were kidnapped by bandits linked to the al-Shabaab terrorist organisation. The SEALS conducted a night-time HALO parachute jump into the area and advanced upon the bandit camp using night vision. Nine hostage-takers were quickly killed and the hostages extracted by 160th SOAR.

ST6 has also been heavily committed to North Africa where operators conduct counter-terrorism missions with local partner forces. In Somalia there are currently two separate SEAL-led components targeting al-Shabaab, numbering around 50 American operators. In fact, ST6 and occasionally 'vanilla' (a term denoting non ST6 SEALs) SEAL Teams – along with JSOC's Intelligence Support Activity (ISA) and the CIA's Special Activities Division (SAD) – have operated in Somalia and neighbouring countries since 2001 targeting al-Qaeda elements. In May 2017, an ST6 operator was killed and two others wounded while conducting a partnered direct action mission in Somalia against an al-Shabaab target.

The unit had conducted two hostage rescue missions into Yemen in 2014 before a fateful January 2017 mission targeting al-Qaeda in the Arabic Peninsula (AQAP) leadership targets. The operation was a joint mission with United Arab Emirates Special Forces. Infiltrated into an off-set LZ (landing zone) by Marine Corps MV-22 Ospreys, the SEALs and Emiratis advanced some five kilometres toward the village of Yakla. UAVs overhead noted significant movement in the village as gunmen took up positions and it became apparent that the operation had been compromised.

Despite the loss of surprise, the SEALs continued into Yakla and met significant resistance. At least three operators were wounded and one died from his wounds. One of two MV-22 tilt-rotor VTOL aircraft, dispatched to evacuate the wounded and insert an IRF, crashed on landing, wounding an additional three operators and adding to the challenges facing the SEALs. US Marine Corps airstrikes and

Super Cobra attack helicopter gun runs allowed the SEAL and Emeriti force to break contact and exfiltrate via additional MV-22s. The crippled MV-22 was destroyed from the air by Marine Harriers.

Although 14 insurgents had been killed in the assault, none was the primary target, the leader of AQAP. Additionally, a large number of civilians were killed, principally by the air support used to allow the SEALs to make their escape, as US Central Command later stated: 'The known possible civilian casualties appear to have been potentially caught up in aerial gunfire that was called in to assist US forces in contact against a determined enemy that included armed women firing from prepared fighting positions, and US special operations members receiving fire from all sides to include houses and other buildings.'

Controversy has dogged the unit in recent years. A number of ST6 operators (along with a pair of Marine Special Operations Command or MARSOC Raiders) were charged in the murder of an Army Green Beret from the 3rd SFG in Mali in June 2017 after the Army soldier discovered that the SEALs were pilfering money meant for local informants. This was not the first time ST6 operators had been investigated for crimes. After the successful hostage rescue of Captain Richard Phillips from Somali pirates in 2009, some $30,000 USD in cash went missing from the lifeboat that Phillips had been imprisoned upon.

There have also been a number of investigations into allegations of war crimes committed by ST6 in Afghanistan and Iraq and the unit has something of a tarnished reputation owing to the regularity of killings that members of other units such as the Rangers and Delta view as unnecessary and outside the Law of Armed Conflict. Culturally, a change occurred within ST6 after the execution of a SEAL on Takur Ghar in 2002 by Uzbek insurgents. From that date onwards, some argue that ST6 has been attempting to exact vengeance against any and all enemy.

ST6 operators use the 9x19mm Glock 19 as their principal assault pistol (replacing the 9x19mm SIG-Sauer P226) with the .45ACP Mk24 Mod0 (a version of the HK45C) used for suppressed shooting. Their assault rifle is the 5.56x45mm HK416, generally suppressed and used with a range of Aimpoint optics. The 7.62x51mm HK417 is also employed as a marksman rifle with one being deployed with the Red Squadron team in Abbottabad during Operation *Neptune Spear* (see pages 338–40).

For suppressed, close range killing, ST6 adopted the 4.6x30mm MP7. The weapon largely replaced the integrally suppressed MP5SD3, which had been in use since the 1980s. Owing to the short effective range of the MP7, operators began carrying sawn-off 40mm M79s to engage targets beyond 100 metres (known as 'Pirate Guns' because of their distinctive profile).

To replace the MP7 the SEALs worked with AAC to develop the Honey Badger in .300 Blackout, a cartridge that offered a greater range (300–400 metres) while maintaining a very low sound signature. Owing to a variety of technical issues, the Honey Badger was never produced beyond a number of operational prototypes and instead the SIG MCX, also chambered for the new .300 Blackout, was adopted to fill the gap.

ST6 snipers use a range of platforms including the .338 Lapua Magnum Surgeon Precision Sniper Rifle and a number of McMillan .338 and .50 bolt action platforms. They will likely also adopt the recently announced multi-calibre Mk21 Advanced Sniper Rifle based on the Barrett MRAD.

Norwegian Special Operations Forces (NORSOF)

Nationality: Norwegian • Branch: Joint • Established: 2014

Norwegian Special Operations Forces or NORSOF, established in a similar manner to US SOCOM, commands two SOF units: the Army's Forsvarets Spesialkommando (FSK or Army Special Commandos – formerly Hærens Jegerkommando or HJK) and the Navy's Marinejegerkommandoen (MJK or Marine Hunter Commandos).

FSK was established in the 1980s, primarily as a counter-terrorist unit (it still retains primary responsibility for the overseas counter-terrorist mission) trained by the British SAS and SBS. However, its remit has now considerably widened and now takes in special reconnaissance, close personal protection and unconventional warfare. Domestic counter-terrorism is the responsibility of the Beredskapstroppen (Emergency Response Unit, but commonly referred to as Delta). It has mainly responded to criminal sieges and shootings, although it responded to the Anders Behring Breivik incident in 2011 (Breivik was a far right terrorist who detonated a number of bombs in Oslo before murdering 69 students on a remote Norwegian island).

The MJK developed from previous combat diver units with an initial emphasis on countering hijack attempts against Norwegian offshore oil rigs. The structure of both units is a well-kept secret, although MJK follows British SBS lines and is believed to include Alpha Squadron, which houses the unit's assaulters and snipers; Bravo Squadron, which provides training; Echo Squadron, which comprises small boat and submersibles; and Lima Squadron, which provides operational and technical support. FSK is believed to be also structured along UK lines with at least two assault squadrons supported by a number of training, logistics and operational support units.

NORSOF deployed 78 FSK and 28 MJK personnel to Afghanistan in 2002 as part of Task Force K-Bar. They deployed special reconnaissance teams in support of Operation *Anaconda* (see pages 320–21). They later deployed under International Security Assistance Force (ISAF) command and conducted operations for the Norwegian-led Provincial Reconstruction Team in the northern Faryab Province between 2004 and 2012. An MJK officer was

killed in action in 2007 in the same year that FSK conducted a successful hostage rescue in Kabul. Four MJK operators were tragically killed in a single IED incident in 2010.

FSK has been conducting mentoring to Afghan National Mission Units including the Crisis Response Unit (CRU) and has been drawn into a number of high-profile operations alongside its Afghan charges. Most well known is the CRU response to the April 2012 attacks in Kabul where Norwegian operators established a base of fire position on the rooftop of a building and directed barrages of LAW (light anti-armour weapon) rockets against Taliban positions.

It was again involved in the recapture of the Intercontinental Hotel in Kabul in January 2018 when the Taliban launched coordinated attacks across the city. The FSK and MJK operators accompanied the CRU, whose members fast-roped to the roof of the hotel and began a methodical clearance of each floor, eventually killing all six Taliban responsible.

MJK has also deployed on counter-piracy missions to the Gulf of Aden. In 2016, a Special Operations Task Group of some 60 operators drawn from both FSK and MJK was dispatched to Jordan to work with the Jordanian JSOC to assist with training anti-Assad Syrian militias.

Unusually, NORSOF maintains a women-only unit, the Jegertroppen (Hunter Troop). The platoon is trained in special reconnaissance including conducting undercover advanced force operations. They also receive language and cultural training to allow them to work as intelligence gatherers, speaking to women in Muslim countries where it is forbidden to speak to an unrelated man.

NORSOF operators, probably from the Norwegian Army's Forsvarets Spesialkommando (FSK), supporting an Afghan National Mission Unit, responding to wide-ranging Taliban terrorist attacks in Kabul, April 2012. The operator in the foreground carries a 7.62x51mm HK417 whilst his colleagues carry the HK416. (Majid Saeedi/ Getty Images)

NORSOF units use both the USP, typically suppressed, and the general issue Glock; the HK416 and HK417 (for many years they used Diemaco – Colt Canada – carbines but the SOF units adopted the HK416 when the Norwegian Army chose it for its issue rifle in 2008 as the 416N); the Accuracy International AWM and the MP5 and MP7 series, again typically suppressed. Both the 5.56x45mm Minimi and 7.62x51mm Mk3 are employed. Beredskapstroppen use the Heckler & Koch P30 sidearm, MP5s and Colt Canada carbines.

Nucleo Operativo Centrale di Sicurezza (NOCS)

Nationality: Italian • Branch: State Police • Established: 1978

The Nucleo Operativo Centrale di Sicurezza (NOCS or Central Security Operations Unit) began as the successor to one of Italy's first counter-terrorist units, the Anti-Commando Unit formed in 1975. Throughout the late 1970s and 1980s, NOCS was at the forefront of operations against the Red Brigades and similar extreme right- and left-wing terrorist groups including Operation *Winter Harvest*, which saw the unit rescue the kidnapped US General James Dozier in 1982 (the US Intelligence Support Activity or ISA had been employed to locate the kidnappers).

Italian NOCS operators parade in 2008. The operator in front carries the 9x19mm integrally suppressed MP5SD3 devoid of its usual assortment of lights, lasers and optics. (Mario Laporta/ AFP/Getty Images)

Through the 1990s, NOCS was increasingly deployed not in traditional counter-terrorism roles but against criminal kidnappers who had become a high-profile scourge. In 2005, the unit was responsible for the capture of one of the plotters of the attacks on the London underground system. More recently, in November 2018 in Macomer, the unit captured an Islamic State-inspired terrorist who was planning to poison the town's water supply. Earlier in 2018, the unit had been involved in high-profile raids targeting an Islamic State facilitator who was recruiting would-be terrorists to drive vans and trucks into tourist sites.

The unit is divided into the Special Team of four assault teams, each of ten operators, and one close personal protection wing, along with various support and headquarters elements for a total of 140 operators. They are supported by the Police Bomb Squad and the 'Neptune' Sharpshooters, a self-contained sniper cell that is typically employed 'to protect dignitaries and sensitive targets at a distance' according to the State Police.

Today NOCS is part of the Divisione Investigazioni Generali e Operazioni Speciali (the General Investigations and Special Operations Division) and now includes its first female operator.

Italy also maintains the Gruppo di Intervento Speciale (GIS or Special Intervention Group), created in 1978, as the counter-terrorist arm of the Carabinieri (a Gendarmerie-like military police organization) and now part of the Comando Interforze per le Operazioni delle Forze Speciali (COFS or Joint Special Forces Command), which also commands Col Moschin. The key difference between GIS and NOCS is that NOCS is focused on the domestic response within Italian borders while GIS can operate internationally.

NOCS carries 9x19mm Beretta PX4 Storm pistols, Aimpoint equipped MP5A3s, M4 carbines and a selection of sniper platforms, including the 7.62x51mm HS Precision and the .338 Lapua Magnum Accuracy International AWM.

PLA Special Operations Forces

Nationality: Chinese • Branch: Army • Established: 1988

People's Liberation Army (PLA) Special Operations Forces (SOF) exist within every military region in China. There are currently believed to be at least nine units, most directly descended from reconnaissance units and each organized to brigade strength – some are independent bridages, while others are held at divisional level. These units conduct direct action raids, long range reconnaissance, airfield seizures and special missions for the PLA district in support of conventional forces. They have little to no training or experience of core special operations activities apart from direct action.

In Western terms, these units are more akin to the Army Rangers of the 1980s in terms of both training and role but the PLA strongly believes in developing SOF as a strategic activity and their training and equipment will only improve. They have certainly the largest body of troops assigned to special operations in the world today. There is as yet no central SOCOM-style command structure and the PLA SOF are held in each of the PLA's five regional theatre commands, leading to obvious duplication and waste in training and logistics.

The PLA had studied the American experience in Vietnam and their own Sino-Vietnamese War saw PLA reconnaissance squadrons successfully conduct direct action special operations against the Vietnamese. In fact for many years, these reconnaissance units were the closest the PLA had to a special operations capability. That began to change in the late 1980s when China began to view SOF as an important strategic tool.

A fascinating image of Chinese operators employing a fibre optic camera to scan for hostiles from the cargo bay of an airliner during a counter-hijack exercise in 2009. (Daily Wong/VCG via Getty Images)

With the rise of international terrorism in the 1970s, the Chinese responded by establishing a police intervention unit, the People's Armed Police (PAP) 772nd Special Squad, after studying Western units like Germany's GSG9 and France's GIGN. The cadre from this unit eventually were employed to teach their skills at the PAP Special Police Institute, laying the groundwork for the development of further special units.

Today, the Chinese People's Armed Police now has several distinct units – Falcon, Snow Leopard and Eagle Special Forces Squadrons, supported by local SWAT and public order teams. Operators from Snow Leopard have conducted close personal protection taskings in Iraq and probably elsewhere. All three units have also been involved in anti-narcotics operations and limited counter-terrorism missions in Xinjiang Province.

The Navy maintains the Xiaolung Assault Squadron, a SEAL/SBS equivalent, which has been deployed a number of times to conduct non-combatant evacuations and on anti-piracy missions in the Gulf of Aden. In 2017, it rescued 19 Filipino hostages held on a cargo ship, although the Somali pirates had fled at the first sign of trouble. It also worked with PAP units to conduct a civilian non-combatant evacuation from Yemen in 2015.

Available imagery of both PLA and PAP units indicates use of standard-issue small arms such as the bullpup QBZ-95 rifle and QSZ-92 sidearm, although they are also likely to employ the suppressed QCW-05 sub machine gun and, for police, the suppressed 9mm CS06/LS06.

Recherche, Assistance, Intervention, Dissuasion (RAID)

Nationality: French • Branch: Police • Established: 1985

Recherche, Assistance, Intervention, Dissuasion (RAID) is the French National Police counter-terrorist and hostage recovery unit. Integrated under the Force d'Intervention de la Police Nationale (FIPN or National Police Intervention Force), which includes the Brigade de Recherche et d'Intervention (BRI or Research and Intervention Brigade) and Brigade de Recherche et d'Intervention – Brigade Anticommando (BRI-BAC or Research and Intervention Brigade – Anti-Commando Brigade), RAID is responsible for interventions in the capital

and for large-scale hostage takings anywhere within France. Since 2016, regional tactical units known as Groupes d'Intervention de la Police Nationale (GIPN or National Police Intervention Groups) were incorporated into RAID in a similar fashion to the GIGN Antenna units.

The unit is composed of two 'brigades', each comprising two 25-man 'sections'. RAID has conducted thousands of operations but most well known would be the response to the November 2015 attack on the Bataclan concert venue in Paris alongside BRI-BAC and a follow-up operation against the surviving terrorists in the Parisian suburb of Saint-Denis.

As the RAID assaulters attempted to conduct an explosive breach into the terrorists' apartment, the charge failed to break down the apartment's reinforced door and the assaulters were taken under fire. Homemade grenades were also lobbed at the RAID team. It was forced to withdraw behind ballistic shields with a number of wounded.

A combat assault dog equipped with a video camera was sent in but was shot and killed. 40mm grenades were used to suppress the terrorists and to blow holes in the apartment's walls to allow snipers to engage those inside. One terrorist detonated a suicide bomb vest, killing herself and a comrade after attempting to lure the police closer. Finally RAID established – through the use of a number of UAVs (unmanned aerial vehicles) and UGVs (unmanned ground vehicles) fitted with cameras – that the terrorists appeared incapacitated and a final assault was launched.

French RAID sniper teams move into place during the siege of the Hyper Cacher Kosher grocery store in Paris following the Charlie Hebdo attacks in January 2015. The spotters (in the lead) both appear to carry HK417 rifles. (Eric Feferberg/AFP/Getty Images)

Three terrorists were discovered dead in the apartment, two blown apart by the vest and one killed under falling concrete. Five other terrorist suspects who had attempted to flee the area were also detained. Unfortunately it now appears that the terrorists were armed only with a single pistol (although a number wore suicide bomb vests) and that RAID's Malinois, Diesel, had been killed by fratricide. Additionally up to five RAID operators may also have been struck by friendly fire. More recently the RAID Strasbourg Antenna unit was deployed during the December 2018 shooting near the Strasbourg Christmas Market and exchanged fire with the terrorist.

Uniquely RAID operators carry two pistols, a Glock 17 with weapon light as their primary and a sub-compact Glock 26. The concept relates to their heavy use of ballistic shields; once one pistol is empty, the second can be drawn rather than attempting a difficult and time-consuming magazine change. The G36C remains the standard assault rifle for RAID, while both the MP5 series and the Molot Vepr-12 semi-automatic shotgun are the standard CQB weapons (the RAID Antenna units also use the folding stock Beretta RS203P shotgun and the SIG 551 as a marksman rifle). The PGM Ultima Ratio sniper rifle was developed in close coordination with the unit.

Regimental Reconnaissance Company (RRC)

Nationality: US • Branch: Army • Established: 1984

A US Army Ranger fires his 5.56x45mm Mk16 SCAR-L on a range in Afghanistan. The Mk16 was combat tested by the Rangers from 2009 but was found to offer no significant capability improvement over the Block II M4A1. The Mk17 in 7.62x51mm was adopted by the Rangers in small numbers as a battle rifle/designated marksman platform and the Mk20 has seen some use as a sniper support or spotter's rifle. (Courtesy US Army, Pfc Dacotah Lane)

The first dedicated reconnaissance unit stood up by the 75th Ranger Regiment was the Regimental Reconnaissance Detachment or RRD, a small element comprising three five-man reconnaissance teams with one team assigned to each Ranger battalion (and known colloquially as Regimental Recon and later as simply 'recce'). Its members served as pathfinders for Ranger airborne operations, emplacing beacons at landing zones, along with the traditional range of special reconnaissance operations. All members were SCUBA and HALO/HAHO (high altitude low opening/high altitude high opening) qualified as well as receiving small boat training.

The core reconnaissance task was conducted by two- to three-man reconnaissance and surveillance teams that would covertly approach a target to monitor and report on movements and enemy strength or the location of hostages or similar objectives. They also trained in extensive close quarter battle shooting to enable an in-extremis capability to secure objectives should a given situation deteriorate before a Ranger assault force was in place.

The RRD often included task-specific attachments from the recce troops of Delta and SEAL Team 6 squadrons along with operators from the Intelligence Support Activity (ISA) who could provide specific capabilities such as signals intelligence gathering and similar technical methods (typically

one to three Special Mission Unit or SMU members would be attached for a specific mission). As the RRD was heavily deployed to Afghanistan and Iraq, its own capabilities expanded and matured to include the use of remote battlefield sensors, including covert unattended ground sensors, limited signals intelligence interception and the employment of a range of UAV (unmanned aerial vehicle) types.

In 2004 the RRD was placed under the direct command of JSOC to increase special reconnaissance and advanced force operations capabilities as the existing reconnaissance units within Delta and SEAL Team 6 were already stretched to meet increasing demand. Within the Ranger Regiment, organic battalion reconnaissance teams were established to meet Ranger needs should the RRD be fully deployed by JSOC.

In 2007, the RRD was renamed the Regimental Reconnaissance Company (RRC). According to SOCOM the unit 'provides worldwide reconnaissance and operation preparation of the environment in support of the 75th Ranger Regiment and other special operations units.' It is believed to have been expanded into at least five five-man reconnaissance and surveillance teams. The RRC is believed to operate with non-standard weapons and equipment, including the HK416, MCX LVAW (replacing the MP7A1) and the Glock sidearm.

Särskilda Operationsgruppen (SOG)

Nationality: Swedish • Branch: Joint • Established: 2011

The Särskilda Operationsgruppen or SOG (Special Operations Task Group) was the result of a merger of two existing Swedish SOF units, the Särskilda Skyddsgruppen (SSG or Special Protection Group), and the Särskilda Inhämtningsgruppen (SIG or Special Collection Group). The SSG had been created in the 1990s to serve as Sweden's primary covert operations unit and given both a wartime special operations and a counter-terrorism mission.

A range of SOF personnel seen during exercises in 2009 – from left: Hungary, Macedonia, Romania, Croatia, Ukraine, Poland and Sweden (in distinctive Swedish M90 camouflage pattern). (Stringer/AFP/Getty Images)

The SIG was founded from elements of the Army's Fallskärmsjägarskolans Insatskompani (FJS IK or Parachute Ranger Rapid Reaction Company) and designated as a special reconnaissance and intelligence gathering entity.

The SOG sits under the command of the Director Special Forces, Joint Special Forces Command, and is composed of two distinct elements: Response Unit 1 dedicated to direct action and counter-terrorism and Response Unit 2 which conducts special reconnaissance and advanced force operations. They are supported by their own integral helicopter and small boat units.

The SSG had deployed to Afghanistan under International Security Assistance Force (ISAF) command and lost two operators in 2005 while the FJS IK had conducted an earlier deployment in 2002. The SOG was deployed since its foundation in 2011 until the Swedish drawdown in 2014. SOG has since been deployed to Iraq since 2015 on the Swedish advise and assist mission.

Domestically, the Nationella Insatsstyrkan (NI or National Task Force) of the Swedish Police has the counter-terrorism intervention mission supported by the Förstärkt Regional Insatsstyrkan (Reinforced Regional Task Force or RRTF), which provides regional tactical support for the local police.

The SOG and NI employ the suppressor-equipped LWRC IC-A5 and the RRTF the IC-E carbine (replacing the G36C within the SOG and NI and the HK53 in the RRTF) and the MP7A1 which has supplemented the MP5A3 and SD3. The SOG also uses the Minimi Para, the HK417, as a marksman rifle and the TRG-42 in .338 Lapua Magnum as its principal sniper platform although the .50 M82A1 is also available and has been seen in SOG hands in Afghanistan.

Sayeret Matkal (Unit 269)

Nationality: Israeli • Branch: Army • Established: 1957

Sayeret Matkal, the General Staff Reconnaissance Unit of the Israeli Army, is Israel's longest serving and best known SOF. Also known as Unit 269 or 'the Unit' (in the same way as Delta Force refers to itself), it was originally developed as a covert reconnaissance and surveillance unit modelled on the British SAS (it still uses the SAS motto), its role diversified into counter-terrorism and direct action tasks. Its most famous operation was the breath-taking hostage rescue at Entebbe in 1976 but Sayeret Matkal has been at the forefront of nearly all successful Israeli special operations.

One of its most famous actions was Operation *Spring of Youth* in 1973 when Sayeret Matkal was ferried to its target, PLO (Palestine Liberation Organization) high-value targets in Lebanon, by the naval commandos of Shayetet 13. Shayetet 13 (Flotilla 13) is the equivalent of the US Navy SEALs or Britain's SBS; a seaborne commando force that has an even older heritage than Sayeret Matkal. Flotilla 13 employs a range of boats including RIBs (rigid inflatable boats), fast boats and covert craft. It also maintains a specialist diving unit known as Yechida Lemesimot Tat-Memiyot (Navy Underwater Missions Unit).

Upon reaching the shore, the Sayeret Matkal was met by Mossad operatives who drove them to their targets. The Army operators carried a mix of AKMs and suppressed Ingram MAC-10 sub machine guns for deniability should any weapons be left behind. In a coordinated assault, the operators breached into a number of locations and killed three PLO commanders and up to 50 other PLO members as well as employing demolition charges to demolish four buildings used as weapons caches.

Other operations were not as successful. Much like Operation *Eagle Claw* for Delta, Maalot lives in infamy as the unit's low point after a 1974 incident when terrorists seized the Netiv Meir School in the Israeli town of Maalot, taking just under 100 hostages. Sayeret Matkal was authorized to conduct a hostage rescue but the dawn operation was fatally flawed as a sniper, whose shot would initiate the assault, only wounded the terrorist leader and the assaulters breached into the wrong floor giving the terrorists time to post grenades into the crowded hostages. Before being killed by the Sayeret Matkal operators moments later, the terrorists murdered 28 hostages and killed one Sayeret Matkal operator.

Operation *Thunderball* followed the June 1976 hijacking of an Air France flight carrying 83 Israelis amongst another 209 hostages, along with a 12-person flight crew. The Air France aircraft eventually landed at Entebbe Airport, Uganda, where the nation's dictator, the infamous Idi Amin, had pledged protection to the hijackers, a mixed Palestinian and German team. Being 3,540 kilometres from Israel, the terrorists believed they were in relative safety, particularly as Amin deployed his soldiers to guard them at the airport.

A classic 1971 image showing the future Israeli prime minister, Benjamin Netanyahu (on the right), and another commando from Sayeret Matkal. Both carry collapsible stock 9x19mm UZIs. Rumour indicates the unit may have used American Ingram MAC-10s rather than UZIs (alongside captured AKs) during the fateful Entebbe raid. (GPO via Getty Images)

After releasing all non-Jewish hostages, the terrorists demanded the release of some 53 terrorists from Israeli custody. An unwieldy rescue plan was hatched by Sayeret Matkal under the title of Operation *Heartburn* but, following a covert photographic reconnaissance flight over Entebbe by an undercover Mossad operative, the plan was redeveloped. It was daring in its scope and audacity.

The Sayeret Matkal operators, again carrying deniable weapons and supported by soldiers from the Golani and Paratroop Brigades, who would secure the airfield, would fly to Entebbe in disguised Israeli Air Force C-130s before landing at the airport at a time when a civilian cargo aircraft was expected. To confuse the Ugandan guards, the operators would drive off the ramps of the C-130s in a black Mercedes sedan, similar to that used by Amin himself and flanked by jeeps carrying his 'security force', actually Sayeret Matkal operators.

The plan, incredibly, went almost without a hitch. The aircraft landed and the convoy approached the terminal but it was challenged by two Ugandan soldiers. They were engaged with a suppressed pistol but only wounded. An operator killed them both with his unsuppressed AKM, the gunfire finally alerting the Ugandans and the terrorists.

Twenty-nine special operators breached into the terminal building, immediately killing all eight hijackers. Unfortunately three hostages stood up during the firefight and were killed in the crossfire. Other Sayeret Matkal teams engaged the Ugandan guard force and placed demolition charges on eight MiG fighter aircraft to ensure the Israeli C-130s were not intercepted on their return journey.

Israeli Sayeret Matkal operators fast-rope from an Israeli Black Hawk during exercises in 2003. (IDF/ Getty Images)

The mission was an incredible success, rescuing 79 hostages along with the flight crew, who had bravely volunteered to stay with the Jewish passengers. Only one Sayeret Matkal operator was killed. The unit had in fact carried out the first successful counter-hijack mission, Operation *Isotope*, in 1972 after a Black September cell hijacked Sabena Flight 571. The hijacking was conducted by four terrorists who forced the aircraft to land at Lod in Israel, where a sixteen-man team of Sayeret Matkal operators (including Benjamin Netanyahu, who was later wounded during the operation) assaulted the aircraft, killing two and capturing two terrorists. Three hostages were wounded (from 90 passengers), one of whom later died of her wounds. It became an early textbook example of a counter-hijack SOF mission. Sayeret Matkal was also responsible for yet another daring mission in 1988 into Tunisia to kill a Palestinian terrorist leader.

Other, more recent, operations are largely unknown on account of pervasive state secrecy that makes UKSF look like an open book in comparison.

There have been hints of deep reconnaissance missions into Syria to surveille nuclear reactor sites and certainly there was the sadly unsuccessful rescue attempt in October 1994 to free a captured Israeli soldier, which ended in his death and the death of a Sayeret element's commander after failed breaches alerted the terrorists.

The terrorists immediately executed the hostage following the failure of explosive charges against a reinforced steel door. The Sayeret had planned three simultaneous explosive breaches, although only one was successful. The first operator through the successful breach was shot and mortally wounded while terrorist gunfire wounded another six Sayeret operators. A four-minute delay in eventually breaching into the stronghold where the hostage was held proved fatal, with the terrorists murdering the soldier before being cut down by operators.

A recent more successful operation allegedly saw Sayeret Matkal infiltrate Syria and provide security while a Mossad Rainbow unit planted technical surveillance in a meeting room used by Islamic State. The intelligence gathered from the operation resulted in the ban on passengers from certain countries carrying laptops onto commercial flights as Islamic State planned to detonate one or more laptops hiding concealed explosives mid-flight.

Sayeret Matkal and Flotilla 13 use the bullpup Israeli Micro Tavor X-95 (MTAR-21), the Tavor carbine variant, the CTAR-21, and ACOG-equipped Colt carbines. Flotilla 13 also still uses captured AKMs both for their reliability in tidal mud and for their deniability if a mission is compromised and a weapon is left behind. For sidearms the Glock 19 is favoured. For heavier firepower the standard Negev light machine gun is used.

Sayeret Matkal and indeed most Israeli special units deploy canines in prominent roles both as combat assault dogs and in explosive detection duties. The Israeli Defence Force (IDF) also has a secret canine unit, Oketz or Sting, trained to carry out covert bombings with devices attached to the dogs in much the same way as the Russians used dogs as a crude anti-tank weapon on the Eastern Front.

Sea-Air-And-Land Teams (SEALs)

Nationality: US • Branch: Navy • Established: 1962

The Sea-Air-And-Land Teams (SEALs) were established in 1962 as naval SOF, specifically to conduct operations against guerrillas and insurgents in littoral environments. Two teams, SEAL Teams 1 and 2, were established from the Navy's Underwater Demolition Teams (UDTs). The UDTs had traditionally performed beach reconnaissance for landing forces, a role that the SEALs would inherit.

They became legendary in Vietnam, operating along the Mekong River interdicting Viet Cong supply lines and striking at staging areas. Individual SEALs were also attached to the Phoenix Programme, a CIA project that targeted Viet Cong infrastructure and conducted fledgling partnered operations with the South Vietnamese Provincial Reconnaissance Units, both efforts reminiscent of the later Omega and partner unit efforts in Afghanistan.

The unit expanded during the Cold War to include SEAL Teams 3, 4 and 5 in 1983 and SEAL Team 8 in 1988. In 1977, SEAL Team 6 (ST6), also known as Naval Special Warfare Development Group (see pages 133–40), had been established as a classified maritime counter-terrorism element. Along with ST6, SEAL Team 4 deployed on Operation *Urgent Fury* to Grenada in 1983 and conducted one of the few successful special operations of the short campaign by carrying out a covert beach reconnaissance mission to ascertain its suitability for a Marine amphibious landing, a classic SEAL mission.

In comparison, their next major operation, Paitilla airfield in Panama, lives in infamy amongst the SEAL community. Before Afghanistan, it was the command's greatest combat loss. The SEAL Teams operated in Panama as Task Force White drawn from Teams 4 and 5 and, according to the official history, included 'five SEAL platoons, three patrol boats, four riverine patrol boats, and two light patrol boats.' Team 4 were assigned a mission to disable Panama's leader Manuel Noriega's personal aircraft to stop him from escaping from Panama.

The SEALs from Team 4 were the assault element for Task Unit Papa, a 62-man force that included three SEAL platoons from Team 4 (Bravo, Delta

A Navy SEAL sniper mans an overwatch position in Day Kundi Province, Afghanistan, 2012. Note the use of MultiCam uniform and AOR1 pattern hat. His sniper rifle is the .300 Winchester Magnum Mk13 with stock folded. (Courtesy US Navy, MC2 Jacob L. Dillon)

Two US Navy SEALs outside Raqqa, Syria, May 2016. Both wear the distinctive AOR-1 camouflage pattern and the right-hand SEAL carries a 5.56x45mm Mk46 light machine gun. (Delil Souleiman/AFP/Getty Images)

and Golf), along with attached combat controllers. Inexplicably, the SEALs of Golf Platoon advanced in the open to the hangar containing Noriega's personal jet before becoming embroiled in a firefight with Panamanian Defense Force (PDF) guards.

Caught in the open, eight SEALs were killed or wounded in the initial contact. The other two SEAL platoons rushed to outflank and suppress the defenders but lost further wounded. The firefight lasted only 12 minutes but four SEALs had been killed and eight wounded. The operators then peppered Noriega's aircraft with 40mm grenades and LAW (light anti-armour weapon) rockets. They held the airfield until that afternoon when 2/75 Rangers relieved the beleaguered SEALs.

Arguably the mission should never have been assigned to the SEALs, and it was indeed initially a Ranger mission. Being an airfield seizure, it fell firmly within the mission set of the Ranger Regiment and sending a unit that was much less experienced in land warfare perhaps indicates that the SEALs were given the mission more for political than tactical reasons. Other SEAL missions during the Panama invasion were more successful, including

Task Unit Whiskey's operation to emplace underwater charges on a PDF patrol boat and the mission of Task Units Charlie and Foxtrot to secure the entrances to the Canal itself.

The SEALs deployed to the Persian Gulf for Operation *Desert Storm* in 1991 and platoons from Teams 1 and 5 contributed to littoral operations, clearing Iraqi sea mines and conducting visit-board-search-seizure operations against ships suspected of supplying the Iraqi regime (the teams had previously deployed to the Gulf in 1987 under Operation *Prime Chance* to counter Iranian minelayers). Along with Army Special Forces, the SEALs were also deployed on the foreign internal defence mission to train and liaise with Arabic Coalition Forces.

In Afghanistan, the SEALs of Teams 2, 3 and 8 deployed as part of Task Force K-Bar, conducting special reconnaissance and sensitive site exploitations, often partnered with Coalition units like the New Zealand SAS and the German KSK. The SEALs' dune buggy-like desert patrol vehicles were found to be unsuitable for the Afghan terrain and HMMWVs were borrowed until specialist ground mobility vehicles could be procured. As the mission switched to a larger counter-insurgency campaign, the SEALs were also involved in direct action raiding and eventually foreign internal defence, working with both locally raised militias and the fledgling Afghan security forces.

A SEAL reconnaissance element drawn from Team 10 was ambushed in 2005 on Operation *Red Wings* with the loss of three of the four SEALs. A 160th Special Operations Aviation Regiment (160th SOAR) MH-47, scrambled with a SEAL Quick Reaction Force (QRF), was shot down by an RPG, killing eight more SEALs and eight Nightstalker aircrew. The resulting book and film, *Lone Survivor*, made the SEALs a household name, despite questions being raised over certain aspects of the retelling.

During the invasion of Iraq, SEALs from Teams 8 and 10 captured offshore oil platforms and seized the vital Mukarayin Dam in a joint operation with Poland's GROM. They were heavily committed to the counter-insurgency in Iraq under Combined Joint Special Operations Task Force – Arabian Peninsula, conducting foreign internal defence and targeting insurgent leaders and bomb-makers in support of conventional forces.

SEAL Task Units consisting of a pair of SEAL platoons were assigned to foreign internal defence, working and living with Iraqi forces. In Anbar Province, the SEALs were instrumental in supporting the eventual 'Anbar awakening' of 2005, which saw tribal leaders turn on the foreign terrorists of al-Qaeda in Iraq and join forces, at least temporarily, with the Americans.

The SEALs have also regularly conducted non-combatant evacuations over recent years, typically alongside Marine fleet elements. In South Sudan in 2013, several SEALs were wounded by gunfire as their CV-22s attempted

US Navy SEALs supporting Iraqi security forces in the re-taking of Mosul, Iraq, from Islamic State in November 2016. The SEALs are firing the 84mm Carl Gustav M3 Multi-Role Anti-Armor Anti-Personnel Weapon System, initially adopted by the SEALs in 1997. (Hemn Baban/Anadolu Agency/Getty Images)

to land to secure US citizens. With critically wounded on board, the CV-22s were forced to divert to land (ironically enough) at Entebbe, Uganda.

The unit has been heavily committed to the fight against Islamic State with Task Force Trident established to command the SEAL advise and assist mission under Operation *Inherent Resolve*. The SEALs have been involved in a number of deadly operations while supporting their Iraqi and Kurdish charges. A SEAL Team 1 sailor, operating as part of a theatre Quick Reaction Force, was shot and killed near Tel Askuf in May 2016 during an operation to relieve besieged Kurdish Peshmerga and their American advisers. Later that year an EOD operator from Explosive Ordnance Disposal Mobile Unit Three attached to SEAL Team 5 was killed by an IED while supporting partnered operations in Mosul.

The SEALs use a number of SOCOM standard weapons. Both SOPMOD M4A1s and the Mk18 CQB-R (Close Quarter Battle Receiver) carbine are employed, as are various iterations of the Mk14 Enhanced Battle Rifle and both the 5.56x45mm and 7.62x51mm variants of the Fabrique Nationale SCAR. MP5s are still held in SEAL armouries but are seldom used. The issue pistol is the 9x19mm Glock 19, replacing the SIG-Sauer P226. Suppressed .45ACP HK45Cs known as the Mk24 Mod0 Combat Assault Pistol are also used.

SEAL snipers deploy suppressed 7.62x51mm M110s, the 7.62x51mm Mk17 and Mk20 SCAR, the bolt action .300 Winchester Magnum Mk13 Mod7, the .338 Lapua Magnum McMillan TAC-338 and the .50 Mk15 Mod0. Machine gunners employ the 5.56x45mm Mk46 and the 7.62x51mm Mk48, which replaced the iconic M60-based Mk43 Mod0/1.

Special Activities Division (SAD)

Nationality: US • Branch: CIA • Established: 1998

Prior to 1998, the CIA relied largely upon contractors or SOCOM and JSOC operators who were 'sheep-dipped' (covertly placed under CIA command with no record made in their military records) and placed on temporary attachment to the agency's Directorate of Operations (DO) and specifically its Special Operations Group to conduct covert actions. Special operators carrying out clandestine operations in Central and South America were 'sheep-dipped' and placed under the direct command of the CIA's DO. In 1998, the pressing need for a more permanent paramilitary capability, driven in large part by the hunt for war criminals in the Balkans, saw the establishment of the Special Activities Division (SAD).

The SAD has '*Tertia Optio*' as its motto, the 'Third Option', after diplomacy and military options are exhausted or inappropriate. SAD is composed of at least three separate components: Ground Branch, Air Branch and Maritime Branch.

The US military operates under Title 10 rather than Title 50 legal authority. This means that the military can conduct operations, including clandestine operations, only in countries deemed as designated areas of hostilities (Afghanistan, Iraq or most recently Yemen, for example) and operations are defined as 'conducted by U.S. military personnel, under the direction and control of a U.S. military commander, preceding and related to anticipated hostilities or related to ongoing hostilities involving U.S. military forces, and the U.S. role in the overall operation is apparent or to be acknowledged publicly.'

Title 50 gives the CIA the capability of conducting covert actions anywhere around the world which are defined as 'an activity or activities of the United States Government to influence the political, economic, or military conditions abroad, where it is intended that the role of the United States Government will not be apparent or acknowledged publicly.' The key difference between Title 10 clandestine operations and Title 50 covert operations is the emphasis in covert operations in obscuring the role of US forces, be they CIA or military special operators.

The October 2008 raid into Syria against an al-Qaeda in Iraq foreign fighter facilitator and the May 2011 Operation *Neptune Spear* targeting bin Laden in Pakistan were examples of operations conducted under Title 50 authorization. At the point the 160th Special Operations Aviation Regiment (160th SOAR) helicopters crossed into

A CIA Special Activities Division (SAD) operative (left) and a 5th Special Forces Group soldier (right) at the infamous Fort of War, Mazar-e-Sharif, Afghanistan, November 2001. Another SAD operative was killed during the Taliban uprising. (CNN via Getty Images)

Syrian or Pakistani airspace respectively, the missions were under CIA control. Another example is when Delta Force operators embedded clandestinely with the Pakistani Special Service Group in the immediate post-9/11 period.

Omega (Counter Terrorist Pursuit Teams) operated as blended teams of locally recruited Afghan militias, CIA SAD personnel and JSOC operators who had been temporarily assigned, or 'sheep-dipped', to the CIA. JSOC personnel were typically drawn from SEAL Team 6 and later the Ranger Regiment. These are currently known as ANSOF or Afghan National Special Operations Force.

Two SAD operatives were killed in 2016 during an operation against Islamic State – Khorasan alongside their ANSOF team. The agency also maintains the paramilitary Global Response Staff (GRS), which is a contractor force that provides close personal protection, force protection and static site security for CIA employees and locations in conflict zones.

Special Air Service Regiment (SASR)

Nationality: Australian • Branch: Army • Established: 1957

The Australian Special Air Service Regiment (SASR) was established in the wake of a number of famous Australian wartime special operations units, principally like its British counterparts to provide a specialist long range surveillance and reconnaissance function. It operated in Malaysia alongside the British and New Zealand SAS before deploying to South Vietnam in 1966. It conducted a number of tours until the wind-down of Australian forces in 1971.

In Vietnam it gained a fearsome reputation and was known by the enemy as 'Ma Rung', the 'Jungle Ghosts' or 'Jungle Phantoms'. The SASR excelled in infiltrating their five-man patrols deep into enemy base areas and gathering intelligence which was vital to planning of conventional operations by the Australian Task Force. It avoided contacts with the enemy if at all possible but if contact was made, it would fire a massive volley to confuse the enemy about the actual size of the patrol, and then break contact as quickly as possible.

Post Vietnam the SASR, also known as 'the Regiment' or more informally as 'SAS Cats', struggled to define a role with imminent disbandment a constant companion. Focusing on its original long range surveillance role, it carved a niche which kept the unit afloat until the late 1970s when it was given responsibility for counter-terrorism, both domestically and internationally. It quickly formed the Interim Tactical Assault Group under the codename Gauntlet in 1979, a 'specialised and dedicated counter terrorist assault team' whose role was to 'subdue the terrorists by force,' according to the briefing document on its formation.

The Tactical Assault Group was formally established the following year along with Nullah, a troop-sized element raised to conduct maritime counter-terrorism operations, including the retaking of offshore oil platforms that were felt at the time to be vulnerable to terrorist attack. Special recovery operations were later added to the mandate of the unit, defined as operations 'to rescue personnel or seize equipment from uncertain or hostile environments and return them to a safe area,' as noted by the same briefing paper from 1979. Along with the counter-terrorist role, the Regiment continued to innovate in its 'green' or conventional warfare techniques.

The long spell since Vietnam was broken in 1999 when SASR deployed to East Timor/Timor Leste, initially as part of Operation *Spitfire* to conduct a non-combatant evacuation and later as the key component of RESPFOR or Response Force, the Allied SOF deployed under the United Nations International Force East Timor (INTERFET) (see page 13). SASR was the first on the ground at Dili Airport and secured the environs for follow-on conventional forces.

The unit was heavily involved in acting both as the theatre Immediate Reaction Force responding to militia incursions and in intelligence-led pre-planned operations including covert surveillance. SASR operators had a number of contacts with the enemy, including a compromised patrol that was forced to fight a five-hour running gun battle to rendezvous with its helicopter extraction, killing a number of militia in the process.

The Regiment's next major deployment was to Afghanistan as one of the first Allied SOF units to arrive. It was immediately employed in special reconnaissance tasks as, unlike most of its peers, SASR had brought its own vehicles with it. Patrols were conducted in Perentie six-wheel LRPVs (long range patrol vehicles) and a collection of quads (all-terrain vehicles) and dirt bikes. A Unimog 'mothership' would resupply the patrols in the field.

The SASR deployed to Afghanistan initially as the Special Forces Task Group (SFTG) and later as the Special Operations Task Group (SOTG) or Task Force 64 to International Security Assistance Force (ISAF) and Operation *Enduring Freedom* command. After rotating all three squadrons through during 2001 and 2002, SASR returned to Australia to prepare for its role in the impending invasion of Iraq. Again operating as Task Force 64, the SFTG for Iraq included 1 Squadron SASR, a platoon from 4th Royal Australilan Regiment (Commando) and the Incident Response Regiment (later renamed the Special Operations Engineer Regiment).

Australian SASR troopers (faces deliberately obscured) pictured with Kuga, their combat assault dog who was later wounded numerous times by insurgent gunfire. He would be awarded the Dickin Medal, the canine equivalent of the Victoria Cross. The SASR trooper to the left carries a 5.56x45mm M4A1 (known as M4A5 in Australia) while his opposite number carries a 7.62x51mm M14 in a Troy MCS chassis, purchased by SASR after its positive experiences with borrowed Mk14s. (Courtesy Commonwealth of Australia, Special Operations Command)

The SFTG conducted mounted patrols to interdict both Iraqi Scuds and fleeing high-value targets heading for the Syrian border, along with direct action missions to capture desert airfields which would soon become forward operating locations for Allied SOF. The Regiment performed admirably and further cemented ties with the UK's 22SAS and the United States' Delta Force, which operated alongside them in the western desert.

The SASR returned to Afghanistan in 2005 as the Taliban insurgency began to grow where they operated closely with SEAL Team 6 and the US Army Rangers. After the deployment of a regular Australian Army Reconstruction Task Force to Uruzgan Province, the SASR returned in 2007 to provide force protection and target insurgents within the province. From 2007 to 2014, SASR, and 2 Commando, conducted continual six-monthly rotations to Uruzgan, although they often operated in neighbouring Helmand.

One of the most notable operations was the June 2010 battle of Eastern Shah Wali Kot. E Troop of 2 Squadron SASR deployed to the village of Tizak, as Alpha Company of 2 Commando fought its own battle in the neighbouring Chenartu. E Troop, reinforced to a 25-man force, arrived in four US Black Hawks to target Taliban high-value targets that had been exposed by the Commandos' action. Even with two Apache attack helicopters in support, the Black Hawks were met by small arms and RPG fire upon their approach, damaging all four of the aircraft.

A massive firefight erupted as the SASR landed and even the aerial sniper teams, normally flying overwatch for the assault elements, were forced to land to reinforce the teams on the ground. It was during this battle that Corporal Ben Roberts-Smith, one of those snipers, conducted actions which would later see him awarded the Victoria Cross for Australia, the country's highest military honour. The official citation noted:

> Two soldiers were wounded in action and the troop was pinned down by fire from three machine guns in an elevated fortified position to the south of the village. Under the cover of close air support, suppressive small arms and machine gun fire, Roberts-Smith and his patrol manoeuvred to within 70 metres of the enemy position in order to neutralise the enemy machine gun positions and regain the initiative.
>
> Upon commencement of the assault, the patrol drew very heavy, intense, effective and sustained fire from the enemy position. Roberts-Smith and his patrol members fought towards the enemy position until, at a range of 40 metres, the weight of fire prevented further movement forward. At this point, he identified the opportunity to exploit some cover provided by a small structure.
>
> As he approached the structure, Roberts-Smith identified an insurgent grenadier in the throes of engaging his patrol. Roberts-Smith engaged the insurgent at point-blank range resulting in the death of the

insurgent. With the members of his patrol still pinned down by the three enemy machine gun positions, he exposed his own position in order to draw fire away from his patrol, which enabled them to bring fire to bear against the enemy.

His actions enabled his Patrol Commander to throw a grenade and silence one of the machine guns. Seizing the advantage, and demonstrating extreme devotion to duty and the most conspicuous gallantry, Roberts-Smith, with a total disregard for his own safety, stormed the enemy position killing the two remaining machine gunners.

The iconic six-wheeled Australian SASR Perentie LRPV or long range patrol vehicle, seen here in Afghanistan. The LRPV was replaced by the Nary, a Supacat HMT variant. (Courtesy Commonwealth of Australia, Sgt Neil Ruskin)

Roberts-Smith joined Corporal Mark Donaldson of 3 Squadron as two of the three recipients of the Victoria Cross for Australia awarded for actions in Afghanistan.

Unfortunately the reputation of the Regiment has been somewhat tarnished by allegations by SASR members of potential war crimes committed by a small number of other SASR soldiers. The allegations include the beating and summary execution of prisoners, including a process to 'blood' junior operators. The allegations are, at the time of writing, under investigation by both the Army and the Australian Federal Police.

Currently SASR maintains three operational squadrons: 1, 2 and 3, along with an Operational Support Squadron that has responsibility for training and selection and a Specialist Support Squadron (also known as Base Squadron) that includes specialist cells including Counter Terrorism. They are supported by 152 Signals Squadron, a specialist communications unit that provides patrol signallers, with each SASR squadron supplemented by a troop of signallers on deployments.

The regiment maintains the Guerrilla Warfare Cell, which conducted low-profile reconnaissance missions (so-called 'grey roles') in Afghanistan, often in Afghan clothing and riding locally procured motorcycles. There have also long been rumours of a fourth SASR squadron tasked with advance force operations and special reconnaissance, perhaps an outgrowth of the Guerrilla Warfare Cell.

Newspapers reports, always denied by the Australian government, describe operations in the Middle East and Africa. The squadron is apparently not based at Swanbourne but conducts much of its training at Swan Island Training Area, an Australian Secret Intelligence Service facility that houses the euphemistic 'Swan Island Army Detachment'.

Under Operation *Augury*, the regiment has also quietly deployed a training team to 'advise and assist' Philippine Army SOF in their fight against Islamic State-affiliated domestic jihadists, particularly in the city of Marawi. The SASR has also been committed to the effort against Islamic State in Iraq, forming part of the Special Operations Task Group under Operation *Okra*.

SASR uses non-standard weapons such as suppressed Colt M4A1s (known as M4A5s in Australian service) and has recently procured the .300 Blackout SIG-Sauer MCX to replace its worn-out MP5SD3s for specialist roles. MP5s are retained but have been largely replaced in the counter-terrorist role by the M4A1s and now MCX.

SASR's standard pistols are the 9x19mm Heckler & Koch USP and Glock 19. After employing borrowed Mk14s in Afghanistan, SASR procured a number of 7.62x51mm Troy SOPMOD MCS (Modular Chassis System) M14s. Snipers employ the 7.62x51mm HK417 (which has replaced the SR-25) and the .338 Lapua Magnum Blaser Tactical 2.

Special Boat Service (SBS)

Nationality: UK • Branch: Navy • Established: 1987

The Special Boat Service (SBS) evolved from the wartime Special Boat Section and a number of other maritime commando units. Following the war, the unit was disbanded, as was the wartime SAS, only to be resurrected by the Royal Marines as the Special Boat Company in 1951; it was renamed the Special Boat Squadron in 1974 as the unit expanded and finally the Special Boat Service in 1987. The SBS has participated in virtually every conflict involving UK forces since World War II and was assigned the initial maritime counter-terrorism response role in 1972.

An unidentified UK Special Forces soldier enters a terrorist-held hotel in Nairobi, Kenya in January 2019. Probably a member of a British Army training team working with the Kenyan Army Special Operations Regiment, he carries the Colt Canada L119A2 fitted with a SIG Romeo 4T optic (rather than the more usual Aimpoint T1 or ACOG), a Surefire suppressor and light mount. His sidearm appears to be a Glock 19. (Kabir Dhanji/AFP/ Getty Images)

The SBS is currently organized into four squadrons – C, M, X and Z. C and X squadrons are small boat specialists while Z maintains institutional knowledge and training of submersibles. M is dedicated to the maritime counter-terrorism mission, although all squadrons are trained for the role and rotate through the on-call counter-terrorist response in six-monthly intervals. All four squadrons are trained in special reconnaissance and conducting unconventional warfare in both conventional and asymmetric settings ('asymmetric' refers to warfare involving counter-insurgencies, counter-terrorist or hybrid warfare activities). All are parachute, HALO/HAHO (high altitude low opening/high altitude high opening) and SCUBA qualified.

In recent years, the SBS was deployed to Kuwait in 1991, where it conducted missions to deny the use of Iraqi Scud missiles and destroy communications lines before deploying to the Balkans during the hunt for war criminals. The unit was also integrally involved in Operation *Barras* in Sierra Leone, the successful hostage rescue operation to recover six soldiers from the Royal Irish Regiment and their Sierra Leone liaison officer who had been snatched by a group of militia. The SBS employed operators to approach the camps where the hostages were held by a small waterway and conducted covert close target reconnaissance. Members were also a part of the D Squadron SAS assault force that rescued the hostages.

Afghanistan would prove to be the largest and longest SBS deployment in its history with two squadrons initially deployed in late 2001. SBS elements were attached to the Delta Force and Green Beret effort at Tora Bora, much to the chagrin of their bitter rivals, the SAS. They were also apparently on the ground before the SAS with a squadron landing at Bagram, also much to the consternation of the local Northern Alliance forces, as no advance notice had been given of their arrival. Operators from M Squadron were also filmed at the 'Fort of War' prison uprising at Mazar-e-Sharif where the United States suffered its first casualty to enemy action, a former Marine working for the CIA's Special Activities Division.

Often forgotten from this time was the successful December 2001 C Squadron intercept of the MV *Nisha*, a cargo vessel suspected of carrying unspecified 'terrorist material', at the time thought to be either chemical/biological agents or a dirty bomb, as the ship crossed the English Channel. Dubbed Operation *Ocean Strike*, C Squadron was reinforced by around 20 SAS operators for the assault. Four Zodiacs transported SBS operators to the ship where they covertly scaled the sides as two Chinooks arrived overhead carrying the mixed SBS/SAS assault team, who fast-roped onto the ship covered by SBS snipers in a pair of Lynx helicopters. After a thorough search the ship was given the all-clear.

In 2003, the unit deployed to Iraq. In the SOF campaign in the north-west, the SBS was called Task Force 7. A large mounted patrol from

These two operators, pictured in April 2005, appear to be from M Sqn, SBS during the second and last Task Force Black rotation of the Special Boat Service. Note the black covert body armour worn under PLCE assault vests in temperate DPM. Both men wear American DCU combats, and both weapons mount thermal-imaging night-vision devices. (Author's Collection)

British Special Boat Service (SBS) operators pictured in East Timor, 1999, deploying as part of the Australian-led INTERFET intervention force. Note the older 5.56x45mm Diemaco C7 assault rifle. (Paula Bronstein/Getty Images)

M Squadron was compromised by Iraqi Fedayeen and was forced into a rolling firefight that saw several vehicles ditched after becoming immobilized before the unit managed to be extracted by RAF Chinook. Two SBS operators who became cut off from the main body evaded capture and escaped across the Syrian border on an all-terrain vehicle.

In the following war against al-Qaeda in Iraq, the unit deployed twice to relieve the hard-pressed SAS who were conducting gruelling six-month tours and suffering many wounded. At all other times, a squadron from the SBS was deployed in Afghanistan and became a key force multiplier both for regular British forces in Task Force Helmand and for the US-commanded Joint Special Operations Task Force. Initially operating as Task Force 84 and later as Task Force 42 under Operation *Kindle*, the SBS was given responsibility for Afghanistan in 2005.

Two operators, one from each unit, were killed in a joint SBS and Special Reconnaissance Regiment (SRR) operation in June 2006, which ignited Helmand Province. Operation *Ilios* was a covert snatch mission to capture a number of local Taliban leadership targets. Upon beginning its exfiltration, prisoners in tow, the joint 16-man SBS/SRR force was ambushed by insurgents. Pinned down, the operators fought against significant odds to finally extricate, with British Apache attack helicopters conducting numerous close air support missions above them. Two of their number were found to be missing and an immediate search was launched with both bodies recovered. Rumours that they had been mutilated by the Taliban have never been confirmed.

More direct action missions followed. A key Taliban leader in Helmand, Mullah Dadullah, was killed in an SBS operation in May 2007. The unit suffered its second casualty of the war in July of that year with an operator killed in Nimruz. Along with direct action raids, the SBS conducted a wide range of special operations in support of both the International Security Assistance Force (ISAF) and Task Force Helmand, including mentoring Afghan Provincial Response Companies and later National Mission Units. Combined mounted operations with SBS Supacats and Toyota Hiluxs mixed with Afghan National Army and Afghan National Police Ford Rangers were not uncommon.

In September 2007, the SBS carried out the hostage rescue of two captured Italian intelligence officers in Farah Province. The SBS was tasked with providing both aerial sniper support and a heliborne cut-off group, should the kidnappers manage to escape. The Italian Col Moschin, or more formally the 9th Paratroopers Assault Regiment, would conduct the actual assault.

The Italian operators conducted an off-set parachute insertion and were approaching the terrorist safehouse when the hostage takers appeared from the building, bundling the two intelligence officers into vehicles, which forced the SBS to act. Eight insurgents were killed in the engagement but both of the hostages, hidden in the trunk of a car, were hit in the crossfire with one later dying of his wounds. An Afghan hostage, reportedly a translator working for the Italians, was also killed in the firefight.

In February 2008, SBS operators shot and killed two Taliban leadership targets in an aerial vehicle interdiction mission that saw the operators dropped into an ambush position ahead of the targets who were travelling on motorcycles. Operation *Beethoven 5* in October 2008 saw a high-value target and three other insurgents killed by members of Task Force 42.

An SBS operator assigned to Task Force 42 was killed in late August 2009 near Gereshk while targeting a bomb-making cell. He was killed and six other operators wounded when an IED detonated during a compound clearance. The following month, an SBS troop supported by a platoon from the Special Forces Support Group (SFSG) launched a hostage rescue mission in Kunduz Province to free a kidnapped journalist and his interpreter. During the operation, an SFSG operator was shot and killed and an Afghan civilian died from an explosive breach. The journalist was recovered but his interpreter was killed, possibly inadvertently by the SBS, as he ran towards them.

In early 2011, a troop from C Squadron was deployed to Libya to effect a non-combatant evacuation of British and other expatriates, mainly oil workers who were under threat of kidnap; this went ahead without incident. In March

British SBS operators seen in an unmarked Land Rover in Kandahar City, Afghanistan, December 2001. Note the operators wear civilian garb. A 7.62x51mm L7A2 GPMG is mounted on a turret ring. (Patrick Aventurier/Gamma-Rapho via Getty Images)

Two SBS operators in civilian dress (to the right) work with 5th Special Forces Group personnel during the Taliban uprising at the 'Fort of War' in Mazar-e-Sharif, Afghanistan in 2001. (Oleg Nikishin/Getty Images)

2012 the unit was involved in an attempted hostage rescue in Nigeria, which failed when the terrorists executed the hostages as the SBS conducted its breach. In the following month the unit was dispatched to Kabul with its partner unit, the Afghan Crisis Response Unit, to clear a tower block of insurgents who were firing RPGs at the surrounding foreign embassies. After a day-long battle fighting alongside the partner unit the building was cleared and all of the insurgents killed.

At the end of 2013, an SBS officer was killed in action during a partnered operation, also with the Crisis Response Unit, targeting suicide bomber cells to the east of Kabul who were planning attacks in the city to disrupt the Afghan elections. Ten insurgents, including one wearing a suicide bomb vest, were killed. An explosives search dog was captured by the insurgents during the action, as were two SBS L119A1 carbines, one with the stock broken off, giving an insight into the ferocity of the fight.

An insurgent hidden amongst boulders shot the SBS operator. His commander explained at the later inquest, 'We had multiple air engagements on this position, we thought most of the enemy were dead. We approached with extreme caution but unfortunately one of the enemy had not been killed. He managed to get a burst off with an AK-47. Two members of the patrol were wounded.'*

In December 2018, the unit conducted a rare domestic maritime counter-terrorist mission in the Thames Estuary to recover a container ship, the crew of which had been threatened by four stowaways armed with knives and metal bars. Amid fears of a hijack, a half-squadron from X Squadron, which was on counter-terrorist rotation, conducted a heliborne visit-board-search-seizure mission, captured the stowaways, and recovered the crew without a shot being fired.

The SBS is armed as per other UKSF units with the L119A2 carbine produced by Colt Canada and the Glock 19 which has replaced the SIG-Sauer P226. MP5s are available, although largely replaced by the .300 Blackout SIG-Sauer MCX. SBS snipers employ the HK417 and a range of Accuracy International platforms.

---

* https://www.telegraph.co.uk/news/uknews/defence/11258477/Special-Forces-soldier-died-in-perilous-raid-on-Taliban-haven.html

Special Forces Command (SFC)

Nationality: Turkish • Branch: Joint • Established: 1992

The Turkish Özel Kuvvetler Komutanlığı (Special Forces Command or SFC) is a multi-service command that oversees the majority of Turkish special operations units within the military, the Gendarmerie and the police. Its primary unit is the Army Special Forces Brigades, which were established under the guidance of the US Army Green Berets and are the largest component of the SFC. They are supported by six commando brigades and three commando regiments which provide a light infantry raiding capability. The SFC also commands the Turkish Navy's special warfare component, the Su Altı Taarruz (SAT or Underwater Offence Group) and Sualtı Savunma (SAS or Underwater Defence Group).

By 2006 the SFC commanded two Special Forces brigades, each consisting of three regiments, which are in turn composed of three battalions each. In each of the Special Forces battalions there are six Special Forces teams structured like a US Special Forces ODA of 12 personnel per team and thus similar in composition to a US Special Forces company. Unlike most SOF in the region, Turkish Special Forces are trained to conduct the full gamut of roles, including foreign internal defence, unconventional warfare and special reconnaissance. Unfortunately, in reality they are mainly deployed in direct action roles against the Kurdish PKK or Kurdistan Workers' Party, an armed organization that Turkey (along with the United States) considers a terrorist group, which has been fighting for an independent state within Turkey for decades.

A Turkish Special Forces brigade soldier conducting a military free-fall (MFF) parachute jump in 2018. (General Staff of the Republic of Turkey/Handout/ Anadolu Agency/Getty Images)

Despite the SFC's historical links with the Green Berets, an incident during the Iraq War soured relations. In 2003, a ten-man Turkish Special Forces detachment was captured by US forces in the heavily Kurdish populated Kirkuk, possibly on an assassination mission to kill the local Kurdish mayor. It led to a rapid deterioration of relations between the SFC and the United States' SOCOM which have never fully recovered.

Turkish Special Forces were also deployed alongside conventional Turkish Army forces during Operation *Euphrates Shield* in support of the Free Syrian Army militias in northern Syria in an operation that, although it claimed to be an offensive against Islamic State, was really an opportunity to drive back the Kurdish Yekîneyên Parastina Gel (YPG or People's Protection Units – Kurdish militias trained and equipped by the US and allied nations).

This resulted in the deployment of US JSOC units, including the Rangers patrolling in Stryker infantry carrier vehicles to Manbij in an attempt to deconflict the area and stop Turkish aggression against the YPG. The Turkish fear both a resurgent Kurdish movement, bolstered by the US-supported YPG, and the encroachment on their borders of Iranian-supported Shia militias.

In a surprising move, the SFC has recently deployed to Somalia in a mentoring role, training local Somali forces after a number of al-Shabaab attacks on Turkish aid workers.

The 2016 coup attempt by a number of Army and Air Force special operators in a plot to kidnap the president and impose martial law led to swift and decisive action against the plotters. Purges have led to reductions of up to a third in many SFC units leaving them critically low on manpower and capability. For some covert tasks, it is expected the government may in the future rely more upon the special units of the Interior Ministry.

Domestically, the Interior Ministry maintains the Special Public Security Command or JOAK, which was established in 2004 as the primary counter-terrorist intervention unit. The JOAK is supported by nine JOH, or Special Operations Battalions, which conduct operations against the PKK. The Turkish Police also maintains its own counter-terrorist response unit, the POH or Police Special Operations.

The Turkish operators employ SIG-Sauer pistols, the Fabrique Nationale P90 and licensed copies of the MP5 and MP5K, HK416 and M4A1 carbines and the SCAR-H battle rifle. Their sniper rifles include both Accuracy International AW in 7.662x51mm and AWM in .338 Lapua Magnum variants. The Special Aviation Group provides organic helicopter support to all SFC units, flying UH-60 Black Hawks, while on the ground the SFC employs Cobra and Kirpi armoured tactical vehicles.

Special Forces Group (SFG)

Nationality: Belgian • Branch: Army • Established: 2003

The Belgian Army Special Forces Group (SFG) is descended from the wartime Belgian SAS and post-war reconnaissance units. A Special Forces Company was formed in 2000 within the 3rd Lanciers Parachutists Battalion but, upon dissolution of the battalion three years later, the independent Special Forces Group was established under the famous motto 'Who Dares Wins'.

Drawing on its SAS heritage, the SFG is organized by insertion speciality: Land (Mountain), Air and Sea, supported by a Special Operations Boat Unit, although all must be qualified in military free-fall parachuting and trained in infiltration by kayak or swimming, along with core close quarter battle and urban combat skills. The SFG has deployed to Chad, the Central African Republic, Afghanistan and Iraq in recent years.

In Iraq, the SFG has operated as a mentoring force for Kurdish Peshmerga and Iraqi Army elements. The SFG has also supported the US Operation *Gallant Phoenix* targeting foreign fighters including Belgian nationals in the region, although it has not been involved directly in kill or capture missions. During the Tal Afar offensive, however, SFG members were seen operating Javelin anti-tank guided missiles against Islamic State armoured suicide vehicles on the front line, despite avowed restrictions on their involvement in direct combat.

Belgian Army Special Forces Group operators pictured prior to deployment to Chad in 2008. The operator to the left carries a 5.56x45mm Fabrique Nationale F2000; the operator to the right is similarly equipped but with the 40mm GL1 grenade launcher mounted on his F2000. The sniper appears to be armed with a 7.62x51mm Accuracy International platform. (Eric Lalmand/AFP/Getty Images)

In 2018, the unit was placed under the command of the newly formed Special Operations Regiment, along with the 2nd Commando Battalion and the 3rd Parachute Battalion. The Special Operations Regiment is also part of the Composite Special Operations Component Command, which is forming a joint NATO Special Forces unit with Denmark and the Netherlands.

The SFG uses primarily Belgian Fabrique Nationale weaponry including the P90, the SCAR in both L and H variants (often suppressed) and as a sniper platform in the form of the Precision model, the Minimi and, uniquely, the Five-seven pistol rather than the more common Glock. A number of B&T MP9s are also used for close protection tasks. The primary sniper rifle is the Accuracy International AXMC in .338 Lapua Magnum although the .50 Barrett M107A1 is also available.

For mounted operations, the SFG has relied upon the JACAM Unimog platform and the Jankel Fox Rapid Response Vehicle (an upgraded Land Cruiser also widely employed by Jordanian SOF), purchased to replace its Volkswagen Iltis fleet. For seaborne operations, the SFG maintains the FRISC or Fast Raiding Interception Special Forces Craft that can carry six operators and their kit at high speeds toward their target. The FRISC is equipped with two MAG58 machine guns that can suppress targets as the boat approaches the objective. Additionally, it can be underslung from a Chinook or carried within a C-130.

Special Forces Support Group (SFSG)

Nationality: UK • Branch: Army • Established: 2006

The newest member of UKSF, the Special Forces Support Group (SFSG) was something of a formal acknowledgement of the long-standing relationship between the SAS and the 1st Battalion of the Parachute Regiment which had deployed on numerous occasions as support to the SAS, most notably during Operation *Barras* in Sierra Leone (see pages 39–40).

Formed around the core of the 1st Battalion, members are also drawn from both the Royal Marines and the Royal Air Force (RAF) Regiment to provide specialist capabilities, including an incident response unit from the RAF to manage chemical, biological, radiological and nuclear threats and an amphibious small boats capability from the Royal Marines. The SFSG is believed to be composed of four infantry companies along with a headquarters company, a sniper and direct fire support weapons company, and a support company which houses the unit's forward air controllers, mortars, patrols, and signals platoons.

The SFSG is officially detailed to 'provide direct support to UKSF intervention operations, as well as reinforcing UKSF in other key capability areas such as provision of specialist training and support to domestic CT [counter-terrorist] operations'.

An additional Ministry of Defence statement confirmed the unit's core responsibilities as the 'provision of supporting or diversionary attacks, cordons, fire support, force protection and supporting training tasks'. It is believed that the SFSG now provides a rotational component to serve as the Counter Terrorist Lead Assault Team for the national UKSF counter-terrorism response.

The unit deployed to both Iraq and Afghanistan in 2006, providing support to the SAS and SBS respectively. In Iraq, where it was known as Task Force Maroon, the SFSG would provide the outer cordon for the SAS as it assaulted target buildings and provided snipers for aerial sniper overwatch. In Afghanistan, it operated alongside the Special Reconnaissance Regiment (SRR) and SBS but also carried out a dedicated mentoring role for the Afghan Territorial Force 444. 2009 saw the unit's first casualty during a hostage rescue in Afghanistan.

A member of the unit became the only living recipient of the Victoria Cross for actions in 2013 in Helmand Province on a joint operation with the US Marines and Afghan Territorial Force 444. While operating as part of the UK's Task Force 42 with the role of 'conducting operations to disrupt insurgent safe-havens and protect the main operating base in Helmand province', as noted in the Victoria Cross citation, the SFSG deployed a number of fire support groups to overwatch the main Marine assault.

The joint force was engaged by insurgent small arms and RPGs as they arrived in their Chinook helicopters. A Marine company commander was immediately wounded and his command element suppressed. The SFSG lance corporal Joshua Leakey dashed through enemy fire to provide first aid and command the medical evacuation of the officer. After doing so, he realized

A rare photo of the British Army Special Forces Support Group in Iraq circa 2006–2007. The range of weapons carried is impressive – the then newly issued 7.62x51mm HK417 (operator third from left in front row carries a HK417 fitted with a brass catcher for ejected rounds, often used by snipers operating from helicopters) along with a number of modified 7.62x51mm G3Ks fitted with suppressors that were used as de-facto marksman rifles until the arrival of the HK417; regular 5.56x45mm L85A2 assault rifles (initially there were too few Diemaco/Colt Canada L119A1 carbines in inventory to equip the newly formed unit); and 5.56x45mm Minimi Para light machine guns. (Author's Collection)

'that the initiative was still in the hands of the enemy, [and] he set off back up the hill, still under enemy fire, to get one of the suppressed machine guns into action. On reaching it, and with rounds impacting on the frame of the gun itself, he moved it to another position and began engaging the enemy'*. He later repositioned another general purpose machine gun under fire, turning the course of the battle.

The SFSG is equipped with a range of standard and specialist small arms. For the first year or two of its existence, members were armed with the SA80A2 (L85A2) standard assault rifle. These were replaced by the Colt Canada L119A1. Owing to a lack of designated marksman weapons, the SFSG pressed into service a number of G3Ks with Trijicon ACOG optics, which were employed until HK417s arrived in theatre. SFSG snipers use both the HK417 and the Accuracy International L115A3 in .338 Lapua Magnum.

Special Operations Command

Nationality: Ukrainian • Branch: Joint • Established: 2015

At the time of the dissolution of the USSR, Ukraine had four Spetsnaz brigades. A SOCOM-style Special Operations Directorate was established in 2008 theoretically to command and control all Ukrainian Army and Naval Special Operations Forces; however, owing to internal politicking, the separate services retained day-to-day command. The 140th Independent Special Operations Centre was raised at the same time and was trained along the lines of the 10th Independent Spetsnaz Detachment, the originator of US Special Forces-style unconventional warfare in the Ukrainian military.

The Naval Spetsnaz formed the basis for the counter-terrorist 73rd Special Naval Center. The unit became a land-focused special mission force with its former maritime role largely eliminated, including the loss of its mini-submersibles and dive training. After the experiences in the ongoing war in the breakaway republics, the Special Operations Division was replaced in 2015 with the Special Operations Command (SOC, which brought all Ukrainian SOF under its direct control.

One unit that remained under the command of the Ministry of the Interior was Counter Terrorism Squad-A or Alfa, the intervention unit of the Ukrainian Security Service (SBU), today known as the SBU Special Operations Centre – A. During the 2000s, Ukrainian SOF saw limited action with NATO and United Nations commitments to Afghanistan and Iraq, as well as peacekeeping operations in Kosovo. SBU's Alfa also conducted extensive

---

*   http://www.thegazette.co.uk/London/issue/61154/supplement/3466

cross-training with its Russian counterparts in Spetsgruppy-A until the February 2014 popular uprising, which saw the overthrow of the government. This led to direct Russian military operations to annex Crimea and continuing operations in the Donbass region supporting pro-Russian separatists.

The Ukrainian Spetsnaz was at the forefront of operations against Russian-backed separatists in the Donetsk and Luhansk regions in 2014. It was particularly valuable in securing key strategic sites. One notable operation saw the 8th Independent Spetsnaz Regiment conduct a heliborne infiltration into the threatened Kramatorsk airfield, which was surrounded by separatist forces. The Spetsnaz maintained the defence of the airfield until it could be relieved a month later.

It was also responsible for the spirited defence of Donetsk Airport, covertly infiltrating a reinforced Spetsnaz company, which, along with a handful of Ukrainian paratroopers, successfully defended the airport against a ground assault led by Russian volunteers (likely themselves Spetsnaz in 'Little Green Men' – see page 119 – mode). Other units were less exemplary. Numerous Alfa detachments refused to take action against the separatists while some operators even defected to the pro-Russian militias.

Not all Spetsnaz operations were as successful either. A July 2014 attempt to recover a downed aviator ended in the deaths of ten Ukrainian operators with a further seven captured. As the war became increasingly conventional, Ukrainian Spetsnaz was employed as elite light infantry to spearhead offensives or shore up weak points. Following the cease-fire agreed in 2015, the conflict has largely degenerated into small unit skirmishes and raids, often conducted by Spetsnaz units, carried out by both sides in contravention of the agreement.

Ukrainian Spetsnaz conducting drills with US 10th Special Forces Group personnel. The Ukrainians (to the centre and right) both carry the recent, domestically produced 7.62x39mm Malyuk bullpup. Other than that, in their MultiCam uniforms and high cut, railed helmets, they are virtually indistinguishable from other Western SOF. Faces have been deliberately obscured. (Courtesy US Army, 1st Lt Benjamin Haulenbeek)

NATO has since provided training to cadre Spetsnaz instructors under the auspices of the Joint Multi-national Training Group – Ukraine. Today there are only two amalgamated regular Army Spetsnaz regiments in existence, along with the 73rd Special Naval Centre, which has regained its maritime roles along with counter-terrorism. The Interior Ministry also retains a number of regional police Spetsnaz units, which are more akin to the Russian Otryad Mobil'nyy Osobogo Naznacheniya (OMON). Prior to the 2014 revolution, one of these units, Berkut, became infamous for atrocities committed against civilian protestors. In the wake of the uprising, Berkut was dissolved.

Ukrainian Spetsnaz detachments feature two companies of 42 operators, each divided into three 14-man groups, following Russian practice, supported by a transport platoon of light vehicles. In terms of weapons and equipment, Spetsnaz still carry the unique Soviet-era Stechkin APS fully automatic pistols with suppressors, some fitted with a weapon light and vertical foregrip, as their favoured sidearm along with the indigenously produced Fort-17.

Suppressed AK-74s of various marks are common, often equipped with EOTech holographic weapon sights and flip-out magnifiers. Israeli MTAR-21 carbines have also seen use, licence-produced in the Ukraine and called the Fort-221. It is unknown whether Ukrainian Special Operations will adopt the new WAC-47 rifle, which combines the features of the American M4 with the use of AK magazines and is slated to become the standard Ukrainian Army rifle. The Spetsnaz has also deployed UAVs (unmanned aerial vehicles) including the Israeli Bird-Eye 400 and appears to have acquired the Chaborz M-6 light patrol vehicle.

Special Operations Command (SOC)

Nationality: United Arab Emirates • Branch: Army • Established: *c.* 2008

Very little is known of the Special Operations Command (SOC) of the United Arab Emirates (UAE). What little has been gleaned is primarily from the UAE's involvement in the wars in Afghanistan and Yemen. According to the US military, the responsibilities of the SOC include 'counterterrorism, direct action operations, special reconnaissance, foreign internal defense, special and sensitive operations, and unconventional warfare.' It appears to include a number of special forces battalions and at least one special operations battalion, reportedly with the counter-terrorism mandate, but its exact composition is shrouded in secrecy.

There are also persistent rumours of a 'contractor battalion' of former Western special operations personnel, although these may be employed as a 'Pretorian guard' or are the Presidential Guard Command (PGC) led by a former Australian SASR officer and head of Australian Special Operations Command (SOCOMD). The PGC itself seems to be the higher headquarters

for the SOC. Both the PGC and the SOC are supported by their own integral rotary air component known as Group 18.

The UAE was the first Arabic country to pledge support to the United Nations International Security Assistance Force (ISAF) mission in Afghanistan and deployed to Tarin Kowt in 2008. The Emirati operators were viewed as widely effective in Helmand Province where they continue to operate alongside US Army Special Forces as Special Operations Task Force 6.

Emirati operators have been deployed to Yemen since 2015 in the conflict against the Houthi insurgents under Operation *Golden Arrow*. In August 2015, UAE Special Forces conducted a successful hostage rescue operation in Yemen, rescuing a British oil engineer who had been held hostage by al-Qaeda in the Arabic Peninsula (AQAP) terrorists. They are reportedly working closely with France's Commandement des Opérations Spéciales (COS) units in Yemen. Intriguingly, the Republic of Korea has deployed a training team (the 'Akh Unit') to work alongside the UAE Special Forces in Yemen. UAE SOC have also deployed to Syria, Egypt and Mali.

The UAE Special Forces are well equipped with M4A1s, G36C and MP5s as well as Minimi light machine guns. They may also employ the Taiwanese T91, modelled after the M4A1 but reportedly offering greater reliability in desert conditions. Their sidearm is the domestically produced 9x19mm Caracal F. They have their own special operations flight of MH-60 Black Hawks and have recently adopted the MRZR and domestically produced Nimr Special Operations Vehicles.

A UAE Special Operations Command (SOC) soldier assigned to Special Operations Task Force 6, Special Operations Task Force – West in Afghanistan. He carries the 5.56x45mm T91 carbine fitted with a Trijicon ACOG optic. (Courtesy US Army, Sgt 1st Class Marcus Quarterman)

Special Operations Group (SOG)

Nationality: Czech • Branch: Army • Established: 2002

Czech operators from the Army's 601st Special Forces Unit during build-up training for their 2004 tour of Afghanistan. The central operator is armed with the integrally suppressed MP5SD3 with twin magazines. (Dan Materna/AFP/Getty Images)

The Czech Special Operations Group (SOG) was a unique unit in that its responsibilities were both domestic and international. Drawn from the Czech Military Police, the unit provided a domestic tactical capability for crimes involving the Czech military and served as the national hostage rescue and counter-terrorist unit for overseas deployments, although the police URNA unit maintained domestic counter-terrorist responsibility.

It deployed to Kosovo as part of the NATO force conducting both close protection and intelligence gathering. The unit later deployed to Helmand Province in 2007 and rotated contingents through for another two years, working with and under the command of the British-led Task Force Helmand. Its members were distinctive in their customized Toyota Hilux trucks with swing mounts and turret ring. They suffered numerous wounded and one operator was killed by a suicide bomber in 2008 when escorting Danish aid workers in Gereshk.

The unit was controversially disbanded in 2009 amid accusations of command issues, although British soldiers who served with the SOG were content with its performance. A Czech Ministry of Defence spokesperson at the time claimed: 'There was an investigation of the operations of this unit in Afghanistan. Thanks to this investigation we know that interpersonal relations in this unit are very bad and during the deployment of this unit in Afghanistan there were conflicts about the mission of this unit and the tasks it should fulfil.' He added: 'They will return to their original purpose. One unit should not mix police and special forces capabilities – it is nonsense.'*

Czech Army 601st SFG is the current Czech SOF unit. It is a full-spectrum unit and is tasked with special reconnaissance, direct action missions and foreign internal defence. The unit has a long history with service in Operation *Desert Storm*, Kosovo, Albania, Iraq and Afghanistan, where it deployed first in 2004, then in 2006 (as Task Force 601), 2008 and 2009, and later, in 2011/2012, as a Special Forces Task Force in Nangarhar Province, where it

*   https://www.radio.cz/en/section/curraffrs/czech-army-special-units-set-for-shake-up-following-afghan-investigation

operated under NATO tasking in support of International Security Assistance Force (ISAF) special operations.

Elements from the unit are currently deployed in the 'advise and assist' role in Afghanistan, training Afghan SOF, and lost an operator and two wounded in late 2018 in Herat, shot by a rogue Afghan Commando in yet another blue on green murder. The unit has forged close ties with both NATO and Israeli units, including cross-training with the Israeli Defence Force's Duvdevan.

The 601st SFG employs a range of weapons including Glock 17 pistols including with detachable suppressors, Bushmaster M4A3 carbines, an upgraded variant of the Vz.58 (conducted by Brügger and Thomet in 2006), the MP5 series and HK417 marksman rifles along with the bullpup Desert Tech Hard Target Interdiction sniper rifle and M60E4 and Mk48 7.62mm medium machine guns. They deploy Land Rover Defender Special Operations Vehicles for mounted operations.

The Rapid Reaction Unit (Útvar rychlého nasazení or URNA) of the Czech Police was established in 1981 as a Spetsnaz unit and later a riot control unit but developed into a fully fledged counter-terrorist unit following the fall of the Communist dictatorship in 1989. URNA also operates against armed criminal gangs in a similar way to Germany's GSG9 or France's GIGN. It is supported by the regional Task Force (Zasahova Jednotka or ZJ).

Both units employ Glock 17 and 26 sidearms, a range of MP5 variants, Benelli M3T shotguns, G36C assault rifles and Sako TRG-22 and TRG-42 sniper rifles while URNA has also a number of domestically produced designs including the CZ805 Bren (also adopted by France's GIGN) and the CZ P-07 sidearm.

Special Operations Regiment (SOR)

Nationality: Kenyan • Branch: Army • Established: 2011

Kenya's Special Operations Regiment (SOR) is composed of two principal units: the 40th (Ranger Strike Force) Battalion and the 30th (Special Forces) Battalion. Originally the 20th (Parachute) Battalion was the Kenyan Defence Force's (KDF) primary SOF-capable unit; however, after allegations of human rights abuses the unit was disbanded and most of its members posted to a conventional light infantry unit. The 20th nevertheless provided the nucleus for the 40th (Ranger Strike Force) Battalion, prior to the establishment of a US-style Ranger School in 2007.

The 20th also housed the secretive D Company, which was believed to act as the KDF's special missions unit with counter-terrorist responsibility before the establishment of the 30th (Special Forces) Battalion. There is also the equally secretive Long Range Surveillance (LRS) unit, about which little is

Kenyan 30th (Special Forces) Battalion soldiers responding to the terrorist attack in Nairobi in January 2019. The soldiers carry the 7.62x51mm Mk17 SCAR-H fitted with EOTech optics. (Simon Maina/AFP/Getty Images)

known. The Kenyan Police Service also has a domestic tactical unit under the Recce Company of the General Service Unit (GSU).

The Army's 30th (Special Forces) Battalion is a full-spectrum SOF unit trained by UKSF and Royal Marine trainers. The Ranger Strike Force is trained and mentored by US units, principally the 3rd SFG and a number of SEAL Team platoons. The Kenyan Navy also maintains the Kenyan Special Boat Unit (KSBU), which is trained by US Navy Special Warfare combatant-craft crewmen who operate alongside the SEALs. In addition, SOR has a strong relationship with Jordan, Israel, Canada and Belgium, which have all assisted in training and mentoring along with the US and UK.

Kenyan SOF have been at the forefront of operations into Somalia since 2011 as part of the African Union Mission in Somalia (AMISOM). SOR units work closely with US Special Forces and Navy SEALs under Operation *Octave Shield*. On one such joint operation in June 2018, a member of the 3rd SFG was killed and four wounded by enemy fire in Jubaland, south-west of the capital.

SOR units responded to the Westgate Mall siege in Nairobi in 2013 when terrorists from al-Shabaab seized the building, although SOR was criticized for taking a reported 12 hours to deploy and for killing a plainclothes GSU officer during the clearance of the facility. SOR elements also deployed in the search for five missing KDF service members after an al-Shabaab ambush near Kismayu, Somalia in 2011.

In the following year, SOR spearheaded the successful capture of the port city from al-Shabaab under Operation *Sledge Hammer*. It has also been active within Kenya itself, hunting the Jaysh Aman al-Shabaab, an al-Shabaab cell organised to operate within Kenya, who use the forested Boni National Reserve on the border with Somalia as a staging point for terrorist attacks in Kenya.

SOR issues both the 9x19mm Beretta M9 and the Browning Hi-Power as a sidearm, although allegedly the .45ACP Glock 30 has been purchased. The KDF uses both the 5.56x45mm M4 carbine and the 7.62x51mm Mk17 SCAR as its primary assault weapon while the Police GSU uses the M16. SR-25s have been seen in use by KDF SOR, as have Accuracy International sniper rifles.

Special Operations Task Force (SOTF)

Nationality: Singaporean • Branch: Armed Forces • Established: 2009

The first Singaporean Armed Forces (SAF) special operations unit was formed in 1969 as the SAF Regular Battalion to signify that it was composed of regular soldiers rather than national servicemen, who make up the bulk of the SAF. It was later renamed the Commando Formation although it only (officially) included one unit, the 1st Commando Battalion.

Members of the Singapore Navy Naval Diving Unit's Special Warfare Group training with their US counterparts in 2006. Note the domestically designed and produced 5.56x45mm SAR-21 assault rifles. (Courtesy US Navy, Mark Allen Leonesio)

In 1991, a then-unknown specialist unit from the 1st Commando Battalion stormed a hijacked Singapore Airlines flight, killing all four Pakistani terrorists and rescuing 123 passengers and crew. The unit, known as the Special Operations Force (SOF), was composed of regular career soldiers rather than the national servicemen who comprise most of the Commando Battalion. It was and remains a relatively small formation with only three platoons of operators.

The SOF had been established in secret in 1984 to act as Singapore's national counter-terrorist unit, along with conducting wartime special reconnaissance, raiding and direct action tasks in common with its parent organization, the 1st Commando Battalion. Members of the Commandos and SOF have deployed in small numbers to Afghanistan under Operation *Blue Ridge*.

The Special Operations Task Force or SOTF was established in 2009 as an overall command for all SAF special operations units in a similar manner to the US SOCOM. Maritime capability is provided by the Naval Diving Unit's Special Warfare Group. Other Navy units are sometimes called upon to provide specific capabilities such as the Clearance Diving Group, the Underwater Demolition Group and the Combat Diving Group.

Supporting the SOTF for counter-terrorism missions in Singapore is the National Police Special Tactics and Rescue (STAR), which was developed with the assistance of the British SAS and Germany's GSG9. The unit maintains an urban Quick Reaction Force mounted on motorcycles to provide an immediate response until a full team can be deployed.

Distinctive in their MultiCam Black uniforms, SOTF units carry a range of small arms including the recently introduced HK416 and suppressed MP7A1s replacing M4 carbines and Fabrique Nationale P90s. Police STAR operators carry Mk17 SCAR assault rifles, MP5 sub machine guns and both Glock and Heckler & Koch USP sidearms. In terms of mobility, both the Spider Light Strike Vehicle Mk2 – an armed dune buggy, which like the MRZR is designed to be carried internally in helicopters – and the Renault Peacekeeper Protected Response Vehicle (PRV) are employed by SOTF.

Special Reconnaissance Regiment (SRR)

Nationality: UK • Branch: Army • Established: 2005

The Special Reconnaissance Regiment (SRR) is one of the newest members of UKSF along with the Special Forces Support Group (SFSG). Established in 2005, the SRR was an expansion of a capability pioneered by 14 Intelligence Company (often known by its cover identity as the Joint Communications

Unit) which operated largely in Northern Ireland during the 1980s and 1980s, surveilling terrorist suspects for later arrest by the security forces.

The need for the expansion was noted by the Ministry of Defence as the 'growing worldwide demand for special reconnaissance capability'.* Although both the SAS and SBS pride themselves on their reconnaissance skills, with the up-tick in operations, a separate organization somewhat akin to JSOC's Task Force Orange or Intelligence Support Activity (ISA) was needed. Although established as a regiment, the operational strength of the SRR is believed to be closer to company strength and it is assumed to be organized into troops following UKSF pattern.

As well as carrying out physical reconnaissance and surveillance, often in local dress and vehicles, the SRR operates a signals and electronic intelligence capability along with more traditional skills in the covert placement of surveillance devices (covert method of entry). This is supported by a range of UAVs (unmanned aerial vehicles) operated by the unit, most commonly the AeroVironment Puma.

The SRR was almost immediately deployed to both Iraq and Afghanistan. In Iraq, the new arrivals faced animosity from some of the veteran SAS operators who already had their own surveillance and reconnaissance cell within the Regiment and felt the SRR was imposing upon a recognized field of excellence within the SAS. The SRR operated alongside the SAS' Task Force Black/Knight as the 'SpR Det' or the Specialist Reconnaissance Detachment.

In Afghanistan in June 2006, a joint operation by the SBS and SRR ended in disaster. Operation *Ilios* targeted a number of Taliban leadership figures and the 16-man element successfully infiltrated and seized its quarry. As it attempted to extract it became engaged in a protracted firefight, which lasted

The berets of the (from left) Parachute Regiment, Special Reconnaissance Regiment, 18 UKSF Signals and the Special Boat Service on display in the National Army Museum. (Leon Neal/Getty Images)

* https://publications.parliament.uk/pa/cm200405/cmhansrd/vo050405/ wmstext/50405m01.htm

for over an hour until Apache attack helicopters and a Gurkha Quick Reaction Force enabled it to escape. During the chaos, an SRR officer and an SBS sergeant were killed in action, their bodies left behind until later spotted by an Apache and retrieved by members of the Parachute Regiment.

Most recently, the unit has been deployed in small numbers to regional trouble spots including Libya, Somalia and Yemen. It has also assisted the civil powers within the United Kingdom on counter-terrorism deployments to Northern Ireland and provided additional (unarmed) manpower in the wake of the July 2007 terrorist bombings in London. Members of the SRR have also been seconded to both the Security Service (MI5) and the Secret Intelligence Service (SIS or MI6).

Special Service Group (SSG)

Nationality: Pakistani • Branch: Army • Established: 1956

The Pakistani Army Special Service Group (SSG), also known colloquially as the Black Storks, serves as the nation's principal special operations force with a history dating back to both the 1965 and 1971 Indo-Pakistani Wars. In the early years the SSG was trained by the US 10th SFG. Following the Munich massacre of 1972 (see page 88), the Pakistani Army's combat diving unit, Musa Company, was incorporated into the SSG and trained as a specialist counter-terrorist intervention force with the assistance of the British SAS.

Today the SSG is composed of eight commando battalions, a combat diver company, a specialist signals (communications) unit (Iqbal Company) and the counter-terrorist company (formerly Musa Company but now renamed Zarrar Company). There is also a maritime counter-terrorist capability in the SSGN or Special Service Group (Navy).

The SSG were involved in a number of counter-hijack operations during the 1980s. The first, in 1980, saw operators posing as ground crew storm a hijacked Indian Airlines airliner in Lahore. All five terrorists were captured and 45 hostages released unharmed. The second operation, in September 1986, saw Musa Company assault a hijacked American Pan Am flight at Karachi.

The Pan Am aircraft was held by four Palestinian terrorists with 350 passengers. The United States had requested and was granted authority to deploy Delta Force's Aztec Squadron to Karachi to stand by for a possible assault but events overtook both Delta and the SSG when a generator on board the aircraft suffered a malfunction, plunging the aircraft into darkness. Believing they were under assault, the terrorists began firing and posting grenades into the passenger compartments.

Musa Company conducted its immediate action drill, racing across the tarmac in its modified Land Rovers and carrying out a hurried assault.

Pakistani Special Service Group (SSG) operators conducting a counter-terrorism exercise, assaulting 'terrorist held' caves by abseiling into position. (Farooq Naeem/AFP/Getty Images)

Some 20 hostages were killed. Ironically the first C-130 carrying the advance elements from the Aztec Squadron landed soon after the gun battle. The SSG was criticized for its equipment choices, namely the use of AKMs and G3 battle rifles which over-penetrated and killed and wounded hostages, and the lack of stun grenades.

A hostage rescue in the Afghan Embassy in 1994 was more successful with all three terrorists killed and all hostages released unharmed. Rumour suggests that the SSG may have been deployed on occasion to Afghanistan, fighting alongside the Afghan mujahideen against the Soviets in a scheme euphemistically referred to as 'Extra Regimental Employment'.

It has operated extensively in coordination with the CIA and JSOC including in direct action operations in the Swat Valley in southern Waziristan (Delta Force operators were clandestinely embedded with SSG teams). Many of these operations were conducted against the Tehreek-e-Taliban Pakistan or TTP, the Pakistani Taliban.

After a cease-fire agreement with the TTP was broken by the insurgents in 2009, the Pakistani military launched a massive operation to retake key areas under TTP control. The SSG conducted much of the advance reconnaissance for the operation and these recce teams frequently ran into TTP insurgents and allied foreign fighters. In May 2009, four SSG operators were captured in one such contact and beheaded.

The SSG was at the forefront of the later assault with operators fast-roped in to seal off the Bunar Valley and the strategic town of Daggar following a series of airstrikes. Additional follow-on forces parachuted in to reinforce the Commandos. Paratroopers pushed the TTP back into the valley and caught the insurgents between them and the SSG, killing a large number of insurgents.

In a related mission, SSGN parachuted into Shangla District, east of Swat, and assaulted a TTP camp, killing over 100 insurgents while losing two operators in the fighting. The SSG were also heavily involved in the operation to retake the Swat Valley. Both the SSG and the Rangers of the Ministry of the Interior (a regional light infantry police unit which includes its own counter-terrorist team, the Ranger Anti-terrorist Wing) conducted a street-by-street clearance of the capitol of Swat, Mingora.

In 2014, the SSG carried out one of the largest successful hostage rescue operations in history when its Zarrar Company conducted a mission to liberate the Peshawar Army Public School, which had been seized by six foreign fighters affiliated with the TTP. Arriving by Mi-17 helicopters, the SSG was forced to conduct an immediate action, storming into the school and engaging the terrorists in close quarters battle. SSG rescued some 960 hostages. One SSG operator was killed by the detonating suicide vest of one terrorist and a number of operators were wounded.

The SSG has taken heavy losses including the 2007 terrorist bombing of one of their bases, which killed 19 operators. The unit has also been involved in the long-simmering proxy war with India and rumours abound that the Mumbai terrorists were trained by the SSG. It has also been accused of operating in league with the Afghan Taliban including persistent accounts of SSG personnel captured or killed on Afghan soil.

It employs the MP5 series (licence-produced in Pakistan) along with Colt M4 and SIG 516 carbines replacing the Steyr AUG which was once standard. The AKM (or Chinese Type 56) is still in use for operations in the Federally Administered Tribal Areas, for instance, owing to its greater range. Sniper platforms include the Steyr SSG-69 and the Accuracy International AWM.

Specialist Firearms Command (Specialist Crime & Operations 19) (SCO19)
Nationality: UK • Branch: Police • Established: 1966

Specialist Firearms Command (Specialist Crime & Operations 19 or SCO19) is the London Metropolitan Police's firearms unit. Within the organization are four tiers of armed officers: the Armed Response Vehicles (ARVs) which patrol the city to provide immediate armed support; the Trojan Proactive Unit which provides armed officers for pre-planned operations; the Tactical Support Teams which are responsible for criminal sieges and armed offenders;

and the Counter Terrorist Specialist Firearms Officers (CTSFOs) who have primary intervention responsibility for terrorist attacks in the capital.

According to the Metropolitan Police, the CTSFOs '… work in teams and provide overt and covert specialist armed support for serious crime and counter terrorist operations. They are designated as the MPS [Metropolitan Police Service] hostage rescue team and form an essential part of the UK contingency to combat terrorism.'* The unit was established in 2012 in advance of the London Olympics and in response to so-called marauding terrorist firearms attacks (MTFAs) such as that carried out in Mumbai in 2008.

Currently there are seven 16-man CTSFO teams within the MPS. Other teams exist at a regional level, forming the CTSFO Network (itself a continuation of the Combined Response Firearms Teams established during planning for Olympics security to ensure that sufficient counter-terrorist police were available to cover multiple concurrent incidents). The CTSFO Network is fully integrated with UKSF with a spokesperson noting: 'We have worked very closely with UK Special Forces to ensure that we are fully interoperable with them; we established working groups involving Special Forces advisers to develop and implement effective tactics for terrorist attacks.'**

Although the on-call CTSFO teams can deploy incredibly quickly, particularly to incidents in Central London, the vanguard against most terrorist attacks remains the three-man Armed Response Vehicles operated by the MPS and the City of London Police, the numbers of which have been significantly increased in recent years: 'The public will have seen this improved response in action during the London Bridge terror attack, when ARVs were able to respond incredibly quickly to stop the attackers without having to wait for specialist officers or Special Forces.'***

The unit employs the Glock 17 as its sidearm and the semi-automatic only 5.56x45mm SIG-Sauer SIG 516 carbine as its primary individual weapon. The CTSFO teams also employ a semi-automatic variant of the .300 Blackout SIG-Sauer MCX, often equipped with integral SRD-556 suppressor.

SCO19 Counter Terrorist Specialist Firearms Officers (CTSFOs) seen in 2018. Both carry suppressed .300 Blackout SIG-Sauer MCX carbines and Glock 17 sidearms. The MCXs in use by CTSFO teams are semi-automatic only, unlike those employed by UK Special Forces who have adopted the weapon to replace the suppressed MP5. (Steve Parsons/PA Images)

---

*   https://www.london.gov.uk/sites/default/files/londons_preparedness_to_respond_to_a_
      major_terrorist_incident_-_independent_review_oct_2016.pdf

**   https://news.npcc.police.uk/releases/national-police-chiefs-council-lead-for-armed-policing-
      has-said-he-is-confident-in-the-ability-of-firearms-officers-to-protect-the-public

*** https://news.npcc.police.uk/releases/armed-policing-numbers-boosted-with-more-specially-
      trained-officers

Previously the unit was equipped with semi-automatic only MP5s and G36C carbines. Its primary sniper platform is the Accuracy International AT308 in 7.62x51mm and the 7.62x51mm SIG 716 DMR, both of which have specialist armour-piercing ammunition available.

Spetsgruppa A (Alpha)

Nationality: Russian • Branch: Federal Security Service (FSB) • Established: 1974

Like many such units, Russia's Alpha or Directorate A of the FSB's Special Purpose Centre was created in the aftermath of the Munich massacre of 1972 (see page 88) under the auspices of the former KGB. Originally formed as a specialist counter-terrorist intervention unit, Alpha's first deployment was to Afghanistan in 1979 where it helped perform a decapitation strike in an effort to assassinate the country's leader.

Along with further deployments during the Soviet–Afghan War and later in Chechnya where it carried out direct action and reconnaissance missions, the unit came to unfortunate prominence at the Dubrovka Theatre siege in Moscow in 2002 and the infamous Beslan School siege in 2004, which ended in the deaths of 334 hostages.

Beslan saw BTR-80 armoured personnel carriers and tanks used for suppressive fire and to breach into the school, and Russian operators may have used RPO (rocket-propelled flamethrower) and RPG (rocket-propelled grenade) launchers to mouse-hole walls, while Dubrovka was resolved with the deployment of an unknown chemical agent that was responsible for the deaths of most of the 130 hostages killed. Although the operators are well trained, and increasingly well equipped, these operations highlighted the Russian mentality that appears to place the deaths of the terrorists over the lives of the hostages.

Other operations have seen Alpha conduct a successful counter-hijack mission in 1983, killing three of the six terrorists, and a 1995 bus assault, which saw the unit use flashbangs for the first time, disorienting the hostage taker long enough to kill him and release the six hostages held on board the bus. In 1997, a gunman took a Swedish government official hostage in the Swedish Embassy in Moscow. Alpha's commander negotiated to take the place of the hostage. Alpha subsequently conducted an assault and killed the hostage taker but the Alpha commander was wounded in the operation and later died from a heart attack.

Despite their hostage rescue and counter-terrorist mandate, it has long been rumoured that Alpha has conducted more deniable operations in Chechnya and Dagestan to include kidnapping and assassination. More recently elements from the unit have apparently deployed to Ukraine in low-profile roles.

Along with Alpha, the FSB (Federal'naya sluzhba bezopasnosti in Russian) officially maintains another two special units: Spetsgruppa V or Vympel (Pennant) and Spetsgruppa S or Smerch (Whirlwind). Vympel, originally part of Russia's foreign intelligence agency, also has a counter-terrorist role and is the national response unit for nuclear or WMD-based (weapons of mass destruction based) terrorism. Smerch is a SWAT-style counter-organized crime unit but may be called upon to support Alpha or Vympel.

The Foreign Intelligence Agency (Sluzhba vneshney razvedki Rossiyskoy Federatsii or SVR) also has a secret unit named Zaslon (Barrier or Screen) that seems to be responsible for high-risk overseas close personal protection and various politically sensitive missions, potentially including targeted killings in a similar manner to the FSB's Vympel. Some have claimed that Zaslon is the SVR equivalent of the CIA's Special Activities Division (SAD). Created in 1998, very little is known of Zaslon; its operators appear to favour low-profile olive-green fatigues and carry a mix of AK-74 and AKM platforms.

Spetsgruppa V or Vympel (Pennant) conduct a counter-hijacking drill in 1994. Of particular interest are the Stechkin APS fully automatic pistols and the 9mm PP-91 Kedr sub machine guns carried and the Altyn steel CQB helmet. (Vladimir Velengurin/AFP/Getty Images)

FSB operators have been seen using the pump action GM-94 grenade launcher, along with the Heckler & Koch MR762 rifle deployed by the Russian Komandovanie sil spetsial'nalnykh operatsii (KSSO) and the VSS/Val family of sniper rifles. For longer range engagements, Alpha snipers use the Accuracy International AWM. They carry Glocks as their primary sidearm and increasingly employ the new AK-12 in replacement of their AK-74Ms. Operators have also been seen with suppressed B&T MP9 sub machine guns, an unusual choice. During the Cold War, Alpha went to extraordinary lengths to acquire MP5s through various intermediaries.

Armed UGVs (unmanned ground vehicles) employed by FSB Spetsgruppy include a wheeled variant known as the Tornado, mounting a PKP medium machine gun and a pair of single shot RPG-29 launchers, which supported an FSB operation (unidentified but possibly Alpha) in December 2016 near Dagestan's capital city of Makhachkala. FSB Spetsgruppy also make extensive use of surveillance UAVs (unmanned aerial vehicles).

The FSB has purchased the imposing ZiL Karatel nicknamed the Falcatus (Punisher), a futuristic black-painted armoured truck with a gun turret typically mounting a PKP, and the Kamaz Viking, another armoured SWAT truck with gun turret. They have also procured the Kamaz Extreme, a dune buggy-style light vehicle with similarities to the American Polaris MRZR.

Spetsnaz

Nationality: Russian • Branch: All • Established: Various

The Spetsnaz, Sily Spetsialnogo Naznacheniya or literally Special Designation, is not the Russian equivalent of the US Army's Special Forces as many commentators have described it over the years. It is instead more akin to the US Army Rangers or the UK's Special Forces Support Group (SFSG) and even these are somewhat inaccurate comparisons as both the Rangers and SFSG are more skilled in a wider array of SOF tasks. The Spetsnaz should instead be considered in the main a well-trained, expeditionary light infantry force.

During the Cold War, Spetsnaz was tasked with strategic reconnaissance and sabotage missions including ambushing NATO personnel in rear base areas, assassinating key commanders, and conducting raids against NATO installations and airfields. Although the much-feared conflict in Western Europe never came to pass, the Spetsnaz saw nearly a decade of brutal combat in Afghanistan following the Russian invasion in 1979.

It was respected by the mujahideen as one of the few Russian units that would conduct active ambushes deep within mujahideen controlled territory. It carried special weapons including suppressed AKM assault rifles and had a fondness for the AGS-17 automatic grenade launcher which was often man-

Russian Army Spetsnaz troops seen outside of Grozny, Chechnya, 1995. Note the heavy use of suppressors. (Alexander Nemenov/AFP/Getty Images)

packed and carried into remote areas when conducting ambushes on mujahideen caravans crossing into Afghanistan from Pakistan.

It also employed what we would now consider 'Non-Tacs', commercial pick-up trucks that would sometimes be covertly infiltrated into an operational area hidden under tarps as part of a seemingly regular Russian Army convoy. The 'Non-Tacs' would be driven from their transporters during a brief convoy halt under cover of line of sight blocking terrain and set off on their mission with any watchers unaware that a mounted Spetsnaz patrol had been deployed.

The two wars in Chechnya and subsequent security operations would see Spetsnaz initially squandered in an infantry role, although during the Second Chechen War, it operated in its traditional roles of deep reconnaissance, sniping and ambushing and was far more successful. It even fell back on tried and tested Afghan tactics such as aerial vehicle interdictions targeting insurgent leaders.

In Georgia too in 2008 the Spetsnaz was deployed in a covert manner to reinforce Russian 'peacekeeping' elements supporting the South Ossetia separatists and paving the way for the eventual deployment of Russian conventional forces under the cover of a controversial military exercise. In Georgia it conducted sabotage and sniping, along with the training and sometimes command of irregular 'nationalist' forces raised by the Glavnoje Razvedyvatel'noje Upravlenije (GRU or Main Intelligence Directorate).

The Russian 'intervention' in Crimea followed a similar pattern to Georgia. According to the US military, 'the Russian GRU dispatched several hundred members of 45th SPETSNAZ Regiment to Crimea to create a "popular uprising" aimed at facilitating Russia's annexation of the region.' In the Ukraine too, Spetsnaz was deployed amongst the 'Little Green Men' or 'Polite People' as they are termed in Russia (see page 119), deniable but obviously Russian soldiers who assisted in seizing key government infrastructure targets and aiding local 'self-defence' militias.

This gives the Russian government the opportunity to claim that any Russian troops in the Ukraine for instance are volunteers and not under Russian state command, although suspicions persist that these 'volunteers', particularly those involved in the Donbas, are paid and equipped by the GRU. This neatly complements the Russian 'relief columns' seen in eastern Ukraine allegedly bringing needed humanitarian assistance but actually carrying ammunition and military supplies.

In fact, Spetsnaz, along with the Russian Komandovanie sil spetsial'nalnykh operatsii (KSSO), has become a vital implement in Russia's new asymmetric strategy of 'hybrid warfare' which includes '(1) use of proxies when possible; (2) deniability to deflect international criticism and domestic political reaction; (3) use of information warfare, including propaganda and cyber warfare; and (4) political preparation of subject populations and manipulation of economic conditions', according to the US military in an unclassified study.

Russian Army Spetsnaz pictured whilst seizing the Ukrainian Belbek Airbase on 22 March 2014. They are equipped with railed AK-74Ms and Vant-VM ballistic shields fitted with high intensity lights. (Oleg Klimov/Epsilon/Getty Images)

In Syria, Spetsnaz has been deployed alongside the operators of the KSSO, principally in a mentoring role for pro-Assad forces. The Spetsnaz in its role as light expeditionary forces is perfectly suited for the task. Along with GRU Spetsnaz, detachments of Spetsnaz from the Federal'naya sluzhba bezopasnosti (FSB or Russian Federal Security Service) Alpha and Vympel, and naval Spetsnaz units, have been noted as operating in Syria since 2015.

Syria has seen the emergence of Spetsnaz practising foreign internal defence, in an advise and assist role, as well as pure unconventional warfare. It has been an important conflict for Spetsnaz as it has allowed it to practise these oft-neglected skills and somewhat bridge the gap between its status as an intervention force and a true special forces capability.

Spetsnaz operators have also been involved in the battlefield trials of new technologies including the Uran-9 UGV (unmanned ground vehicle) and a range of UAVs (unmanned aerial vehicles) as the Russian government sees the Syrian conflict as an ideal testing ground. Most recently, Spetsnaz troops deployed to Al-Safa in southern Syria in November 2018 to support a Syrian Arab Army offensive where they were again embedded in an advisory capacity with the local forces.

Today there are eight officially acknowledged Spetsnaz brigades, most composed of a mix of conscripts and contract soldiers, one Spetsnaz regiment, and four naval Spetsnaz brigades, which include combat divers and mini-submarine units and are comparable to the regular US Navy SEAL Teams. In another recent move (2017), the first dedicated Spetsnaz electronic warfare detachment has been created with a focus on counter-UAV operations.

In each Spetsnaz brigade there are three Spetsnaz detachments, a combat support detachment and a specialist communications/signals detachment. A detachment has three companies of operators, a sniper/surveillance cell and a communications company. The Spetsnaz companies themselves are composed of three groups similar to US Special Forces ODAs or Marine Special Operations Command (MARSOC) Marine Special Operations Teams (MSOTs).

The combat support company provides integral mortar and ATGM (anti-tank guided missile) capabilities, operates the brigade's UAVs and includes an electronic warfare element to disrupt enemy radio and GPS signals and conduct tactical signals intelligence. The combat support company also houses two platoons of BTR-82A wheeled armoured personnel carriers for protected mobility in more conventional operations.

The Spetsnaz groups are 14-man strong with two attached signallers. Like ODAs or MSOTs, these groups are designed to operate in smaller sub-elements termed patrols if necessary. This is a reduction in Cold War manning levels where Spetsnaz platoons were often 25-man strong.

The sniper/surveillance cell is also typically parcelled out into smaller elements of one or two sniper 'pairs' to the relevant Spetsnaz group as needed. They operate in a Western fashion, with the primary sniper equipped with the sniper rifle and supported by a spotter with a suppressed assault rifle or 'light sniper rifle' like the VSS.

The Spetsnaz is equipped with the issue AK-74M but will be amongst the first to be issued the new AK-12. The suppressed VSS and Val rifles are commonly seen, as is the SR-3 sub machine gun, also often equipped with a sound suppressor. Along with a range of UGVs (unmanned ground vehicles) and UAVs, Spetsnaz operate a number of vehicle types including the Tigr-M armoured patrol vehicle, the Patriot technical, the Typhoon MRAP (mine resistant ambush protected vehicle) and the Rys, a licensed version of the Iveco LMV or light multi-role vehicle.

Takavaran

Nationality: Iranian • Branch: Army • Established: 1959

An Iranian Takavaran commando guarding Iranian shipping in South Sudan armed, ironically enough, with a 9x19mm UZI sub machine gun. Note also the locally produced copy of the American UCP/ACU pattern camouflage uniform he wears. Iranian Quds Force members dressed in such copies of US uniforms conducted a raid in Karbala in 2007 during the Iraq insurgency which resulted in the deaths of three US servicemen. (Ashraf Shazly/AFP/Getty Images)

Iran has a number of special operations units known generically as the Takavaran within both the Iranian Army and the notorious Islamic Revolutionary Guard Corps (IRGC). The Army appears to have at least five Special Forces brigades although most are far closer to airmobile or parachute infantry rather than true SOF. There are also three independent commando brigades, again more akin to light infantry.

The only unit that could be at all comparable to its Western contemporaries is the 65th Airborne Special Forces Brigade. Prior to the downfall of the Shah following the Iranian Revolution of 1979, Iranian Army Special Forces were trained by both the French and US Army Special Forces as part of the Military Assistance Advisory Group Iran programme. The 65th Brigade still wears a green beret reminiscent of its original instructors.

Nicknamed 'The Powerful Ghosts' after a 'red team' exercise that saw it stealthily seize key government buildings in the nation's capital, the 65th Airborne Special Forces Brigade is widely believed to be the premier Iranian SOF unit. The 65th is composed of three battalions with attached information operations/

psychological warfare and counter-terrorist companies. It is unknown if the battalions are formed into a US-like structure with ODA-style teams.

The unit fought and suffered horrendous casualties during the Iran–Iraq War. The 65th now has both a counter-terrorism and traditional special operations mission set and has seen limited action in Syria from 2016 in support of pro-Assad elements (prior to this, Quds Force had trained and supported Iranian-backed pro-Assad militias). Another recent operation was the 2018 hostage rescue of four Iranian fishermen captured by Somali pirates.

The Islamic Revolutionary Guard Corps has its own units including the Saberin Takavar Battalion, which appears to be a commando-like raiding force. The IRGC also directs the Quds Force, a clandestine group that trains and supplies militants and terrorists across the Middle East including supplying Hezbollah and pro-Assad militias.

Quds Force cells, or Special Groups as they were termed by the US, actively trained and supplied insurgents in Iraq during the insurgency, including supplying more lethal IEDs. They have also financed and organized a number of the Shia People's Militia units that have ironically fought alongside Iraqi forces during the war against Islamic State. The Navy too has at least one special operations unit nestled amongst its Marine units, the Niruye Daryai Sepah-e Iran (NEDSA) or Sepah Navy Special Force (SNSF), whose members appear to be trained as combat divers and marine raiders.

The Iranian Ministry of Intelligence maintains its own special operations capability but even less is known about its composition and role. It is alleged to have been involved in a hostage rescue of an Iranian government envoy in Yemen in 2015. The Law Enforcement Force of the Ministry of the Interior maintains a domestic counter-terrorist unit called the NOPO or Counter-terrorism Special Force but historically has been used as a public order tool against dissidents, although it is now understood that the unit was involved in the response to the Islamic State attack on Iran's Parliament building in 2017.

The Special Forces, like all of the Iranian military, suffer from poor equipment. The Army units' two principal forms of transport are the domestically produced Samir light truck which is employed as a technical, and a range of commercially acquired quad bikes or all-terrain vehicles. Motorcycles are also employed for mounted reconnaissance tasks.

The Army units carry a range of small arms including the Iranian-produced copy of the MP5 and MP5K, the Tondar-9 and Tondar-9K, locally produced G3 battle rifles (likely to be replaced by AK-103s) and the Sayyad 5.56, a copy of a Chinese copy of the M16A1. More recent models have included rails systems allowing optics and vertical foregrips to be attached. Sidearms appear to be a mix of Browning Hi-Powers and Beretta 951s. The NEDSA appears to employ a mix of Israeli UZIs, Spanish Star Z-84s and Tondar-9s.

Task Force 777

Nationality: Egyptian • Branch: Army • Established: 1977

The Egyptian Army maintains six Special Forces regiments, the Al Sai'qa (Lightning) Para-Commandos of the 27th Parachute Battalion, and a number of naval commando brigades whose role includes counter-mine warfare, beach reconnaissance, force protection and visit-board-search-seizure. The Thunderbolt Special Forces Command also comprises Task Force 777, Task Force 999 and the newly created Task Force 888, which gives the Egyptian Rapid Deployment Forces its own SOF capability.

Task Force 999 conducts close personal protection duties, along with more traditional special operations tasks such as special reconnaissance and guerrilla warfare. Task Force 999 has been active in operations in Libya against Islamic State. It has also been active in the Sinai against Islamic State-linked jihadist groups. The Ministry of the Interior also maintains its own domestic counter-terrorist unit, Task Force 333, otherwise known as the Hostage Rescue Force.

Task Force 777 is the primary counter-terrorist intervention force and has been involved in two counter-hijack operations, which can only be described as unmitigated disasters. The first occurred in 1978 after a pair of Palestinian terrorists assassinated an Egyptian newspaper editor in Cyprus. They took hostages to ensure their escape and were given access to a Cyprus Airways DC-8 airliner to leave the country. Amongst the hostages was a single Egyptian national.

Seventy-four members of Task Force 777 were immediately dispatched to Larnaca and planned an Entebbe-style assault; they were to land in their C-130 Hercules and before it even slowed to a halt the commandos would leap out and run toward the hijacked aircraft, hopefully catching the terrorists

Egyptian operators likely drawn from Thunderbolt Special Forces Command's Task Force 999 that conducts close personal protection along with more traditional counter-terrorist missions. They are both armed with the elderly but reliable 5.56x45mm SIG SG551 SWAT carbine. Note the double magazine couplers. (Khaled Desouki/AFP/Getty Images)

by surprise. Unfortunately as the operation had been neither cleared with nor sanctioned by the Cypriots, the Cypriot National Guardsmen surrounding the hijacked aircraft took the Egyptian commandos as terrorist reinforcements and opened fire on them.

The resulting firefight resulted in 15 dead Task Force 777 commandos and several dead Cypriots. Three of the Egyptian C-130's crew perished when it was engaged by a Cypriot 106mm recoilless rifle. Ironically, just as Task Force 777 touched down, the Cypriots had negotiated the surrender of the two terrorists.

The second disaster occurred in 1985 when EgyptAir Flight 648 was hijacked by the Abu Nidal Organization and landed in Malta. Although this time it had the agreement of the national authorities, the outcome was similar. Task Force 777 assaulted the aircraft using a large breaching charge to blow a hole in the ceiling of the aircraft. A number of hostages were killed in the explosion. Egyptian commandos then lobbed in chemical smoke grenades, which incurred more casualties amongst the hostages as the commandos fired at vague shapes inside the aircraft. The terrorists also began throwing fragmentation grenades.

The final grim total was over 50 dead hostages and scores wounded. In a sad postscript, Delta Force had forward deployed its Aztec counter-terrorist squadron as there were nine American hostages on board but was refused permission by the Maltese government to conduct the operation. Soon after, Task Force 777 was disbanded but it was reconstituted a decade later. In a bizarre operation in 1998, Task Force 777 deployed to conduct a visit-board-search-seizure boarding of a commercial ship that had failed to pay for passage through the Suez Canal and had fired shots at Egyptian Coast Guard vessels.

Task Force 777 members are typically armed with MP5 sub machine guns and SIG 552 series assault rifles, although during the 1985 operation to storm EgyptAir Flight 648, they were primarily and inappropriately armed with AKMs. The unit's operators are distinctive in olive-green uniforms with black plate carriers and helmets.

Terrorelhárítási Központ (TEK)

Nationality: Hungarian • Branch: Interior Ministry • Established: 2010

The Terrorelhárítási Központ (TEK or Counter Terrorism Center) is Hungary's national body responsible for counter-terrorism, police tactical response to armed criminals and close personal protection of diplomatic staff. The unit is divided into three directorates: the Intelligence Directorate, the Personal Protection Directorate and the Operations Directorate. The last of these provides the national intervention capability with six teams based in Budapest and seven regionally.

Hungarian TEK members stand alongside their customized BTR-80 armoured personnel carriers, complete with police light bars. (Attila Kisbenedek/AFP/ Getty Images)

In 2012 the TEK Operations Directorate conducted a hostage recovery in Syria to rescue three former police officers held by unidentified gunmen. More recently the unit has been involved in raids against the far-right terrorist groups which are re-emerging in Europe and in combating Russian illegal arms smuggling. It also carried out the successful capture of a criminal bomber whose device wounded two police officers in Budapest in 2016.

The Hungarian Defence Forces maintain the 2nd Special Forces Brigade, which is composed of the 34th Special Operations Battalion, established in 2005 from a former long range reconnaissance battalion and trained by US Army Special Forces, and the airmobile 25/88th Light Mixed Battalion established in 2004, which acts as a Ranger element for the 2nd. Both units are supported by the Mi-17s of the 86th Szolnok Helicopter Base.

The 34th focuses on unconventional warfare and has deployed to Afghanistan since 2004 (as the unit was just being established) and 'NATO Training Mission – Iraq' in 2005. The first Hungarian Special Operations Task Unit (SOTU) deployed to Afghanistan in 2009, working with the 10th SFG under Task Force 1/10 on a four-month tour under Regional Command East. In 2013, the Hungarian SOTU took command of Task Force 1/10 for the first time.

TEK uses Glock 17 and 19 pistols and MP5A3s as its primary assault weapon. The unit snipers employ the HK417 and the Accuracy International AWM. The 34th Special Operations Battalion also uses the Glock along with Colt M4A1s, while the 25/88th Light Mixed Battalion relies upon a modernized Hungarian AKM variant, the AK-63MF. Both M249 SAWs and Russian PKM medium machine guns are employed.

Tiger Force

Nationality: Syrian • Branch: Air Force • Established: 2012

The Syrian Arab Army (SAA) does not have SOF units in the Western sense. Much like its Russian allies with Spetsnaz, the SAA has a number of units that are named and designated as Special Forces divisions but that operate in a manner closer to Western air-assault or Ranger-type formations, being relatively elite light infantry. Nor does the SAA have any units that are specifically assigned the counter-terrorist role. Its Special Forces Command has two such special forces divisions and a number of small special forces regiments. The Syrian Interior Ministry maintains a unit known as the Special Mission Forces, which conducts force protection and security operations to counter Islamic State terrorist activities.

The Syrians also have the irregular Tiger Force (Qawat al-Nimr) and the similar Cheetah Force (Qawat al-Fahoud), which they designate as special operations (although in reality they are better termed 'shock troops'), which operate under the command of the Syrian Air Force's Intelligence Directorate and were created as a direct result of the ongoing Syrian civil war.

In reality, these are groups of thugs who, although of generally more uniform appearance (in copies of US Woodland pattern also worn by Hezbollah), are little better trained than the average Syrian soldier. They are equipped to a generally higher standard and have been seen carrying modern Russian small arms including AK-74Ms, GP-30M under barrel grenade launchers and even the later AK-103 and carbine length AK-104.

Russian Komandovanie sil spetsial'nalnykh operatsii (KSSO) and Spetsnaz units have operated in close concert with the Tiger Force in Syria (including providing close protection parties for its leaders), often 'advising and assisting' by embedding operators within the militias. They also act as a vital link to Russian airpower for the militias. The Tiger Force, which numbers roughly a battalion in strength, has been accused of a wide range of war crimes and is known for its brutality against civilian and jihadist alike.

Hamza Division irregulars, affiliated with the Free Syrian Army, being trained as 'special forces', February 2018, Syria. (Free Syrian Army/Handout/Anadolu Agency/Getty Images)

Unit Interventie Mariniers (UIM)

Nationality: Dutch • Branch: Navy • Established: 1973

The Royal Netherlands Navy maintains its Maritime Special Operations Forces or MARSOF. One of the country's principal counter-terrorist units is drawn from MARSOF, the Unit Interventie Mariniers or UIM, also known as M Squadron (one of three MARSOF squadrons: M Squadron for counter-terrorism, C Squadron for unconventional and irregular warfare and T Squadron for training).

UIM can trace its history through the Bijzondere Bijstandseenheid Mariniers (BBE-M or Special Support Unit), which was famously responsible for the successful simultaneous rescue of hostages held by terrorists on a train and at a school in June 1977. The assault on the train near De Punt has been rightly hailed as a textbook example of conducting a tubular assault. After a particularly low flypast by Dutch fighter aircraft and the detonation of an explosive charge to draw attention to the front of the train, BBE-M snipers opened fire on visible terrorist targets. Six assault teams then boarded the train and methodically fought through each carriage. Within moments, the nine terrorists were killed or captured and 52 hostages were freed. Only two hostages died in the operation.

Dutch MARSOF UIM (formerly BBE) operators practise counter-hijack tactics. Note the Fabrique Nationale P90 and the SIG-Sauer P226 used by the shield-man. (Courtesy Dutch Ministry of Defense, CC0)

The famed BBE-M was renamed the UIM in 2006 although operators still refer to the unit as BBE-M. Today UIM comprises 30 personnel divided into three assault platoons. The platoons are further divided into six-man assault teams supported by snipers. Some are also combat divers and operate closely with the British SBS on maritime counter-terrorist tasks as 7 Troop (sometimes known as the Dutch SBS). Others specialize in urban climbing and rope work, in heavy breaching or as covert entry specialists. The unit often operates with the Explosieven Opruimingsdienst or Explosives Clearance Team, which provides specialist EOD capabilities.

The UIM is the pinnacle of Dutch counter-terrorism; however, it is supported by a range of other SOF units, which are also under the command of the Dienst Speciale Interventies (DSI or Special Interventions Service), part of the Dutch Ministry of Home Affairs. The Border Guard has a unit styled like Germany's GSG9 that conducts

high-risk tactical operations along with close personal protection. Known as the Brigade Speciale Beveiligingsopdrachten (BSB or Special Security Assignments Brigade), it is recruited from both the Border Guard and the military including operators from Korps Commandotroepen (KCT or Army Commando Corps) and UIM.

Members of UIM and BSB (along with the National Police Arrestatieteams) also operate as a joint unit called UI (Unit Interventie or Intervention Unit), which is tasked with resolving armed criminal situations such as sieges or mass shootings or arresting terrorists. UIM is used for the rescue of hostages from terrorists and other exceptionally high-risk tasks. UIM has also operated overseas including conducting a 2010 joint MARSOF and UIM rescue of hostages held on a German cargo vessel by Somali pirates. The unit also deployed to Afghanistan and operated alongside KCT under Task Force 55.

The Arrestatieteams, which are similar to other police tactical teams such as the French Brigade de Recherche et d'Intervention – Brigade Anticommando (BRI-BAC) or German Spezial Einsatzkommandos (SEKs), also deploy in immediate action teams to the scene of any terrorist incident within the Netherlands as Rapid Response Teams (RRTs) similar to those established in Paris by the BRI-BAC. All of the DSI units are also supported by a sniper cell held in the DSI's Expertise en operationele ondersteuningseenheid (Expertise and Operational Support Unit).

The UIM primarily uses the HK416 along with the P90, normally suppressed and used by the lead scout; the MP5 series; and SIG-Sauer P226 pistols. Integrally suppressed .300 Blackout Sig-Sauer MCXs have also been recently introduced. BSB operators use both the Glock 17 and sub-compact 26, the Fabrique Nationale P90, the MP5 series (including the MP5K briefcase model), the MP7A1 and both Diemaco (Colt Canada) C8A1 and HK416 carbines. The RRTs and Arrestatieteams use the MP5, HK416 and the SCAR-L. All carry the Glock 17 as their standard sidearm.

Yamam

Nationality: Israeli • Branch: Border Police • Established: 1973

Although Sayeret Matkal and Sayeret 13 are the better-known Israeli special units, there are several others very worthy of mention. Amongst these is the Israeli Border Police Yamam unit (also known either as Hayehida HaMeyuhedet LeLohama BaTerror, translated as the Special Counter Terrorist Unit, or as Yechida Mishtartit Meyuchedet, translated as the Special Police Unit), which has the responsibility for hostage rescue and associated counter-terrorist missions within Israel (pre-1967 borders).

The Army's Sayeret Matkal in comparison operates predominantly outside Israel, although often in contested Israeli territory. Formed in 1973, the Yamam is broadly similar to the FBI's Hostage Rescue Team or Germany's GSG9, with which it trains extensively (it also maintains a close relationship with France's GIGN) and is structured along Delta or SAS lines with troop-strength detachments (known as *mahlakah* in Hebrew).

Perhaps Yamam's most celebrated success was the March 1988 'Mother Bus' hostage rescue, so named as most of the 11 hostages were mothers who had just dropped off their children at school. After managing to crawl close to the hijacked bus, the terrorists executed three hostages, leading to a daring daylight Yamam assault. This was sniper initiated, and two terrorists fell from precision rifle fire before the pistol-armed assault team made rapid entry, hurling flashbangs and smashing in the side windows. Within seconds, all three terrorists were dead in a textbook example of a bus assault.

A November 2018 operation into Gaza resulted in the death of a senior officer, an unnamed lieutenant colonel believed to be from Yamam. The objective of the mission, which included operators disguised in women's clothing, was to emplace technical surveillance devices at the property of a Hamas leader. In the resulting firefight, the lieutenant colonel was killed and an operator wounded before the unit managed to exfiltrate under the cover of airstrikes. Hamas later displayed a suppressed Glock 19 at a press conference, allegedly left behind by the Yamam operators.

The Border Police also maintains a unit similar to the Belgian Directorate of Special Units (DSU) Quick Reaction Force in the form of the Yasam (Yechidat Siyur Meyuchedet), whose members travel to incidents at high speed on motorcycles, and district response units including Yoter Avtacha (More Security but commonly known as Unit Yoan), which was created in 1997 to protect public transportation following a wave of bombings and stabbing attacks. They patrol in marked police cars in a similar way to the Armed Response Vehicles of the UK police.

An undercover special unit known as Yamas (Yechidat Ha'Mistaarvim Shel Mishmar Ha'Gvul or Border Guard Undercover Unit) also operates under the command of the Border Police, mirroring the tasks carried out by the Duvdevan (Cherry) unit within the Army (see below). Duvdevan and Yamas operators are sometimes seen wearing civilian jeans and tee-shirts with a *keffiyeh* hiding their features although more elaborate disguises have been employed, including dressing as women. Performing a dangerous role, the undercover units have suffered numerous fratricide incidents, including cases where operators have been killed by Israeli snipers who mistook them for terrorists based on their clothing.

Cherry was first established in 1987 with responsibility for the West Bank; many original members were drawn from Shayetet 13. It specialized in surveilling and capturing Palestinian terrorists. In one well-known mission, its

operators posed as an American ABC news crew to capture a young insurgent. A second sister unit, Shimshon (Samson), established in 1988, operated in the Gaza Strip but was dissolved in 1994 as parts of the Gaza Strip were transferred to Palestinian control (and one of its former commanders was charged with manslaughter). A third unit, Gideon, was established in 1995 to operate in East Jerusalem.

Yamam uses the Micro Tavor X-95 (MTAR-21), suppressed M4 variant carbines fitted with EOTech optics, SR-25 and Barrett MRAD sniper rifles and suppressed P90s equipped with Israeli-designed Meprolight 21 reflex sights. Although formerly equipped with domestically produced Jericho pistols, the unit appears to now use the Glock.

The unit has always been equipped with an interesting range of small arms. During the 1980s and 1990s, the Browning Hi-Power was the standard issue, along with suppressed .22 Berettas, and a range of Uzis (Micro, Mini and fixed stock full sized variants) were in use. A closed bolt semi-automatic Uzi with suppressor and loaded with subsonic ammunition took the role of the MP5SD. Snipers used both the Galil Galatz and the Austrian Steyr SSG-69.

The Army and Border Police undercover units employ Mini Uzi and Micro Uzi sub machine guns as they are compact enough to conceal under clothing (or as in one famous Yamas operation, in false beer bellies!) along with Glock pistols. Micro Tavor X-95s are often hidden in their vehicles for greater range and penetration.

The Mossad, Israel's external security service, also includes a direct action unit known as Kidon or Bayonet, a unit responsible for external targeted

Former Israeli President Shimon Peres visits Yamam in 2011 and tries his hand at a suppressed P90. (Amos Ben Gershom/GPO via Getty Images)

killing operations. Founded in 1969, it was made famous during the 1970s and 1980s as it tracked the Black September terrorists responsible for the Munich massacre of 1972 (see page 88). Bayonet is supported by the Rainbow units who can conduct covert break-ins and plant technical surveillance.

Israeli special units have attracted as much criticism as praise although much of this is down to the Israeli willingness to conduct targeted killings as a primary means of national self-defence. Unfortunately this has resulted in civilian deaths including cases of mistaken identity and bombings which have killed civilians along with their targets. Along with Mossad's Bayonet, the undercover units in particular have been criticized as operating as 'death squads' by assassinating Palestinians in the street without warning or attempt to capture.

Yekîneyên Antî Teror (YAT)

Nationality: Kurdish/Syrian • Branch: Syrian Democratic Forces • Established: 2014

The Yekîneyên Antî Teror (YAT or Anti-Terror Unit) operates as the Syrian Democratic Forces' counter-terrorist and direct action unit. It comprises members drawn mainly from the Kurdish Yekîneyên Parastina Gel (YPG or People's Protection Units) and the Yekîneyên Parastina Jin (YPJ or Kurdish Women's Protection Units). Although created as a counter-terrorist unit it has taken on a range of SOF tasks.

One of its most celebrated operations was conducted with Marine Special Operations Command (MARSOC) and the 5th SFG in March 2017 when it conducted an operation to capture the strategically vital Tabqa Dam, a precursor to any assault on Raqqa, the Islamic State's de facto capitol. The areas surrounding the dam had been transformed into a key Islamic State training and logistical hub since its capture in 2013. Islamic State was confident that the Coalition would not hit the dam with airstrikes on account of the possibility of catastrophic collateral damage should the dam itself be damaged.

The operation involved US special operators and YAT, along with other YPG units, conducting a heliborne assault on the dam alongside MARSOC and SEAL operators who infiltrated by the newly acquired high-speed Combat Craft Medium Mk 1. Following the assault on the dam, a secondary follow-on mission was conducted to seize the nearby Tabqa airbase, which involved the support of unidentified UKSF (likely SAS as its distinctive Bushmaster vehicles were photographed in the area).

The unit faces threats other than pro-Assad jihadists and Islamic State. The YAT's first leader was assassinated by an IED in 2016, along with his two YAT bodyguards, allegedly by Turkish security forces who regard the Kurds, and the YPG and YPJ in particular, as extensions of the PKK or

Kurdistan Workers' Party which they view as a terrorist organization.

The YAT maintains a particularly close relationship with 5th SFG and Delta Force, which in some individual contacts dates back to 2002 and the preparations for the Iraq invasion where the US operators worked closely with the Peshmerga. YAT was initially trained, equipped and mentored by Delta but today works with a range of US SOF units. SEALs, for instance, have been embedded with the YPG and their YAT units. Although they attempt to blend in by wearing MultiCam Black uniforms, their non-standard weapons including Mk17 SCARs, along with their helmets and plates carriers, are simply too distinctive to miss.

The Kurdish Yekîneyên Antî Teror (YAT) acts as the Syrian Democratic Forces' direct action SOF unit. Here operators can be seen rather uniformly equipped with folding stock 7.62x39mm AKMs. (Courtesy YPG, Creative Commons CC BY 2.0)

As well as the typical range of AK variants, the YAT has been seen carrying M4 carbines with EOTech holographic sights and PEQ-2 laser illuminators, and M249 squad automatic weapons, small arms which were likely provided by the CIA or JSOC. They are often seen dressed in black fatigues but have donned USMC pattern MARPAT for operations, including the Tabqa Dam seizure, partly to reduce the risk of fratricide.

Another primarily Kurdish SOF unit is the Counter Terrorism Group or CTG, sometimes known informally by its motto, '*Lexoman Parastin*', 'those who give their lives to protect their people'. CTG was formed from a unit originally trained by the 10th SFG during the preparations for the invasion of Iraq and Operation *Viking Hammer*. Since then it has been mentored by both the United States' Delta and the UK's 22SAS – its training pipeline is even known as the Operator Training Course in obvious emulation of Delta.

The CTG was heavily involved in the war against al-Qaeda in Iraq and operated in concert with the JSOC task forces in the north of Iraq. Following the 2010 departure of US forces, the CTG found itself fighting what would soon become the Islamic State. It acts as shock troops for the Peshmerga, assaulting particularly resistant strongholds using both IAG Guardian armoured vehicles and MRZR buggies along with its own dedicated helicopter fleet of EC-135 helicopters.

Visually, with its EOTech-equipped M4 carbines and Crye MultiCam uniforms, the CTG is virtually indistinguishable from US special operators. CTG snipers employ a range of .50 Bushmaster BA50 and Barrett M82A1s, and the .338 Lapua Magnum B&T Advanced Precision Rifle.

WEAPONS

Accuracy International AWM

Type: Sniper Rifle • Nationality: UK • Calibre: .338 Lapua Magnum • Weight Unloaded: 6.8kg • Length: 1270mm • Magazine: 5

Accuracy International has led the field in precision sniper rifles for the special operations market for many years. They first began hand-manufacturing 7.62x51mm PM bolt action rifles for both the SBS and SAS, before winning the British Army contract for a new sniper rifle, the L96A1, in 1982. In the United States, Accuracy International rifles were also adopted by the likes of Delta, including in an integrally suppressed variant known as the Covert, and by many European counter-terrorist units.

Their Arctic Warfare Magnum rifle was a .338 Lapua Magnum calibre long range sniper rifle that was developed with input from UKSF. After several years of service with the SAS and SBS in Afghanistan and Iraq, the weapon was adopted by the wider British Army as the L115A3. It is also in service with a wide range of special operations units including the Czech 601st Special Forces Group, the Dutch Korps Commandotroepen (KCT), the Israeli Sayeret Matkal, Italy's Col Moschin, the Norwegian Special Operation Forces units, the Polish Grupa Reagowania Operacyjno Manewrowego (GROM) and even the Russian Spetsgruppa Alpha unit (Alpha may also be the source of a number of AWMs – Arctic Warfare Magnums – seen in use by Syrian Army Tiger Force).

The rifle is commonly equipped with a sound suppressor and is capable of precision fire to 1,500 metres although shots have been taken in Afghanistan at

A US Army Special Forces soldier fires a 40mm M320 in stand-alone mode. Note the grenade is visible on its way to the target. (Courtesy US Air Force, Airman 1st Class Jeff Parkinson)

The .338 Lapua Magnum AWM or L115A3 in British service. Note the user-adjustable stock and the massive muzzle brake used to tame the blast from the .338 round. (Courtesy Accuracy International)

even greater ranges. A modernized variant, the AXMC, is a multi-calibre design capable of firing the 7.62x51mm, the .300 Winchester Magnum and the .338 Lapua Magnum by employing a conversion kit that the individual sniper can use to swap calibres quickly (UKSF adopted the AXMC338 in 2014).

Barrett M82A1

Type: Anti-materiel Rifle • Nationality: US • Calibre: .50 BMG • Weight Unloaded: 13.5kg • Length: 1200mm • Magazine: 10

The Barrett M82A1 is the father of all modern anti-personnel rifles. First developed in 1982, among their first orders were the US Army Special Forces and Navy SEALs. The first known combat action for the Barrett was in Operation *Desert Storm* in 1991 although the SEALs planned an operation in Panama two years earlier that would have used the rifle to destroy Panamanian ruler Manuel Noriega's personal plane.

The US Marine Corps (USMC) also purchased the rifle just before *Desert Storm* and the weapon proved popular thanks to its outstanding range and destructive capabilities. During the 1990s, the Barrett was purchased in larger quantities by the US SOCOM and was issued to Army Ranger snipers along with the standard M24 and, during the late 1990s, the SR-25. It proved popular internationally and was procured by a wide range of units from the UK's 22SAS and the German GSG9 to the German KSK (as the G82) and the Dutch KCT.

It was eventually adopted by the US Army as the M107 and M107A1 and served extensively in both Iraq and Afghanistan. The weapon was also enthusiastically adopted by both military and police EOD teams as a means of safely disrupting a device from considerable distances. The longest-range known engagement by a Barrett was by Australian 2 Commando snipers in Helmand Province in 2012, hitting a Taliban insurgent at 2,815 metres.

There is a range of other anti-materiel rifles available, a number of which have served with SOF. The McMillan TAC-50 (also known as the Mk15 Mod0 in US service) is perhaps the best known. A sniper from Canada's JTF2 took a shot in Iraq with a TAC-50 (actually the Canadian issue variant, the C15) at the incredible range of 3,540 metres. Also common is the Accuracy International AW50F, which is known for its accuracy and has seen use with both Australian and British SOF.

A range of specialist .50 ammunition is available for anti-materiel rifles including the Raufoss Mk211 Mod0, which provides both an incendiary and light armour-piercing capability for snipers. The round includes both a tungsten steel penetrator and a small amount of high explosive packed in zirconium powder. When the round penetrates an armoured vehicle, for instance, the tungsten penetrator will go through the armour plate and five milliseconds later the incendiary component will ignite, sending burning fragments through the inside of the vehicle.

The .50 BMG Barrett M82A1 in service with the US military as the M107 SASR or Special Applications Scoped Rifle. (Courtesy US Army, Thomas Alverez)

Blaser R93 Tactical 2

Type: Sniper Rifle • Nationality: German • Calibre: .338 Lapua Magnum • Weight Unloaded: 5.8kg • Length: 1230mm • Magazine: 4

The German-made Blaser is a straight-pull bolt action design which speeds up chambering a new round and has less effect on the sight picture as the sniper does not have to work a bolt to lock it into place, instead just sliding the bolt back and forward to chamber a new round. It is available in a range of calibres but is most commonly encountered in .338 Lapua Magnum. The rifle is designed, however, to allow easy conversion to other calibres such as .300 Winchester Magnum or 7.62x51mm. In its .338 guise, the Blaser can strike targets in excess of 1,500 metres.

A sniper from Australia's 2 Commando Regiment maintains overwatch with his .338 Lapua Magnum Blaser R93 Tactical 2 sniper rifle in Afghanistan 2011. (Courtesy Commonwealth of Australia/ SOCOMD)

The weapon was originally designed for long range competition shooting but after SIG-Sauer purchased the Blaser's parent company, a sniper variant was developed. The rifle has seen significant combat in Afghanistan with Australian snipers from 2 Commando and SASR as well as being in service with the Danish Politiets Aktionsstyrke (AKS or Special Intervention Unit), the French BRI-BAC and the Ukrainian Counter Terrorism Squad-A.

.338 Lapua Magnum has proven increasingly popular with special operations snipers, particularly since the mid-2000s when the environment in southern Afghanistan often allowed shots to be taken at ranges exceeding the 800–1,000-metre range of most 7.62x51mm sniper rifles. The .338 offers a compromise between the power and range (and weight!) of the .50 and the accuracy of 7.62x51mm systems. A new calibre, the .338 Norma, is showing even more promise as a sniper and medium machine gun round, particularly as it reduces the excessive barrel wear associated with the .338 Lapua Magnum.

Colt Canada L119A1/A2 (C8 Special Forces Weapon)

Type: Assault Rifle • Nationality: Canadian • Calibre: 5.56x45mm • Weight Unloaded: 2.7kg • Length: 760/840mm • Magazine: 30 • Cyclic Rate: 900 RPM

Colt Canada (formerly Diemaco) makes a number of M4A1-based designs that equip several international units. UKSF use the Colt Canada L119A1 and L119A2 carbines while the C8SFW is employed by the Norwegian Forsvarets Spesialkommando (FSK) (although being replaced by the HK416) and Canada's JTF2 and CSOR. The New Zealand SAS also formerly used the C8SFW until it was recently replaced by the LMT MARS-L.

The 5.56x45mm Colt Canada L119A2 produced specifically for UK Special Forces. UKSF trialled a number of weapons but decided to keep the basic L119A1 (C8SFW) platform but upgrade it. (Courtesy Colt Canada)

22SAS adopted the weapon in 2000 to replace its ageing collection of M16A1s and Colt Carbines. The unit trialled a number of weapons including SIG 551s and the Heckler & Koch G36 but settled on the-then Diemaco C8SFW. Two separate upper receivers were supplied, one with a 254mm (10-inch) CQB barrel and one with a 398mm for the standard carbine. The British Army noted:

> The L119A1, C8 is a versatile 5.56mm assault rifle developed for the Special Forces with a range of 600m. It can also be assembled with a short barrelled upper receiver to make the [CQB] Carbine which can be used at up to 300m range. When fitted with a Picatinny rail hand guard it can be adapted for various uses with the addition of lasers, lights, UGLs, down grips, in fact almost anything with a Picatinny fitment. It is usually used in conjunction with the ACOG 4x optical sight or EOTech holographic sight.

UKSF were scheduled to begin trials in 2014 to replace the L119A1 Special Forces Individual Weapon (SFIW); however, it was felt that the rifle was the equal to all current contenders and instead an upgrade to the L119A2 was ordered. The L119A2 was supplied with two different upper receivers again offering both CQB and full length barrel configurations. The new weapons feature ambidextrous firing controls and a full length monolithic rail along the receiver and barrel amongst other improvements.

More recently the L119A2 has been seen in action carried by SAS assaulters in the UK during the response to the London Bridge, Manchester and Newcastle operations against Islamic State-inspired terrorists. It appears the Aimpoint Micro T2 has since been adopted, some in use with Aimpoint x3 magnifiers, which can be flipped to the side when not required. They are also often seen mated with Surefire suppressors.

Colt M4A1

Type: Assault Rifle • Nationality: US • Calibre: 5.56x45mm • Weight Unloaded: 3.6kg • Length: 757/838mm • Magazine: 30 • Cyclic Rate: 700–950 RPM

The M4A1 carbine is the primary weapon for the majority of American and allied special operators. Developed from the CAR-15 of Vietnam War fame, the carbine is a shortened version of the M16 assault rifle and unlike the original M4, it is capable of fully automatic fire (the M4 had instead a three-round burst setting).

Featuring a flat top receiver, the M4A1 allows the mounting of a wide range of optics to the receiver. It was additionally enhanced by the issue of the Special Operations Peculiar Modifications (SOPMOD) kit beginning in the late 1990s and first issued to US Army Special Forces ODAs. The SOPMOD kit contained a range of optics, vertical foregrips, and most importantly a rail adapter system, which replaced the hand guards on the barrel with Picatinny rails. Once fitted, weapon lights and infrared lasers could be added to the hand guard.

Many of the SOPMODs enhancements were later rolled out to the wider US Army while other SOCOM units received both the SOPMOD Block I and the SOPMOD Block II kits which added new thermal day/night sights and optics including the EOTech 553 and Trijicon ACOG. The SEALs were issued both kits whole, while the Rangers were issued a standard of elements so that each Ranger M4A1 was largely identical using the M68 Aimpoint red dot sight which had become the issue red dot sight for the US Army.

The SEALs also used a shortened version of the M4A1 called the Mk18 Close Quarter Battle Receiver (CQB-R), a replacement upper receiver that reduced the barrel length to just 262mm (10.3 inches), making it ideal for the SEAL primary mission of visit-board-search-seizure (VBSS).

US Navy SEALs on their range at Little Creek in 2007 firing the 5.56x45mm SOPMOD Block I M4A1 fitted with Knight's Armament QD suppressor and M68 Aimpoint optic. (Courtesy US Navy, Lt Cmdr Shawn Eklund)

Previously the SEALs had employed MP5s for such missions. The SEALs also developed a variant known as the Recce Rifle for their snipers, an M4-based design that incorporated a 406mm (16-inch) match grade barrel and was later formalized into the Mk12 Mod0 and Mod1.

The Rangers have since modified their M4A1s with SOPMOD Block II rails from Daniel Defense with both 368mm (14.5-inch) and 261mm (10.3-inch) barrels, the latter for use in close quarter battle and by dog handlers. They use a number of optics including the Elcan Specter which can be switched between a one-power CQB optic to a four-power magnified optic for longer ranges and the EOTech 553 holographic weapons sight with EOTech magnifier on a swing-out mount.

Concerns about the performance of the 5.56x45mm round from short barrelled carbines increased during the Iraq and Afghan wars. The problem stems from a reduction in velocity and accuracy from the shorter barrels. The short barrels also effected the potential for a round to yaw in the target, and thus increase lethality, rather than to punch straight through.

Several new bullet designs have largely alleviated the issue, with the heavier 77-grain Mk262 and the 62-grain Mk318 both seeing widespread and successful use. A specialist CQB round has also been developed – the Mk255 – which almost eliminates overpenetration, a key factor when firing within ships or with hostages in the vicinity.

A US Army Ranger at the range in Afghanistan 2014 firing his 5.56x45mm SOPMOD Block II M4A1 fitted with EOTech holographic weapon sight and M3X weapon light. (Courtesy US Army, Pfc Dacotah Lane)

Fabrique Nationale Minimi Para

Type: Light Machine Gun • Nationality: Belgian • Calibre: 5.56x45mm • Weight Unloaded: 6.5kg • Length: 914/766mm • Magazine: 50/100/200 • Cyclic Rate: 800 RPM

The Minimi, or M249 as it is known in US service, has been the most successful post-war light machine gun design. Firing the 5.56x45mm round, the Minimi is a lightweight and handy source of suppressive fire feeding from box magazines that can hold up to 200 rounds. The Para variant typically used by SOF has a shortened barrel and collapsible stock making it ideal for operations in urban terrain.

With its standard length barrel, its effective range is around the 400-metre mark; with the shortened Para barrel, that range is effectively halved. It has also been criticized by some for its lamentable accuracy beyond short range with groupings expanding dramatically. This has led to its retirement from the British Army although it is probably still in UKSF armouries. US SOF have developed their own version of the weapon in the form of the Mk46 Mod0 and Mk46 Mod1, the latter in service with the US Navy SEALs. The Mk46 weighs a quarter of a kilogram less than the Para and features multiple Picatinny rails for mounting lights, infrared lasers and vertical grips.

A 7.62x51mm variant was also produced at the urging of the United States' SOCOM. The Mk48 is obviously larger and heavier than the Mk46 but it offers the increased range and ballistic effects of the 7.62x51mm. It has been adopted by both UK and Australian SOF (where it is known

A US Navy SEAL carrying the 5.56x45mm Mk46 Mk1 variant of the Minimi, pictured in 2010. Note the shortened barrel, ATPIAL (AN/PEQ-15) laser and vertical foregrip. (Courtesy US Navy, Mass Communication Specialist 2nd Class John Scorza)

simply as the 'Maximi') along with the majority of SOCOM units including the Rangers. Fabrique Nationale currently markets a similar modernized version as the Minimi 7.62 Mk3. The Polish GROM and the Belgian SFG currently field the Mk3.

The Minimi has often been employed during aerial vehicle interdiction missions as it can deliver a large number of rounds into a target's engine block, or should it fail to comply, the vehicle itself. It is also a favourite of SOF teams deployed as cut-off or cordon groups around a targeted compound as it can provide, within its noted range limitations, a very effective beaten zone to dissuade insurgents until mortars or air assets can be employed.

Fabrique Nationale P90

Type: Personal Defence Weapon • Nationality: Belgian • Calibre: 5.7x28mm • Weight Unloaded: 2.68kg • Length: 500mm • Magazine: 50 • Cyclic Rate: 900 RPM

The P90, like the Heckler & Koch MP7, is a product of the NATO Personal Defence Weapon trials of the late 1980s and early 1990s. It fires a 5.7x28mm round at impressively high velocities and is able to penetrate Level IIIA soft armour and most ballistic helmets as it was designed to be used by non-frontline personnel against Soviet infantry. It will not, however, penetrate a modern SAPI (Small Arms Protective Insert) or similar trauma plate.

The weapon has negligible recoil making it very easy to shoot, is supremely compact and fires from an unusual helical 50-round translucent magazine mounted over the stock. Its Picatinny rails mean that the normal range of accessories such as lights and lasers can be fitted. With a sound suppressor and subsonic ammunition, the weapon is very quiet indeed.

In its suppressed form, it has found favour with a number of SOF units around the world, most prominently the Belgian Directorate of Special Units (DSU) and Belgian Army SFG, the French GIGN and RAID and the Italian Col Moschin although its first operational use appears to have been with Peruvian naval commandos when they retook the Japanese ambassador's residence in 1996. It is commonly employed by lead scouts as they require a handy weapon that can provide a high level of firepower. It has also been adopted by a number of units specifically for close personal protection, another role where its short overall length and high firepower is an advantage.

A combat swimmer from the Austrian Jagdkommando (Army Special Operations Task Group) which has served in Afghanistan and Mali. He is armed with the Fabrique Nationale P90 fitted with Aimpoint optic. (Dieter Nagl/AFP/Getty Images)

The calibre itself is still largely unproved as there are few actual shooting reports to draw upon. Fabrique Nationale also issued a pistol in the same calibre, the Five-seven, which is also considered to be very light in the recoil department and holds an impressive 20 rounds. The Five-seven has been seen in use by the Belgian DSU although the Glock still dominates.

Fabrique Nationale SCAR-H (Mk17)

Type: Battle Rifle • Nationality: Belgian • Calibre: 7.62x51mm • Weight Unloaded: 3.59kg • Length: 711mm/901mm • Magazine: 20 • Cyclic Rate: 625 RPM

The Special Operations Forces Combat Assault Rifle or SCAR was developed by Fabrique Nationale at the request of the United States' SOCOM, which was looking to replace its M4A1 carbines in the mid-2000s. A modular weapon system that could be used in a range of both calibres and roles was required. The SCAR family was initially procured in a number of these variants.

The 5.56x45mm Mk16, also known as the SCAR-L, was purchased as a direct replacement for the M4A1; the 7.62x51mm Mk17 or SCAR-H was expected to replace the numerous designated marksman rifles in service with SOCOM units while also serving as a sniper weapon in the form of the 7.62x51mm Mk20. Initial field testing by Army Rangers in Afghanistan did not highlight enough of an evolutionary improvement from their M4A1s to justify the procurement and the Mk16 was cancelled.

MultiCam clad operators from the Belgian Special Forces Group carrying 5.56x45mm SCAR-L (Mk16) rifles mounted with suppressors (the suppressors are fitted with Manta suppressor covers to reduce heat), vertical foregrips, lights and infrared lasers. The optic appears to be the Aimpoint T-1 Micro. (Olivier Matthys/Getty Images)

The Mk17 was well liked and offered a capability in between the M4A1 and marksman rifles like the SR-25 and M110. It has since been adopted by all SOCOM units and is typically seen with Special Forces ODAs and SEAL platoons with one or two Mk17s complementing the majority M4A1s. A small number of the 5.56x45mm Mk16s remain in service with the SEALs, who also widely employ the 7.62x51mm variants including the Mk20 Sniper Support Rifle.

A new sub-compact variant, the suppressor-ready SCAR-SC, has been developed in both 5.56x45mm and .300 Blackout with an overall length of just 536mm (21 inches) with the stock retracted. As more units adopt suppressed .300 Blackout platforms to replace their suppressed sub machine guns, the SCAR-SC will be another contender. It is perhaps instructive to note, however, that none of the special mission units like SEAL Team 6 or Delta Force have deployed with any variant of the SCAR family.

Users currently include Belgium's Directorate of Special Units (DSU) intervention unit, the Belgian Army SFG, France's GIGN and a number of French Army and Navy Special Forces units.

Glock 17

Type: Pistol • Nationality: Austrian • Calibre: 9x19mm • Weight Unloaded: 625g • Length: 186mm • Magazine: 17

The 9mm Glock 17 has become the most widely employed pistol by both military and police special operators the world over. Originally the polymer-based pistol was developed for an Austrian Army trial to identify a suitable replacement for its ageing Walther P38s. The Glock, designed by a man with no previous firearms experience and more at home designing curtain rails, unexpectedly won. Adopted by the Austrian Army as the Pistole 80, the Glock was slowly procured for a number of European counter-terrorist units but large-scale military adoption eluded it.

During the 1980s and at the height of international terrorism, Glock suffered from a number of hysterical newspaper reports, claiming that the 'plastic pistol' could evade airport X-ray scanners. A number were even allegedly purchased by Colonel Gaddafi of Libya for terrorist groups that he sponsored. The truth of course is that the Glock is just as visible to X-rays as any other pistol.

Instead the pistol became incredibly popular with US law enforcement, later riding the wave of the .40 Smith & Wesson, which was becoming the calibre of choice for US police (Glock had introduced the Model 22 and 23 to capitalize on the popularity of the round). Influential special operations units like the French GIGN and eventually Germany's GSG9 adopted the 9mm version, replacing a range of .38 Special and .357 Magnum revolvers and 9mm Heckler & Koch pistols.

A US Army Ranger aims his AAC suppressed Glock 17 on an operation in Helmand Province, Afghanistan, 2012. Note the lanyard connecting the pistol to his belt kit and that he also carries an Mk17 SCAR as his primary weapon. (Courtesy Department of Defense, US Army Spc Justin Young)

Its first US military use was in the hands of Delta Force, which began to supplement its custom Caspian .45ACP pistols with the Glock in the late 1990s. By the time of the Iraq insurgency, Delta was employing STI 1911 designs in both .45ACP and .40 Smith & Wesson along with Glock 22s in .40 Smith & Wesson. Eventually the STI guns were dropped largely owing to magazine-induced stoppages and the Glock 22 was retired as, with the tremendous number of rounds fired by Delta operators, the guns were literally falling apart under the strain.

The 9mm Glock replaced the STIs and Glock 22s in a number of models including the Model 34 designed originally for sporting use. The compact Glock 19 version is also commonly employed by Delta. Other US military special operators began to migrate to the Glock 19 and today it is the standard pistol for SOCOM units including Marine Special Operations Command (MARSOC) and Army Special Forces (although a number of SFGs had already made unit purchases of Glocks for use in Iraq). A recent contract will see all SOCOM Glocks modified with mini red dot sights, weapon lights and threaded barrels for suppressors, mimicking the Glocks that Delta carries.

French special operators have long preferred the Glock and special versions designed to operate after being submerged under water are used by Commando Hubert. GSG9 combat swimmers use a similar version. The US Army Rangers have used both the .40 Smith & Wesson and 9mm versions with suppressors and the Austrian pistol remains the standard Ranger sidearm. UKSF and the SEALs adopted the Glock 19 in recent years, replacing their well-worn SIG-Sauer P226s. The Glock is even used by Russian counter-terrorist forces.

A number of intriguing variants exist. The Glock Model 18 is a fully-automatic version which feeds from an extended 33-round magazine but has seen little commercial success. One was recovered with Saddam Hussein by Delta Force and presented to former President George W. Bush. A number of sub-compact designs have also been developed for deep concealment including the 9mm Glock 26 and .40 Smith & Wesson Glock 27. A Glock narrowly lost the competition for the US military's Modular Handgun System with its Glock 19X entrant, a hybrid featuring the frame of a Glock 17 and the slide of a Glock 19.

Heckler & Koch 416

Type: Assault Rifle • Nationality: German • Calibre: 5.56x45mm • Weight Unloaded: 4.11kg • Length: 900/804mm (with 14.5-inch barrel) • Magazine: 30 • Cyclic Rate: 850 RPM

The HK416 was designed for the US Army's special mission unit, Delta Force, which was looking for ways to improve the performance of its M4A1 carbines, particularly in increasing reliability after extended firing and with the use of suppressors. Heckler & Koch and the Unit worked together to develop specifications for what was initially termed the HK M4. The name was changed to the 416 when Colt issued a lawsuit over the M4 trademark.

The 416 differs from the M4 and M4A1 in that it uses a short stroke gas piston action that reduces the amount of carbon build-up in the weapon's action. Initial testing at Delta was positive, including a 15,000-round torture test with zero stoppages, and the first batch from the production line was sent to Iraq with a Delta squadron in 2004.

Field reports were equally positive and the Unit transitioned to the 416 as its primary assault rifle. Both the original 10-inch barrel and 14.5-inch barrel were employed, dependent on task. Both were often utilized with a sound suppressor. During the early years of the Iraqi insurgency, Delta typically used EOTech holographic weapons sights and a custom-designed vertical foregrip, manufactured by KAC, which featured buttons to activate attached weapons lights and infrared lasers. Later the Schmidt & Bender CQB Short Dot optic was adopted after the scope was developed in conjunction with Delta.

An operator from France's 3e RPIMA carrying a 5.56x45mm HK416A5. The HK416 has been selected to replace the FAMAS as the standard issue rifle for French forces but variants of the weapon have been in use by both French military SOF and units such as GIGN for a number of years, being used in Afghanistan, Mali, Iraq, Libya and Syria. This example is fitted with an EOTech holographic weapon site and a x3 power magnifier that can be flipped to the side when engaging close-range targets. (Ludovic Marin/AFP/Getty Images)

The Navy's special mission unit, Naval Special Warfare Development Group, more commonly known as SEAL Team 6, also adopted the 416 and the rifle was famously responsible for the shots which ended the life of Usama bin Laden. Many other special operations units have procured the weapon in the years since Delta's first adoption. These include the German Army's KSK with the HK416A7, which replaced their G36Ks, known as the G95 in Bundeswehr service; Poland's GROM, which replaced its Bushmaster M4s with the 416 (including KAC vertical foregrips as GROM has close ties to Delta); and the majority of French Army and Naval special operations units. Australian SOCOMD purchased a number for the Tactical Assault Group – East but is in the process of retiring them as it has experienced difficulty sourcing replacement barrels.

The 416 was included in the US Army's Individual Carbine competition for a replacement for the issue M4 and M4A1 carbines. The Heckler & Koch weapon performed admirably with as few as a quarter of the stoppages of the M4A1 but the procurement programme was cancelled before a winner was announced. Other nations' armies have adopted the weapon, including the French as the HK416F and the Norwegians as the HK416N.

A compact version known as the HK416C was developed to compete in UKSF trials in 2010 for a new compact carbine known as the Ultra Compact Individual Weapon, which required a 5.56x45mm carbine no longer than 558mm (22 inches) in overall length. Unfortunately the 416C was not adopted and the LWRC M6A2 was eventually procured. The 416 has been continuously improved from user feedback and the current range now sports the latest variants the HK416A5 and A7. Both are available in a range of barrel lengths. A .300 Blackout variant named the HK337 has been introduced, likely as competition against the SIG-Sauer MCX.

Heckler & Koch 417

Type: Battle Rifle • Nationality: German • Calibre: 7.62x51mm • Weight Unloaded: 4.45kg • Length: 905/985mm • Magazine: 20 • Cyclic Rate: 600 RPM

In the mid-2000s, a 7.62x51mm version of the HK416 was introduced, the HK417. Based on the AR-10 but using the gas piston of the 416 family, the 417 was intended both as a battle rifle for units requiring the penetration of the 7.62x51mm, and as a marksman's rifle to equip snipers. It was the first rifle from Heckler & Koch built from the ground up to incorporate the use of a sound suppressor with a simple gas block to improve reliability during suppressed firing. Three models were initially offered with differing barrel lengths for specific roles. Unusually, the 417 also features a fully automatic selector setting.

Surprisingly, the 417 was never adopted by Delta, which continued to use its custom-honed SR-25s, but saw widespread use by many other special operations units including UKSF, the Australian SASR and Commandos, Germany's KSK, Ireland's Army Ranger Wing (ARW) and SEAL Team 6 (although SEAL Team 6 is apparently currently replacing its 417s with the Wilson Combat Super Sniper based on the AR-10 platform). The Spanish Grupos de Operaciones Especiales (GEO) has purchased a number of the 12-inch (305mm) barrel variants for their assaulters who may face terrorists wearing body armour. The French GIGN faced a similar quandary after the Bataclan siege in 2015 and adopted the Czech CZ806 Bren 2 in 7.62x39 as it exhibited lower recoil characteristics.

The 417 has been extensively trialled with the 6.5mm Creedmoor, which has been adopted by the US SOCOM as its new intermediate sniper calibre, with the new 6.5mm 417 called the M110A1 or Compact Semi-Automatic Sniper System (CSASS) in SOCOM service. Perhaps the most surprising user has been Russian special operators including Komandovanie sil spetsial'nalnykh operatsii (KSSO), Alfa and Vympel who employ the civilian semi-automatic variants of both the 416 and 417: the MR556 and MR762 respectively.

An Australian SASR sniper fires his 7.62x51mm HK417 fitted with a Schmidt & Bender/Accuracy International variable power scope. (Courtesy Commonwealth of Australia)

Heckler & Koch G36

Type: Assault Rifle • Nationality: German • Calibre: 5.56x45mm • Weight Unloaded: 3.3kg • Length: 615mm/860mm (K) • Magazine: 30 • Cyclic Rate: 750 RPM

The Heckler & Koch G36 was designed to replace the German Army G3 as its standard service rifle after the promising caseless G11 concept was scrapped owing to funding difficulties. The G36 is a largely polymer-based design and in its standard version includes an integrated magnified optic and red dot sight in the carrying handle.

The most common models of the G36 seen in the hands of special operators is the G36K and G36C, both shortened versions which are offered with flat top receivers mounting a Picatinny rail for optics and side folding stocks. The G36C is the shortest, measuring just 500mm with the stock folded, while the G36K measures in at 615mm with stock folded.

Along with German Army, Air Force and Navy special operators, variants of the G36 are employed by GSG9 and most German police tactical units. It was widely procured by European counter-terrorist units including the French GIGN, the Italian Nucleo Operativo Centrale di Sicurezza (NOCS) and the Spanish Naval Unidad de Operaciones Especiales (UOE). It was also adopted by a large number of armies as their principal individual weapon including Spain, Lithuania and Saudi Arabia.

French RAID operators with their 5.56x45mm G36C assault rifles fitted with EOTech holographic weapon sights. (Kenzo Tribouillard/AFP/Getty Images)

Some controversy has recently dogged the G36 with allegations of the weapon suffering stoppages and seizing up during a protracted firefight in Afghanistan. Like the M4, any rifle will be degraded by firing excessively – in this case some examples had six magazines fired through as quickly as possible. It appears much of the controversy was actually politically driven.

Today the G36 series is being replaced in the German Army's KSK and Navy Kommando Spezialkräfte Marine (KSM) service by an HK416A7 variant called the G95. Within France's GIGN, the G36 has largely been superseded by the HK416 and the 7.62x39mm CZ806 Bren 2, a weapon that was procured after the November 2015 Paris terrorist attacks to counter-terrorists wearing body armour, although the French RAID continues to use the G36 as its primary assault rifle. Germany's GSG9 has also adopted the HK416 although it continues to field examples of the G36C, particularly versions equipped with special stocks to allow the use of ballistic helmets with face shields.

Heckler & Koch M320

Type: Grenade Launcher • Nationality: US • Calibre: 40mm • Weight Unloaded: 1.5kg • Length: 350mm • Magazine: Single Shot

The Heckler & Koch M320 is the US military's version of the German 40mm AG36, a single shot underbarrel grenade launcher that has largely replaced the M203 in SOCOM use. The primary advantage of the M320/AG36 is its swing out design, allowing longer 40mm rounds to be chambered to take advantage of medium velocity designs that offer far greater range.

The weapon can be employed with its own detachable shoulder stock as a stand-alone launcher and is widely employed in this guise by US SOCOM units; in fact the Rangers are one of the few units which typically employ it as an underbarrel launcher. Accuracy is reportedly greater as a stand-alone and it allows the launcher to be easily swapped out amongst teammates. Specialist holsters have even been designed to carry the weapon in stand-alone mode.

Other grenade launchers are employed, although the M320/AG36 and other variants produced by Heckler & Koch are the most widely encountered. The British SAS and SBS for example use the L17A1, the British Army name for the AG-C compact launcher, under the barrels of their L119A1 and A2 carbines.

The Heckler & Koch HK69A1 is also still encountered – a break-open stand-alone design, it is often seen fielded by European counter-terrorist units. Even the venerable M79 of Vietnam fame makes the occasional appearance. US Army Special Forces and Navy SEALs during the Iraq insurgency favoured the M79 thanks to its superior accuracy over the M203. It is used by SEAL Team 6 in a vastly modified form based on models used by

A superb close-up of the 40mm M320 based on the Heckler & Koch AG36. Note the large external safety, folding foregrip and collapsible stock. (Courtesy US Army)

MACV-SOG (Military Assistance Command Vietnam – Studies & Observations Group): the 'Pirate Gun', an M79 with its barrel cut back and stock sawn off, turning it into something approaching the appearance of a pirate's matchlock, hence its name.

Multi-shot launchers also abound, with SOCOM adopting the M32 and M32A1 based on the South African Armscorp/Milkor MGL-6 model. The M32 series looks like an oversized revolver with a forward grip and M4-style stock. It can deliver six 40mm grenades in seconds out to a range of more than 100 metres. Russian special operations units have fielded a similar design, the RG-6.

The Russians more commonly use the GM-94, a three-round pump action design. Naval Spetsnaz also deploys the unique DP-64, an over-and-under-style design that launches grenades specifically designed to counter enemy SCUBA divers; the SG-45 signal grenade is designed to mark the swimmer's location and the FG-45 fragmentation grenade to destroy the swimmer.

Heckler & Koch MP5

Type: Sub Machine Gun • Nationality: German • Calibre: 9x19mm • Weight Unloaded: 3.1kg • Length: 690/550mm (A3) • Magazine: 30 • Cyclic Rate: 800 RPM

The MP5 is, alongside the Israeli UZI, perhaps the most recognizable sub machine gun design in the world today. For many, the first exposure to the MP5 was during televised news reporting from the Iranian Embassy siege in London in 1980. Black-clad assaulters from B Squadron 22SAS dramatically used frame charges to blow in windows, all the while carrying the MP5, a hitherto little-known 9mm sub machine gun that was already in the armouries of units such as Germany's GSG9 and the US Delta Force.

The MP5 had been developed in the 1960s, initially for a German Army requirement to replace its issue UZIs, known as the MP2. The MP5 was first adopted by GSG9; the weapon's effectiveness was highlighted to the UK's 22SAS during GSG9's 1977 takedown of the hijacked Lufthansa Flight 181 (see page 90) and it was soon standard issue for the 22SAS Pagoda counter-terrorist teams. Previously they had been using the open bolt 9mm Ingram Model 10, which was far from a precision weapon.

The MP5A2 and later MP5A3 adopted by the British SAS fired from a closed bolt meaning that the action of the weapon did not move when first fired, adding to the accuracy. In simple terms, the round is already seated, the bolt forward, and the only action required to fire that first round is to engage the firing pin with the trigger. In open bolt weapons, the bolt slams forward, chambering and firing the first round in the same action.

The early versions of the MP5 featured a straight magazine rather than today's more familiar curve. The magazine was modified following feedback

A rare MP5K, in its purpose-designed briefcase enabling the weapon to be fired from within, recovered from one of Saddam Hussein's palaces in April 2003. (Mario Tama/Getty Images)

French naval commandos from Commando Montfort display a selection of MP5s including an MP5K (figure 1), an MP5 PDW (figure 2) and an MP5A3 fitted with a B&T stock for use with ballistic visors (figure 3). Note also the Glock 17 in Hera Arms carbine kit allowing the mounting of an EOTech and folding foregrip along with sound suppressor (figure 4). (Frank Perry/AFP/Getty Images)

from GSG9 to improve the feeding reliability of hollowpoints and specialist 9mm rounds like the armour-piercing THV. Other improvements were made and soon specialized variants became available, often developed to the specifications of end users like GSG9.

An integrally suppressed MP5 was manufactured which reduced the sound from the weapon's report, slowing the velocity of the 9mm bullet to subsonic levels and thus eliminating the telltale crack of the bullet breaking the sound barrier. This variant, the SD or Schalldämpfer, was produced in several core types; the SD1 with no stock, the SD2 with a fixed plastic stock, and the SD3 with a collapsible stock. Further variations were added with different trigger groups including one designed for the Navy SEALs, which added a three-round burst option. Interestingly enough, the SD also made its British SAS debut at the Iranian Embassy in 1980.

The other major variant was the K or Kurz indicating the shortened version. The MP5K in its original configuration was only 325mm (12.8 in) in total length and was available with a shoulder holster system to carry the weapon under a coat. A briefcase firing device was also produced, allowing the MP5K to be fired from within – very James Bond! Further variants were produced including the KA1 which dispensed with the standard sights to reduce any snag as the weapon was being presented. The MP5K is still occasionally encountered today in the hands of special operators conducting close personal protection duties.

The MP5 was enthusiastically received by all branches of the US military's special operations community and a Navy-led project was established to develop the next generation of the MP5. These included SMG II its later iteration, the MP2000. The SMG II was an attempt to produce a modular weapon that could fulfil the roles of the standard MP5, the SD and the K, all in one package. The SEALs decided to stay with their existing MP5 stocks, while only one unit – Delta – had around 60 SMG IIs produced by Heckler & Koch. These were issued and used in service until the late 1990s when Delta transitioned across to 5.56mm carbines for the counter-terrorist role.

Heckler & Koch MP7A1

Type: Sub Machine Gun • Nationality: German • Calibre: 4.6x30mm • Weight Unloaded: 1.9kg • Length: 380mm/590mm • Magazine: 20, 30, 40 • Cyclic Rate: 950 RPM

The Heckler & Koch MP7A1 was developed as a PDW or personal defence weapon for NATO requirements in the late 1980s. The idea of the PDW was to equip non-frontline troops with a light, handy weapon that they could use to defend themselves and that offered greater range than a pistol. A key requirement was for the PDW to be able to penetrate then-Soviet helmets and body armour.

The PDW concept, and funding, eventually ground to a halt. The MP7A1 emerged from the trials where it competed against the Fabrique Nationale P90 and was marketed as the replacement for the MP5. It unfortunately found few takers, particularly owing to the expense and short track record of its 4.6x30mm calibre.

The MP7A1 did, however, find a niche with SEAL Team 6 as a suppressed CQB (close quarter battle) weapon to replace its older MP5SD series of integrally suppressed sub machine guns. The SEALs employed the MP7A1 widely in Afghanistan using it to equip both dog handlers and the breaching

A German SEK (Spezial Einsatzkommando or Special Deployment Commando) operator carries a 4.6x30mm MP7A1 fitted with EOTech sight and B&T stock. (picture alliance/dpa/Sven Hoppe)

teams who stealthily entered insurgent compounds. The noise levels produced by the MP7A1 were even lower than the 'industry standard' of the MP5SD using subsonic rounds.

Where the MP7A1 fell down was its limited range. If the SEALs engaged in a longer range firefight, the MP7A1 was close to worthless, having an effective range of around 200 metres at best. The lethality of the round itself was also open to question with SEALs emptying magazines into adversaries to ensure a lethal effect.

The SEALs looked to a new calibre, the .300 Blackout, and firstly to the AAC Honey Badger, an integrally suppressed carbine, before settling on the SIG-Sauer MCX Black Mamba, which was adopted by both SEAL Team 6 and Delta Force as the low visibility assault weapon. The advantage of the .300 Blackout is that it can be used with subsonic loads for close range engagements and, with the switch of a magazine, swap to supersonic loads which are effective out to 400 metres.

The MP7A1 was also adopted by a number of European counter-terrorist units including France's GIGN and Germany's GSG9, although typically for close personal protection duties. It is also used by the German Army's KSK special operations unit, often with a suppressor, and the weapon remains as standard issue to the German Army as a PDW.

Heckler & Koch PSG1

Type: Sniper Rifle • Nationality: German • Calibre: 7.62x51mm • Weight Unloaded: 8.1kg • Length: 1208mm • Magazine: 5/20

In the aftermath of the Munich massacre in 1972 (see page 88), two sniper rifles were developed with the police or counter-terrorist sniper distinctly in mind, the bolt action Mauser SP66 and the semi-automatic PSG1. The PSG1 was revolutionary – although based on the tried and true G3 action, it incorporated a free-floating barrel (meaning the barrel does not touch the forward hand guard to eliminate minute vibrations), a user adjustable stock and a specialist tripod that acted as a stabilizer, resulting in phenomenal accuracy.

It and/or the SP66 was adopted by the majority of Western counter-terrorist units in the 1970s including the German GSG9 and the UK's 22SAS, specifically for the urban counter-terrorist role. The weapon was far too fragile (and heavy) for conventional warfighting. One of the few complaints about the PSG1 was that it was solely designed to use the Hensoldt 6x42 scope; no other could be fitted. The updated PSG1A1 was introduced in the mid-2000s with a side folding stock, relocated charging handle and a new standard Schmidt & Bender optic, along with the provision of a B&T custom suppressor.

A lighter and more robust version was also introduced in the form of the MSG90 and later MSG90A1 and A2 iterations (both of which added a Picatinny rail for the optics). The original MSG90 featured the more common at the time Weaver rail (this was the most common form of mounting system before the development of the Picatinny rail) and was threaded for use with a suppressor (it also featured a patented silent bolt closing device). It was also significantly cheaper than the PSG1 and was adopted by many European counter-terrorist units as a supplement or replacement for the PSG1.

Another G3-based rifle which saw some use in SOF was the G3SG/1, a G3 with a new trigger (that incorporated the provision of altering the trigger pull without recourse to an armourer), a fixed Zeiss optic and an integral bipod that folded into the hand guard. The rifle was adopted by SEAL Team 6 and used during operations in Grenada in 1983.

A GSG9 sniper in 2015 armed with the 7.62x51mm MSG90, the updated and more robust modern version of the iconic PSG1. (John Macdougall/AFP/Getty Images)

Heckler & Koch USP

Type: Pistol • Nationality: German • Calibre: 9x19mm • Weight Unloaded: 720g • Length: 194mm • Magazine: 15

An excellent view of the .45ACP Mk23 Mod0 in the hands of a US Navy SEAL. This example is fitted with the laser aiming module and Knight's Armament Company suppressor. (Greg Mathieson/Mai/Mai/The LIFE Images Collection/Getty Images)

The USP, or universal self-loading pistol, was introduced by Heckler & Koch to provide a modern alternative to its classic designs like the P9 and P7 and to offer a pistol in the then-popular .40 Smith & Wesson, a relatively new cartridge that was finding much popularity in American law enforcement. The USP, first sold in 1993, can be fired either single- or double-action and features a de-cocking lever which acts as an external safety, although there are now more than a dozen variants available with the user's selection of action and safety.

The USP formed the basis of the design for the .45ACP Mk23 Mod0 'Offensive Handgun Weapons System – Special Operations Peculiar' which was developed for a US SOCOM contract, complete with laser and light module and Knight's Armament suppressor. The Mk23, while impressively accurate and reliable, was heavy and overly large. It was appreciated by the SEALs, who conducted operations with submersibles and in SCUBA, as the weapon was optimized for reliability in maritime environments.

The USP Tactical was designed as a more manageable Mk23 alternative, aiming at the military SOF market. Initially offered in .45ACP, 9x19mm and .40 Smith &Wesson versions were added to the line. The Tactical was developed using the best features of both the USP and Mk23 and threaded for a suppressor. The USP Compact is also available in 9x19mm, .40 Smith & Wesson and .45ACP.

The most recent additions to the family are the .45ACP HK45 and HK45 Compact. The HK45C has been adopted by the SEALs as the Mk24 Mod0 Combat Assault Pistol and is used as their preferred suppressed pistol as the .45ACP round is subsonic. The USP Tactical has been adopted by all Australian SOF including the two Tactical Assault Groups, as well as the French 1er Régiment de Parachutistes d'Infanterie de Marine (1er RPIMa) and the German KSK (in suppressed .45ACP form as the P12).

Israeli Weapon Industries Tavor

Type: Assault Rifle • Nationality: Israeli • Calibre: 5.56x45mm • Weight Unloaded: 3.3kg • Length: 725mm • Magazine: 30 • Cyclic Rate: 700 RPM

The bullpup (meaning the magazine is located behind the pistol grip to reduce overall length) Tavor family of assault rifles was initially developed as the TAR-21, with the intention of replacing the range of Galils, M16A1s, Colt Carbines and M4A1s used by the Israeli Defence Force (IDF), and officially became its new service weapon in 2006. It had been trialled by numerous Israeli SOF and although the designers of the Tavor had copied the placement of the M4A1 selector settings to ease training on the weapon, by and large the SOF stayed with their tried and true M4A1s, particularly thanks to the large number of accessories available for the Colt pattern rifle.

The CTAR-21, a compact variant, was developed at the behest of SOF and found more favour. The CTAR was 85mm shorter and threaded for a sound suppressor. A third version, the MTAR or Micro Tavor, now known as the X-95, finally found its place with Sayeret Matkal. It was only 590mm long and weighed just under 3 kilograms, incorporating all of the best features of the M4A1 and the TAR-21. It is now commonly seen fitted with a suppressor and a range of close combat optics (but typically the Mepro MOR that cleverly incorporates both a red dot optic and a visible/infrared laser illuminator). It has since become the standard assault rifle of the Israeli Army.

The 5.56x45mm TAR-21 Tavor fitted with Meprolight M21 reflex sight. (Courtesy US Army, Staff Sgt Samuel Northrup)

Along with the Israeli special units, the Tavor family is in use with various Colombian SOF, the Indian Marine Commandos (MARCOS), the Mexican Police Grupo de Operaciones Especiales (GOPES) and the Portuguese Grupo de Operações Especiais (GOE). A recent development by IWI is a 12-gauge bullpup variant of the Tavor, the TS12. Uniquely the shotgun feeds from three rotating magazine tubes, giving it a 15-round capacity. It will be interesting to see if the semi-automatic TS12 makes its way into the hands of Israeli special operators in the near future.

Kalashnikov Concern AK-103

Type: Assault Rifle • Nationality: Russian • Calibre: 7.62x39mm • Weight Unloaded: 3.8kg • Length: 943/705mm • Magazine: 30 • Cyclic Rate: 600 RPM

Russian OMON operators pictured in 2018 – the centre operator carries the 7.62x39mm AK-74M. The operator to the left appears to carry the 9x19mm PP-19-01 Vityaz sub machine gun whilst the lead operator uses the Vant-VM ballistic shield. (Alexander Ryumin/TASS via Getty Images)

The AK-103 is the modern variant of the AK-74M rechambered for the older 7.62x39mm round. Specifically designed for export, it uses black plastic furniture to reduce weight. It is also offered as the AK-101 in 5.56x45mm and the AK-105 in 5.45x39mm. The AK-103 is employed by a number of SOF units globally, including the Pakistani Special Service Group (SSG) and Saudi Special Forces. Iranian Special Forces (and likely Quds Force) have also received the AK-103. The original AK-74M still soldiers on in 5.45x39mm and is standard issue to most of Russia's Spetsnaz units, although this is reportedly soon to change.

The AK-12 (fitted with an unusual two-round burst setting) and AK-15 are being introduced to replace the AK-74M in general service while the Degtyarev A-545 in 5.45x39mm and the A-762 in 7.62x39mm are being procured for all Spetsnaz and similar special designation units. The A-545 and A-762 are both

thoroughly modern updates to the classic Kalashnikov design featuring an ambidextrous Heckler & Koch-style fire selector, Picatinny rails and an improved flash suppressor.

Another AK design, the AK-308, has recently been unveiled. This is another model aimed at export markets that may find its way into the hands of some SOF. As the name suggests, it is chambered for 7.62x51mm NATO and has the appearance of an AK-103 but is built from a design based on the frame of the RPK light machine gun for durability with the heavier recoiling round.

The RPK-74, now largely eclipsed by the PKP Pecheneg (an upgraded PKM) in Russian SOF use, is being replaced by the RPK-16, a brand new design that shaves weight and length from the RPK-74 and modernizes the design with Picatinny mounts (including a rail mounted bipod), two barrel lengths in a similar manner to the Minimi, and the provision of a sound suppressor.

Knight's Armament Company SR-25

Type: Marksman Rifle • Nationality: US • Calibre: 7.62x51mm • Weight Unloaded: 4.9kg • Length: 1158mm • Magazine: 20

The Knight's Armament Company SR-25 was the first widely successful 7.62x51mm marksman rifle issued to US SOCOM units and to allied units around the world. Prior to the introduction of the SR-25 in the 1990s, teams requiring a precision semi-automatic 7.62x51mm rifle were limited to the Heckler & Koch G3/SG1 and PSG1 family, both excellent rifles but heavy and, in the PSG1's case, not durable enough for military combat use.

A US Army Ranger sniper fires the 7.62x51mm M110 Semi-Automatic Sniper System, a variant of the original SR-25. (Courtesy Michael Bottoms, USSOCOM Office of Communication)

The 7.62x51mm M110 Semi-Automatic Sniper System. (Courtesy US Army, Thomas Alverez)

The SR-25 was developed partly at the behest of Delta Force, which had realized the need for a 7.62x51mm rifle during Operation *Desert Storm* when it was forced to rely upon a number of scoped M14s. The basic SR-25 platform went through innumerable modifications based on feedback from Delta, including a shortened version that was known as the SR-25K. Many of the weapons still used by Delta are 'Frankenstein' creations with numerous modifications and improvements created by Knight's specifically for the unit.

The rifle was type-classified as the Mk11 in US service and was issued to all SOCOM units including the Rangers. Australian Commandos also carried early SR-25s when they deployed to East Timor in 1999; however, the combat debut for US forces was Afghanistan in 2001 where Delta Force carried the SR-25 into the mountains of Tora Bora (along with one operator who preferred his HK21 medium machine gun). The SEALs including Team 6 and Army Special Forces also employed the SR-25 along with the Australian SASR.

The success of the SR-25 and Mk11 saw the weapon adopted by the wider US Army as the M110 Semi-Automatic Sniper System or SASS. Today the SR-25 continues to be employed by Delta, Poland's GROM and the Australian SASR and Commandos (although the HK417 has been procured to supplement and in some cases replace the worn SR-25s) and units such as the Israeli Sayaret Matkal deploy the Mk11 variant.

Manurhin MR73

Type: Revolver • Nationality: French • Calibre: .357 Magnum • Weight Unloaded: 1050g • Length: 264mm • Magazine: 6

The Manurhin is a French-made .357 Magnum revolver originally designed for competition shooting. It was built both for ruggedness and for accuracy, the perfect combination for a fighting revolver. Its all-steel construction could withstand the constant use of full-power .357 Magnum ammunition while the cold hammered barrel and hand-built specification maximized accuracy.

France's GIGN issued a 5.25-inch (133mm) Sports barrel version as its first sidearm when the unit was formed. Other variants included an optic and bipod-equipped 8-inch model (203mm), available for close-range urban sniping, and a 3-inch (76mm) Gendarmerie version, used for undercover work. It was also originally issued by RAID when the unit was first created in 1985 and by the Austrian Einsatzkommando (EKO) Cobra until it transitioned to 9x19mm Glocks.

The German GSG9 also used revolvers in its early years (Smith & Wesson Model 66s and snub-nosed Model 19s in .357 Magnum) including during Operation *Fire Magic* in Somalia although they later adopted the 9x19mm Heckler & Koch P7. Even SEAL Team 6 employed stainless Model 66s for waterborne operations for many years because of their reliability in maritime conditions.

A GIGN operator pictured in 1994 poses with the 5.25-inch (133mm) Sports barrel version of the Manurhin MR73 fitted with an early laser sight. (Jean-Michel Turpin/Gamma-Rapho via Getty Images)

At the time, revolver calibres such as the .357 Magnum and .38 Special offered a wide range of ammunition, from hollowpoints to specialist training loads, all thanks to the widespread use of revolvers by American police and sports shooters. Available 9x19mm hollowpoints and the first generation of fragmenting rounds like the Blitz Action Trauma were often less than 100 per cent reliable in automatic pistols (and automatic weapons – allegedly GSG9 asked Heckler & Koch to modify the magazine of the MP5 to the now familiar banana shape as it increased reliability with hollowpoints).

Unfortunately, despite what various stories on the internet would lead you to believe, the MR73 is today more of a symbolic trophy for recruits completing GIGN selection and for use during the famous confidence-building ritual known as the 'Trust Shot' to ensure complete mutual confidence in the new member. A GIGN member clad in body armour has a clay pigeon attached to his vest. The recruit fires his MR73, using full-power loads, to strike the clay without wounding his fellow operator. The last major operation which saw the MR73 in action was the counter-hijacking of Air France 8969 in 1994 (see pages 311–13).

PGM Mini Hecate

Type: Sniper Rifle • Nationality: French • Calibre: .338 Lapua Magnum •
Weight Unloaded: 7.3kg • Length: 1010/1286mm • Magazine: 10

OPPOSITE French naval commandos from Commando Montfort display the tools of their trade including the .50 PGM Hecate in the right foreground and the .338 Lapua Magnum PGM Mini Hecate directly behind it. (Frank Perry/AFP/Getty Images)

The French firm of PGM Precision produces a range of sniper platforms that have seen extensive service with European counter-terrorist and SOF. The Mini Hecate, or PGM 338, is chambered for the .338 Lapua Magnum round and is based upon the company's Ultima Ratio platform, distinctive because of its skeletonized stock.

The Ultima Ratio (Final Option) is the standard 7.62x51mm design although it is also available in calibres such as .300 Winchester Magnum. The Integral Silencieux Commando model is, as the name suggests, integrally suppressed and features a side folding stock. Intervention and Commando variants differ primarily on the type and length of barrel employed; the Intervention employs a fixed muzzle brake while the Commando models use fluted barrels with fixed or detachable muzzle breaks. The weapon was designed with significant input from the French RAID counter-terrorist unit.

The Hecate II is the .50 anti-materiel variant, which can be equipped with an Ops Inc. suppressor and features a collapsible carrying handle and removable stock to aid in transporting the massive weapon. The Hecate II in common with the Mini Hecate and Ultima Ratio has a free-floating barrel to minimize vibrations from the stock and is supplied with Picatinny rails.

The Ultima Ratio is employed by the French RAID, Lithuanian Anti-terrorist Operations Unit (ARAS), and Israel's Yamam; the Mini Hecate is also deployed by RAID and French military SOF. The Hecate II is used by Austria's EKO Cobra, France's GIGN and RAID and the German GSG9, along with French Commandement des Opérations Spéciales (COS) units.

Remington M870

Type: Pump Automatic Shotgun • Nationality: US • Calibre: 12 Gauge • Weight Unloaded: 2.5kg • Length: Varies • Magazine: 8

The Remington M870 is widely used by both military and police special operations units. Based on a design dating to the 1950s, the M870 is tough and reliable. Pump action designs are generally more widely favoured for special operations as they allow the use of breaching and less than lethal rounds along with standard buckshot.

Semi-automatics are used such as the Benelli M1014; however, they often require specialist loads such as bean-bag rounds (these are filled with lead and cause only blunt trauma impact) or CS gas to be hand-cycled as the pressure

French GIGN operators seen in June 2004 perched upon the ramp of a HARAS (Height Adjustable Rescue Assault System) during a demonstration for the unit's 30th anniversary. From the left, the operators carry an MP5, a P90, a Glock and a Remington 870 shotgun. (Xavier Rossi/Gamma-Rapho via Getty Images)

is not great enough to cycle the semi-automatic action. With the pump action, rounds are manually cycled with the pump being brought to the rear and thus are better suited for so-called 'low impulse' rounds.*

The Remington M870 MCS or Modular Combat System is a recent iteration of the classic shotgun for US SOCOM. Supplied in kit form, the MCS can be configured as a stockless entry shotgun with shortened barrel or in various forms as a stocked or folding stock model. US Army Special Forces have received the MCS while other SOCOM units use a mixture of 870 variants.

Shotguns are principally employed by special operations units to quickly and relatively safely ballistically breach doors without recourse to explosive charges. A number of manufacturers produce shells designed for this purpose such as the Shok-Lok or Hatton – all work in much the same way, being frangible rounds that dissipate much of their energy shattering the hinge or lock without overpenetration risks.

The Remington M870 is probably the most popular design with units like the Rangers. The British 22SAS and the US Delta Force still employ relatively

---

* Hand-cycled means that each round has to be fed and ejected before another can be fired, negating the semi-automatic capability. Manually cycled means that the pump action is manually actioned to eject a spent round and feed another into the chamber.

primitive sawn-off models that can be quickly slung to the side and out of the way after a successful breach. These pistol-grip 870s normally hold only four rounds, although this is usually sufficient for breaching purposes. SAS and SEAL examples often feature vertical foregrips and EOTech holographic weapon sights.

A number of recent designs have quietly revolutionized the combat shotgun, including the new Israeli Tavor TS12, the Crye Six12 and the Origin 12. The former two are bullpup designs, meaning the action and magazine sit behind the pistol grip to shorten the overall length of the weapon. The Six12 can also apparently be suppressed with a SilencerCo suppressor and mounted under an M4A1 carbine in the manner of the older Master Key designs trialled by Delta back in the 1990s.

Remington M2010

Type: Sniper Rifle • Nationality: US • Calibre: .300 Winchester Magnum • Weight Unloaded: 5.5kg • Length: 1180mm • Magazine: 5

The M2010 Enhanced Sniper Rifle is the latest bolt action sniper rifle to be issued to US Army units. It has replaced the M24 series of sniper rifles used by the US Army since the late 1980s. The M2010 is essentially a re-barrelled and re-stocked M24, now chambered for the more potent .300 Winchester Magnum round rather than the 7.62x51mm, increasing effective range to around 1,200 metres. The USMC has also transitioned from the 7.62x51mm M40A6 to the .300 Winchester Magnum Mk13 Mod7, a platform used by both the SEALs and Marine Special Operations Command (MARSOC) units for many years (including by the 'American Sniper', former SEAL Chris Kyle).

The rifle has been seen in use with Army Green Berets and Rangers in Syria and Iraq but made its combat debut in Afghanistan. The United States' SOCOM attempted to procure its own sniper rifle under the Precision Sniper Rifle (PSR) programme but the eventual winner, the Remington MSR

The .300 Winchester Magnum Enhanced Sniper Rifle now issued to US SOCOM units. The weapon was developed from the 7.62x51mm M24 and is essentially a re-barrelled and re-stocked M24, now chambered for the more potent .300 Winchester Magnum round rather than the 7.62x51mm, increasing engagement ranges to around 1,200 metres. (Courtesy US Army, Charles Rosemond, Training Support Team Orzysz)

(Modular Sniper Rifle), was deemed not to match contracted quality standards and the procurement was discontinued.

A new SOCOM sniper rifle procurement, the Advanced Sniper Rifle (ASR) has replaced the failed PSR programme. The ASR will be a multi-calibre platform capable of firing the 7.62x51mm, the .300 Norma Magnum and the .338 Norma Magnum (SOCOM is also looking at a new machine gun – the Lightweight Medium Machine Gun – in .338 Norma Magnum).

SOCOM has also announced that it will be rechambering all of its existing semi-automatic sniper rifles such as the Mk20 used by the SEALs and the M110 variant of the SR-25, along with the newly adopted M110A1 or Compact Semi-Automatic Sniper System (CSASS) based on the Heckler & Koch HK417. The Precision Intermediate Caliber programme identified the 6.5mm Creedmoor, a relatively new cartridge that retains its velocity for far longer at extended ranges and offers greater terminal effects at these longer ranges than the 7.62x51mm. It also produces less felt recoil than the 7.62x51mm.

It appears that SOCOM will look to the newly adopted 6.5mm Creedmoor as the calibre of choice for its Mk46 and Mk48 replacement, the Intermediate Calibre Assault Machine Gun. Informed observers suggest this could be another Fabrique Nationale product, and indeed may be a rechambered Mk48.

Saiga-12

Type: Semi-Automatic Shotgun • Nationality: Russian • Calibre: 12 Gauge • Weight Unloaded: 3.6kg • Length: Varies • Magazine: 5/7/8 or 12 or 20 round drum

The Saiga is another Kalashnikov design based on the AK-47 receiver and operating controls. Instead of 7.62x39mm, however, the Saiga fires the potent 12 gauge shotshell. The Saiga is semi-automatic and can be fired as quickly as the trigger is pressed. Recoil is surprisingly milder than expected, likely due to the weight of the weapon.

The standard Saiga-12 can be fired from box magazines of varying capacities or large, unwieldy drum magazines that can hold up to 20 shotshells. To counter issues with cycling low power rounds such as less-than-lethal riot control or Shok Lok or similar breaching rounds, the shotgun has two user selectable gas settings to allow reliable functioning of both buckshot and low powered specialist rounds.

The Saiga-12 can be fitted with any number of folding and collapsible stock types and is available in a number of different barrel lengths. The Saiga-12K is the most popular with police and SOF, featuring a side-folding stock, a 430mm (17 inch) barrel and rails allowing optics to be mounted. The 12K has seen service with Western SOF units including RAID and GIGN.

The Saiga-12K semi-automatic shotgun produced by Kalashnikov Concern (the 'K' denoting the shortened variant). The shotgun has been adopted by a number of European counter-terrorist units (as has the similar Vepr-12) along with Russian SOF including the elite SSO. (Courtesy Kalashnikov Group/Kalashnikov Media)

A rival Russian firm manufactures the similar Vepr-12 which is based on a modified RPK receiver. A number of variants exist including the compact VPO-205-03 with a 305mm (12 inch) barrel and side-folding stock. Another type features an M4 style collapsible stock. All are equipped with Picatinny rails attached to the receiver allowing optics to be mounted. The Vepr family are also employed by French and Russian SOF units.

Sako TRG-22

Type: Sniper Rifle • Nationality: Finnish • Calibre: 7.62x51mm • Weight Unloaded: 4.7kg • Length: 1000mm • Magazine: 10

Sako of Finland (now owned by Beretta of Italy) have an impressive and long-standing record of manufacturing some of the world's most accurate rifles. The TRG-21 was their first offering designed for the sniper market in the late 1980s. It is based on their successful .308 Winchester target rifle and uses a free-floating cold hammer forged barrel for maximum accuracy.

The TRG-21 was improved upon with the TRG-22, now a standard bolt action sniper platform with many European SOF units. The TTRG-22 featured a redesigned stock, adjustable trigger and bipod mounting. An integrally suppressed variant was also produced in the UK called the LEI TRG-SPP in 7.62x51mm. The TRG-22 is also available in the new favourite US SOCOM calibre of 6.5mm Creedmoor.

The TRG-42 was introduced in .338 Lapua Magnum as a contender for various European sniper rifle trials as increasing numbers of countries adopted the heavier calibre over the 7.62x51mm. The TRG-42 is distinctive (like the Accuracy International AWM) because of its prominent muzzle brake. Both the TRG-22 and TRG-42 can be supplied with a skeletonized folding stock. The Czech 601st SFG and Útvar rychlého nasazení (URNA) both employ Sako TRG rifles as do Danish SOF, French Commando Parachutiste de l'Air no10 (CPA-10), the Italian Col Moschin and Gruppo Intervento Speciale

The .338 Lapua Magnum Sako TRG-22 seen here being fired from a helicopter by an Italian sniper providing aerial overwatch during operations in Herat, Afghanistan, 2013. (DoD photo courtesy US Army)

(GIS), Norwegian Special Operations Forces (NORSOF), Polish Grupa Reagowania Operacyjno-Manewrowego (GROM), and the Spanish Grupos de Operaciones Especiales (GEO).

A multi-calibre variant called the M10 was developed to compete in the SOCOM Mk21 Precision Sniper Rifle trials, which were won (and later lost) by Remington's Modular Sniper Rifle. The M10 took the best features from both weapons and incorporated them with a new side folding stock and lightweight chassis in a platform that could be configured to fire 7.62x51mm, .300 Winchester Magnum or .338 Lapua Magnum (ten-round magazine for the 7.62x51mm, seven for the .300 Winchester Magnum and five for the .338).

SIG-Sauer MCX

Type: Assault Rifle • Nationality: US • Calibre: 7.62x35mm (.300 Blackout)/5.56x45mm • Weight Unloaded: 2.6kg • Length: 730mm • Magazine: 30 • Cyclic Rate: 700 RPM

One of the most important new firearms adopted by a number of prestigious units has been the SIG-Sauer MCX in the new calibre of .300 Blackout (termed 7.62x35mm in UK service). The weapon was developed as a response to a competing design by AAC, known as the Honey Badger, which was first publicly unveiled in 2012. The Honey Badger had been developed at the request of SEAL Team 6 based on its experiences in Afghanistan.

The SEALs wanted a replacement for their MP7 and MP5SD sub machine guns. The disadvantage of the MP5SD series that was in common use with US special operators was that if a suppressed option was needed for a particular task such as stealthily clearing compounds, the MP5SD variant would have to be carried in addition to the operator's standard rifle so that he could engage targets at extended ranges beyond the 100 metres or so effective range of the suppressed MP5.

A similar issue occurred with the MP7 that SEAL Team 6 employed, initially to replace its MP5SDs. Designed for close quarter battle shooting, the weapon was very quiet with a suppressor but was next to useless if the SEALs were contacted during their infiltration to or exfiltration from the objective. SEALs took to carrying the sawn-off M79 grenade launcher, nicknamed the 'Pirate Gun', to provide some longer range suppressive capability when carrying the MP7.

The advantage of the .300 Blackout was that it could be very effectively silenced with the use of subsonic ammunition but just as simply fire standard supersonic rounds with a magazine swap, giving the operator a weapon with similar range capabilities to the AK-47 out to 400 metres. With the stock retracted the Honey Badger was no larger than an MP5SD.

A rare sighting of the MCX 'in the wild'. A JSOC operator on close personal protection duty (second from left), most likely drawn from Delta, is pictured shadowing former Delta and JSOC chief General Scott Miller in February 2019. The operator carries the version of the MCX adopted by JSOC, the .300 Blackout LVAW or low visibility assault weapon fitted with a suppressor. (Sylvie Lanteaume/AFP/Getty Images)

The AAC weapon was positively tested by the SEALs but mismanagement at AAC meant there was no way to incorporate the changes requested by the operators. In the meantime, SIG-Sauer had developed what was later dubbed the 'Black Mamba' in response to a Delta-led request for a low visibility assault weapon (LVAW). The LVAW also needed to be no larger than an MP5 and be able to fire rifle calibre ammunition, ideally with the capability of swapping calibres between .300 Blackout, 5.56x45mm and 7.62x39mm, dependent on circumstance.

The United States' JSOC officially adopted the MCX as the LVAW in 2015, with earlier variants being trialled for a number of years beforehand with changes incorporated from Delta feedback in much the same way as the SR-25 was developed. Examples have been spotted in Delta hands in Syria. The MCX has since been adopted by the British SAS and presumably the SBS in .300 Blackout with integral suppressor. The London Metropolitan Police's SCO19's CTSFO (Counter Terrorist Specialist Firearms Officer) teams were another early adopter. SEAL Team 6 employs the MCX but rumour suggests that a .300 Blackout HK416 variant, possibly a prototype HK337, has also been tested by the unit.

SIG-Sauer has also produced the MPX which is the sub machine gun or PDW (personal defence weapon) variant of the MCX, manufactured in 9x19mm and aimed at replacing ageing stocks of MP5s, particularly in organizations that employ the MCX (it has been adopted by the Indonesian SAT-81 for instance). Another ultra-short variant called the Rattler has been developed to meet a SOCOM request for a PDW). SIG-Sauer has also won the contract for the Suppressed Upper Receiver Group (SURG) for SOCOM that will see 5.56x45mm MCX-style upper receivers with integral suppressors mated to existing M4A1 carbines.

SIG-Sauer P226

Type: Pistol • Nationality: Swiss • Calibre: 9x19mm • Weight Unloaded: 870g • Length: 196mm • Magazine: 15

The Swiss SIG-Sauer P226 was first developed to compete in US military pistol trials during the 1980s to replace the venerable .45ACP M1911A1. It matched the eventual winner, the Beretta M9, in all respects apart from price. Despite this setback, the P226 was soon adopted by the Navy SEALs, including SEAL Team 6 in 1989. At the same time, UKSF were looking to replace their 9mm Browning Hi-Powers and also chose the P226 and its compact variant, the P228.

The P226 was known for its accuracy and reliability and functioned well after being submerged but was comparatively heavy thanks to its stainless steel frame. The SEALs adopted an improved version with a rail under the barrel to allow the user of weapon lights in the form of the P226R or Mk25 Mod0 in Navy use. The 9mm SIG-Sauer P239 also found favour with the SEALs. A compact eight-shot pistol, the P239 was often used as a concealable pistol when operating under cover or as a back-up to their main weapon.

With the SEALs replacing their Mk25s with Glock 19s and UKSF and New Zealand SAS doing likewise, the days of the P226 may be numbered, although the Canadian CSOR and JTF2 continue to employ P226Rs as does the Irish Army Ranger Wing and a host of European police units.

The winner of the US military Modular Handgun System trials was the SIG-Sauer M320, type-classified as the M17 in standard size and M18 in compact. These are replacing all M9 Berettas across the military and are supposed to replace the Glocks and SIGs used by SOCOM units.

A classic display of 1990s SEAL small arms. Along with the MP5-N, clockwise there is the 9x19mm Heckler & Koch P9S threaded for a suppressor, the .357 Magnum Smith & Wesson Model 686 (which replaced earlier stainless Model 66s carried by the Teams), the .22LR Ruger Mk2 (also commonly suppressed), the iconic .45ACP M1911A1 and the 9x19mm SIG-Sauer P226 (or Mk25) in the centre which has only recently been replaced by the Glock 19 as the SEALs' primary sidearm. (Jim Sugar/Corbis via Getty Images)

EQUIPMENT

Body Armour

SOF body armour poses a number of challenges compared to standard military combat body armour. Chief among these is size and weight. Issue infantry body armour, for example, usually comprises a heavy Kevlar lined vest with front, rear and side trauma plates, with optional neck and groin protectors. While offering excellent protection against bullets and fragmentation, such ensembles are hot and heavy and considerably slow down the wearer.

Because of the nature of their role, SOF cannot be encumbered by this kind of heavy armour and thus choose smaller, more lightweight chest plates manufactured by the likes of Crye and Paraclete which cover the heart and lungs with a trauma plate rated to stop 7.62x39mm bullets fired from close range. Additional side plates are available but are seldom used owing to their increased bulk and weight.

For specialist roles during counter-terrorism missions, operators may well incorporate additional protective measures beyond the simple plate carrier. Delta Force in Iraq, for instance, often added groin protectors and side plates when conducting building clearance operations. Breachers will also often wear heavier armour including neck protectors.

Body armour has also been supplemented by ballistic shields. The British SAS employed such devices during raids in Iraq and they have now become a standard part of its counter-terrorism kit. They are typically carried by the

Operators from the French BRI-BAC counter-terrorist unit display the Ramses wheeled ballistic shield that was deployed during the Bataclan assault in Paris, November 2015. It was struck more than two dozen times by AK-47 rounds. (Kenzo Tribouillard/AFP/Getty Images)

lead man who will be armed only with a pistol (some operators will carry two pistols, as reloading while carrying a shield is difficult, to say the least, and it is easier to simply drop and empty one pistol and draw their back-up than attempt a reload). Designs now feature high-intensity LED lights which can be set to strobe to momentarily distract an enemy upon entry.

Others are heavy, multi-part wheeled designs used to provide protection for the entry element as they approach the door to an objective. One such wheeled shield, the Austrian-made Ramses, was famously used by France's Brigade de Recherche et d'Intervention – Brigade Anticommando (BRI-BAC or Research and Intervention Brigade – Anti-Commando Brigade) and RAID unit as they breached into the Bataclan Theatre in November 2015. The Ramses took 27 hits from 7.62x39mm-calibre weapons with none penetrating.

Camouflage

All military (and some police) SOF use some form of camouflage uniform, both to aid in hiding themselves from visual detection and to distinguish each other from the enemy. Traditionally military SOF have worn the same camouflage as their parent armies. For instance the British SAS wore Disruptive Pattern Material (DPM) for many years until it began transitioning to specialist camouflage during the counter-insurgency war in Iraq.

Members of 22 SAS in Baghdad circa 2006 sporting a range of camouflage patterns. The use of US patterns was initially to help disguise the fact that 22 SAS were operating in Iraq post the invasion but later became a question of using whatever was available due to their high operational tempo (Crye MultiCam, following Delta's lead, was adopted in the following year). Patterns visible include US ACU/UCP (Army Combat Uniform/ Universal Camouflage Pattern, far left), US Navy AOR 1 (Area Of Responsibility, second from left), and British Desert DPM (Disruptive Pattern Material, far right). Elements of the US DCU or Desert Camouflage Uniform are also worn by each operator. (Author's Collection)

Today, the most common camouflage pattern is Crye MultiCam which is a complex blend of greens, browns, blacks and even white and seems to work equally well in both desert and less arid conditions. Delta Force was the first to adopt the pattern to replace its three-colour Desert Camouflage Uniforms (DCUs) in Iraq in around 2005. The British SAS and SEAL Team 6, both working closely with Delta, followed suit.

SEAL Team 6 and the 'vanilla' (a term denoting non ST6 SEALs) SEAL Teams also developed their own arid and temperate patterns known as AOR1 and AOR2 (AOR for Area of Responsibility) which resemble the US Marine Corps' digital MARPAT (Marine Pattern) patterns (although without the Marine 'globe and anchor' emblem embedded in the design to deter reproductions). Both AOR patterns have been also employed by Delta and even Marine Special Operations Command (MARSOC).

Black Nomex flight suits were once the standard in counter-terrorism operations; however, these have largely been replaced by MultiCam or MultiCam Black fatigues (a pattern which resembles a set of MultiCams which have been dyed black so that the original pattern is still discernible) or black or dark blue specialist uniforms from the likes of Arc'teryx. Some units such as Belgium's Directorate of Special Units (DSU) have adopted olive-green uniforms largely in an effort to distinguish themselves from black-clad and balaclava-wearing terrorists.

Although the choice of camouflage is largely driven by operational requirements, there is also undoubtedly a 'cool guy factor' present. By wearing specialist patterns, SOF make themselves stand out, whether inadvertently or not. The British SAS operated covertly and successfully in Bosnia by wearing then standard-issue DPM and carrying SA80s. Now anyone in an unusual camouflage pattern and carrying an unusual or suppressed weapon is an obvious operator.

Counter-IED

Very little detailed information can be provided on counter-IED (improvised explosive device) measures as most are rightfully classified. In broad terms, the counter-IED systems used by SOF are either man-portable or vehicle mounted and perform similar functions. Systems such as the US Warlock Green and Warlock Red provide an electronic umbrella, which jams the detonation of IEDs. A disadvantage of their use is that they often interrupt *all* radio and electronic signals, including friendly signals equipment.

Such man-pack units are also carried by counter-terrorist teams, although these units typically perform multiple functions, jamming mobile (cell) transmissions, radios, and radio or electronic IED detonators. Vehicle-based

A US Army 5th Special Forces Group multi-purpose canine (MPC) and handler search for IEDs in Deir Ezzor Province, Syria, October 2018. (Courtesy US Army, Sgt Matthew Crane)

systems are more powerful and operate at greater range. They can be supplemented by physical systems mounted upon the vehicle, which prematurely detonate IEDs triggered by infrared beams by interrupting the beam and setting off the device in front of the vehicle.

IEDs fall into three broad categories: PPIEDs, RCIEDs and CWIEDs. The distinctions are based on the method of triggering the device. Pressure plate IEDs (also known as victim operated IEDs) are the simplest, constructed with an ad hoc pressure plate (often made from wood or plastic to disguise the IED from non-ground penetrating radar-equipped mine detectors), which detonates when stood upon.

RCIEDs are detonated by remote control. This may take the form of radio signals or a mobile (cell) phone call. RCIEDs are typically larger devices and are the safest for the terrorist or insurgent as they can be triggered from non-line of sight. They are, however, the easiest to jam with counter-IED technology.

Finally CWIEDs are command wire detonated, meaning the device is triggered by a physical means such as detonating cord. These are not favoured by the enemy as they require significant camouflage and are limited by the length of the command wire. Operators will be constantly scanning for such wires as will their attached dog teams.

The best method of countering the IED threat is to 'attack the network'. This is done through meticulous detective work by weapons intelligence personnel who look for clues to the identity of the bomber by examining recovered components. From this, the bomber can be tracked through the use of sophisticated data mining and similar techniques, which map the relationships between terrorists. Once the target is housed, an SOF raid is conducted to kill or capture the bomb-maker.

Grenades

A wide range of both hand and launched grenade types are used by SOF. The most common is the humble flashbang or stun grenade. First developed by Project Pagoda for the British SAS, early types detonated with a single thunderous bang and a brief but blinding flash. More recent examples provide multiple blasts and are commonly referred to as 'eight bangers' or 'nine bangers' dependent on the number of detonations. These multiple-bang types have increased the momentary edge such distraction devices provide.

Flashbangs are largely non-lethal, although earlier designs were pyrotechnic and were responsible for starting the fire in the Iranian Embassy, for example. The fire was spread rapidly by these early pyrotechnic grenades and eventually gutted the building, leading to extensive renovation. This was the reason Germany's GSG9 demurred from using them during its counter-hijack mission in Mogadishu in 1977. Today's designs will not typically start fires but can cause serious injuries or even death if detonated in contact with a person.

The Scalable Offensive Hand Grenade used by SOCOM. The grenade can be 'dialled up' by clipping up to three devices together to increase the blast, dependent on the target. (Courtesy US Army, Angie DePuydt)

Flashbangs can also be fired from 40mm launchers or attached to 'bang sticks', giving the operator versatility based on the operational requirements. CS gas grenades, commonly but erroneously called 'tear gas', can also be launched from 40mm launchers and are often introduced to wear down an opponent prior to an entry. Concussion grenades are utilized to reduce fragmentation risk (although still highly lethal in enclosed spaces) and are especially effective under water. They are also more effective than flashbangs when used in the open.

Fragmentation grenades are of course still used, although rarely in counter-terrorist operations. Mini grenades like the golf ball-sized Dutch V40 were used for many years by JSOC units as a means to limit the kill radius of a fragmentation grenade. A recent development is the enhanced tactical multi-purpose (ET-MP) grenade, which can be switched from fragmentation to concussion by the operator. A similar development, seen recently carried by some US operators, is the scalable offensive hand grenade HGO 115-3, 5 produced by Nammo. The explosive effect of this grenade can be doubled or tripled by the addition of extra grenades, which can be simply screwed together.

The final category of grenade used by SOF is the thermobaric grenade, typified by the Mk14 anti-structure munition (ASM) Grenade. The Mk14 detonates producing a massive wave of concussion and thermal effects and is particularly suitable for use in structures and caves. In use by US and Australian SOF in Afghanistan, the device will literally demolish a small building, killing all inside.

Helmets

All SOF wear helmets to provide both bump and ballistic protection on operations. For many years, units relied upon plastic skate-style helmets as they judged that the greatest risk was smashing their heads when climbing through a window or other enclosed space. This thinking was up-ended with the events of Operation *Gothic Serpent* in Mogadishu where the plastic ProTec helmets that the Delta operators wore provided zero protection against bullets and fragmentation.

European counter-terrorist units had been wise to this fact since the early 1980s when a French operator was shot in the face by a criminal armed with a handgun. They adopted both ballistic helmets and clear ballistic visors, which became a trademark of France's GIGN and Germany's GSG9. After Mogadishu, significant research was conducted to develop SOF-suitable ballistic helmets, by combining both the light weight of the skate helmet and the protective abilities of Kevlar.

This resulted in a number of designs manufactured by the likes of Gentex and later Crye. SOF ballistic helmets now typically leave the ears clear to allow the use of the likes of Peltor headsets which act as hearing protection and as radio earpieces and which are cut high at the back to allow the operators to fire their weapon from the prone position.

The Ops-Core and Crye helmets which have since cornered the market also feature rails (mounting attachments fitted to the sides of the helmet) and attachment points allowing night vision goggles, cameras, lights and strobes to be easily attached. Some can also be up-armoured as the typical ballistic helmet is still intended to protect against fragmentation and rifle rounds fired from some distance (and thus having significant lost velocity). The SLAAP Plate by Velocity Systems for example can be attached to an Ops-Core helmet and provides protection against close range strikes from 7.62x39mm AK-47 rounds.

Increasingly, counter-terrorism teams including the UK's SAS have begun wearing face masks that incorporate respirators such as the Ops-Core SOTR (Special Operations Tactical Respirator) which according to the manufacturer, Gentex, offers '99.97% filtration efficiency against airborne particulates including lead, asbestos, fentanyl, lubricant mist, and explosive gunfire residue.'* Such masks were originally employed by EOD and breaching personnel but have now been procured for counter-terrorist assaulters.

This 10th Special Forces Group soldier in Afghanistan wears an Ops Core ballistic helmet with rails to allow cameras and lights to be fitted. The high cut around the ear is designed to facilitate the use of Peltor and similar integrated communications and hearing protection headphones. (Courtesy US Army, Sgt Connor Mendez)

* https://shop.gentexcorp.com/content/Ops-Core-SOTR-Data-Sheet.pdf

Less than Lethal

Formerly known as non-lethal weapons, less than lethal includes a range of devices intended to subdue or capture a target without resorting to lethal force. In SOF use, such devices are typically used in counter-terrorism rather than warfighting operations; however, they may be employed to disperse hostile crowds.

The flashbang or stun grenade is the most commonly used and is covered under its own entry (see pages 249–50). Similar grenades, known as Sting Balls, spray 180 .32 calibre rubber balls at high velocity on detonation. Variants of the base design can include irritants like CS gas, while others can combine flashbang effects. Sting Balls were carried for crowd control by Delta Force in Somalia in 1993.

Next are less than lethal munitions. They take the form of bean-bag rounds (these are filled with lead and cause only blunt trauma impact) and similar rounds that are fired from 12-gauge, 40mm or proprietary devices such as the 17.3mm Fabrique Nationale FN 303 which fires a range of projectiles including bean-bag, pepper-spray irritant and paint marker from a rotary 15-round magazine. The FN 303 has been widely employed by Belgium's Directorate of Special Units (DSU) when attempting to capture terrorist suspects.

A range of flashbang grenades including the US military issue M84 (centre). (Paul J. Richards/AFP/Getty Images)

Capsicum or pepper sprays are also used. These operate on a similar principle to the smaller compact units used by police officers but are backpack mounted and can deliver an overwhelming incapacitant effect, particularly in enclosed spaces. The US military have purchased the Pepperball, an M4-style carbine that fires paintballs impregnated with irritants.

Tasers are sometimes employed; both the standard police X26 version and a shotgun-delivered variant called the X12, which increases stand-off range, are available. Again these have greater utility in law enforcement but may be employed during counter-terrorism operations to subdue a target, although with the increasing use of suicide bomb vests the discharge of a Taser into a terrorist might have disastrous consequences.

Method of Entry (MOE)

Method of entry or MOE is a catalogue of techniques which are used to gain access to a contested objective, such as a terrorist stronghold. These range from ballistic breaching with shotguns to explosive method of entry (EMOE) techniques using explosive or cutting charges. The simplest method is the Halligan Tool, first developed by New York firefighters. This is a pry bar that can be used to physically force a door or window open. It has the advantage of being lightweight and relatively quiet. Similar devices known as 'glass

10th Special Forces Group soldiers prepare to employ a breaching card to gain entry during explosive method of entry (EMOE) training in 2017. (Courtesy US Army, Sgt Brandon Franklin)

breakers' can be used to bust open glass windows quickly, reaming out the shattered glass to reduce injury risk to operators.

Ballistic breaching using shotguns firing specialist Hatton or Shok-Lok rounds has the advantage of speed but is very noisy and only used in conjunction with distraction devices. Hydraulic breaching tools offer the greatest stealth with some models being virtually silent. The Door Raider by Libervit can be quietly emplaced and then activated by remote control if necessary, hydraulically breaching even reinforced doors in seconds. Their HR5 model is less bulky and is fitted across the door, literally to pop open even multiple-lock doors.

Explosive breaching charges are obviously the most dangerous form of breaching and can easily result in unintended injury or death. During the 2009 hostage rescue in Afghanistan by the SBS (see page 165), an Afghan civilian was killed as he stood behind a door that was breached by an explosive charge. Different types of charges, which funnel or direct the blast, can be fashioned and master breachers are adept at using exactly the right configuration of charge to accomplish the breach.

Explosive charges may also be mounted on 'boom sticks', telescoping poles, to allow for stand-off breaching – for instance breaching an upper-storey window. They can also be used to disorient or distract hostage takers by causing a blast at a tactically advantageous location. For maritime operations where explosives pose too great a risk, companies such as Libervit produces underwater versions of their hydraulic tools and specialist thermal lances can be used to cut through bulkheads.

Finally there are rifle grenades. Although standard 40mm high explosive dual purpose rounds can be used, there are a number of specialist products which shape the blast and reduce collateral damage. Chief amongst these is the Israeli Simon and the similar US-issued M100 Grenade Rifle Entry Munition. These operate on the principle of World War II-era rifle grenades but with a stand-off rod fitted that causes the charge to detonate at the optimum distance from the door to channel the blast.

Military Working Dogs (MWDs)

The use of military working dogs (MWDs) has expanded tremendously in both conventional and SOF units. There are a number of specialist roles dogs are trained in but in the case of SOF there are three principal types: the combat assault dog (CAD), the explosives detection dog (EDD) and the multi-purpose canine (MPC).

CADs are trained to conduct active reconnaissance of an objective ahead of assaulters. They are often equipped with body armour and a video camera

in a special harness to transmit real-time footage of the interior of the target. CADs will also be used to sniff out hidden insurgents and chase down 'squirters' or those insurgents who attempt to escape the cordon.

EDDs are, as the name implies, employed to detect gunpowder and explosives either in concert with an assault team or in support of an attached EOD element. The MPC is a combination of a number of traits – able to chase down insurgents and sniff out hidden bombs. All dogs assigned to SOF undergo training to be able to accompany their handlers in helicopters, fast-roping if necessary, and in some cases are trained to parachute into a target area tethered to an operator.

Much of the early development of SOF dogs was pioneered by European counter-terrorist units such as the Belgian Escadron Spécial d'Intervention (ESI) – now known as the Directorate of Special Units (DSU) – who began the SOF use of a particular breed – the Belgian Shepherd or Malinois. Known for its intelligence and resilience, the Malinois makes a good choice for specialist training.

Today all JSOC units, for instance, have their own kennels and dog handlers. In fact the Rangers have one of the most effective and mature training programmes for their dogs with a number attached to each battalion. Delta also has four dogs attached to each squadron. Delta even took its dogs to western Iraq in 2003 in specially air-conditioned cages. Indeed, a CAD called Cairo accompanied SEAL Team 6 into Abbottabad.

One of the latest losses was an MPC named Maiko who operated with 2/75 Rangers and was killed during an operation in Nimruz Province in November 2018; sadly a Ranger sergeant was also killed in this operation, probably shot accidentally by a member of the Afghan Partner Unit.

A US Navy SEAL combat assault dog (CAD) during a training exercise – note the fearsome muzzle! SEAL Team 6 deployed the famous Cairo, a Belgian Malinois, during the operation to kill Usama bin Laden in 2011. (Courtesy US Army National Guard, Terra C. Gatti)

According to a US military Ranger biography of Maiko, 'Maiko was killed in action while leading Rangers into the breach of a targeted compound. Maiko's presence and actions inside the building directly caused the enemy to engage him, giving away his position and resulting in the assault force eliminating the threat.'

Night Vision Goggles (NVGs)

A German KSK soldier wearing the famous L-3 GPNVG-18 Ground Panoramic Night Vision Goggles which deliver an unparalleled 97-degree vision through four individual image intensifier tubes which blend the image seen by the operator into one. (picture alliance/dpa/Kay Nietfeld)

Night vision goggles or NVGs (also known as night observation devices or NODs in the United States) have come a long way in the last 20 years. Once likened to looking through a dirty window through a toilet roll inner, NVGs today offer a wide range of capabilities; some have almost 100-degree field of vision, others can project information onto the lens of the goggle. The principal disadvantages, however, remain – they are heavy, cause headaches after even brief use and require a counterweight mounted to the back of the helmet to alleviate pressure on the neck.

Brought into the public consciousness by the film *Zero Dark Thirty* detailing Operation *Neptune Spear* into Abbottabad, Pakistan to kill

Usama bin Laden in 2011, the L-3 GPNVG-18s are the most expensive NVG system currently on the market with prices starting at upwards of $40,000 USD a pair. The Ground Panoramic Night Vision Goggles (GPNVGs) offer 97-degree vision through four individual image intensifier tubes which blend the image seen by the operator into one.

Developed originally for US special operations aviation, including the 160th Special Operations Aviation Regiment (160th SOAR), the GPNVGs have also been purchased by a number of other nations, notably including Germany's GSG9; even the Russian KSSO has been seen sporting the quad-goggles. The GPNVG is in selected use by US SOCOM and JSOC units, and particularly by the 160th SOAR using the aviation model, but its increased weight and bulkiness is problematic for lengthy ground operations. For snipers and personnel maintaining blocking positions around an objective, however, it makes eminent sense thanks to its massively increased field of vision.

The PVS-21 Low Profile Night Vision Goggles used by UKSF are another option which, although restricting vision to 40 degrees, have a number of features which make them better suited for assaulters than the GPNVGs. For one they are much more compact and offer 'see-through optics' which regulate the image intensifier based on the amount of light, meaning that the goggles will not suffer 'white-out' should the operator move from darkness into a lit room, for instance. They can also thus be used with weapon optics like Aimpoints and EOTechs without having to rely upon the infrared laser from the operator's laser illuminator. The PVS-21s are also favoured for 'blackout' driving as they offer the greatest depth perception.

The next generation of enhancement to night vision will likely be a clip-on tactical augmented reality (TAR) viewer that can be used in conjunction with the PVS-21 and will be based on the heads-up display principle used in fighter aircraft and attack helicopters. The TAR will project the same kind of real-time information on enemy and friendly locations and movements that operators normally receive through vehicle-mounted Blue Force Tracker viewers. It may also be able to sync with a weapon-mounted camera that allows a split-screen view for the operator, allowing him to monitor one direction with his weapon while looking another way.

For the most part, SOCOM operators such as the Rangers are choosing the newer AN/PVS-31 series for their light weight and clarity of vision to replace their legacy PVS-15s which have equipped the SEALs and Rangers for most of the War on Terror. The PVS-21 is still favoured for its 'see-through optics' and compactness for close quarter battle while the GPNVG-18s are for specialist roles.

Unmanned Aerial Vehicles (UAVs)

UAVs or unmanned aerial vehicles play a vital role on today's special operations battlefield. From their genesis with Israeli operations in the early 1980s, UAVs have become both smaller and more capable with each passing year. The best known is the MQ-1 series Predator, which was deployed (at that time unarmed) to hunt Usama bin Laden in Afghanistan a year before the 9/11 attacks. The armed MQ-1A carried out the first interdiction during October of 2001 and was used for the first time as close air support for embattled Rangers on Takur Ghar several months later (although the Israelis beat the US Air Force to the punch on the first UAV 'kill' by several years).

UAVs became integral during the counter-insurgency in Iraq. The US Army history notes that JSOC:

> ... [began] the war with only two helicopters equipped with full-motion video cameras, by April 2005, the addition of Predator unmanned aerial vehicles and manned aircraft enabled the number of dedicated orbits for other special operations forces to reach 4.21 (each orbit is defined as the ability to cover a single target continuously for a 24-hour time period). By March 2006, the total had reached 6.25 orbits, and imagery-related intelligence had come to be considered as important as signal-related intelligence.

Although the Predator and its replacement the Reaper receive the most press, for SOF a range of intelligence, surveillance, targeting and reconnaissance (ISTAR)-dedicated tactical UAVs are their constant companions. The most common SOF platform is the RQ-20A Puma, which offers a lightweight UAV that can transmit real-time video in harsh weather environments for up to two hours. The Puma can be man-packed but is more likely to be carried into the battlespace by a ground vehicle such as the Flyer 60 or a quad bike.

Micro UAVs are increasingly employed, such as the PD-100 Black Hornet used by Australian and UK SOF. These are tiny UAVs designed to be carried by individual operators and used to provide unmanned reconnaissance of buildings and terrain features. Increasingly systems are being developed to operate in GPS-denied environments (for example, against a peer enemy that operates electronic warfare systems). The quadcopter American Shield AI Nova micro UAV can be operated autonomously with no GPS requirement and can create maps of the interior of a target, along with real-time video capture.

Known euphemistically as 'long loiter munitions' or 'kamikaze drones', kinetic strike UAVs are a relatively recent phenomenon. Israeli examples include the Harpy and Harop but the most well-known is the American AeroVironment Switchblade which, as its manufacturer explains, provides a

'back-packable, non-line-of-sight precision strike solution with minimal collateral effects'.* The Switchblade has seen combat experience since 2011, being employed by both US Army Special Forces and conventional troops in Afghanistan.

Available as a single man-portable UAV or in a six-pack configuration that can be mounted upon a ground vehicle, the Switchblade can even be launched from an aircraft. Its warhead is equivalent to a 40mm grenade in lethality but can be detonated above a target for airburst effect. The huge advantage of the Switchblade is that it provides both an ISTAR and indirect fire capability for operators, all in a package that weighs just over 2 kilograms and can be carried into an objective.

An unidentified US SOF member launches an AeroVironment Switchblade 'long loiter munition' during Operation *Roundup* outside the Hajin Pocket, Syria, January 2019. (Courtesy US Army, Spc Christian Simmons)

* https://www.avinc.com/uas/view/switchblade

UAVs have also descended onto the sea and below with the development of unmanned surface vehicles (USVs) and unmanned undersea vehicles (UUVs), which offer additional capabilities to maritime-focused SOF. AeroVironment's Blackwing, for example, offers a stealthy, low-signature UAV with underwater-to-air capability designed to be launched from a submersible.

Unmanned Ground Vehicles (UGVs)

Along with unmanned aerial vehicles (drones), SOF are increasingly relying upon remote-controlled ground vehicles to conduct reconnaissance into hostile areas. Originally developed from EOD droids, the field of unmanned ground vehicles or UGVs has exploded in recent years as their potential has been realized in ever smaller and more capable units.

One such UGV is the Throwbot, a mini UGV that looks like a flashbang grenade with wheels, which can be literally thrown through a door or window. It is equipped with both real-time video and audio capture and what it sees and hears is transmitted back to the operator deploying the UGV. Throwbots were employed by the French GIGN and RAID during operations following the Paris terrorist attacks and are becoming a common item amongst counter-terrorist units. They are also on trial with UKSF. A similar tracked variant called the FirstLook has been purchased for US SOCOM units.

Most of the mini UGVs weigh only a couple of kilograms, meaning they can be attached to an operator's assault pack and used when the situation dictates. The video and audio they transmit can be viewed via the handheld tablet device. Improvements are mooted which will enable the vision to be transmitted to other operators on the team via their tactical augmented reality goggles or the NVGs' (night vision goggles) clip-on devices. Other innovations include a microphone, which will allow an operator's commands to be broadcast from the UGV – useful when dealing with civilians or hostages or in law enforcement siege scenarios.

Armed UGVs have also become available with variants mounting anything from a 7.62x51mm medium machine gun to anti-tank guided missiles. Several Russian models were battle-tested in Syria although the results were reportedly somewhat less than encouraging, with operators losing contact with the UGVs and the devices occasionally spontaneously shutting themselves down. Endeavor Robotics have recently debuted the Kobra, mounting an M240 medium machine gun on a remote weapon station, which was developed from their successful line of EOD droids and appears to be likely trialled by SOCOM.

A US soldier deploys a Throwbot unmanned ground vehicle through a building window. The latest version of the device offers audio in addition to streaming video. (Courtesy US Army)

VEHICLES

CV-22 Osprey

Nationality: US • Type: Tilt-rotor Aircraft

The CV-22, distinctive thanks to the fuselage bulges, is the US Air Force Special Operations Command (AFSOC) variant of the Osprey. The CV can also be refuelled in mid-air from a tanker, extending the range of the airframe. The aircraft can accommodate up to 32 operators or can internally carry the GMV (ground mobility vehicle) 1.1 Flyer 60 or the MRZR ground vehicles and a reduced complement of operators.

The tilt-rotor is only lightly armed, typically with a .50 or 7.62x51mm machine gun mounted on the ramp in a similar fashion to the Chinook. Currently work is under way to add a retractable weapons pod on the belly of the aircraft, likely armed with some form of minigun to allow the crew to engage targets in emergency situations, such as when they are transitioning into hover mode to land at a contested LZ (landing zone). This modification is still unfortunately a number of years away.

The CV-22, although not an airframe flown by the US Army's 160th Special Operations Aviation Regiment (who traditionally transport US special operators to their targets), has seen increasing use in Iraq and Syria. Flown by the US Air Force's 7th SOS (Special Operations Squadron), the Osprey appears to be competing with the MH-47 for landing JSOC operators into denied environments.

An Estonian Special Operations Forces operator is hoisted up to a US Air Force CV-22 Osprey during fast-rope training. (Courtesy US Army, Staff Sgt Matt Britton)

A USAF pararescue jumper (PJ) fast-ropes from a USMC MV-22 Osprey. Ospreys have been damaged in a number of SOF operations in both Yemen and in East Africa. (Courtesy US Marine Corps, 1st Lt Christin St. John)

In some cases, the Marine Corps variant is used, particularly if the task force is staging from offshore. In Yemen in January 2017, a Marine MV-22B crash-landed during the exfiltration of a SEAL Team 6 raiding force, resulting in three injured SEALs. The exact circumstances of the crash have not been released, although it is believed it was not caused by enemy fire.

The 2013 attempted non-combatant evacuation of US citizens in South Sudan ended in three AFSOC CV-22s riddled with some 119 rounds of 7.62x39mm and 12.7x108mm from rebel assault rifles and DShK heavy machine guns. Four SEALs were wounded during the operation with rounds punching through the unarmoured airframe, although all three CV-22s successfully made it to their divert location (all the injured SEALs survived). The mission resulted in the devolvement of a composite armour kit called the Advanced Ballistic Stopping System that could be relatively quickly and simply installed in the cargo area of a CV-22.

M1126 Stryker

Nationality: US • Type: Infantry Carrier Vehicle

In 2005, the 75th Ranger Regiment received 14 Stryker infantry carrier vehicles, an M1133 medical evacuation Stryker and an M1130 command variant. These were officially loaned to the Ranger Regiment to provide a protected mobility capability greater than its standard Ranger special

operations vehicles (RSOVs – modified Land Rovers) for its 2005 Afghan tour. It appears the Rangers never gave them back and indeed heavily modified the Strykers for their unique mission sets.

The Strykers employed by the Rangers have received a number of upgrades. Chief amongst these is appliqué composite armour in a similar fashion to current Delta Pandurs. Although classified, it is assumed that the Stryker armour is proofed against at least 14.5mm heavy machine gun rounds. They do not feature the so-called Stryker Reactive Armour Tiles (SRAT), which provide explosive reactive armour (ERA) useful against RPGs and recoilless rifles, probably because of the close proximity in which dismounted Rangers will be working with the Strykers.

Although Ranger Strykers deployed in the past to Iraq and Afghanistan have been equipped with a full set of bar armour (which works to trap and detonate RPG warheads before they strike the actual vehicle), those seen more recently in Syria feature either only one section of bar armour covering the frontal aspect of the Stryker to protect the driver or none at all.

The other most obvious enhancement has been an AGMS (armoured ground mobility system) Pandur-style driver's module, which sits the driver behind ballistic glass and allows far greater situational awareness. Ranger Strykers also feature additional lights – likely able to be operated in the infrared spectrum as well as visible white light – and a suite of anti-IED electronic countermeasures.

Ranger Strykers seen in Syria in June 2017. Note that the lead vehicle mounts a 7.62x51mm M134 minigun, possibly to counter the use of weaponized commercial drones flown by Islamic State. (Delil Souleiman/AFP/Getty Images)

Rangers deployed to Afghanistan in 2010 return to their modified M1126 Strykers. Note the slat or cage armour deployed on the Stryker to interdict RPG warheads before they strike the vehicle. (Courtesy US Army, Spc Joseph Wilson)

In terms of weapons platforms, the vehicles are a curious mix of CROWS (Common Remotely Operated Weapon Station) II remote weapons stations mounting .50 M2 heavy machine guns and Mk47 automatic grenade launchers, and open-topped manned armoured turrets, at least one of which has been seen in Syria mounting a 7.62mm M134 minigun, possibly to counter the drone threat. The use of the minigun makes sense in an environment where insurgents employ commercial drones fitted with grenades or mortar bombs. It also provides incredible suppressive capability against unarmoured targets.

M1165A1 GMV (Ground Mobility Vehicle)

Nationality: US • Type: Patrol Vehicle

The GMV or ground mobility vehicle began life as a largely field-expedient solution by the US Army's 5th Special Force Group, although work on a special operations variant of the HMMWV had begun as early as 1985. Faced with the prospect of deploying to Kuwait and potentially Iraq in 1991, 5th SFG's mobility specialists began working on modifying standard M988 and M1026 HMMWVs to suit their unique requirements. These initial experiments were christened the DMVS or Desert Mobility Vehicle System, occasionally referred to simply as the 'Dumvee'. The suspension was improved, as was the engine, and additional stowage racks and weapons mounts were added to the vehicles.

Delta also modified its own HMMWVs with similar modifications and these entered the western deserts of Iraq along with their customized Pinzgauer special operations vehicles (SOVs) in the famous Scud hunt to track down and destroy Iraqi mobile ballistic missile systems. This was the only time Delta deployed its DMV variant HMMWVs which were not as successful as its Pinzgauers, later replacing them with commercial non-standard tactical vehicles.

The M1025A2 TOW missile carrier and the standard M998 eventually formed the basis of the first production GMVs produced after *Desert Storm*. Variants were produced for each service within SOCOM. The Army Special Forces received the GMV-S (Special Forces), the SEALs the GMV-N (Navy), the Air Force the GMV-ST (Special Tactics) and the Rangers the GMV-R (Ranger). When Marine Special Operations Command (MARSOC) was established, a GMV-M (Marine) was subsequently produced. All differed slightly in their load capacities, up-armouring and weapons load.

The base GMV was produced with an improved suspension, a turbo-charge diesel engine, a radiator designed for desert use, increased payload capacity, extra stowage racks and infrared headlights. Some versions offered complete 'black-out' driving with a switch to eliminate all internal lighting. Each also had a main weapons mount in a turret ring, typically mounting a .50 M2 heavy machine gun or Mk19/Mk47 automatic grenade launcher. Some also featured swing arms mounting an M240 medium machine gun for the passenger and weapons mounts in the rear tray.

A US Army Special Forces GMV-S mounting a .50 M2 heavy machine gun in central turret ring and 7.62x51mm M240L in rear tray swing-arm. (Courtesy US Army, Visual Information Specialist Erich Backes)

Now known as the GMV 1.0 (after the development of the GMV 1.1 based on the General Dynamics Flyer), the GMVs in service with SOCOM forces are of three distinct types rather than service specific: the M1165A1 with B3 armour package, the standard M1165A1, and the M1113, all with special operations modifications.

The M1165A1 B3 is the standard up-armoured variant seen in Syria and Iraq and provides a level of protection greater than the M1114 armoured version used by conventional forces during the Iraq insurgency (with the B3 kit, the M1165A1 can withstand strikes from explosively formed projectile – EFP – IEDs). The M1165A1 base model has reduced protection and is designed to provide maximum range and mobility; it is closer to the original GMVs employed by 5th SFG during the invasion of Iraq. Finally the M1113 is a modified variant of the standard M1113 Expanded Capacity Vehicle and is able to be under-slung by an MH-60 Black Hawk.

Despite the introduction of the GMV 1.1, the older GMV is still a common sight in Afghanistan and Iraq/Syria. Images of the 5th SFG near al-Tanf taken in 2018 show a mix of GMVs and GMV 1.1s. The older-pattern GMV also offers the ability to now 'conceal in plain sight' alongside Afghan or Iraqi Army HMMWVs as both nations now employ the HMMWV, hiding the presence of US special operators amongst their allies.

M1288 GMV 1.1 (Ground Mobility Vehicle)

Nationality: US • Type: Patrol Vehicle

One of the key requirements for the GMV 1.1 programme (a programme to equip US SOF with a new light vehicle begun in 2012) was for a light vehicle that could be easily transported internally within a Chinook helicopter but that offered greater range and capacity than an ATV (all-terrain vehicle). Named GMV 1.1 in recognition of the earlier GMV 1.0, the HMMWV-based ground mobility vehicle, the programme saw six competing designs go into extensive trials.

General Dynamics' Flyer 72 won the competitive tender and began production in 2015. Along with a ring mount for the vehicle's primary weapons system, the Flyer can be fitted with several additional swing-mounted machine guns although a trial version equipped with a 30mm M230LF cannon has been displayed. The Flyer can carry up to five wounded on stretchers or else up to six operators, all under the protection of modular armour if necessary, along with the three-man crew.

The modular armour package gives operators the option based on the threat assessment with base armour protecting up to NATO STANAG Level 1 (fragmentation and small arms). The GMV 1.1 can be stripped down with

no doors or armour to conduct reconnaissance or 'buttoned-up' for direct action missions. Examples have been spotted in both Afghanistan and Syria operated by US Army Special Forces and US Navy SEALs.

A smaller version, the Flyer 60, is currently under examination for SOCOM procurement as the Advanced Light Strike Vehicle. It can be carried internally within the MV-22 Osprey tilt-rotor as it is only 60 inches (152cm) wide (for comparison the Flyer 72 is obviously enough 72 inches or 182cm wide). The Flyer 60 can carry four operators. Stripped down, two Flyer 72s can be carried within an MH-47 Chinook.

UK Special Forces are trialling the Flyer 72 as part of Project Westerley, an effort to procure a lightweight, Chinook-transportable special operations vehicle to replace or supplement the Mendacity Supacat platform, and a number are in service with Italy's Col Moschin and reportedly the Polish GROM. A modified variant has also been adopted by the US Army for airborne forces as the M1297 Army Ground Mobility Vehicle (AGMV).

Members of 5th Special Forces Group manning a GMV 1.0 (front) and GMV 1.1 (rear) at al-Tanf, southern Syria in November 2017. (Courtesy US Army, Staff Sgt Jacob Connor)

MH-6/AH-6 Little Bird

Nationality: US • Type: Assault/Attack Helicopter

The Little Bird concept was originally conceived during the planning of a second hostage rescue into Tehran in 1980 (see pages 318–19). A need existed to fly assaulters into a dense urban area from a small helicopter that could be transported to the region in a C-130 Hercules. A planner remembered the by-then obsolete OH-6 Cayuse of Vietnam fame and tracked a number down in a National Guard storage yard. In the capable hands of the pilots of Task Force 158, soon to be Task Force 160 (the first version of what would later become the 160th SOAR and the

The MH-6 Little Bird seen here during a capabilities exercise in 2018 with soldiers, probably Army Special Forces, perched on the 'people pods' to either side of the helicopter. (Courtesy Michael Bottoms, US SOCOM Communication Office)

The AH-6M armed Little Bird, also known as the Six Gun or Killer Egg, equipped here with 2.75-inch unguided rocket pods and 7.62x51mm miniguns. (Courtesy US Army, Patrick A. Albright)

component command which would provide helicopter support during the *Eagle Claw* mission), and fitted with an early version of FLIR (forward-looking infrared) they became the first iteration of the famed Little Bird.

During the development of these original Little Birds, Delta snipers found they did not have enough room to shoot accurately from the helicopter and an ingenious solution was found: 55 gallon fuel drums were sliced in half and mounted to both skids. Six of the OH-6s were also converted into attack helicopter configuration with a minigun mounted on one side and an unguided rocket pod on the other. These became the first AH-6s.

The aircraft, now called the MH-6, evolved over time with the fuel drums replaced with what was officially termed the External Personnel System or unofficially as the 'People Pod', a folding plank-like attachment that allowed up to two operators to be carried externally. This suited the operators as it minimized any delay in getting off the helicopter at the objective. A detachable fast rope system was also fitted should a landing be unfeasible.

The AH-6 was also refined. The current AH-6M is fitted with FLIR and a suite of radios including satellite communications. The standard armament is now an M134 minigun and a 70mm (2.75in.) rocket pod on either stub wing. Both the MH and AH-6 are fitted with Blue Force Tracker, which allows aircrew to deconflict enemy and friendly forces on the ground.

MH-47G Chinook

Nationality: US • Type: Medium Lift Helicopter

Based on the older MH-47E, the MH-47G is the standard Chinook variant flown by the 160th Special Operations Aviation Regiment (160th SOAR). It can be refuelled in-flight (the distinctive refuelling probe makes spotting a 160th SOAR MH-47G easy), and can carry a reinforced platoon of operators (between 30 and 50 dependent on how much equipment is carried). For the 160th it has become the preferred platform to insert a large assault force quickly.

It features a fully digital avionics package and is equipped with multi-mode Raytheon AN/APQ-174A radar and a Raytheon AN/AAQ-16 forward-looking infrared (FLIR) which enables the flight crew to see 'through' darkness, smoke and rain, allowing the MH-47G to be flown in almost all conditions. Even with a full load, the MH-47G can reach speeds of between 120 and 170 knots, often out-pacing escorting Apaches.

The MH-47G is equipped with an electrically powered 7.62x51mm M134 minigun on each side and a spade-grip M60D on the rear ramp. It also features a common missile warning system that gives audio and visual warning of SAM launches, the Advanced Threat Infrared Countermeasures system

US Army Rangers prepare to board an MH-47 to infiltrate them into a target area to conduct a kill or capture mission, Afghanistan, 2014. (Courtesy US Army, Spc Michael G. Herrero)

which uses a laser to divert the incoming missile off-target, an electronic countermeasures suite to deal with enemy radio jamming, and the XM216 flare dispenser which can confuse heat-seeking missiles.

The MH-47G has seen extensive action around the globe but particularly in Iraq and Afghanistan where airframes flew multiple missions nearly every single night. The advantages of the MH-47G are its superior payload capacity (vehicles like the GMV 1.1 and MRZR, non-standard commercial vehicles and even the older Ranger RSOV or Ranger special operations vehicle can be internally stowed, while larger and heavier vehicles like the GMV or ground mobility vehicle can be sling-loaded under the helicopter) and its operational range and speed.

Although the MH-47G presents a large target when landing near an objective, AC-130s, armed UAVs (unmanned aerial vehicles) and attack helicopters are normally present to scan the landing zone and confirm the presence of hostiles long before the Chinook arrives. If the helicopter does come under fire, the crew can escape quickly thanks to the speed of the twin-rotor airframe.

For the Abbottabad raid to capture or kill bin Laden in 2011 (see pages 338–40), consideration was actually given to infiltrating the SEALs in MH-47Gs using terrain masking (flying so-called nap of the earth) which would hide the Chinooks from Pakistani air defence radars and minimize their signature as they approached the objective. For what appears to have been political reasons relating to authorization of the mission, the MH-X Silent Hawks were instead chosen.

At least two MH-47Gs flew a Ranger Quick Reaction Force along the Afghan border during the operation in case the SEALs ended up surrounded and needed reinforcement to exfiltrate. Additionally three MH-47Gs penetrated Pakistani airspace alongside the Silent Hawks, two equipped with fuel bladders to conduct refuelling of the MH-Xs for the return flight to Jalalabad and the other carrying additional SEALs to act as an Immediate Reaction Force for the assault element.

MH-60 Black Hawk

Nationality: US • Type: Medium Lift Helicopter

Since the formation of the 160th Special Operations Aviation Regiment (160th SOAR), US Army special operations Black Hawks have been configured with a number of mission-specific enhancements. The two current models in use are the MH-60K and the MH-60L. All feature common elements such as night vision capable cockpits, a FLIR (forward-looking infrared) pod, air-to-air refuelling capability (with the MH-60's distinctive probe), optional external fuel bladders and a defensive suite including two M134 miniguns.

The 160th also pioneered and is the only unit to fly the MH-60L direct action penetrator or DAP. The concept for the DAP is two-fold. One, it serves as an armed escort for other MH-60s and MH-47s infiltrating troops (a task it carried out in the first lifts of Special Forces ODAs into Afghanistan). Two,

An MH-60M from the 160th Special Operations Aviation Regiment hovers as Special Forces soldiers fast-rope onto a simulated enemy-held vessel. (Courtesy Michael Bottoms, US SOCOM Communication Office)

it can orbit around the objective and can thus either support armed Little Birds by securing an outer perimeter or, if the objective is at a height which makes the Little Bird unfeasible, act in the direct close air support role.

The DAP can carry a wide assortment of weapons systems. A typical load-out would include one 30mm M230 cannon, a pair of forward-firing M134 miniguns and either unguided 70mm (2.75-inch) rocket pods or Hellfire anti-tank guided missiles. Increasingly, the 160th is using the Advanced Precision Kill Weapon System (APKWS), which gives the 70mm rockets laser guidance.

All versions of the MH-60 can attain speeds of up to 178 knots with a standard range of 450 nautical miles, which can be increased by the provision of air-to-air refuelling and/or use of external long distance tanks. The latest MH-60 variants are equipped with advanced AN/APQ-187 Silent Knight radar for terrain avoidance and both electro-optical and infrared (FLIR) cameras for flying in any weather or light environment.

A contingent from the 160th is based at the legendary Area 51 and flies the so-called MH-X or Silent Hawk stealth variant of the MH-60 Black Hawk. This was the helicopter used to ferry SEAL Team 6 operators into Abbottabad to kill Usama bin Laden in 2011. The programme originally stemmed from work conducted to develop a 'stealthy' Little Bird and progressed to build two 'signature reduced' Black Hawks for clandestine infiltrations into non-permissive environments. What made them 'stealthy', however, also made them difficult to fly and, most importantly for infiltrations, to hover.

SOCOM had actually cancelled the programme by 2011 with only the original two highly experimental helicopters built. Since then, the programme has been re-started and as many as six Silent Hawks now exist. They were rumoured to have been flown in at least one Delta operation into Syria in 2014. Apart from the tail rotor assembly seen in the aftermath of the crash at the Abbottabad compound in the 2011 Operation *Neptune Spear*, no reliable imagery exists of exactly what these helicopters look like.

Non-Standard Commercial Vehicle (NSCV)/Non-Standard Tactical Vehicle (NSTV)

Nationality: US • Type: Covert Utility Vehicle

Commonly referred to as a 'Non-Tac', the non-standard commercial or tactical vehicle (NSCV/NSTV) is a modified civilian pick-up truck which can blend into its environs. According to the United States' SOCOM, non-standard commercial vehicles 'provide SOF with a low visibility vehicle capability to conduct operations in politically or operationally constrained permissive, semi-permissive, or denied areas.'

Early examples of such vehicles were purchased directly from Toyota and Land Rover and modified by contractor firms to accommodate special operations equipment such as Blue Force Trackers, SATCOM radios, and run-flat tyres. Immediately following the 9/11 attacks, US Army Special Forces even purchased Toyota Tacoma trucks from dealerships around Fort Bragg and refitted their own modifications including winches and weapon mounts.

In recent years SOCOM has purchased a large number of NSCVs – mainly Toyota Land Cruiser 79s (perfectly suited for Africa, Syria and Libya) and the venerable Toyota Hilux (which blends in for operations in Afghanistan and Pakistan, for example). Ford Rangers have also been purchased as these are increasingly used by Iraqi and Afghan security forces. SUV (sport utility vehicle) variants of the Land Cruiser 76, 78 and 200 series have also been purchased (these have been seen in both Niger and Syria with US Army Special Forces).

The Navistar Special Operations Tactical Vehicle (SOTV) series is a development of the Navistar Non-Standard Tactical Truck first introduced in 2008. The SOTV is an armoured Non-Tac that can be up-armoured with appliqué armour panels, depending on threat, and can be internally carried within an MH-47 Chinook.

The SOTV comes standard with blackout capability meaning that it can be driven with infrared headlights and all other vehicle lights switched off, allowing for highly covert operations at night. Two variants are offered, both of which have been purchased by SOCOM, the SOTV-A and SOTV-B.

A US Army Special Forces soldier mans a .50 M2 heavy machine gun sporting a Surefire HellFighter weapon light mounted upon a Toyota Hilux in Syria, May 2016. (Delil Souleiman/AFP/Getty Images)

The difference is primarily that the B model is designed for deniable operations such as those carried out under Title 50 authority and can be configured to visually match any common model of commercial SUV.

The SOTV-A can also be reconfigured to visually simulate another make but is more obviously a militarized SUV with its integral ring mount for machine guns or automatic grenade launchers. The SOTV-A could easily pass inspection at range as just another technical while the SOTV-B would be able to endure much closer examination, perhaps allowing suitably disguised operators to negotiate checkpoints without revealing their identity. Future variants will include transparent armour, giving greater protection, but still appearing as a local vehicle at range.

UKSF operate a range of types but have been spotted in Libya in 2016 using recent models of the Toyota Hilux – this was most likely the SBS. These vehicles were white with typical racing stripes (and some seemingly crudely camouflaged with mud) and mounted both .50 M2s with distinctive Trijicon ACOG optics and Heckler & Koch GMG automatic grenade launchers. Others have been seen in Afghanistan in less obtrusive colours mounting both single and twin 7.62mm general purpose machine guns. Even the Russian Komandovanie sil spetsial'nalnykh operatsii (KSSO) has been spotted operating Toyota Tundra SUVs in Syria, although the domestically produced Patriot is a more common platform.

Oshkosh M1245 (MRAP All-terrain Vehicle or M-ATV)

Nationality: US • Type: Mine Resistant Ambush Protected (MRAP) Vehicle

The MRAP (mine resistant ambush protected) all-terrain vehicle or M-ATV was developed both to increase the off-road capability of the current generation of MRAPs and to improve upon the 'top-heavy' rollover risk of earlier designs. It was designed from the ground up with environments such as Afghanistan in mind. Developed to operate in high-threat IED areas, the M-ATV is built upon a V-shaped hull to direct the blast upwards and away from the vehicle.

The US SOCOM variant of the air-conditioned 4x4 vehicle can carry five including the crew; it is normally manned by the operators themselves who complete the MRAP course before deployment. The SOCOM M-ATVs have an acoustic counter-sniper system for detecting enemy fire and all sport a range of electronic counter-IED measures to jam or disrupt IEDs.

Today's versions invariably feature the M153 CROWS (Common Remotely Operated Weapon Station) II remote weapon system mounting a .50 M2 heavy machine gun or 40mm automatic grenade launcher that can be fired from inside the vehicle (and sometimes matched with the Boomerang counter-sniper system, which can detect and note the direction of incoming small arms fire)

while most earlier versions featured the Objective Gunner Protection Kit (OGPK) with an open, manned turret. Most used by US special operators is the later M1245A1 variant that features the UIK or Underbelly Improvement Kit, which adds extra armour to counter IEDs and mines.

The M-ATV has seen significant service in northern Iraq and Syria in the campaign against Islamic State. During operations to retake Mosul, a number were painted black to blend in with the black-painted HMMWVs of the Iraqi Counter Terrorist Service which the Green Berets were mentoring and supporting with embedded operators trained as JTACs (joint terminal attack controllers). Three particular tan-painted vehicles operating around Mosul humorously sported the names of Disney princesses on their doors.

In Syria the vehicles have been seen in both standard tan and in a locally applied camouflage pattern. They were amongst the first US special operations vehicles spotted in Syria and have been seen operating alongside 'Non-Tac' commercial SUVs (sport utility vehicles). A number of these Special Forces M-ATVs have been significantly upgunned with additional weapons platforms including Mk47 grenade launchers and M240L medium machine guns on swing-arm mounts in the rear cargo compartment.

Other MRAPs are in use by SOCOM, including the M1239 special operations variant of the RG33 Armored Utility Vehicle. Older RG31A1s are also still in use. The M1245 and M1239 are both often seen fitted with a range of counter-IED measures, such as IED jammers to provide an electronic umbrella which disrupts remote detonation based on radio or mobile (cell) phone signals and Rhino, a boom that extends ahead of the vehicle to prematurely detonate IEDs emplaced to be triggered by infrared sensors, effectively initiating the device before the vehicle passes by.

Two US Army Special Force M1245A1 M-ATVs spotted outside Mosul in October 2016. The M-ATVs were initially painted black to help them blend in with the black-painted HMMWVs used by the Iraqi Counter Terrorist Service (CTS); similarly some operators wore Crye Black MultiCam in an effort to 'hide in plain sight' alongside the black-clad CTS operators. (Yunus Keles/Anadolu Agency/Getty Images)

Pandur Armoured Ground Mobility System (AGMS)

Nationality: US • Type: Armoured Personnel Carrier

Following the experiences of using unarmoured HMMWVs during the battle of Mogadishu, Delta Force began looking at whether a light armoured carrier could be adopted to ferry its operators to urban targets. The argument bitterly divided Delta, with one camp arguing that acquiring light armour would lead to missions being planned based on its inclusion and thus limiting JSOC's options when deploying the unit. They also argued that precious maintenance and training time would be eaten up by the vehicles, as the operators would have to train on operating and maintaining the vehicles rather than working on their core skills.

The question was finally answered in the late 1990s with Delta purchasing a number of modified Austrian Pandur 6x6 armoured personnel carriers from General Dynamics Land Systems. An initial order for 12 was later supplemented by another order in 2006 for an additional 11 vehicles. Christened the AGMS or Armoured Ground Mobility System, but known within Delta as simply the Pandur, the vehicles were an immediate success.

A column of Delta Force Pandur AGMSs pictured in Baghdad, October 2003. The early versions used a simple gun shield while current versions seen in Syria use remote weapons stations. The fabric taped to the front of each vehicle is possibly an ad hoc identification-friend-or-foe measure and may be fashioned from a VS-17 marker. (Patrick Baz/AFP/Getty Images)

It appears that the unit deployed to Afghanistan in 2001 with its Pinzgauer special operations vehicles but the AGMS debuted in Iraq soon after. The AGMS could ferry up to seven Delta operators under armour to an objective and, more importantly, get them and any prisoners back out again. The AGMSs initially mounted a simple gunshield for their M240s and Mk48s but some were later fitted with remote weapons stations mounting the .50 Browning heavy machine gun and the Mk47 automatic grenade launcher.

More recently a version was seen in Syria armed with a TOW II anti-tank guided missile system to counter armoured suicide vehicle-borne IEDs (SVBIEDs), literally armoured car bombs including versions built from APCs (armoured personnel carriers) and tanks that are employed by the Islamic State. All AGMSs feature a number of counter-IED electronic countermeasures and appliqué armour kits that can be increased or decreased based on the perceived threat. They can also be equipped with specialist surveillance equipment.

According to former operators, the Pandur AGMS is also used as a rolling resupply vehicle with operators able to store their water, ammunition and other essentials on board. Some leave their 'go-bags' of ammunition and grenades on the vehicles when they strike an objective, others take the 'go-bag' with them to allow immediate resupply. Another big advantage is the capability of extracting wounded operators under fire; the AGMS can accommodate two litters (stretchers) in the rear passenger compartment.

One Delta AGMS was destroyed in 2005 by a massive IED constructed of multiple anti-tank mines on the Syrian border. Three veteran operators were killed, along with a Ranger corporal. Several other vehicles have suffered multiple RPG and IED attacks. The platform is used only by Delta, and on occasion by SEAL Team 6, for example during the rescue of Private Jessica Lynch in Iraq 2003,* and has become something of a signature platform as it is distinctive enough to telegraph Delta's presence in a combat zone, a point made by former Delta operators who were against the procurement for that very reason.

The British SAS wished to purchase its own AGMS vehicles but reportedly the lead-time from the manufacturer was too long for the regiment's pressing needs and instead the Australian Bushmaster was procured; this is known as the Escapade, probably from the procurement programme name. According to a 2019 SOCOM briefing paper, a replacement for the AGMS known as the 'Next Generation' AGMS is scheduled to enter service in 2022/23.

---

* Private Lynch was captured by Iraqi forces after the supply convoy in which she was driving took a wrong turn and was ambushed. She was later rescued by SEAL Team 6.

Polaris MRZR

Nationality: US • Type: Patrol Vehicle

Polaris has had great success with its range of all-terrain vehicles (ATVs), the ubiquitous 'quad', which many special operations units have employed as a resupply, casualty evacuation and even route reconnaissance vehicle. Variants have been produced with specially configured mufflers to deaden the sound of the engine and with infrared filters on the headlights to allow the vehicles to be driven at night using night vision goggles.

In an update to the classic ATV, Polaris developed the MRZR-2 and MRZR-4 in response to a SOCOM request for an ATV that could carry additional cargo and weapons while still seating between two and four operators. Officially termed the light tactical all-terrain vehicle (LTATV) and based on the civilian RZR model, the MRZR now comes in two variants based on load capacity.

Both feature swing-mount fitted weapons stations to allow M240L and Mk48 medium machine guns to be fired by the passenger and can move at speeds of almost 100 kilometres an hour. They have been modified from the commercial RZR to accommodate litter-carrying capability, run flat tyres, an infrared light system and a winch for self-recovery. A further variant, the DAGOR or Deployable Advanced Ground Off-Road, has also been developed.

All appear visually as beefier descendants of the SEAL M1040/M1041 desert patrol vehicle (DPV) and the SAS' Light Strike Vehicle, essentially armed dune buggies that were trialled during the 1990s (the SEALs last used a DPV operationally in 2001 in Afghanistan but they were famously photographed during the liberation of Kuwait in 1991).

US Special Forces MRZR light tactical all-terrain vehicles (LTATVs) seen near Mosul, Iraq, May 2016. Note the Javelin missile and Command Launch Unit standing by ready to fire. The coloured panels are for aerial recognition. (Yunus Keles/Anadolu Agency/Getty Images)

Both the MRZR-4 and MRZR-2 can be internally carried in a range of airframes, including the MH-47 Chinook and the MV-22 Osprey making the vehicle very attractive for units using these airframes. Being able to be easily flown into an objective, it can serve as a light fire support platform or as a resupply vehicle, or to evacuate casualties back to a helicopter landing zone.

Along with deployments to Northern Iraq and Syria, the MRZR-4 has been spotted with US Army Special Forces operators arriving in Libya in 2015. The MRZR-4 has also been adopted by the Canadian Special Operations Regiment (CSOR) and JTF2 as the Ultra-Light Combat Vehicle (ULCV) and Australia's SASR and 2 Commando Regiments in the form of the DAGOR.

Germany's GSG9 has purchased a small number of MRZRs, as has the Portuguese Força de

Operações Especiais (FOE) for their operators, while the French have adopted a similar vehicle to the MRZR-2, the two-seat Unac RIDER (Rapid Intervention Droppable Equipment for Raiders), designed with two weapon mounts and which can be parachuted into an objective.

Supacat HMT 400

Nationality: UK • Type: Surveillance and Reconnaissance Vehicle/Offensive Action Vehicle

The UK firm Supacat was established in 1981 and worked on a number of specialist vehicular engineering projects for the UK Ministry of Defence (MOD). In its earlier days, its best-known product was the 6x6 All Terrain Mobile Platform or ATMP, a sort of predecessor to the quad bike or ATV (all-terrain vehicle) designed to move supplies over rough terrain at the front line. In the late 1990s, Supacat responded to a tender from the MOD for a replacement vehicle for the Land Rover-based 'Pinkies' and 'Dinkies' used by the SAS and SBS. Supacat won the tender with the High Mobility Transporter or HMT 400.

The HMT 400 was designed to meet the requirements of what were originally specifications for two separate vehicles, a surveillance and reconnaissance vehicle and an offensive action vehicle. Commonalities included the need for excellent handling over desert and mountain terrain, including the ability to raise or lower the suspension based on the terrain; an open-top design for visibility matched with roll-over survivability; a number of weapons stations and integrated satellite communications; and the ability to be transported within a Chinook helicopter.

Sixty-five HMT 400s were purchased by UKSF for use by both units, and their Land Rover platforms were retired in the aftermath of the invasion of Iraq. Acquired under Project Mendacity, the UKSF vehicles were first deployed to Afghanistan's Helmand Province in 2006. In far more urban Iraq, the SAS replaced its ageing (and unarmoured) 'Pinkies' with borrowed American up-armoured HMMWVs, until such time as they could purchase a number of Australian-designed Bushmaster protected mobility vehicles (they had originally wanted the same vehicle Delta Force used in Iraq – the Austrian Pandur – but the manufacturers could not match the aggressive delivery requirements of the SAS).

Delta itself was suitably impressed with the new SAS vehicle and ordered 47 HMT 400s based on the Mendacity specification to replace their 6x6 Pinzgauer 718 special operations vehicles. The highly modified Delta Pinzgauers had been operational since *Desert Storm* (and had deployed to Afghanistan in 2001 and Iraq in 2003) but were approaching the end of their service life. Delta fittingly code-named their version the Marauder.

The Australian variant of the Supacat HMT 400 Extenda known as the Nary in honour of an SASR warrant officer who was killed in Kuwait in 2005. (Courtesy Commonwealth of Australia, Sam Birch)

The British Army was also looking for a replacement for its armed Land Rovers known as the WMIK (Weapon Mounted Installation Kit). Following positive feedback from UKSF, a version of the HMT 400 was trialled and adopted as the MWMIK for Mobility WMIK or Jackal 1. At the time of adoption, controversy surrounded the deployment of largely unarmoured vehicles like the WMIK and Jackal to Helmand with its high IED threat. A second version of the MWMIK known as the Jackal 2 was procured with Afghanistan-inspired improvements, including increased chassis armour and blast seats.

A 6x6 version, called the HMT 600, was also purchased by UKSF as a 'mothership' resupply vehicle to replace their ACMAT and Unimog trucks that had also served since *Desert Storm*. The wider British Army also procured a version of the HMT 600 called the Coyote as a 'tactical support vehicle', intended to carry resupplies for Jackal patrols. This HMT 600 design also led to a third version being adopted by special operations units including the Australian SASR, the Danish Jægerkorps and most recently the Norwegian Army.

Called the HMT (E) Extenda, this unique design allows a third axle to be added, converting the HMT 400 into a 6x6 version. It offers obvious operational flexibility, allowing the vehicle to be converted to suit specific requirements (the Australian SASR for instance favour a 6x6 platform for desert patrolling and replaced its distinctive six-wheeled Perentie Long Range Patrol Vehicle with the Extenda).

In fact, one of the latest adoptions of a Supacat design has been the Extenda, with 89 vehicles purchased for Australia's 2 Commando Regiment. This Special Operations Vehicle – Commando or SOV-Cdo can be reconfigured into any of four different configurations: Troop, Mortar, Command and Control and Logistics. New Zealand SAS too have adopted the Extenda as the Special Operations Vehicle – Mobility Heavy (SOV-MH).

Swimmer Delivery Vehicle (SDV)

Nationality: US • Type: Submersible

Swimmer delivery vehicles (SDVs) offer a covert infiltration option for naval SOF. Resembling large torpedos, SDVs are submersibles that can carry a reconnaissance or assault team into enemy-held ports or beaches or provide a hidden approach to a hijacked ship. They are launched from submarines, allowing a vessel to stay in international waters while infiltrating operators.

The latest model coming into service is the SDV Mk11 Shallow Water Combat Submersible (SWCS). Three have been purchased for the British SBS, which currently employs the MkVIII Mod1 SDV, the same model that has been in use with the SEALs. The Mk11 can carry six operators and be deployed from the dry deck shelter of a suitably equipped submarine. The Russians have also introduced a so-called Special Mission submarine, which carries its own complement of midget submarines that can be used by special operators.

STIDD submarine diver propulsion devices (DPDs) are also used by many maritime SOF. The DPD resembles a cross between a torpedo and a sled and can carry two operators and their equipment. The SEALs also employ a range of stealthy, high-speed boats and the Combat Rubber Raiding Craft (CRRC), more commonly known as the Zodiac.

The outboard-powered CRRC can typically carry ten operators and their equipment. The latest version includes Armorflate, an inflatable soft armour system. The CRRC offers a fast approach to an enemy ship and can be dropped from a C-130 or an MH-47. The latest Combatant Craft Assault or CCA is the Mk1 operated by Special Boat Team 20 assigned to Naval Special Warfare Development Group. Air-droppable by C-17A Globemaster, the CCA Mk1 is designed with stealth in mind. It is built from radar-reflecting composites and, like the F-35, has no protrusions to register on enemy systems. It is even equipped with combatant craft forward-looking infrared (CCFLIR) for operations at night and in inclement weather.

A heavily armed Special Operations Craft–Riverine (SOC-R) crewed by Special Warfare combatant-craft crewmen attached to Special Boat Team 22. (US Navy photo by Mass Communications Specialist 2nd Class Jayme Pastoric)

TACTICS

Advanced Force Operations (AFO)

All SOF conduct a range of reconnaissance activities and indeed strategic or special reconnaissance has been a core skill for many units since World War II. Advanced force operations (AFO) differ from even clandestine reconnaissance in wartime as they are typically covert activities conducted in civilian dress or even enemy garb and designed to remain secret. Even if discovered, clothing and weapons will typically be deniable, meaning they have no identifying marks or serial numbers to trace back to the country of origin.

The CIA Jawbreaker teams who entered Afghanistan ahead of the Army Special Forces in 2001 were conducting an AFO activity, wearing civilian clothes and carrying deniable AK-47s and Browning pistols. Likewise units such as Delta Force and SEAL Team 6 place increasing emphasis on the covert infiltration of operators to conduct anything from environmental reconnaissance to the traditional CTR, or close target reconnaissance, of an objective.

Such deniable operations have always had a designated, specially trained element in many large SOF organizations. In Delta, the Operational Support Troop conducted such operations. In the Australian SASR, the Guerrilla Warfare Cell was trained and equipped largely for covert AFO-type tasks. Today, AFO has become a core role with separate squadrons or teams assigned to the task such as E Squadron within 22SAS, G Squadron of Delta or 4 Squadron of SASR.

This is also a growth area for the employment of females within SOF units. Delta was one of the first to employ women within its Operational

Soldiers from the 7th Special Forces Group conduct surveillance of a target during exercises in 2016. Note the sniper in his Ghillie Suit to the right. There are no known images of AFO members. (Courtesy US Army, Tech Sgt Efren Lopez)

Support Troop in the late 1980s and the experiment paid dividends during the hunt for war criminals in the Balkans where male and female pairs were much less obtrusive. The women complete a specialist version of the Operator Training Course which focuses on surveillance, reconnaissance and close quarter battle skills.

AFO has also blended into other traditional SOF activities. Covert or advisory training teams may be infiltrated into a country to work with either an insurgent or government force in a purely deniable manner. An example of this was the embedding of JSOC operators within Ethiopian forces who entered Somalia in 2007 to combat al-Shabaab and al-Qaeda elements who were taking refuge in the war-torn nation. Another example was the small JSOC presence attached to Pakistan's Special Service Group (SSG) in the immediate aftermath of the 9/11 attacks. These operators cultivated long beards and wore Pakistani uniforms, although their non-standard weapons became a distinctive signature for the trained eye.

Aerial Vehicle Interdiction (AVI)

Aerial vehicle interdiction (AVI), sometimes known simply as VI or vehicle interdiction, is the interdiction of a target in a ground vehicle by precision fire from a helicopter. It is used in both hostage rescue and direct action scenarios where the aim is to capture the occupants of the vehicle. Indeed the concept was driven by counter-terrorism operations and specifically the need to halt escaping vehicles. The German GSG9 and French Groupe d'Intervention de la Gendarmerie nationale (GIGN or National Police Intervention Group) were experimenting with the tactic as far back as the 1970s.

One of the earliest examples of AVI as a special operations tactic was its use by Task Force Ranger in Mogadishu in 1993. One of its targets was captured by an AVI consisting of Delta snipers aboard Black Hawks. Units such as France's Commando Parachutiste de l'Air no10 (CPA-10) train extensively in the AVI role. The French commandos use the 7.62x51mm HK417 fitted with an EOTech holographic weapon sight which allows operators to keep both eyes open when firing. They also use shotguns to fire flares as a warning to their targets to stop their vehicles and to destroy enemy drones in flight.

Delta Force consistently employed scoped SR-25s in Iraq, firing armour-piercing rounds to penetrate the engine block. It would also employ the miniguns mounted on the MH-60 helicopters flown by the 160th SOAR to riddle a vehicle's engine block. The miniguns on both the MH-60s and the AH-6 Little Bird attack helicopters would also be used to fire warning bursts ahead of the enemy vehicle in an attempt to capture the target bloodlessly.

Once the vehicle was stopped, operators, often carried on the 'people pods' of MH-6 Little Birds, would land ahead and behind the vehicle and conduct the capture operation with the snipers overwatching from above. AVI was also used by SBS snipers during a 2007 hostage rescue in Afghanistan; the insurgents made off with the hostages in two SUVs (sport utility vehicles), which were disabled from the air by the SBS snipers, allowing a cut-off force to encircle and kill the hostage takers.

The tactic has been used by the Delta Force elements of the Expeditionary Targeting Force in Iraq and Syria. 2019 media reports on an Islamic State chemical weapons production effort detail an AVI against one of the scientists responsible in a February 2016 operation. Four helicopters were used, two as firing platforms with snipers engaging the tyres and engine block of the car, and two others landing with the capture team, including a combat assault dog, which held the target until he was restrained and hooded by the operators.

A US Navy SEAL practises firing from a helicopter. Note the suppressor and Night Force optic on his modified 7.62x51mm Mk11. Although this image shows the helicopter over water, an aerial vehicle interdiction would follow the same principles. (Courtesy US Navy, Seaman Apprentice Brian Read Castillo)

Building Clearance

Another key skill used by all SOF is building clearance and close quarter battle (CQB). SOF units are trained and conduct exercises in specially built urban ranges known as 'Shoot Houses' or 'Killing Houses'. Operators spend hundreds of hours each year honing their skills in these buildings, which allow furniture and individual room layout to be changed to suit a particular scenario or to mirror a real-world location.

These indoor ranges include sophisticated closed-circuit video systems, allowing instructors to monitor techniques, and rubber walls to stop bullets, with industrial-strength fans to extract gunpowder and explosive residue. MOE (method of entry) buildings are also used to train teams in a wide range of breaching techniques.

Some units have access to modified civilian passenger aircraft, buses and train carriages allowing them to conduct training in the most realistic way possible. Role players or other unit members often play the part of terrorists or insurgents and hostages or local civilian inhabitants. In the United Kingdom, the Royal Family regularly attend familiarization sessions which include the royalty sitting in a darkened room while operators conduct an assault around them with live ammunition and flashbangs.

Building clearance is also trained for urban operations in conventional or counter-insurgency operations. Mock-up Iraqi or Afghan villages have been constructed purely for this purpose. Although SOF are not typically involved in the clearance of enemy-held cities, a role for the infantryman, they do deploy in support or conduct shaping operations for conventional forces. During the second battle for Fallujah, for example, SEALs, Green Berets and Delta operators all embedded with Marine and Army infantry units.

US Army Rangers from 2nd Battalion, 75th Ranger Regiment, conduct building clearance exercises in a US Army 'Shoot House'. Note the Remington 870 shotgun carried by the breacher to the left and the SOPMOD Block II M4A1 carbines. The yellow muzzle attachments are blank firing adapters. (Courtesy US Army, Staff Sgt Teddy Wade)

Clearly villages held by insurgents have also become an ever more likely scenario for SOF deploying to conflict zones to snatch an enemy leader or recover intelligence information, such as the 2017 SEAL Team 6 raid into Yakla in Yemen (see pages 138–39). Although planned as a fast direct action mission targeting designated compounds, the SEALs found themselves in a large-scale battle against armed civilians and al-Qaeda fighters. Similar battles in Afghanistan have resulted either from targeted high-value target missions being compromised or from incorrect intelligence.

Climbing

SOF make extensive use of climbing as a means of infiltration and exfiltration. One of the more obvious techniques is that of fast-roping from a hovering helicopter. This enables a team to deploy quickly onto an objective without the necessity of finding and securing a landing zone. As a means of extraction, particularly of hostages, a device known as an AirTEP (Airborne Tactical Extraction Platform) can be used. This resembles an upside-down umbrella constructed of Kevlar which opens to provide a platform for the hostages to clamber onto before being whisked away under a helicopter.

Tactical rappelling is also a famous SOF skill. Typically used during counter-terrorist operations such as at the Iranian Embassy in 1980, it allows operators to access entry points that are otherwise unreachable relatively quickly and quietly. They can then employ glass breakers or similar MOE (method of entry) tools to make entry through the window or door and attack from an unexpected direction. Climbing is also important for SOF snipers who must find the most advantageous position to provide overwatch for the assaulters.

Members of the South Korean National Police Special Operations Unit practice the so-called 'Australian' or forward rappel designed to allow the operator to see any threats as he or she descends down the building and to engage a target is necessary. It has also proven to be a significantly faster method of descent that than traditional rappelling. (Youn Jae-Wook/ AFP/Getty Images)

Maritime SOF operations probably require the most extensive use of specialist climbing skills and equipment. A rope is attached either by a covertly infiltrated advance element (who have likely scaled the sides by the use of magnetic hand and foot clamps) or by using a compressed air operated grapnel launcher, which can fire a grapnel with attached rope up to 50 metres. Versions also exist that automatically unfurl a climbing ladder in their wake, allowing operators to ascend quickly. To scale a ship quickly and quietly, a device known as a powered tactical ascender is used. A motorized device, it remotely ascends or descends the rope at several speeds and can be used to insert an assault team quickly and near silently.

The ascender can allow hands-free operation of the rope by an operator designated to emplace a breaching charge or 'bang stick' on an external window of a target building. The ascender is instead controlled by a fellow operator from the rooftop. Similar systems can be used to extract wounded personnel or hostages.

Telescopic poles with a hook device are also used in both maritime operations and in urban combat and counter-terrorism missions. The hook is attached to a rope to allow an ascender to be used or a caving ladder that can be immediately employed to climb onto the deck. These are only a few of the techniques used to infiltrate an assault team covertly onto a hijacked ship or similar target.

Combat Search and Rescue (CSAR)

In all active conflict zones, particularly those involving Coalition air campaigns such as Syria, a risk exists that an aircraft will be shot down and the aircrew placed at risk of capture or worse. Particularly in such grey zones between war and counter-terrorism, SOF are often given the task of providing a combat search and rescue or CSAR presence.

The role is to fast-rope, parachute or otherwise insert into the site of a downed aircraft (and sometimes vehicles struck by IEDs), provide immediate medical aid and free any crew trapped in the wreckage before stabilizing the wounded for extraction. Often all of this must be accomplished while in the middle of an ongoing firefight.

Within dedicated special operations task forces, a component unit will normally be tasked with CSAR, such as US Air Force Special Tactics pararescue jumpers (PJs) and combat controllers (CCTs), often supported by an SST or Search and Rescue Security Team of operators. During Operation *Gothic Serpent* for instance, the CSAR element of PJs and CCTs from the 24th Special Tactics Squadron (24th STS) was accompanied by a mixed Delta Force and Ranger SST.

In established theatres such as Afghanistan, the CSAR mission is entirely run by dedicated US Air Force Rescue Squadrons flying the HH-60G Pave Hawk (with many similarities to the specially configured MH-60s of the 160th Special Operations Aviation Regiment or 160th SOAR); these are often known by the callsign 'Pedro' in Afghanistan and respond to casualties from both conventional and SOF units. The Rescue Squadrons normally operate in a package of two HH-60s supported by a pair of A-10A Warthog ground attack aircraft along with intelligence, surveillance, targeting and reconnaissance (ISTAR) assets, with top cover provided by a pair of fighter escorts.

Air Force Special Tactics are integrated into the local special operations task force. Army aviation units also provide aeromedical evacuation but do not conduct dedicated CSAR missions. In some cases, the closest unit is the one that responds, however. In July 2017, when an Afghan member of a CIA partner unit operating under ANSOF (Afghan National Special Operations Force), otherwise known as Omega, was shot, it was Army Aviation 'medevac' Black Hawks that responded, evacuating the casualty and braving enemy fire to land a second time in an attempt to save an Army Ranger who had been hit moments before.

An HH-60G Pavehawk and pararescue jumpers (PJs) of the USAF's 82nd Expeditionary Rescue Squadron conduct casualty evacuation training in an undisclosed location in East Africa in 2018. (Courtesy US Air Force, Staff Sgt Corban D. Lundborg)

Counter-insurgency (COIN)

COIN is, according to US Army doctrine, the 'military, paramilitary, political, economic, psychological, and civic actions taken by a government to defeat an insurgency.' In SOF terms, this means that operators must conduct their missions, whether training local forces or direct action against insurgents or terrorists, within a COIN environment. Essentially this means that, for a COIN campaign to be successful, SOF must understand and use appropriate techniques and tactics to minimize harm to the local civilian population and encourage them to side with the government.

In Afghanistan, critics of SOF and in particular their direct action operations, argued that conducting night raids on villages was counter-productive to the overall COIN strategy. They point out that the deaths of civilians and livestock and the damage to infrastructure that are the inevitable result of at least a percentage of such operations all play into the hands of the insurgents. Culturally night-time raids were regarded as an affront by the average Afghan family, particularly when they involved the detention, however temporary, of male family members in front of other family members. President Hamid Karzai eventually banned such operations in 2012, until he was guaranteed that such missions would be Afghan-led and use verbal 'call-outs' in an attempt to limit civilian deaths.

Subsequently SOF units were moved from direct action to supporting village stability operations (VSO) (see pages 322–23), which was a COIN programme directed by former JSOC commander and later commander of

A US Army Special Forces soldier meets with locals during a Shura with elders in Uruzgan Province, Afghanistan, 2013. His patch denotes both his 'zap number' and blood type. (Courtesy US Army, Sgt Jessi Ann McCormick)

all US forces in Afghanistan General Stanley McChrystal. As a result, villagers were supported by civil affairs initiatives and local militias (the Afghan Local Police or ALP) were raised to counter-insurgent influence. Although some ALP descended into banditry, many of the VSO initiatives became the greatest chance for COIN stability in Afghanistan, largely owing to the efforts of a range of SOF units.

Counter-narcotics (CN)

Although not a core mission for SOF, counter-narcotics is often an ancillary role as SOF frequently operate in regions and against enemies that finance their operations through the cultivation and sale of illicit narcotics. Chief amongst these is the Taliban, which controls much of the Afghan heroin trade, and the so-called 'narco-terrorists' in Central America, who often work hand in glove with local insurgencies.

For US Army Special Forces operating in Central America, they are often partnered to train and mentor local anti-drug units drawn from the police or military. In 2017, for example, the 7th SFG trained the Honduran Tropa de Inteligencia y Grupos de Respuesta Especial de Seguridad (TIGRES or Intelligence and Special Security Response Groups Units) in close quarter battle. Other training packages have focused on small unit tactics, first aid and mission planning as part of their foreign internal defence role.

Other units operate more closely with partner forces in theatre. Famously, a revolving detachment from Delta Force and SEAL Team 6 was involved in training and mentoring a Columbian police unit tasked with hunting down

Operators from the DEA's Foreign-Deployed Advisory and Support Teams (FASTs) dressed in MultiCam fatigues and carrying M4A1 carbines and Glock sidearms during a counter-narcotics operation in Kandahar Province, Afghanistan, 2008. (Courtesy US Drug Enforcement Administration)

notorious drug kingpin Pablo Escobar. Surveillance intercepts from the US Intelligence Support Activity or ISA (then known as Centra Spike) were integral in the eventual location of Escobar. Rumours alluding to Delta involvement in his subsequent killing have proven to have no basis in reality.

Both US and Australian SOF have accompanied American Drug Enforcement Administration (DEA) personnel on missions in Afghanistan. The DEA maintained five Foreign-Deployed Advisory and Support Teams (FASTs), which were trained by SOCOM until the unit was disbanded in 2017. According to the agency, 'One of these is permanently stationed in the Afghanistan theatre of operations to conduct CN and counter-terrorist missions, with the support of a second FAST team that is rotated through.'

Along with Afghanistan, where they deployed from between 2008 and 2015, FASTs have been active in a number of Central American countries, assisting local units against 'narco-terrorist' cartels. During such missions in Honduras in 2012, the deployed FAST was involved in three shooting incidents which raised a number of questions, including the possibility that a number of alleged smugglers killed by FAST agents were in fact local people with no connection to the cartels. The unit was subsequently disbanded.

In counter-insurgency (COIN) missions, prosecuting the counter-narcotics mission may in fact be counter-productive as the British discovered in Helmand Province. The Taliban used the counter-narcotics missions as 'proof' that the British were aiming to take away the livelihoods of the local population and effectively bolstered their own narrative that the NATO forces must be opposed.

Counter-proliferation (CP)

Counter-proliferation (CP) are SOF operations to 'to curtail the conceptualization, development, possession, proliferation, use, and effects of weapons of mass destruction (WMD), related expertise, materials, technologies, and means of delivery by state and non-state actors', according to the United States' SOCOM. CP became a core SOCOM mission only in late 2016, taking over from the nuclear command Strategic Command (STRATCOM). SOCOM has now established the Counter-Weapons of Mass Destruction-Fusion Center to coordinate all actions relating to WMD.

Before this, however, the mission of making safe WMD was a principal mission for JSOC (known as the '0400' mission as opposed to the '0300' on-call counter-terrorist mission). Since its inception, the command had focused on operations against nuclear armed terrorists, working with a secretive Department of Energy element known as the Nuclear Emergency Search Team or NEST. Much of its training revolved around locating, seizing and making safe a 'dirty bomb' or similar radiological device smuggled into the United States.

During the 1990s, the mission evolved to seizing nuclear facilities overseas, a threat that has only grown with time. The Rangers were on stand-by several times in the 2000s – most recently in 2008 – to conduct just such an operation should Pakistan fall to jihadist elements. Today there are broadly three key mission types related to WMD: 1) the 'traditional' threat of attack on the homeland or allied state by a smuggled WMD; 2) a rogue state acquiring and employing a WMD; and 3) the Pakistan example, state-owned WMD being seized by terrorists or insurgents.

The core mission of breaching such sites fell to the heavy breachers of Delta and SEAL Team 6 while the task of making safe such a device was the responsibility of specialist EOD personnel within both units. The lead nuclear 'render safe' mission was eventually assigned to SEAL Team 6 in 1998. There have long been rumours of an alleged mission by SEAL Team 6 during the 1990s that resulted in the interdiction of a North Korean freighter carrying some form of WMD, although some sources argue that the cargo was ballistic missiles bound for Iran.

Other nations have also added counter-proliferation to the responsibilities of their respective SOF. In the wake of 9/11, Australia established the Incident Response Regiment, for instance, which later morphed into the Special Operations Engineer Regiment with responsibility for tackling WMD. UKSF employ specialist EOD technicians (known as 'High Risk Ammunition Technical Officers or ATOs'), from Alpha Troop of 821 Field Squadron (EOD).

A US Army Special Forces soldier clad in chemical, biological, radiological, nuclear (CBRN) protective clothing and equipment. (Courtesy US Army, Visual Information Specialist Jason Johnston)

Direct Action (DA)

Direct Action (DA) has long been a core SOF task dating back to the activities of the British Commandos and US Army Rangers in World War II. Australian Special Operations Command (SOCOMD) states that the role of Australian SOF, for example, is to conduct 'special reconnaissance, special recovery,

Raiders from US Marine Special Operations Command (MARSOC) conduct direct action training in close quarter battle. Note the older Woodland pattern favoured, although these are produced by Crye. The operators' faces have been deliberately obscured to protect their identities. (Courtesy US Air Force, Senior Airman Joseph Pick)

support operations (including proxy and guerrilla warfare and special shaping operations) and direct action (including precision strike).'

Likewise it is one of the 12 core missions of US SOCOM, who define DA as 'Short-duration strikes and other small-scale offensive actions employing specialized military capabilities to seize, destroy, capture, exploit, recover, or damage designated targets.'

The US Army's Ranger Regiment is perhaps the preeminent DA force with an ability to seize opposed airfields, conduct counter-terrorist raiding and carry out behind the lines 'marauding' such as the Team Merrill operations in Afghanistan. Other nations have similar capabilities, with Ranger- or Commando-like units, although these are often somewhat subjugated to a supporting role for special mission-style SOF units.

In Iraq and Afghanistan, all SOF have conducted DA to a greater or lesser degree. The JSOC campaign against al-Qaeda in Iraq for instance was essentially one long-term DA mission. The key discriminator of 'short-duration' was also upended in Afghanistan where units would conduct solely DA missions for their entire deployment. The Rangers have developed to such a point that they can now conduct relentless DA taskings for as long as is operationally necessary.

Following years of relentless campaigns in Iraq and Afghanistan, observers have noted that the DA role has become the de facto core mission of SOF, often to the detriment of other, arguably more valuable skills such as foreign internal defence (FID) or unconventional warfare (UW). Indeed SEALs were initially unimpressed to be given a FID mission in Iraq and later Afghanistan under the village stability operations (VSO) programme (see pages 322–23). DA is certainly the more exciting end of SOF but FID is the more impactful. Marine Special Operations Command (MARSOC) on the other hand embraced the tasking, largely as they were seen initially as 'second cousins', and made it their own.

US Army Special Forces have recognized that their Green Berets have become too DA focused and an effort is being made to realign. The Army has also noted the ever-increasing operational tempo of its SOF and have created non-SOF Security Force Assistance Brigades to take on some of the FID mission. The future of SOF is certainly one of FID, although DA will always remain as a necessary capability. Even against peer or near-peer enemies, there will always be a need to raise and support guerrilla movements or conversely to mentor and train security forces.

Foreign Internal Defence (FID)

Foreign internal defence or FID, defined by the US Army as 'activities that support an HN's [host nation] internal defense and development (IDAD) strategy and program designed to protect against subversion, lawlessness, insurgency, terrorism, and other threats to their internal security, and stability, and legitimacy', is one of the oldest SOF missions and for America's Green Berets, one of its foundation stones.

During Vietnam, US Army Special Forces worked alongside local units including irregulars. El Salvador is often used as an example of a successful multi-generational FID mission. Certainly to some degree, Iraq can also be seen as a successful example of FID, although the poor performance of many Iraqi units during the onslaught of Islamic State in 2014 somewhat calls this into question. In Afghanistan, FID has been of limited success with only a small percentage of the Afghan National Army able to plan, launch and conduct unilateral operations.

FID is typically classified as not involving the SOF component working with the host nation forces in actual direct combat, although on today's battlefields this is often impossible, with foreign SOF accompanying their local allies into the field on operations to mentor and advise. A number of US Special Forces soldiers have been killed and wounded in recent years conducting exactly such missions.

More broadly speaking, SOF FID is focused not just on the tactical employment of host nation forces but also on providing them with the skills to develop essential planning

US Army Special Forces soldiers deploy to the Philippines in 2002 as part of Operation *Enduring Freedom* – Philippines (OEF-P), a more than a decade-long commitment to supporting the battle against al-Qaeda- and Islamic State-inspired terrorists. Note the early MICH helmets and SOPMOD Block I M4A1s. (Patrick Aventurier/ Gamma-Rapho via Getty Images)

and logistics processes. In addition, skills focusing on combat medical care including medical evacuation are often included in FID 'packages'. Today FID is often implemented in concert with security force assistance (SFA), which is now a separate core mission as SOCOM notes: 'FID and SFA may support training, advising, and equipping HN security forces as an element of a COIN [counter-insurgency] operation.' Many of the operations conducted in Mali, Niger and Somalia by both US and multi-national SOF fall into this category – often characterized as 'train, advise and assist'.

The UK deploys training teams, both conventional and SOF, to many countries to conduct FID and SFA, as do the majority of NATO allies. Many European SOF gained valuable experience in the FID and SFA mission during the International Security Assistance Force (ISAF) campaign in Afghanistan and more recently in Iraq against Islamic State. Such missions also present their own unique challenges. The US Special Forces ODA ambushed in Niger in 2017 (see pages 344–45), for example, had to rely upon a civilian contractor to provide aeromedical evacuation and were unable to communicate with French Air Force aircraft overhead owing to the language barrier.

Hostage Rescue

The most dangerous of all special operations, hostage rescues, rely upon speed, surprise and overwhelming force to succeed (or as Delta Force says, speed, aggression and surprise). The standard tipping point for an assault is the imminent or actual death of a hostage. Once a hostage has been killed by the terrorists, a psychological barrier has been broken and an assault is generally the only way to ensure more hostages are not killed.

When an SOF unit deploys on a hostage rescue, two plans are developed. The first is the immediate action (sometimes known as the emergency action) plan or IA. This is quickly sketched out and briefed and will be the plan enacted should the terrorists immediately begin killing hostages. As the IA is further refined and developed, through the addition of further intelligence and reconnaissance, for example, it becomes the DA or deliberate action plan.

The DA plan is the preferred option, allowing the operators to conduct the operation at a time of their choosing. It allows all supporting elements to be put in place (such as overwatching sniper teams, EOD personnel, a hostage reception area, and any specialist breaching techniques) before being triggered. A DA offers the best chance of success. Obviously when conducting pre-planned, intelligence-led, hostage rescues in active combat zones such as Yemen or Syria, a DA is part of the planning process for the operation.

The use of the correct weapons, ammunition and distraction devices is obviously essential. This may seem to be common sense; however, a SEAL

Team 6 operator accidentally killed a British hostage during a rescue attempt in Afghanistan in 2010. The SEAL, new to SEAL Team 6, posted a fragmentation grenade at an insurgent and killed the hostage in the process. Stun grenades or flashbangs, which the SEALs also carried, would obviously have been far preferable. It was later learnt that the team had not conducted any refresher hostage rescue training prior to its deployment but in any case this fundamental rule should not have been broken.

Once the authority to begin the operation is given, speed is the key. The operators must breach into the location, typically by more than one entry point if possible, and swarm into the terrorist stronghold, quickly dominating the environment and killing the terrorists. To do so, distraction and deception are often used; at the Iranian Embassy siege in 1980, road workers using jackhammers covered any sound of the preparations for the assault.

In Mogadishu in 1977 during the German GSG9's famous assault on a hijacked Lufthansa flight (see page 90), a fire was lit to draw all of the terrorists to the cockpit. In Marseilles in 1994, following the hijacking of an Air France flight (see pages 311–13), the French GIGN managed to get all of the terrorists to the cockpit through the ruse of a press conference. Anything that will give the assaulters extra vital time or that will help congregate the terrorists in one place, preferably away from the hostages, is essential.

Operators from Austria, Croatia, the Czech Republic, Hungary, Slovakia and Slovenia coordinate in a hostage rescue exercise in 2018 as part of the Atlas Network Common Challenge: an organization that shares training and knowledge across European counter-terrorist units. (Joe Klamar/AFP/Getty Images)

French GIGN operators seen conducting the successful assault on the hijacked Air France flight at Marseilles. Moments after this image was taken, the standing assaulter's sidearm was struck by a terrorist bullet and he tumbled back down the Airstairs. (Thierry Orban/Sygma via Getty Images)

In tactical terms, distraction devices are also an essential element. These may take the form of flashbangs; 'boom sticks' that affix a flashbang or an explosive charge to a telescoping pole that can be used to breach or confuse the hostage takers; CS gas and similar irritants (often fired into the stronghold by the cordon team using Ferret 12 gauge or 40mm ammunition which can breach windows and most doors); and even ballistic shields fitted with blinding strobe lights. Again, anything which provides an extra second or two to facilitate the entry of the operators is considered at the planning stage.

Once the stronghold has been breached, overwhelming force is necessary to quickly identify and kill the terrorists. Unless a terrorist is unarmed and clearly surrendering, all need to be eliminated as quickly as possible to reduce the threat of more hostages being killed or an IED or suicide bomb vest being triggered. Even a supposedly surrendering terrorist may be wearing such a device and thus it is unlikely that any terrorists will survive the assault once under way. Consider SEAL Team 6's successful rescue of two aid workers in Somalia in 2012 – all nine hostage takers were killed within moments of the assault being launched.

Once the terrorists have been killed, EOD personnel are introduced as soon as practicable to render safe any suspect devices as the hostages are firmly and speedily moved out of the stronghold. Another key lesson from the Iranian Embassy siege was the importance of hostage reception procedures, ensuring that hostages (and any potential terrorists) can be secured and identified. In the case of the 1980 mission, one terrorist did manage to escape detection and was subsequently arrested after being identified by another hostage. If such an incident were to occur today it could have far more devastating consequences on account of the use of suicide bomb vests.

A similar example was the recovery of US deserter Bowe Bergdahl by Delta Force operators in Afghanistan in 2014. The operators thoroughly searched Bergdahl before escorting him to a waiting MH-60 and allowing him on board, aware of the chance of a hidden Taliban device. At Forward Operating Base Chapman, again in Afghanistan, a double agent recruited by the CIA and Jordanian General Intelligence Directorate detonated a suicide vest as he was greeted by a CIA team eager to debrief him. Seven CIA officers, a Jordanian and a local Afghan hire were killed in the blast, the single worst loss suffered in the history of the CIA.

Another lesson learned at the Iranian Embassy siege was the impact of media, and specifically television crews. At one vital point as the assaulters prepared for the go brevity code, a television crew transmitted the black-clad operators. Fortunately the terrorists were not watching television at the time inside the strongpoint but the operation could have easily ended in disaster if they had been.

Obviously this mainly applies to operations conducted in permissive environments but operational security must always be considered. A civilian living in Abbottabad 'live Tweeted' that helicopters were hovering over a compound in the city followed by explosions as Operation *Neptune Spear*, the SEAL mission to kill bin Laden, began. If the information had been transmitted quickly to the Pakistani authorities, the SEALs might have experienced considerable difficulties on their exfiltration back to Jalalabad.

Kill or Capture

Kill or capture operations are a sub-set of direct action (DA) missions. Although the term was used during the insurgency in Iraq during the 2000s, it become synonymous with special operations in Afghanistan where the Afghans termed them 'night raids'. The aim was to kill or capture, not necessarily in that order, enemy high-value targets – typically leadership figures, financiers, bomb-makers and foreign fighter facilitators.

This type of operation reached an early zenith in Iraq under General Stanley McChrystal's JSOC task force, which ran thousands of such missions between 2003 and 2010. They were instrumental in the destruction of al-Qaeda in Iraq and certainly saved many civilian and military lives in the process, for example, by decimating the terrorist car-bombing network in and around Baghdad. After the task force, and specifically the British SAS component, began targeting the network, car-bombings in the city fell by over half.

When by 2008 operations focused on Afghanistan, where a lower-key kill or capture was already in place, the success of the Iraq mission could not be repeated. The key barrier was the almost complete lack of telecommunications infrastructure in Afghanistan. The targets simply did not log onto the internet

A US Army Special Forces soldier fires on the enemy during a partnered operation against Taliban high-value targets in Logar Province, Afghanistan, July 2018. An Oshkosh M1245 M-ATV can be seen in the background. (Courtesy US Air Force, Staff Sgt Nicholas Byers)

at net cafés or use mobile (cell) phones to any great degree. Signals intelligence, so vital to identifying targets in Iraq, was far less effective. The tribal networks and allegiances were also far more difficult to identify and map.

There is some evidence that such missions have affected the operators who executed them over the long term during multiple deployments. War crime investigations in the United States, the UK and Australia seem to point to a dehumanizing effect generated by both the pace of such missions and the frequent lethal violence required. Some also point to the 'revolving door' of the admittedly corrupt Afghan justice system, which often saw known enemy released. Some operators may have decided that killing the target on the objective, whether armed or unarmed or indeed posing a threat, was preferable.

There was also the frustration of not reaching the same kind of successful operational tempo that SOF had in Iraq. The lack of strong signals intelligence, the Afghan justice system, and operators who were becoming psychologically burnt out all likely contributed to the needless deaths of both Afghan civilians and unarmed enemy.

Whether kill or capture can actually win a counter-insurgency is open to debate. Certainly in Iraq it was eventually paired with a form of encouraged social change that saw former nationalist insurgents turn against the outrages of al-Qaeda and become unlikely allies of the Americans. A kill or capture campaign in isolation can degrade the technical and leadership capabilities of the enemy but it will not attain a semblance of peace. Even General David Petraeus noted, 'You don't kill or capture your way out of an industrial-strength insurgency.'*

---

*   http://www.pbs.org/wgbh/frontline/article/interview-general-david-petraeu

Parachuting

Parachuting is but one insertion method practised by SOF. The method provides a number of unique advantages and disadvantages. In the plus column, parachuting is near silent and can be difficult to detect on radar, and units can jump from an aircraft in one country and, using steerable chutes, land in a neighbouring country. In terms of negatives, it is difficult to keep anything larger than a relatively small group from scattering and it vastly reduces the amount of equipment which can be inserted into the area of operations. Although light vehicles like the MRZR can be parachuted in, this is never without risk.

SOF practise several methods of parachuting. The most common is the static-line jump used by units like the Parachute Regiment and Ranger Regiment when large numbers of soldiers need to be parachuted into an area. Next is high altitude low opening or HALO, which sees operators jump at upwards of 30,000 feet with oxygen and free-fall until at a relatively low altitude before releasing their chutes.

HALO provides two major advantages. One, it reduces the amount of time the operators are visible with deployed chutes both by the human eye and by radar (chutes obviously making a larger radar return than a free-falling individual). Secondly, experienced parachutists can keep together as they free-fall, meaning that when they do deploy their chutes, they can land close together.

The third method is similar to HALO but the chute is opened at high altitude, thus high altitude high opening or HAHO. Although this negates some of the stealthiness of HALO, it allows operators to steer their chutes for many miles before landing. SEAL Team 6 conducted one operation into the Pakistan border regions by using this method as their transport aircraft did not have to cross into Pakistan air space.

Combat jumps are today a fairly rare occurrence. Most are in support of other larger special operations, for example to seize a remote location to allow for the refuelling of helicopters bound for an assault on an objective. HALO jumps have been used on a handful of occasions to access locations that either tactically or logistically were otherwise difficult such as SEAL Team 6's jump along the Somali border during its 2012 hostage rescue (see page 343) or a late 2001 Delta operation that saw operators HALO ahead of retreating Taliban in order to call in airstrikes.

A rare shot of a Delta Force operator preparing for a HALO (high altitude low opening) jump in 1988. (Greg Mathieson/Mai/Mai/ The LIFE Images Collection/ Getty Images)

Sniping

Snipers have always been an essential component of SOF organizations. In counter-terrorism operations they provide a useful set of highly trained eyes to monitor the location and behaviour of the terrorists while also offering a precision strike capability. In wartime special operations, they form an important intelligence, surveillance, targeting and reconnaissance (ISTAR) tool which often outweighs their offensive role. They also offer a tremendous advantage in counter-insurgency operations as a target can be eliminated by a single well-placed round rather than calling in an airstrike.

Many units, particularly counter-terrorist intervention teams, group their snipers and reconnaissance specialists within one sub-unit that can be attached in packages of varying sizes to assault teams as required. SOF snipers work in pairs with one manning the primary sniper rifle and the second operator acting as his or her spotter. In wartime operations, the snipers will likely be reinforced by a security element to ensure they are not flanked by the enemy and to give the team more offensive punch should they be forced to shoot their way out of a hide site.

On direct action assault operations, snipers provide overwatch, relaying intelligence on enemy movements as well as interdicting any enemy who attempt to escape from or reinforce an objective. The snipers may be mounted in helicopters, which allows them also to act as a cut-off group that can be landed ahead of fleeing insurgents or to reinforce assault teams on the ground.

SOF snipers are also used for more politically, and some would argue more morally, dubious tasks which amount to assassination of designated insurgents or terrorists. Delta snipers in Iraq, for example, operated from modified locally procured vans. Once they had identified their target, for instance in traffic, the sniper would take the shot, killing the target and leaving the scene covertly before advising Iraqi police or a local ground-holding unit.

Belgian Army Special Forces Group snipers descend mountainous terrain during a NATO sniping course. A suppressed Accuracy International AXMC in .338 Lapua Magnum is carried by the soldier on the left and a suppressed Mk20 Sniper Support Rifle in 7.62x51mm is carried by his spotter on the right. (Courtesy US Army, 1st Lt Benjamin Haulenbeek)

A US Navy SEAL sniper provides overwatch in Afghanistan during a partnered operation in 2011. He wears AOR 1 (Area of Responsibility 1) in contrast to AOR 2 pattern, which is designed for jungle and woodland environments. His rifle appears to be the Mk13 Mod5 chambered for the .300 Winchester Magnum round, fitted with a suppressor. (Courtesy US Air Force, Staff Sgt Ryan Whitney)

They are also used in aerial vehicle interdictions. Most such operations fall into the kill or capture category with the aerial sniper fire aimed at engine blocks to immobilize the target vehicle. Should resistance be met, lethal force can be applied. Force protection is also a role for the SOF sniper. In Syria, for example, snipers would perform overwatch at SOF bases to identify and engage Islamic State suicide car bombs. As the war progressed, however, these SVBIEDs (suicide vehicle-borne IEDs) would be up-armoured to counter sniper and small arms fire and thus Coalition SOF began to use Javelin and TOW 2 anti-tank guided missiles to destroy them at a safe distance.

Special Reconnaissance (SR)

Special reconnaissance or SR is another of the core SOF tasks outlined by the likes of SOCOM which it defines as 'actions conducted in sensitive environments to collect or verify information of strategic or operational significance.' It is a key wartime role for special operators who will support conventional forces by achieving 'eyes on' an otherwise denied target.

During Operation *Iraqi Freedom*, the 5th SFG mirrored its essential role in Operation *Desert Storm* by conducting a large number of both mounted

US Army Special Forces snipers are often employed to conduct reconnaissance and surveillance of targets, lying concealed in hides for days or weeks monitoring an objective. The sniper closest to the camera mans a .50 Barrett M107 anti-materiel rifle. These soldiers are deployed in support of Syrian Democratic Forces. (US Air Force, Staff Sgt Corey Hook)

and dismounted SR operations to confirm the location and strength of enemy units. SR can also be used to monitor a target to understand the 'atmospherics' of the local population and likely responses of any garrisoned enemy.

SR tasks and advanced force operation (AFO) tasks are intrinsically linked and some AFO tasks could well be regarded as SR in disguise: for example, operators conducting reconnaissance of an area in local dress, such as those carried out by the British SAS in Basra, Iraq. Such missions are obviously fraught with danger – in Basra two SAS operators were captured while conducting surveillance on a corrupt member of the Iraqi Police.

Closely related to both SR and AFO is what is known as CTR or close target reconnaissance. This is a covert reconnaissance task undertaken in advance of a planned assault on an objective to gain an intimate understanding of enemy dispositions, location of non-combatants or hostages and even such minute but vital details as which way a particular door opens or whether a skylight is unlocked.

In all such operations, it is imperative that the SR team remain undetected to civilian and enemy alike. Infamously both the British Bravo Two Zero patrol in 1991 (see pages 38–39) and Operation *Red Wings* conducted by SEAL Team 10 in 2005 were compromised by civilian animal herders. SOF reconnaissance teams learn to establish hide sites that are camouflaged to all but the most curious of passers-by but must be ready to withdraw immediately to a previously agreed extraction point should they become compromised.

Unconventional Warfare (UW)

Unconventional warfare or UW is yet another key SOF task: the United States' SOCOM's own declassified unconventional warfare 'Pocket Book' defines UW as 'Activities conducted to enable a resistance movement or insurgency to coerce, disrupt or overthrow a government or occupying power by operating through or with an underground, auxiliary, and guerrilla force in a denied area.'

UW is the mirror to foreign internal defence (FID). Instead of supporting a security force to defeat an insurgency, in unconventional warfare SOF become the insurgents and work with local resistance fighters to overthrow a government. An excellent recent example of unconventional warfare has been in Syria where SOF have worked with the Kurds in a UW environment to defeat the 'occupying power', namely Islamic State. Another example was the work of both Army Special Forces and CIA operatives working alongside the Northern Alliance to overthrow the Taliban in 2001.

Indeed SOCOM provides its own relevant examples: 'UW has a wide range of applications in the contemporary environment, whether a textbook approached operation supporting the Syrian resistance, preparing a partner state ahead of potential occupation, or enabling a tribal group to resist Da'esh [Islamic State] occupation in an Iraqi city.'

A US Army 5th Special Forces Group soldier with faithful military working dog pictured in Syria conducting unconventional warfare with the Kurdish YPG in October 2018. (Courtesy US Army, Sgt Matthew Crane)

Historically, during the Cold War, the UW mission was intended to enable US Special Forces to raise guerrilla armies in occupied territories should the Russians have invaded Western Europe. To facilitate this, future resistance leaders were recruited and arms caches hidden. In the event of open war, the Green Berets would act as 'stay-behind' parties and conduct sabotage operations alongside the local resistance. As an adjunct to that role, Special Forces were trained in the use of so-called 'backpack nukes' or special atomic demolition munition (SADM) to target enemy headquarters and logistics nodes.

Many such UW missions conducted by US SOF are under covert Title 50 authority meaning that the mission itself is secret and deniable. Larger multi-national UW operations may operate under Title 10 as they are clandestine rather than covert (see page 157 for more on Title 50 and Title 10). In classic Special Forces training, the final exercise is conducted in 'Pineland', a fictional nation state. In the scenario, Special Forces must covertly infiltrate and meet with resistance leaders, a scenario not dissimilar to the opening days of Operation *Enduring Freedom*.

Visit-Board-Search-Seizure (VBSS)

The rather innocuous sounding visit-board-search-seizure or VBSS is actually a fairly wide-ranging term for any operations which require service members to board an unknown or enemy vessel. The world's coast guards and navies perform VBSS missions every day, often to stem the flow of people smugglers, piracy or drug transportation. In the realm of SOF, VBSS typically means an opposed operation to infiltrate and seize a maritime vessel.

The target of such a VBSS could be a hijacked cruise liner or a North Korean freighter suspected of carrying WMD (weapons of mass destruction). The British SBS carried out such an operation in December 2018, conducting a textbook VBSS against a hijacked cargo ship in the Thames Estuary. The Australian SASR and Royal Australian Navy Clearance Divers seized the North Korean freighter, the *Pong Su*, which was carrying heroin in 2003. The operators conducted a simultaneous assault by fast-roping to the deck from a Seahawk helicopter and assaulting up boarding ladders from three rigid hull inflatables.

The US Navy SEALs have conducted hundreds if not thousands of similar non-compliant VBSS actions in the Middle East in an effort to thwart weapons being smuggled to and from the likes of Iran and Syria. Although the template used for the VBSS differs understandably based on the target, most use a combination of helicopters and fast boats to insert the assault teams.

In a maritime hostage rescue scenario, the target ship will be flooded with operators who, as in any hostage rescue mission, will focus on eliminating the hostage takers before they can kill hostages or trigger an explosive device. The difficulty of course is that the target is a ship at sea. Such operations pose challenges as a cargo or cruise ship offers many hiding places and there are restrictions on what breaching methods can be safely employed. Many teams with a maritime counter-terrorist (MCT) responsibility train with thermal lances and similar high-tech cutting equipment that enables them to cut through heavy steel bulkheads.

Ukrainian 73rd Special Naval Center operators work with US Navy SEALs in a VBSS exercise in July 2017. (Courtesy US Navy, Staff Sgt Henry Gundacker)

OPERATIONS

Air France Flight 8969 (French)

Hostage Rescue in Marseille • December 1994

One of the most famous counter-hijack operations conducted by a special operations unit was undoubtedly the storming of Air France Flight 8969 at Marseille–Marignane Airport in France. Four terrorists of the Groupe Islamique Armé (GIA or Algerian Armed Islamic Group) hijacked the flight on Christmas Eve 1994 at Algiers' Houari–Boumediene Airport. The hostage takers had disguised themselves as Air Algérie security personnel to talk their way onto the aircraft but soon produced AK-47s and a Micro UZI shouting 'Allah Akbar' and pronouncing that the flight was now under the control of the GIA.

Two passengers, one an Algerian police officer, were immediately executed to show their intent. Negotiations began with the Algerian Interior Minister. The demand was for the release of two imprisoned leaders of the banned Islamic Salvation Front. Negotiations dragged on as the Algerian Groupement d'Intervention Spécialise (GIS or Special Operations Group) counter-terrorist unit took up positions around the aircraft. Eventually some headway was made and 63 hostages, women and children, were released leaving 173 crew and remaining passengers.

Meanwhile, in France, GIGN received the alert at its base to the south of Versailles. Two intervention groups of assaulters reinforced by snipers boarded an Air France Airbus A300, similar to the type of aircraft that had been

GIGN operators can be seen assaulting the hijacked Air France flight moments before activating the emergency slides to evacuate the aircraft while their comrades engage the terrorists in a close quarter firefight near the cockpit. (Georges Gobet/AFP/Getty Images)

hijacked, and headed for Algiers. Immediate action plans were drawn up during the flight and the teams practised their drills.

In Algiers, the French government negotiated with the Algerians, who were keen to employ GIS, to allow GIGN to provide at least technical assistance. The Algerians, fearful of the political repercussions of allowing French special operators on Algerian soil, demurred and the GIGN flight was diverted to Mallorca, Spain where it refuelled.

The terrorists had by now altered their demands and given up on the release of the two terrorists. Instead they wanted to be allowed to fly the aircraft to Paris. In the years since the hijacking many have theorized that had this been allowed, the terrorists might have used the aircraft as a missile in the manner of the 9/11 hijackers or blown the aircraft from the sky over Paris. This view was reinforced by the presence of commercial dynamite amongst the terrorists.

After continued arguments with the Algerians, who wanted to keep the aircraft on the ground in Algiers, the terrorists grew frustrated and executed another hostage. Soon after they were cleared for take-off.

Ostensibly for refuelling before continuing on to Paris, the hijacked Airbus landed at Marseille–Marignane Airport in France. GIGN was already on the ground and moving into position while negotiations were opened by the French police.

As part of the negotiation, cleaners and catering staff were allowed onto the aircraft. These were in fact unarmed GIGN operators dressed as airport workers. They conducted a close target reconnaissance and checked for IEDs or any obstructions at likely entry points as well as emplacing a number of technical surveillance devices. The terrorists were convinced to hold a press conference on the aircraft and the forward galley and first class were cleared of hostages, who were moved to the rear of the Airbus, ostensibly so that the camera crews of the world's press could set up.

Increasingly frustrated with the delays, the terrorists suddenly began taxiing the Airbus and demanded to be immediately allowed to take off for the capital. To reinforce their intent, one fired his AK-47 at the control tower. At this point, GIGN received the order to stand by and three entry teams clambered onto mobile Airstairs to begin their approach, covered by several snipers hidden in and around the airport buildings.

Given the go code, the three Airstairs were driven up from behind the aircraft as GIGN knew the terrorists were clustered in the cockpit. One hostage saw the operators pass by his window as they approached the forward right door. This team, Team 1 led by the GIGN commander, would head straight for the cockpit to neutralize the terrorists.

Two other Airstairs followed and pulled up by the rear doors on either side of the Airbus. A coordinated breach was made with the two rear teams, each consisting of 11 GIGN operators, racing into the aircraft, lobbing flashbang grenades and shouting in French and English for the hostages to stay down.

One of the terrorists spotted Team 1 approaching on their Airstairs and opened fire with his AK-47. In television footage, sparks from the impacting rounds can be seen. The operators crouched farther down as the Airstairs finally arrived at the forward door. They ran into difficulty getting the door open and one operator bravely swung the lock open with his body weight, hanging in mid-air until his compatriots had made entry before following them in.

The eight operators of Team 1 were immediately met by a crescendo of automatic fire directed out of the cockpit. Six of the GIGN operators were wounded in the initial fusillade although the lead operator, armed with GIGN's distinctive Manurhin MR73 .357 Magnum revolver, managed to kill two of the terrorists at extremely close range before he was hit by AK-47 fire.

A flashbang grenade thrown from the assaulter on the tarmac missed its mark and detonated harmlessly on the ground. Although the snipers could occasionally spot the terrorists, they held their fire as the flight crew were interspersed with their targets. The terrorists managed to post several homemade grenades into the galley, again wounding the lead GIGN operator who lost most of one hand in the blast of a grenade. He would be pinned down, peppered with shrapnel and bleeding from gunshot wounds, for another 12 minutes.

At the rear of the aircraft, Teams 2 and 3 had secured the area and deployed the escape chutes. Passengers began to race from the aircraft to be met by the cordon team and moved to safety. The faster the hostages could be cleared from the aircraft the less chance remained of their being hit by a terrorist bullet from the cockpit where the firefight still raged.

Team 1 threw flashbangs into the cockpit but the enraged terrorists blind-fired into the galley. The co-pilot took the opportunity of the distraction to escape from the cockpit window, falling to the tarmac. The snipers, unaware the pilot was still in the cockpit, began to engage the terrorists, killing one. A second team moved up the forward Airstairs and began throwing flashbangs into the aircraft. The Manurhin carried by the lead operator was struck by a round fired from the surviving terrorist and blown from his hand.

The second team eventually managed to break into the cockpit and kill the last surviving terrorist. Just 22 minutes after the operation began, it was all over. The GIGN commander transmitted, 'The operation is terminated. Damage limited.' All of the passengers and crew had been rescued although 13 suffered various minor injuries and wounds. Eleven of the GIGN operators had been wounded by gunfire or grenade fragments. In a grim postscript, a number of hours after the successful operation GIA terrorists in Algeria murdered four Catholic priests to avenge the dead hostage takers killed by GIGN.

Operation *Desert Storm*

Special Operations in Kuwait and Iraq • 1991

In August 1990, Iraqi forces invaded and occupied neighbouring Kuwait after years of wrangling over debts incurred by Iraq while fighting the Iran–Iraq War (1980–88). Western nations led by the United States were invited into Saudi Arabia to defend the kingdom from any further aggression (much to the chagrin of none other than Usama bin Laden who volunteered his 'Afghan Arabs' for the task). After seven months of occupation, Operation *Desert Shield* transitioned into Operation *Desert Storm* with a ground invasion of Kuwait beginning in mid-February 1991.

The first SOF unit to cross the border into western Iraq was the British SBS, joined later by the SAS. Their primary targets were both the actual Iraqi mobile ballistic missile sites, including the Russian-designed Scud, and the Iraqi communications networks supporting their launch. Such a two-tiered objective aimed to shut down the ability of the Iraqi military to launch Scuds into Israel, which threatened the fragile Arab coalition fighting alongside Western forces.

Delta Force deployed into Iraq after the early success of the SAS forced the hand of General Norman Schwarzkopf, commander of the Coalition forces, who had a dim view of SOF because of negative experiences in Vietnam. Delta conducted mobile patrols mounted in both HMMWVs and modified

US Navy SEAL Desert Patrol Vehicles (DPVs) equipped with both .50 M2 heavy machine guns and 7.62x51mm M60E4 light machine guns along with AT-4 anti-tank rockets deployed in Kuwait City, 1991. (Patrick Durand/ Sygma via Getty Images)

Pinzgauers in a closely coordinated effort with the SAS. Schwarzkopf's negative opinions of SOF, and in particular direct action SOF missions, affected not just Delta but also the Rangers and SEAL Team 6, who were largely sidelined during the campaign.

US Army Special Forces were, however, heavily committed, primarily in their traditional role of mentoring and training allied armies as Coalition Warfare Support Teams (CWSTs), an important task that Schwarzkopf could see the value in handing to the Green Berets. These CWSTs were embedded within all partner nation forces to coordinate their forces with Western forces. An additional task was providing the ground component of the combat search and rescue (CSAR) effort for any aviators downed over land. The SEALs received the maritime CSAR role.

US Army Special Forces also conducted a number of long-range special reconnaissance missions into Kuwait and Iraq itself. One of the most dangerous was the 'emergency exfiltration' of ODA 525. An eight-man special reconnaissance team from 5th SFG, the ODA were compromised in their hide site by civilians and were soon being flanked by a company-strength enemy force. 'Danger close' airstrikes by F-16s helped stall the Iraqis' advance until the 160th Special Operations Aviation Regiment (SOAR) could extract the ODA at last light.

The Army Rangers were put forth for a number of missions but only one major operation – Operation *Ranger Run* – was actually conducted by them, a heliborne assault on an Iraqi microwave relay facility. The operation was a success but whether the target was of any strategic importance is still debated. Otherwise the Rangers acted as the Quick Reaction Force for Delta should one of their mounted patrols run into a sizeable enemy force.

The US Navy's SEALs (drawn largely from SEAL Teams 2 and 5) conducted their traditional mission of advanced reconnaissance for proposed amphibious landings on the Kuwaiti coastline. These covert missions discovered the beaches were heavily mined. They also conducted possibly the most successful deception operation of the war. A small element infiltrated in Zodiac small boats in late February to emplace timer initiated explosive charges and buoys to deceive the Iraqis into thinking a major amphibious operation was under way. The ruse worked magnificently with two Iraqi divisions diverted to the area.

The SEALs were also famously photographed entering Kuwait City in their distinctive Chenowth Desert Patrol Vehicles and were involved in securing the US Embassy, while their British compatriots in the SBS fast-roped into the UK Embassy. The SEALs also conducted at least two successful combat search and rescue missions in the waters of the Persian Gulf, recovering downed aviators, and SEAL Team 2 manned a 'maritime interdiction force' to conduct opposed boardings of Iraqi vessels in the Gulf.

Not all SOF missions during *Desert Storm* were successful. The infamous Bravo Two Zero patrol to monitor Iraqi military traffic saw an eight-man 22SAS patrol compromised and on the run across western Iraq. Four were eventually captured, two died of hypothermia, one was killed in a contact with the enemy and a single operator managed to escape on foot across the border into Syria. A decade later, during the 2003 invasion of Iraq, two SBS operators repeated this incredible feat, although with the assistance of an all-terrain vehicle and Coalition air cover.

Operation *Eagle Claw*

Hostage Rescue in Iran • 1980

In November 1979, in the wake of the overthrow of the Shah, anti-American protesters seized the American Embassy in Tehran, taking over 100 hostages, amongst them 67 US citizens including Marines and CIA personnel. The hostage taking surprised the American Administration, which initially struggled to develop a military option. Delta Force was still in its infancy and awaiting final certification and establishment. There were no specialist helicopter or air transport units.

Despite this, Joint Task Force 1-79, with Delta Force as its key component and operating as Task Force 79.1, began planning and training for an eventual hostage rescue attempt. Under the control of the Joint Chiefs of Staff's Special Operations Directorate, the team worked up an ambitious plan under Operation *Ricebowl*.

1/75th Rangers would land in MC-130s to seize a remote airfield code-named Desert One, which would act as a launchpad for the assault force, along with a vital forward refuelling point, organized and managed by Air Force combat controllers. Follow-on aircraft would bring the assault elements and EC-130s loaded with fuel. Navy RH-53 helicopters would launch from the USS *Nimitz* aircraft carrier and rendezvous at Desert One for refuelling before loading the assault teams for the movement to the forward staging area.

Once at the forward staging area, Delta would transfer to locally sourced ground transport to move covertly to the Embassy and Ministry of Foreign Affairs to conduct their assault. Two AC-130s would provide overhead support should Iranian reinforcements arrive. Once the now 53 hostages were secured (a number of hostages suffering from illness had already been released), the RH-53s would land at the Ajadieh Stadium near the Embassy and extract both the hostages and the assault teams back to a second site at Manzariyeh, which would be secured by the Rangers as a forward refuelling point for the helicopters and C-130s on their exfiltration from Iran.

Special Forces soldiers from the Berlin-based Detachment A would conduct undercover advanced force reconnaissance and participate in the actual rescue with responsibility for the three hostages held at the Iranian Ministry of Foreign Affairs. Delta operators would also conduct their own

undercover close target reconnaissance of the Embassy before the assault teams arrived. It was a complicated plan, which relied upon precise timing and not a small amount of luck. Authority to launch was received on 25 April 1980 under Operation *Eagle Claw*.

One RH-53 was forced to return to the *Nimitz* with mechanical problems and a second was forced to ditch owing to unexpected weather conditions. The remaining six made it to Desert One, running late owing to dust clouds slowing their arrival. Unfortunately one of the six also developed a mechanical issue meaning it was unsafe for it to fly. In planning, it had been decided that the mission could not proceed if fewer than six RH-53s were available.

With the mechanical difficulties reducing the number of helicopters available both to ferry in the assault forces and to fly out the hostages, the difficult decision was made to abort the operation. As preparations were made to collapse the Ranger security perimeter and load the assault forces for the flight out of Iran, a grim and unexpected radio message was relayed, according to the SOCOM history of the event: 'We have a crash. A helo crashed into one of the C-130s. We have some dead, some wounded, and some trapped. The crash site is ablaze; ammunition is cooking off.'

During the exfiltration, an Air Force EC-130 refuelling aircraft and a Navy RH-53 helicopter had collided at Desert One and eight servicemen had been killed. The exploding ammunition had disabled three more RH-53s, leaving only one in serviceable condition. Nonetheless, the Rangers and the assault force were flown out after efforts were made to recover as much classified material as possible from the stricken airframes. In the immediate aftermath, the US hostages were scattered across Tehran in an attempt to forestall any further rescue attempts.

Robat-E Posht-E Badam, Iran, better known as Desert One, the refuelling and staging site for Operation *Eagle Claw*. Visible in the background right is one of the scuttled RH-53s. (Bettmann/Getty Images)

The mission had simply been too complicated with far too many moving parts requiring expert coordination between the services and units, which were not experienced at working together. A similar hostage rescue operation planned today would be much simpler and managed by an integrated command such as the JSOC, formed in the immediate aftermath of *Eagle Claw*, which has its own organic air transport and helicopter capability. *Eagle Claw* was a vitally important if painful learning point for US special operations. It underscored the fact that only units which trained intensively together, to the point of 'knowing each other's jobs', would be successful.

Although none of the blame was apportioned to Delta, the Unit felt the failure keenly, none more so than its commander, Colonel Charlie Beckwith. It was only amplified by the success of 22SAS' siege-breaking Operation *Nimrod* at the Iranian Embassy in London less than a month later. Planning quickly resumed for another attempt under the codename Operation *Honey Badger*, a pre-existing programme that was evaluating techniques and equipment for the JTF (or Joint Task Force which conducted the operation but was replaced by the formal activation of JSOC). A cell under *Honey Badger*, called Snowbird, conducted the actual planning. One key failing was the lack of CIA human intelligence confirming hostage locations and no attempt at rescue could be made without this.

In July 1980, a requirement was raised to form a human intelligence activity within the Department of Defense; this would become the Field Operations Group (FOG), precursor to the Intelligence Support Activity (ISA), which was established under a joint Army and CIA programme. The FOG deployed into Iran and generated significant intelligence on the location of the hostages.

An Army aviation element was stood up, drawn from the 101st Airborne and equipped with Black Hawks and Chinooks, which would provide direct organic capability to the JTF under the name of Task Force 160. The Air Force established the 1st Special Operations Wing, equipped with the MH-53 Pave Low, and began intensive training in night flying. Another key requirement was for a light reconnaissance helicopter that could be carried within the confines of a C-130 or C-141 transport aircraft for immediate deployment.

First attempts at modifying the Army's OH-58 Kiowa were successful; however, attention soon focused on the even smaller OH-6 or Loach. Although obsolete, six airframes were tracked down in a National Guard facility, found eminently suitable, and returned to active service within days. Other OH-6s were located and eventually a fleet of 20 airframes was made available.

JTF 1-79 would be disbanded in November 1980 and a new command, JSOC, would be raised. Responsibility for *Honey Badger* also passed from the JTF to JSOC the following month. Option X, informally known as 'the Godzilla option', was fast becoming the preferred mission template should another rescue be launched. A massive undertaking, Option X would see the

Rangers seize a number of airfields in Iran to allow the landing of C-141s carrying OH-6s, now nicknamed 'The Little Bird'.

Delta would then launch against the main hostage locations via the Little Birds and under constant AC-130 cover. Other Delta elements would use Chenowth fast attack vehicles (armed dune buggies) to reach a number of hostages who had been scattered in small groups. However, on 20 January 1981, the hostages were finally released by the Iranian government. Debriefings confirmed that Delta's assault plans would have succeeded had they made it back into Iran.

Operation *Enduring Freedom/Freedom's Sentinel*

Special Operations in Afghanistan • 2001 to present day

Operation *Enduring Freedom – Afghanistan* (OEF-A or OEF) officially began in October 2001 with a series of air and cruise missile strikes on Taliban and al-Qaeda targets known as Operation *Crescent Wind*. Two weeks earlier, however, CIA operatives from the Special Activities Division (SAD) and Counter Terrorist Center (CTC) had deployed into Afghanistan to pave the way for the strikes and for the arrival of Army Special Forces.

The first Green Beret ODAs were infiltrated in mid-October, linking up the CIA teams and their Afghan allies, the Northern Alliance. At the same time as the first ODA touched down on Afghan soil after flying in from neighbouring Uzbekistan, two night-time operations were conducted to the south of the country. The first was the publicly acknowledged Operation *Rhino*, which saw the Rangers of the 3rd Battalion conduct a combat jump onto a desert airfield in a show of force to the Taliban.

Conducted in far more secrecy was the concurrent strike against Objective Gecko, a Delta Force operation to raid the residence of Mullah Omar, the

A fascinating image of a US Army Special Forces ODA taking up residence in the former Kandahar home of the late Taliban leader Mullah Omar in December 2001. This compound was known as Objective Gecko, the site of an earlier Delta Force operation that October. Note the ubiquitous Toyota Hilux. (Paula Bronstein/Getty Images)

leader of the Taliban. Although various tales have been told over the years, it appears that Delta's B Squadron (reinforced with a troop from A) took down the compound unopposed. An MH-47E clipped a wall as it landed and at least one operator was wounded by fragments from a friendly grenade, which penetrated the thin walls of the building. There were, however, zero enemy on the objective and, after a sensitive site exploitation (SSE), Delta was exfiltrated.

The Green Berets on the ground, alongside their CIA compatriots, began making serious headway against the Taliban. The combination of precision airstrikes by the Americans and the anti-Taliban fervour of the Northern Alliance combined to collapse the Taliban government. Instead of the six to 12 months many analysts predicted, most of Afghanistan had fallen to the Northern Alliance in a mere 49 days.

Although the Taliban had been toppled in record time, the job for SOF was not yet over. Multi-national units joined American SOF in conducting a series of reconnaissance missions to track al-Qaeda remnants. Green Berets followed the trail of Usama bin Laden himself into the mountains of Tora Bora. With the operation handed to Delta Force, the Americans and their locally recruited allies fought against al-Qaeda remnants believed to be protecting bin Laden.

The al-Qaeda leader escaped thanks to the duplicity of those locally recruited allies when a cease-fire, meant to facilitate the surrender of the foreign fighters, was actually used as a ruse to ferry bin Laden away. Other reconnaissance operations were ongoing and in early 2002 one of these discovered a large number of fighters using the Shahikot Valley in eastern Afghanistan, a former mujahideen sanctuary, as a safe haven. Located along the Pakistan border, the al-Qaeda and Taliban fighters were hiding in the caves which criss-crossed the valley walls.

In March 2002, Operation *Anaconda* was launched as a joint mission to seize the valley and eliminate the foreign fighters and Taliban elements. Although originally an SOF mission, it morphed into a daytime conventional air assault, much to the consternation of the SOF operators. Teams from Task Force Dagger with the Northern Alliance would be used to flush out the enemy, forcing them to retreat into the guns of the conventional forces who would be helicoptered into the valley while reconnaissance units from Task Forces Sword and K-Bar would call in airstrikes on any large concentrations to seal the valley.

Poor planning and pure bad luck plagued the operation from the start with a 5th Special Forces ODA embedded with Afghan militia erroneously engaged by an AC-130. When promised pre-planned airstrikes did not eventuate, the Afghans decided to withdraw. This initial action accomplished little apart from

Senior Chief Special Warfare Operator (SEAL) Britt K. Slabinski, known as Slab, of SEAL Team 6 photographed on the peak of Takur Ghar after the conclusion of Operation *Anaconda*. Note his SEAL 'Recce Rifle', a customized M4 with a 16-inch barrel. His attached Special Tactics CCT, Master Sergeant John A. Chapman, was subsequently posthumously awarded the Medal of Honor. Some suggest the SEALs left "Chappie" on the peak, wounded but perhaps unconscious. Chapman later engaged a number of insurgents around and in the bunkers before finally being killed moments before the Ranger Quick Reaction Force arrived in Razor 01. (Courtesy US Navy)

serving as an early warning to the enemy. Miraculously the enemy were still caught napping when the air assault was conducted and only after the Chinooks had lifted off were the first sounds of small arms and RPG fire heard.

The operation descended into a fierce firefight with the conventional forces trapped on the valley floor until night fell. The same mission saw the infamous battle of Takur Ghar occur on a neighbouring peak with the deaths of seven SOF personnel after a SEAL Team 6 recce team erroneously landed in a hornet's nest of insurgents.

By mid-2002, conventional forces replaced many of the SOF components in theatre and the job of hunting al-Qaeda remnants fell to a handful of SEALs and Rangers and a rotational Army Special Forces element which was also tasked with training the fledgling Afghan security forces. The focus, and available assets, had shifted to Iraq.

The Taliban did not lose focus, however, and by 2005 there were signs that the insurgency was gaining ground. Multinational forces under the NATO International Security Assistance Force (ISAF) began to deploy SOF and greater numbers of conventional forces. For instance the French deployed Task Group Ares composed of elements drawn from 1er Régiment de Parachutistes d'Infanterie de Marine (1er RPIMa), Commando Parachutiste de l'Air no10 (CPA-10) and the 13e Régiment de Dragons Parachutistes (13e RDP or 13th Parachute Dragoon Regiment, a long range reconnaissance and surveillance unit providing a capability not unlike the UK's Special Reconnaissance Regiment or the US JSOC's Ranger Reconnaissance Company). Ares operated in both Kandahar and Nangarhar provinces between 2003 and 2006.

Most US and ISAF SOF were tasked with mentoring Afghan security forces and conducting direct action raids in support of ISAF conventional forces. As the 'Surge' in Iraq began to pay dividends, efforts were refocused on Afghanistan and a special operations surge was implemented from 2008 with both operators and strategic assets like Reaper UAVs (unmanned aerial vehicles) redeployed. A US SOCOM policy document explained at the time the divergence of roles: 'We layer with other SOF units to effectively disable the insurgent infrastructure and support the populace. TF-310 and ISAF SOF work on the head (insurgent leadership), and we [SOCOM SOF] work on the body (denying time and space to the facilitators and supporters) of the insurgent infrastructure.'

An exceedingly rare image of two Delta Force operators making their way up a dry stream bed in Tora Bora, December 2001. Both wear a mix of civilian cold weather clothing and Afghan Pakol hats. (Robert Nickelsberg/Getty Images)

A 2018 image of a Coalition forward operating base in Nangarhar Province, Afghanistan. Visible are US Special Forces soldiers driving the M1128 GMV 1.1 (foreground right and rear) and the MZRZ (centre). (Wakil Kohsar/AFP/Getty Images)

JSOC, who operated generally unilaterally for OEF but also on occasion in support of ISAF, was now organized into four Iraq-style geographic commands – the Ranger-led Task Forces South and Central, SEAL Team 6's Task Force East and Delta's Task Force North, under an overall Task Force 310 (sometimes called Task Force 3-10). Following the special operations surge into Afghanistan, by 2010 most units were conducting a minimum of six kill or capture missions every night. The British SAS and SBS were on a similar punishing regime. Just under half of JSOC's missions were considered successful (known as 'jackpots') with shots fired on less than 10 per cent of operations.

Units were also tasked with implementing village stability operations (VSO) to recruit, train and accompany locally recruited militia to protect their local environs as part of a wider 'clear, hold and build' counter-insurgency (COIN) strategy implemented by General Stanley McChrystal and later General David Petraeus, the architect of the Iraq Surge. As the US Army noted, there were two distinct missions for SOF: 'CJSOTF-A tactical operations, which were initially called the community defense initiative, or CDI, then became the local defense initiative, or LDI, and in May 2010 became VSO; and a foreign internal defense, or FID, mission with partnered ANSF.'

While VSO enjoyed some success, it was not enough to turn the tide of the insurgency. Increasingly ISAF and OEF looked for a negotiated settlement. Indeed a 2012 US government report saw little sign of the Taliban, overtly and covertly supported by Pakistan, agreeing to a cease-fire: 'Though the Taliban suffered severely in 2011, its strength, motivation, funding, and tactical proficiency remains intact. Despite numerous tactical setbacks, surrender is far from their collective mindset. As opposed to years past, detainees have become more confident in not only their potential to win, but the virtue of their cause.'

ISAF was dissolved at the end of 2014 and all multi-national SOF are now under the command of Operation *Resolute Support*, which has subsumed both OEF and ISAF. Despite the drawdown of forces, SOF still conduct a wide range of mentoring and direct action missions and are likely to continue to do so for the foreseeable future.

In August 2016, for instance, SEAL Team 6 conducted a night-time HALO (high altitude low opening) parachute jump to rescue two kidnapped professors, one American and one Australian. The rare combat use of a HALO jump indicates that the target location was probably in a geographic position where a helicopter-borne assault would have been compromised. Seven insurgents were killed on the objective but unfortunately the hostages had already been moved from the location.

Increasingly US SOF have been targeting ISIS-K or the Khorasan Group, an Islamic State affiliate active in eastern Afghanistan and in open conflict with the Taliban. In April 2007, two Rangers platoons and a reinforced platoon from one of the Afghan National Mission Units launched a night-time ground assault against an ISIS-K redoubt in Nangarhar Province. Some 35 Islamic State fighters were killed, as were two US Army Rangers from the 3rd Battalion of the 75th Ranger Regiment. Amongst the enemy killed was the raid's primary target, the ISIS-K leader in Afghanistan.

Operation *Gothic Serpent*

Special Operation in Somalia • October 1993

Task Force Ranger, a Joint Special Operations Task Force (JSOTF) composed of a company of Rangers, a squadron from Delta Force and elements from Air Force Special Tactics and the Army's 160th Special Operations Aviation Regiment (160th SOAR), the Intelligence Support Activity (ISA) and a handful of SEAL snipers from SEAL Team 6, was dispatched to Mogadishu, Somalia in August 1993. Its mission was to locate and capture a Somali warlord responsible for the deaths of United Nations peacekeepers in the war-torn nation.

The task force completed six operations to varying degrees of success before 3 October when rapidly developing intelligence indicated that two of

Bravo Company, 3rd Battalion of the 75th Rangers, pictured on the beach adjacent to their hangar in Mogadishu immediately prior to the mission on 3 October 1993. (Courtesy US Army, 75th Ranger Regiment)

Delta Force Master Sergeant Norm Hooten's F-Team pictured with their AH-6 Little Bird prior to the October mission. All carry Colt carbines (one equipped with an M203) with early Aimpoint optics and jury-rigged light mounts. (Author's Collection)

the warlord's chief lieutenants would be meeting in downtown Mogadishu that afternoon. It was too good an opportunity to pass up. The operators planned to be on the ground for no more than 30 minutes.

A daring daylight raid was launched, with the Delta assaulters to be infiltrated into the target on MH-6 Little Birds while the Rangers and the Delta command element would fast rope from MH-60 Black Hawks and establish blocking positions around the perimeter of the objective. A Ranger Ground Assault Force in HMMWVs and trucks would rendezvous at the target to exfiltrate the assault force and their prisoners back to their base at Mogadishu's dilapidated airport.

Despite one Ranger falling from the fast rope and having to be evacuated by a small column of HMMWVs, the mission was going according to plan, although the task force was encountering more small arms and RPG fire than on previous missions. Delta had successfully seized its prisoners and was in the process of loading the warlord's men onto the trucks for the return journey when one of the Black Hawks overhead, carrying a four-man Delta sniper team, was struck by an RPG.

The MH-60 crashed to the north-east of the target building. A composite force of Rangers and operators made its way on foot towards the crash site, racing Somali crowds. The vehicle convoy attempted to drive to the crash site but was repeatedly ambushed and ran into makeshift barricades. An MH-6 managed to land and recover two of the wounded snipers.

Just as the first Rangers reached the crashed helicopter, the CSAR (combat search and rescue) helicopter arrived, disgorging its mixed team of pararescue jumpers, Delta medics and Ranger security force. The combined force managed to establish a perimeter and push the Somali militia back to allow work to begin to extract the bodies of the Black Hawk's aircrew who had perished in the crash.

Meanwhile the Ranger ground convoy was becoming increasingly combat ineffective with increasing numbers of wounded and vehicles which were being shot to pieces. Directions transmitted from helicopters above arrived too late owing to a relay, only adding to the chaos and confusion. Eventually, the Ranger battalion commander decided that the only option was to return to base and regroup.

The situation was exacerbated by the downing of a second Black Hawk over the city. This time, the helicopter crashed to the south-west. With the CSAR team already deployed and the Rangers and operators either fighting a pitched battle at the first crash site or on the ground convoy, there were few options left.

The only known image taken during the battle from Chalk 1's blocking position looking back at Chalk 3's blocking position in the distance. On the right top can be seen the perimeter wall around the target building. The gate into the interior courtyard into which Delta breached can also be seen (light blue wall section). (Courtesy US Army)

While the ground convoy struggled through ambush after ambush, a second ground convoy constituted from Rangers left at the airport tried to fight its way through to the second crash site but also fell prey to Somali ambushes and roadblocks. The two Ranger convoys inadvertently ran into each other and, with mounting dead and wounded, decided to return to the airport.

A pair of Delta snipers volunteered to land near the second crash site and provide security until a reinforced and reorganized ground column, hopefully with UN armoured vehicles, could punch its way through. The two snipers managed to protect the wounded aircrew for around 20 minutes until the weight of fire became overpowering and both were shot and killed. The pilot of the Black Hawk was miraculously captured alive.

Work continued at the first crash site to release the bodies of the aircrew, while at the airport a hastily agreed plan was put into action. Both Malaysian and Pakistani armoured vehicles, along with American infantry and a small composite force of Rangers and operators, drove back out into the city to fight their way through to the crash sites. Just after midnight, the UN convoy broke through and linked up with Task Force Ranger.

While the wounded and the dead were transferred to the armoured vehicles, the second crash site was searched but no trace of the aircrew or the Delta snipers could be found. Eventually, just as dawn was breaking, operators managed to cut loose the body of the dead pilot at the first crash site and loaded his remains upon a vehicle. The massive convoy then made its way back out of the city as the sun rose above it.

In a final challenge to the men of Task Force Ranger, a number of Rangers and operators were forced to make part of the journey on foot to their destination, a UN-controlled soccer stadium, as the vehicles were overloaded and a number of the Malaysian armoured vehicles drove off leaving the men to fight their way out. A Ranger NCO realized the problem and returned with an HMMWV patrol finally to pick up the last survivors as they ran from the city.

The operation resulted in the deaths of five Delta operators (a sixth was killed several days later in a mortar strike on the airport), five members of the

160th, six Rangers and two members of the 10th Mountain Division, along with two Malaysian soldiers killed. Task Force Ranger suffered an incredible 83 wounded while 10th Mountain suffered 22 wounded during the desperate battle to link up with the besieged Rangers and operators. The captured pilot, Mike Durant, was eventually released into Red Cross custody after 11 days.

Operation *Inherent Resolve*

Special Operations in Iraq and Syria • 2014 to present day

Following the onslaught of the so-called Islamic State in both Iraq and Syria, multi-national SOF deployed in support of both Iraqi security forces and Syrian irregulars. They also began targeting Islamic State high-value targets in a campaign reminiscent of the JSOC 'industrial counter-terrorism' efforts in Iraq in the early 2000s. The overall SOF mission is known as Special Operations Joint Task Force – Operation *Inherent Resolve* with the JSOC element probably operating as Task Force 27 (although this designation has also more than likely already been changed).

The first publicly acknowledged SOF deployed to Syria in 2015 with a small number of US Army 5th SFG ODAs later followed by both SEAL and Marine Special Operations Command (MARSOC) elements although the overall mission was and is still largely Army Special Forces-led. Their role was to advise and assist the Kurdish Peshmerga and anti-Assad rebels known as the Syrian Democratic Forces (SDF). Along with mentoring, the Americans brought with them Air Force combat controllers to harness US airpower to support the Kurdish and Syrian Democratic Forces offensives. The CIA had already established its own competing training programme, which also funnelled weapons and equipment to the SDF.

American forward operating locations were established at several sites including Kobani on the Turkish border, another near Hasaka in the north-east and another at Deir al Zour, which would later be famously attacked by a mixed force of Iranian-backed jihadists and Russian mercenaries. These bases range from fully equipped airstrips such as at Kobani to forward refuelling and rearmament sites for helicopters, including the Bell 407s flown by Echo Squadron, at Hasaka. The sites are colloquially known as SOC FWDs: Special Operations Command, Forward.

While SOCOM units continue to advise, assist and accompany SDF and Peshmerga units, often calling in air support or artillery fire from Marine batteries to support them (and supplying EOD support – an EOD technician attached to 5th Special Forces was killed in Syria in 2016 working with the Kurds), JSOC maintains a small force of around 200 personnel in Syria, mainly drawn from Delta, the Rangers and the Intelligence Support Activity

(ISA). The JSOC elements are conducting both targeted operations against Islamic State and training and advisory duties with fledgling special operations units drawn from the SDF and Kurds.

The Expeditionary Targeting force (ETF) is likely operating as part of the overall JSOC Task Force 27 and although based in northern Iraq has conducted numerous operations into Syria. One of the first was a July 2014 hostage rescue attempt to recover an American humanitarian volunteer, Kayla Mueller, and Western journalists Steve Sotloff, Peter Kassig and James Foley, who were being held by Islamic State.

In its first publically acknowledged mission into Syria, Delta launched a night-time raid with the assault force infiltrated by the so-called MH-X or Silent Hawk, stealth Black Hawks, with a pair of direct action penetrators (DAPs), heavily armed MH-60 variants, and two armed Predator UAVs (unmanned aerial vehicles) flying overwatch above them. Unfortunately the hostages had been recently moved. Delta killed a number of terrorists and conducted a sensitive site exploitation (SSE), recovering items which proved the hostages had been recently at the site, before re-boarding their aircraft and making a getaway back across the border. A 160th Special Operations Aviation Regiment (160th SOAR) DAP pilot was hit in the leg by an insurgent round but kept flying. He was the only casualty incurred.

In May 2015 the ETF again launched to capture or kill a high-ranking Islamic State leadership target in al-Amr. Infiltrating in MH-60s with MV-22 Ospreys assigned to both the combat search and rescue and immediate reaction force missions, the assaulters stormed a multi-storey building, killing a number of terrorists and eventually the target himself when he attempted to fire upon them. His wife, who was also an Islamic State member, and an imprisoned sex slave were loaded onto the helicopters and the assault force exfiltrated without casualties.

A 2018 image of members of the 5th Special Forces Group and a Jordanian Black Hawk at an undisclosed location in Syria. Note the range of vehicles in use: the GMV 1.1 (far right), the MRZR (centre) and the older HMMWV-based GMV 1.0s. (Courtesy US Army, Staff Sgt Jacob Connor)

A soldier from 5th Special Forces Group scans for Islamic State suicide car bombs through the Command Launch Unit of his FGM-148 Javelin anti-tank guided missile at an undisclosed location in northern Syria, October 2018. (Courtesy US Army, Sgt Matthew Crane)

Delta launched an ambitious hostage rescue mission alongside Kurdish Peshmerga to free over 70 prisoners being held by Islamic State in Hawijah, south-west of Kirkuk, Iraq in October 2015. Intelligence, surveillance and reconnaissance (ISR) indicated that mass graves had already been dug and that the prisoners – a mix of captured Iraqi security forces and Peshmerga – would be executed the following morning.

Delta and the Peshmerga Counter Terrorism Group (CTG) operators infiltrated in 160th SOAR Black Hawks and conducted explosive breaches to enter the prison. During the firefight, some 20 Islamic State terrorists were killed but sadly a Delta master sergeant was shot and killed as he assisted the CTG in clearing the objective, the first US casualty in combat under Operation *Inherent Resolve*. All hostages were safely extracted.

More recently, in January 2017, unnamed Islamic State leadership targets were killed during an aerial vehicle interdiction mission in the village of Kubar, Deir al Zour Province. Reports state that the assault force was supported by AH-64D Apache attack helicopters, which destroyed two Islamic State vehicles heading toward the objective to reinforce their comrades. Some 25 terrorists were killed by Delta at the target location. Several months later, in April 2017, an Uzbek associate of the Islamic State leader al-Baghdadi was killed in another ETF operation in Deir al Zour.

These missions were of course not the first time Delta had operated in Syria. In October 2008, a foreign fighter facilitator was targeted in a rare daylight operation across the Syria border from the insurgent hot-spot of Al-Qaim (where a number of operators had been killed over the years). Foreshadowing Operation *Neptune Spear*, which targeted bin Laden in 2011, the mission was planned and executed by JSOC until the operators crossed the border. At that point, it came under CIA control to meet congressional requirements (in Syria, the ETF operates under CIA Title 50 authority to meet with US law but is command and controlled by JSOC operationally).

While a pair of AH-6 Little Birds kept watch overhead, two MH-60 Black Hawks deposited the assault force. They stormed the objective, killing the target and a number of insurgents before conducting a thorough sensitive site exploitation (SSE) and exfiltrating by Black Hawk with the body of the dead insurgent leader and a trove of documents.

United Kingdom Special Forces, principally from the SAS, have been deployed to Syria since at least 2015. Photographs showing British operators in Jordanian al Thalab long range patrol vehicles at Al-Tanf airbase at a strategic point on the Syria–Iraq–Jordan border in June 2016 were published by the BBC. Al-Tanf later became another key Coalition special operations base.

Other videos from anti-Assad rebels have shown unidentified Westerners with British accents firing Javelin anti-tank guided missiles. In addition, their distinctive up-armoured Australian Bushmasters have been filmed alongside a Delta Force Pandur at the Tabqa Dam in May 2017 and in a convoy of at least three outside the de facto Islamic State capitol of Raqqa in July 2017. According to reports from Syrian journalists, Coalition 'special forces' were seen fighting alongside their Syrian and Kurdish allies. Even a US government spokesperson for Operation *Inherent Resolve* was forced to admit that 'Coalition SOF are in Raqqa, and they are close to the front lines.'

In March 2018, a member of the British SAS and a Delta Force operator were killed by an IED while conducting a covert infiltration in a civilian van. Their target was an Islamic State high-value target hiding out near Manbij. The official statement released by CENTCOM (US Central Command) only noted: 'Coalition forces, in an advise, assist and accompany capacity with our partners, were conducting a mission to kill or capture a known ISIS member when they were struck by an improvised explosive device.'

Reports suggest that a number of Kurdish Peshmerga were working with the joint element and were wounded in the blast, along with five other Delta and SAS soldiers. In August 2018, an aviator from the 160th SOAR was killed during a night-time assault mission supporting Delta Force north of Sinjar in northern Iraq. His MH-60, carrying seven operators along with the four-man crew, crashed, wounding all on board but two.

Apart from the publicly announced mentoring operation from 2016 with Syrian Democratic Forces (SDF), French special operators were first committed in 2018 under Operation *Chammal* in a more direct action role although there is convincing evidence that elements may have been deployed earlier than this, perhaps as early as 2015 following the Paris terrorist attacks. Certainly General Directorate for External Security (Direction Générale de la Sécurité Extérieure or DGSE) operators have been in Syria since this time, albeit in an advisory and liaison role. French operators have been seen in Nexter Aravis MRAPs (mine resistant ambush protected vehicles) conducting joint operations with US Army Special Forces mounted in M-ATVs in and around Manbij late in 2018.

Manbij itself has been under threat from Turkey along with pro-Assad jihadists who want to eliminate the Kurdish population, and was the site of a very public display of force projection initially from US Army Rangers in Stryker infantry carrier vehicles flying large American flags. The Rangers were replaced by what appear to be Army Special Forces. Both Strykers and Pandurs were seen outside Raqqa in 2017, perhaps as part of the same operations that the British SAS was conducting in its Bushmasters.

In January 2019, the US suffered four casualties from the Special Operations Joint Task Force in Manbij after a suicide bomber detonated a

US Army Special Forces seen around Deir Ezzor, near the Syrian border with Iraq, in 2018. Both MRAPs are the M1245A1 M-ATV variant with enhanced counter-IED protection. Note the non-standard commercial vehicle to the right. (Delil Souleiman/AFP/Getty Images)

device in a restaurant being frequented by the Americans. Along with 15 local civilians, the bomber killed a 5th SFG operator, an Arabic-speaking Navy intelligence specialist, a former SEAL contracting to the Defense Intelligence Agency and a civilian Syrian-American interpreter.

Other Coalition nations have deployed SOF into Iraq and Syria. Belgian Army SFG has been active in both countries in mentoring operations since 2016. SFG operators have been filmed operating Javelin anti-tank guide missile systems in northern Iraq. Belgian military intelligence, the ADIV (Algemene Dienst Inlichtingen en Veiligheid or General Intelligence and Security Service), is operating in Syria in support of the US-led Operation *Gallant Phoenix* tracking foreign fighters. These ADIV elements are believed to be protected by small teams of SFG operators.

There have also been persistent rumours of German KSK involvement with an alleged party of some 50 operators working alongside US, French and British trainers; however, the German government was unequivocal in its response: 'There are no German special forces in Syria. The accusation is false.' Certainly no pictures have yet emerged of obviously German operators besides the German military contingent conducting training and mentoring in Iraq.

Although the Australian government has strenuously denied direct ground combat participation by Australian forces, the author has spotted an Australian Bushmaster in Mosul during the efforts to retake the city. It is known that Australian operators from the 80-strong Special Operations Task Group committed to Iraq have provided terminal guidance for Coalition aircraft in support of Iraqi offensives against Islamic State.

Canadians, including elements from the Canadian Special Operations Regiment (CSOR) and the JTF2 counter-terrorist unit have also been employed in mentoring operations that have skirted the official line denying involvement in actual combat. CSOR operators accompanied Peshmerga fighters into the battle for Mosul while JTF2's snipers entered the record books in 2017 with the longest range sniper kill in history, let alone Iraq, at an astounding 3,450 metres.

The Jordanians have also certainly deployed into Syria as members of the 5th SFG next to a Jordanian Black Hawk at what is now officially known as Al-Tanf Garrison, which has been recently reinforced by a company of US Marines. Jordanian operators have also accompanied Delta Force on a number of missions within Syria and have worked alongside the British SAS out of Al-Tanf. They also conducted a sadly abortive hostage rescue attempt to recover a Jordanian pilot before he was savagely executed by Islamic State by being burnt alive.

The Israelis too have conducted at least one and probably several long range special missions into Syria. One, conducted by Sayeret Matkal, was carelessly exposed by President Trump to a Russian delegation at the White House. The operation saw Israeli operators penetrate Syria and place technical surveillance devices in an Islamic State headquarters. The intelligence they gained prompted the targeted ban on laptops being carried onto passenger aircraft as an Islamic State external operation was discovered that had planned to use an explosive-laden laptop to destroy an aircraft mid-flight.

The Israeli Air Force of course have carried out any number of airstrikes upon both Syrian and Iranian forces in Syria including targeting Syria's secret nuclear processing plant. Mossad and Agaf HaModi'in (AMAN – Israeli Defence Force or IDF military intelligence) operatives were involved in both inadvertently learning of the construction of the site, and advising where best to strike to destroy the capability from the air. Doubtless the Israeli Sayeret Matkal was involved in some form of close target reconnaissance.

Operation *Iraqi Freedom*

Special Operations in Iraq • 2003–10

Officially the ground component of Operation *Iraqi Freedom* began on 20 March 2003. The night before, the first American special operators from Task Force Wolverine crossed the border and headed into the deserts of western Iraq. The task force was drawn from Delta's C Squadron and commanded by an operator who had fought in the famed battle of Mogadishu. Its members were mounted in a mix of Pinzgauer SOVs (special operations vehicles), Polaris ATVs (all-terrain vehicles) and 'Non-Tac' commercial vehicles and were equipped with their own UAVs (unmanned aerial vehicles)

Two Australian Commandos from the then-4RAR (now 2 Commando Regiment) conduct clearing operations around a captured Iraqi airfield in April 2003. (Courtesy Commonwealth of Australia, Defence Photographer JC)

and a complement of combat assault dogs carried in air conditioned comfort on one of their 'mothership' vehicles.

Their mission was initially to support the 5th SFG, which was assigned the western desert to target mobile Scud missile launchers but Delta soon expanded beyond that remit, and conducted 'marauder' operations to confuse and tie up Iraqi units, stopping them from reinforcing their comrades in the south fighting against two US Army- and Marine-led offensives. Wolverine also hunted down fleeing Iraqi generals and high-ranking Ba'ath Party members who attempted to escape to Syria.

The Green Beret ODAs of the 5th SFG were hunting the Scuds and providing strategic intelligence from mounted reconnaissance missions deep into Iraqi territory in the western and southern JSOAs or Joint Special Operations Areas, operational boxes assigned to specific units. Wolverine, along with the Australian SASR's Task Force 64 and the United Kingdom's Task Force 14, composed of elements of two SAS squadrons (B and D), was assigned the northern JSOA abutting Syria.

Farther north operated another British unit, M Squadron of the SBS, which entered Iraq from Jordan to make contact with an Iraqi commander who had been convinced to surrender by operatives from the Secret Intelligence Service (SIS) and CIA. Instead it ran into Iraqi patrols, supported by armour, which had been given the specific task of hunting down Coalition special operations incursions.

A rolling firefight developed that eventually saw the SBS operators extracted by Chinook, leaving behind a number of vehicles that had become bogged. The Land Rovers had been set for demolition but inexplicably the charges had failed to detonate. Also left behind were two operators who had become separated from the main body and were forced to evade into Syria on a Polaris ATV (all-terrain vehicle) where they were captured. They were later released after the personal intercession of none other than then-Prime Minister Tony Blair.

Farther to the north-east, Task Force Viking conducted a difficult ground movement into northern Iraq, employing its Kurdish Peshmerga allies. In the year previously, teams from ODA 066 of the 10th SFG along with CIA and Intelligence Support Activity (ISA) elements covertly infiltrated into Kurdistan to begin training and liaising with the Peshmerga along with conducting strategic reconnaissance. They were also instrumental in laying the ground work for the planned surrender of the Iraqi 5th Corps that the SBS was eventually tasked to manage.

After the collapse of the Iraqi military and government, SOF began the hunt for what were known as Former Regime Elements or FREs: high-ranking Ba'ath Party members and senior military staff. In the official history of US military operations in Iraq, scant mention is made of this effort; it simply notes that 'Portions of a separate special operations task force, the Rangers, and the 160th Special Operations Aviation Regiment, started to transition from operations against Iraqi military and paramilitary forces to hunting high-value regime targets'.

As the insurgency gained strength through the later stages of 2003, JSOC was given the mission to hunt down insurgent leadership and logistical figures while the British SAS, much to its frustration, was relegated to the FRE mission. JSOC in Iraq, although officially termed the Counter-Terrorism Special Operations Task Force, operated under a bewildering and ever-changing range of designations from Task Force 20 to Task Force 121 to Task Force 626 to Task Force 145 to Task Force 77 to Task Force 88 before finally setting on Task Force 16. This was the overall command for a number of sub task forces, each assigned a geographic area of responsibility.

Task Force Green was Delta-led; along with a Ranger company, it was assigned Task Force Central, while Task Force West was the responsibility of a squadron from SEAL Team 6 (Task Force Blue), again supported by Rangers. Task Force North or Task Force Red was Ranger-led with a troop from Delta in support while Task Force Black was the eventual UKSF contribution. Other supporting units such as the 160th Special Operations Aviation Regiment (160th SOAR) were known as Task Force Brown while Britain's Special Forces Support Group (SFSG) was Task Force Maroon.

As the insurgency grew, so too did JSOC operations. Led by General Stanley McChrystal, the task force forged a new operating principle, bringing together disparate elements from a multitude of intelligence agencies to work alongside the special operators in tackling the insurgents. McChrystal believed that 'It takes a network to defeat a network'* and he set about creating this unique structure to facilitate the destruction of both nationalist insurgent groups and the emerging al-Qaeda in Iraq (AQI).

In his memoir, McChrystal notes that the network was enabled through a strict focus on what he called FFFEA or 'find, fix, finish, exploit, and analyse':

> The idea was to combine analysts who found the enemy (through intelligence, surveillance, and reconnaissance); drone operators who fixed the target; combat teams who finished the target by capturing or killing him; specialists who exploited the intelligence the raid yielded, such as cell phones, maps, and detainees; and the intelligence analysts who turned this raw information into usable knowledge. By doing this, we speeded up the cycle for a counterterrorism operation, gleaning valuable insights in hours, not days.**

Soon JSOC teams were conducting multiple missions every night. The British SAS eventually joined them although disagreements on prisoner handling procedures restricted British access to the full target list until January 2006. Along with both Sunni and Shia sectarian insurgents, the task force was focused on destroying AQI and its notorious leader, the Jordanian terrorist Musab al-Zarqawi.

The official US Army history hints at the violence of the campaign although the majority of objectives were secured without a shot being fired:

> Demonstrating the level of insurgent resolve, a handful of SOF raids had to be extracted under pressure with the support of AC-130 and rotary wing fires. This resulted in the increased use, on some missions, of a 'call out', in which a megaphone was used to instruct non-combatants to leave a surrounded building. If the fighters inside did not surrender, or if they opened fire, the building would then be reduced with an airstrike rather than risk troops' lives.

The Rangers of Task Force North almost captured High Value Target-1, al-Zarqawi, in early 2005:

> On February 20, 2005, other special operations forces were following Zarqawi's movements with one ISR [intelligence, surveillance and reconnaissance] platform. Just as Zarqawi's location appeared to be confirmed, the video camera on the ISR platform malfunctioned and

---

*   https://foreignpolicy.com/2011/02/21/it-takes-a-network/

**   https://foreignpolicy.com/2011/02/21/it-takes-a-network/

needed to be reset, a process that took only 23 seconds. In that short time, Zarqawi himself was able to disappear from sight, escaping capture from an assault force that arrived seconds later. While the team's main prize was gone, it did capture Zarqawi's vehicle and many of his personal possessions, including his laptop, seven thumb drives, and 50,000 euros.

Despite narrowly missing the 'emir' of AQI, the Rangers and Delta had a tremendous effect on the terrorist networks:

> … in Mosul over the summer of 2005, when Abu Talha and Abu Zubayr, AQI's regional emir and his replacement, were killed along with numerous subordinate AQI leaders. By November 7, four more replacement leaders, including the sixth emir of Mosul, Abu Sayf, had also been killed, and AQI's Mosul branch began to grind to a halt.

A rare image of Delta Force in its distinctive Austrian-designed Pandurs, officially the Armored Ground Mobility System, adopted in 2000 after years of often heated debate within the unit. This ground assault force is pictured in Baghdad in October 2003. (Karim Sahib/AFP/Getty Images)

Al-Zarqawi was finally killed in June 2006 after then-Task Force 145 tracked him and launched an airstrike that obliterated his safehouse in the AQI heartland of Baqubah. Despite sustaining major wounds from the impact of two 500lb bombs, the terrorist leader was still alive as Delta operators flying in on MH-6s arrived. Rumours have long circulated that operators may have 'finished off' al-Zarqawi.

By 2006, there were on average 50 terrorist incidents, both sectarian and anti-Coalition, every day in Baghdad. Car bombings, both suicide and static VBIEDs (vehicle-borne IEDs), were at an all-time high, with as many as three a day occurring in Baghdad alone. The 'Surge' was the US military's response to this ever-increasing violence against civilian and soldier alike. Large numbers of conventional forces were surged into Iraq in an attempt to swamp the insurgency using the 'policeman on every corner' analogy. With them came more special operators.

General David Petraeus, a champion of counter-insurgency thinking, was at the helm of the 'Surge' and encouraged his troops to 'live with the people'. US forces – both conventional and SOF – were pushed out to over 100 combat outposts and forward operating bases instead of living on the huge bases at Balad or Baghdad International. Green Beret ODAs, and some SEAL Teams, took on the role of developing joint combat outposts, living alongside the Iraqi security forces and in the midst of population areas in an effort to encourage the 'inkblot' counter-insurgency strategy.

The idea was that by placing security forces out amongst the population, small hamlets of relative safety could be established, and as these grew they began to resemble inkblots on a page, spreading their influence outward as neighbouring communities saw the benefits of supporting the security forces, including the considerable financial incentive of trading with the Americans and Iraqi security forces. Many combat outposts were also constructed using local labour, again adding to the affluence and thus stability of the area.

Although Petraeus was an enthusiastic supporter of JSOC's operations against AQI he knew that:

> ... we would not be able to kill or capture our way out of the industrial-strength insurgency that confronted us in Iraq. Hence we had to identify those insurgents and militia members who were 'reconcilable', and we then had to persuade them to become part of the solution in Iraq rather than a continuing part of the problem.*

The Special Forces implementation of the 'inkblot strategy' was one of the little-heralded successes in Iraq as it allowed the 'Anbar awakening' of 2005 and similar popular uprisings against al-Qaeda and the foreign fighters. Spurred on by AQI brutality, the combat outposts meant that local leaders who wanted to align with the security forces could do so. One of the best known of these programmes was the 'Sons of Iraq', a programme spearheaded by a UKSF officer that was intended to 'deputize' local militias to protect their own communities. Although the militias were paid and sometimes equipped by the Americans, the system had several distinct benefits.

Chief amongst these was that it drained the insurgency of recruits by enlisting these often rag-tag community militias into a recognized security programme that ostensibly benefited their local community rather than the Coalition 'occupiers'. Secondly, it provided paid employment for the throngs of unemployed youth, again depriving the insurgency of recruits and raising local living standards; thirdly it offered a ready-made intelligence network of people who knew the language and could quickly identify outsiders. It did of course mean that many nationalist insurgents and local gang members became 'Sons of Iraq' and former adversaries ended up on the government payroll but this will naturally occur in any successful counter-insurgency.

5th SFG and a number of SEAL Teams were also involved in yet another numbered task force under JSOC command, Task Force 17, the so-called 'CII' or 'Counter Iranian Influence' unit targeting the Iranian Quds Force and its agents, who were actively supporting the insurgency, particularly in the Shia-dominated south.

The special operators also supported conventional operations such as *Phantom Fury* in Fallujah. Army Special Forces and Delta were both active in shaping the

---

* https://foreignpolicy.com/2013/10/29/how-we-won-in-iraq/

battlefield before the offensive, conducting reconnaissance and marking targets. They later conducted a range of tasks during the operation. Both ODAs and Delta would attach themselves in small groups to Marine and Army infantry units and provide a type of mentoring in the field, helping the young soldiers survive the brutal cauldron of urban warfare against often fanatical jihadists. The SEALs too would see considerable action in Ramadi conducting operations in support of the local 'ground-holding' units as they attempted to pacify the area. This included providing sniper cover and raiding suspected insurgent safehouses or bomb-making factories.

Army Special Forces also spent many years in one of their most traditional roles – that of foreign internal defence. Green Beret ODAs trained and mentored Iraqi forces, including Iraqi Special Operations Forces (ISOF), which would later take the brunt of the fighting against Islamic State. The ODAs and later SEALs also trained police and Ministry of the Interior SWAT units, which enjoyed considerable success against both nationalist and AQI insurgent cells. Some US units found handing missions off to the Iraqis difficult as, in the case of the SEALs particularly, they were more focused on direct action than foreign internal defence. Iraqi forces ended up being little more than a cordon force in some cases.

The kill or capture strategy to deprive the insurgency, and particularly AQI, of its leadership, its logisticians, its bomb-makers and its most experienced terrorists worked hand-in-glove with the reconciliation strategy exemplified by the 'Sons of Iraq'. Neither in isolation would end in success but taken together, almost as a carrot and stick approach, there were strong indicators that the tide was turning in Iraq.

General Petraeus later noted of the JSOC operation:

> Looking back, it is clear that what the American and British special operators accomplished, aided enormously by various intelligence elements, was nothing short of extraordinary. Their relentless operations, employment of unmanned aerial vehicles and other advanced technology, tactical skill, courage, and creativity were truly inspirational.*

US military operations in Iraq ended in August 2010 after disagreements over status of force negotiations, although US special operators continued mentoring their Iraqi charges until late 2011.

US Army Special Forces seen patrolling in April 2003 in north-west Baghdad. Note the SOPMOD Block I M4A1s with QD suppressors and EOTech optics. (Scott Nelson/Getty Images)

---

* https://foreignpolicy.com/2013/10/29/how-we-won-in-iraq/

Operation *Neptune Spear*

Capture/Kill in Pakistan • 2011

After narrowly missing Usama bin Laden at Tora Bora in 2001, US SOF and the CIA had continued the hunt for the al-Qaeda leader. Although the resources committed to 'High Value Target 1' waned over the years as JSOC and the CIA focused on al-Qaeda in Iraq and its former leader, Abu Musab al-Zarqawi, a dedicated element at the CIA finally hit the jackpot, leading them to a compound in Abbottabad, Pakistan in late 2010.

Opinions differed within the CIA and the National Security Council on whether this was the hiding place of bin Laden but eventually a mission was 'green-lit'. Discussions included using a Reaper or manned aircraft to conduct a precision strike, an undercover mission by the CIA's Special Activities Division or a ground SOF assault. Needing to confirm the death of the target and his identity, the SOF option offered the best chance of an accurate battle damage assessment. From the start, a capture option does not appear to have been seriously considered, primarily as it was thought bin Laden would potentially be wearing a suicide vest.

Red Squadron of SEAL Team 6 was recently back from Afghanistan and was conducting a squadron rearming and refitting and thus was available for the special mission. According to Admiral Bill McRaven, JSOC commander at the time, the choice was based on available leaders: his other choice, a Delta Force squadron commander, had already deployed to Afghanistan so Red Squadron and its squadron commander, known publicly only by his callsign of 'Romeo 66', received the prestigious mission.

The plan evolved to include a small SEAL element infiltrated into Pakistan using the so-called Silent Hawk stealth variant of the MH-60. A Ranger Quick Reaction Force drawn from the Rangers assigned to JSOC's Task Force 310 in Afghanistan would forward deploy along the border in MH-47s as a precaution, along with an orbiting armada of electronic countermeasures and strike aircraft. Additional MH-47s would establish a Forward-Armament-And-Refuelling Point (FARP) site in Pakistan itself to refuel the Silent Hawks for the return leg of the journey. The FARP itself would be protected by an ST6 element that could act as an immediate reaction force if required.

Once they reached the compound in Abbottabad, the SEALs would fast-rope from the Silent Hawks, breach the compound and, if he was positively identified, kill bin Laden. A hasty SSE (sensitive site exploitation) would be conducted and any intelligence material, along with bin Laden's body, would be flown back to Afghanistan, all before the Pakistani military could react to the incursion (it was felt that any pre-warning to the Pakistanis could risk the operational security of the mission).

The mission was launched on the night of May 1, 2011 and went largely according to plan until the Silent Hawks arrived over the compound. One of the experimental helicopters was caught in a freak 'vortex ring state' which forced it to crash-land inside the compound walls. The SEALs quickly escaped the wreckage and continued with the mission thanks to the flying skills of the 160th SOAR pilots. One of the MH-47s from the FARP site was subsequently flown to Abbottabad where it held some five minutes' flying time away from the target, ready to be called in to exfiltrate the SEALs from the crashed Silent Hawk.

With a dog team of one handler and a Belgian Malinois named Cairo keeping back curious locals, the assaulters breached into both the main and secondary building known as the guest house. A power failure engineered by other government agencies saw the target compound and the surrounding neighbourhoods plunged into darkness. The SEALs wore the then newly developed quad night vision goggles, the GPNVG-20s, which turned the night into a green-tinted approximation of daylight.

The operators shot any who opposed them, using their suppressed HK416s and were involved in a brief firefight with bin Laden's courier (whose existence had led to the ultimate unravelling of bin Laden's location). As the SEALs climbed the stairs to the top floor in the main building, bin Laden himself peeked out from the master bedroom. The lead SEAL fired two shots, which missed. The operators burst into the bedroom, and as the lead SEAL tackled two of bin Laden's wives out of the way (and was forced to shoot one in the leg), the second SEAL through the door shot bin Laden twice in the head, followed by a 'security shot' as the body lay twitching on the floor.

Re-enactors display the weapons and equipment worn on the raid – Crye AOR1 desert digital camouflage, GPNVG-20 quad night vision goggles and 5.56x45mm HK416 carbines fitted with EOTech optics and ATPIAL infrared laser illuminators.
(MILpictures by Tom Weber/ Getty Images)

As the MH-47 was called forward, the SEALs grabbed what intelligence they could in the short time available and the attached EOD technician set charges on the crashed Silent Hawk. The assaulters spent 38 minutes on the ground before they clambered aboard the surviving Silent Hawk and the back-up MH-47 and headed for the FARP, bin Laden's body secreted on the floor of the stealth MH-60. They refuelled and safely crossed the border into Afghanistan before the first Pakistani Air Force interceptors were airborne.

Although the mission has been described as one of the greatest special operations in modern history, apart from the location in the 'non-permissive environment' of Pakistan, it was in fact a simpler mission template than many of the thousands of raids that Red Squadron, and ST6 as a whole, had conducted in Afghanistan. Even the failure of the helicopter was not a particularly uncommon occurrence owing to the high tempo of operations in the preceding decade. That long experience, however, allowed the SEALs to adapt quickly and overcome such obstacles and successfully prosecute the mission.

Operation *Nimrod*

Hostage Rescue in London • May 1980

On 30 April 1980, just after the US tragedy at Desert One during Operation *Eagle Claw*, six Iranian separatist terrorists with Iraqi backing (an Iraqi intelligence officer was suspected of orchestrating the operation) seized the Iranian Embassy at 16 Princes Gate, South Kensington, London. Holding 26 hostages, they demanded a mass release of political prisoners and the establishment of an Arabic homeland in Iran.

With the Iranian government refusing to entertain such demands, negotiation was left to the Metropolitan Police. An armed cordon had been put in place by the then-D11, the Force Firearms Unit and the predecessor to today's SCO19; however, an assault would be handled by UKSF as D11 had neither the manpower nor specialist expertise at that point to manage such an operation.

An advance element from B Squadron, 22SAS, the on-call counter-terrorist squadron at Hereford, was dispatched by its commander, Lieutenant Colonel Mike Rose (who would later be instrumental in UKSF operations in the Falklands). The rest of the squadron followed later that day, bringing with them breaching and climbing equipment, and began developing an immediate action (IA) plan at an SAS holding area at Regent's Park Barracks.

The IA initially comprised teams making their way onto the Embassy roof from neighbouring buildings and sledge-hammering their way in before following the standard urban warfare tactic of fighting down through the building. After the discovery of reinforced glass in externally facing windows and doors, the plan was modified to include explosive method of entry

Serving members of 22SAS pose in period 'black kit' equipment used during Operation *Nimrod* for a television documentary in 2000. Note the Streamlight torch (flashlight) mounted upon the second MP5 from the right – one of the first efforts to integrate a light with a weapon. (John Rogers/Getty Images)

(EMOE) techniques. Negotiations slowly saw the release of a handful of hostages as the SAS further developed their deliberate action (DA) plan.

After a hostage was executed six days into the siege, control of the incident was signed across from the Metropolitan Police to the SAS and, moments later, B Squadron struck. Two elements, Red Team and Blue Team, prepared to storm the Embassy. In a simultaneous assault, teams would enter from the ground floor, the rooftop skylight and the second-floor balconies which would be accessed by abseil. A further team would climb across to the first-floor balconies from an adjacent building.

When an operator (the Scottish Sergeant Tommy Palmer, who would sadly later die in a car accident while on operations in Northern Ireland in 1983) was caught up in his abseil rope, the use of a frame charge was precluded and the roof team was forced to resort to its sledgehammers to batter its way in. This was because when Palmer had become entangled, another operator had attempted to reach him and in the process had broken a window, inadvertently alerting the terrorist.

Once entry was achieved, the teams followed their methodical drills, lobbing in flashbang grenades in their first operational use (Germany's GSG9 had been provided with the grenades for the 1977 Lufthansa hijacking – see page 90 – but had decided not to use them for fear of setting the aircraft alight) and clearing each of the more than 50 rooms inside the Embassy, in the process killing five of the terrorists.

A police officer taken hostage had managed to keep his jacket on for the six days, concealing his issue Smith & Wesson Model 10 revolver. He had struggled with the leader of the terrorists as the SAS broke in, finally rolling away when ordered to by an operator who gunned the terrorist down. Another died after he tried to escape amongst the hostages as they were shepherded out down the main stairway. An SAS trooper recognized him from earlier intelligence briefings and managed to club him with his MP5 sending him tumbling down the stairs where he was hit by several magazines' worth of MP5 fire. In his hand was a Russian RGD-5 grenade, the pin thankfully still in place.

The hostages were moved to the rear garden of the Embassy where they were restrained and secured by other SAS operators until their identities could be confirmed. The single surviving terrorist was also discovered, having managed to escape with the hostages. Stories abound of an SAS operator preparing to haul the terrorist back into the Embassy to 'finish him off' until spotting the camera of a television crew but veterans dispute the account. Instead, the terrorist was transferred to the custody of the Metropolitan Police. Minutes later the objective was declared secure and management of the incident returned to the police with operators dropping their weapons into evidence bags for later forensic matching with terrorist wounds.

An SAS operator clambers over the balcony at the front of the embassy following the detonation of the first frame charge. The barrel of his 9x19mm MP5 sub machine gun is just visible. (Rolls Press/Popperfoto/Getty Images)

The operation had taken 17 minutes with five of the six terrorists neutralized and 19 hostages rescued. (One further hostage had been murdered as the SAS commenced their assault.) The operation was an overwhelming success, a textbook example of a hostage rescue against a multi-storey terrorist stronghold with a comparatively large number of hostages and terrorists.

Operation *Octave Shield*

Special Operations in Somalia • 2006 to present day

When Ethiopia invaded Somalia in 2006 to wipe out the Islamic Courts Union (ICU) who had captured the capitol Mogadishu, small teams of JSOC operators were embedded with their forces. Their attached combat controllers guided in AC-130 Spectre gunship strikes on al-Shabaab and al-Qaeda targets. At least one Spectre strike resulted in SEAL Team 6 operators landing in Little Birds to recover the body of a high-value target.

An operation in June 2007 resulted in a small team of SEAL Team 6 operators and an attached combat controller from the 24th Special Tactics

Squadron calling in naval gunfire support from an offshore US Navy destroyer to allow them and their Somali partner unit to escape from encircling al-Shabaab forces.

Operation *Octave Fusion* was put in place in January 2012 to rescue an American non-governmental organization (NGO) worker and her Danish co-worker involved in land mine clearance held by al-Shabaab elements. Blue Squadron of SEAL Team 6 which was the Trident on-call counter-terrorist rotation conducted a HALO (high altitude low opening) parachute drop and approached the target on foot. It swiftly engaged and killed the nine hostage takers and rescued both NGO workers unharmed. 160th Special Operations Aviation Regiment (160th SOAR) helicopters exfiltrated the team and the hostages to safety.

In October 2013, SEAL Team 6 carried out a covert beach landing by small boat outside the town of Barawe. Consisting of a reinforced troop, six operators entered the target building to snatch an al-Shabaab leader responsible for external operations including terrorist acts in Kenya, while the remaining SEALs established a perimeter. By chance an insurgent who walked outside for a cigarette spotted them and a firefight ensued. The SEALs broke contact because of the presence of large numbers of civilians on the objective and exfiltrated from the beach. It appears from equipment left behind that at least one SEAL was wounded.

US SOF (and more recently the British SAS) have been instrumental in training local Somali SOF including Danab ('lightning'), which is officially a rapid reaction unit that functions along the lines of the US Army Rangers,

US Army Special Forces soldiers driving a Polaris MRZR while conducting foreign internal defence operations with Nigerian SOF, March 2015. (Pierre Terdjman/Paris Match via Getty Images)

and Gaashaan ('the shield'), which consists of two US-trained units: Alpha and Bravo, Somalia's designated counter-terrorist intervention forces. Alpha was initially trained in the US by Naval Special Warfare while Bravo was trained locally in Mogadishu.

In 2015, US Army Green Berets and SEALs, including Team 6 operators, were amongst AMISOM (African Union Mission in Somalia) forces that conducted wide-ranging offensives against al-Shabaab. One SEAL-led operation saw them engaged by small arms, machine guns, anti-aircraft guns, RPGs, mortars, and IEDs.

In May 2017, a SEAL Team 6 operator was killed and two others (one another SEAL, the other an American translator) wounded during a night-time partnered advise and assist operation with Danab in Daarasalaam, west of Mogadishu. The objective of the mission was to kill an al-Shabaab leader and destroy his radio broadcaster used for al-Shabaab propaganda.

After silently killing three insurgent lookouts during the infiltration, the Danab forces searched the target location and killed another two al-Shabaab ensconced in a camouflaged trench. Unbeknownst to them, a third insurgent crouched in the trench waiting. It appears that the SEALs were brought forward to conduct a sensitive site exploitation (SSE) when the hidden insurgent opened fire, killing the SEAL.

A US Army HUMINT (human intelligence) specialist attached to the 3rd SFG was killed in action in June 2018 by al-Shabaab mortar fire when accompanying ANISOM forces during an offensive south-west of Mogadishu. The aim of the mission was to establish a combat outpost following the 'ink-blot' strategy of counter-insurgency to be manned by Kenyan and Somali troops.

Operations in Somalia and regional countries like Mali and Kenya are largely the preserve of SEAL Team 6, although US Army Special Forces ODAs and regular SEAL Teams are routinely deployed in training and mentoring tasks. They also conduct partnered operations, as tragically illustrated in Niger in 2017 when an Army Special Forces OSA was ambushed and four operators killed during such an operation. Most of these operations fall under the auspices of Combined Joint Special Operations Task Force – Arabian Peninsula (CJSOTF-AP) although JSOC missions are run unilaterally.

Operation *Juniper Garrett* was a JSOC-led operation targeting al-Qaeda high-value targets in the East Africa region but centred upon Somalia while Operation *Juniper Shield* was the codename for all US special operations carried out in East Africa. It was under this operation that the ambush of a 3rd SFG patrol occurred near the village of Tongo-Tongo in Niger in October 2017.

In that operation, ODA 3212 from 3rd Group was ambushed by a numerically superior force of Islamic State – Greater Sahara (IS-GS) insurgents who opened fire upon the mounted patrol with DShK heavy machine guns from technicals, RPGs, mortars and small arms fire. The ODA was in unarmoured 'Non-Tac' pick-ups and were quickly surrounded and engaged in a pitched firefight by the hundred or so insurgents. The patrol was scattered and four American and five Nigerian soldiers were killed before a complement of French special operators from neighbouring Mali arrived to reinforce the Green Berets.

The ODA was in Niger to conduct an 'advise and assist' mission with Nigerien partner forces – the newly raised Nigerian Counter Terrorism Company – but had been diverted to support a joint French and JSOC operation targeting a IS-GS high-value target in Operation *Obsidian Nomad*. When it was realized one of the American bodies was missing and feared captured, a SEAL Team 6 element deployed to Djibouti in anticipation of a rescue mission.

A former commander of US Special Operations Command Africa noted in 2018 that along with casualties in Niger and Somalia, American operators had also been wounded in operations in Kenya and a number of other locations: 'We had them [casualties] in Tunisia. We had them in Mali. We had them in Niger, Nigeria, Cameroon, and Chad. But those were kept as quiet as possible. Nobody talked about it.'*

In January 2019, five al-Shabaab terrorists attacked an international hotel in Nairobi, Kenya. In the light of the shortcomings identified after the 2013 Westgate shopping centre siege also in Nairobi, the response of the Kenyan SOF was far more nuanced.** Also present was a UKSF operator, identified in the press as being from the SAS but much more likely an SBS operator from the SBS training team working with the Kenyan Army Special Operations Regiment (SOR). A similar attack in 2016 in Burkina Faso saw a pair of Delta operators respond alongside unidentified French Commandement des Opérations Spéciales (COS) operators.

In Nigeria in 2012, Britain's SBS launched a hostage rescue to recover a kidnapped British citizen and an Italian hostage held by terrorist group Boko Haram in the city of Sokoto. Unfortunately the raid ended in failure as both hostages were executed after a Yemeni APC (armoured personnel carrier) was used to breach the gates of the target compound and before the SBS operators could reach the two men. All of the Boko Haram cell were killed by the SBS and the Nigerian special operators (who may have been drawn from Nigeria's own Special Boat Service).

In Libya, both Delta and SEAL Team 6 along with French and British special operators have been active. In October 2017, SEAL Team 6 snatched another Libyan wanted in connection with the 2012 Benghazi attack. Three years earlier in June 2014, Delta had successfully captured another terrorist leader responsible for the assault on the Consulate and CIA Annex (see page 24).

---

* https://news.vice.com/en_us/article/a3my38/exclusive-the-us-has-more-military-operations-in-africa-than-the-middle-east

** In September 2013, four jihadists conducted a roving shooting attack within the Westgate shopping centre, killing 71 and wounding over 200. The Kenyan SOF response was slow and confused, and resulted in at least one friendly fire incident.

A Special Forces ODA was embarrassingly caught on camera in 2015 during a failed infiltration into Libya. The Pentagon has admitted: 'The US is providing unique capabilities – notably intelligence, surveillance, and reconnaissance (ISR) and precision strikes – that will help enable GNA-aligned forces to make a decisive, strategic advance. A small number of US forces have gone in and out of Libya to exchange information with local forces, and they will continue to do so as we strengthen the fight against ISIL and other terrorist organizations.'

Small detachments from SEAL Team 6 have been operating for a number of years alongside French and Malian SOF in Mali to counter al-Qaeda in the Islamic Maghreb (AQIM) and Islamic State – Greater Sahara (IS-GS). Operating in blended teams with the Intelligent Support Activity (ISA), the SEALs have accompanied the French 1er RPIMa and CPA-10 on operations targeting jihadist leadership and logistical nodes.

In anti-piracy operations off the African coastline, Danish Frogmen launched an operation in February 2010 to retake a hijacked merchantman, rescuing the 25-man crew and capturing five Somalis with only warning shots fired. In May 2010, Russian Spetsnaz – possibly KSSO operators – conducted an under way visit-board-search-seizure operation on a crude oil tanker seized by Somali pirates. Ten pirates were captured and one killed in a brief firefight as the Spetsnaz regained control of the vessel. Most famously, in 2009, SEAL Team 6 rescued the captain of the Maersk Alabama with snipers engaging and killing the pirates holding him.

Operation *Row/Paradoxical/Crichton*

Special Operations in Iraq • 2003–09

UKSF deployed to Iraq in 2003 for the invasion phase under Operation *Row*. Their role was two-fold. To the west, two squadrons of 22SAS would launch vehicle-mounted operations to seize key terrain such as airfields; tie down Iraqi forces from reinforcing to the south; and in a reprise of their 1991 role, hunt for mobile Scud launchers, again to keep Israel out of the war and to reduce the Iraqi's capability to launch chemical attacks against the invasion forces.

To the north, an SBS squadron, known as Task Force 7, would be infiltrated again in vehicle-mounted patrols to attempt to resolve the surrender of an Iraqi Army corps, the leaders of which had been contacted by the CIA and UK Secret Intelligence Service (SIS) and seemingly convinced to return to barracks once hostilities began. Of the two UKSF missions, the SAS' was far more successful.

The SBS was dealt a difficult if not impossible mission; its operators soon ran into Iraqi patrols and were forced to fight a running gun battle, including against Iraqi T72 main battle tanks, to an emergency rendezvous where they were helicoptered to safety. Two operators who became separated from the main force were forced to flee to Syria on a quad bike (ATV or all-terrain vehicle) with Iraqi pursuers at their heels. The Iraqi propaganda machine made much of their captured equipment including quads, a desert patrol vehicle (DPV), a Stinger surface to air missile and a number of small arms.

The SAS task force, composed of B and D squadron, operating as Task Force 14, also ran into difficulties on its first mission. Its target was a suspected chemical weapons dump near al-Qaim, a border town close to Syria and the future site of many bloody fights as it became both a key transit station for foreign fighters entering Iraq and a safe haven for al-Qaeda in Iraq. B squadron had infiltrated Iraq from Jordan in an extended mounted patrol, while D squadron was airlifted in by Chinook, complete with its DPVs.

The first assault on the chemical dump was repulsed and one of the vehicles immobilized by enemy fire. Eventually airstrikes were called in to subdue the defenders. Soon after, in concert with the Australian Task Force 64, the SAS captured two key Iraqi airfields, providing a vital forward launch pad for Coalition operations. It also worked with the Australians in intercepting senior Iraqi officers and Baath Party officials who were attempting to escape to Syria.

After the invasion phase was concluded, UKSF went looking for work. Initially they conducted close personal protection for SIS and UK diplomatic staff in Baghdad and supported raids hunting the illusive weapons of mass destruction. Later they began to hunt down senior Baathists and Iraqi officers wanted by the Americans and made famous by the advent of the infamous deck of playing cards, which illustrated their top targets, the so-called 'Former Regime Elements' or FREs.

By this stage the SBS had been rotated home and only an understrength G Squadron remained of the SAS presence. In an intelligence vacuum, it created its own unit of native Iraqis modelled on the CIA's Scorpion Force, which had assisted in intelligence gathering during the invasion. The small team of locals, tasked with both interpreting and conducting surveillance missions for the SAS, was called the Apostles. It would become one of the most important elements in the war against the insurgency and al-Qaeda in Iraq.

British 22SAS 'Blade' (right) and unidentified JSOC operator (left) in Iraq c. 2005. The SAS trooper carries the L119A1 while the JSOC operator carries an HK416. Note that although dressed in a mix of camouflage to blend in with the British, he wears both Union Jack and US flag patches on his Paraclete plate carrier. The SAS soldier also wears a squadron patch – the bear's paw of B Squadron. (Author's Collection)

As the SAS chipped away at the playing card deck, its members began to form closer relationships with Delta Force and the Rangers with whom they shared accommodation in one of Saddam Hussein's former palaces. In October 2003, they conducted one of their first joint operations with Delta, targeting foreign fighters, with the SAS leading the assault. It did not go well. The assault force was contacted by small arms and RPG fire as it entered the target compound, which resulted in a number of assaulters wounded and one man killed, an attachment from the SBS and the first UKSF soldier to be killed in Iraq.

Delta and their cordon force of Bradley infantry fighting vehicles opened fire on the target building after a courageous effort by two SAS operators rescued one of the wounded men lying outside. After 'reducing' the target, Delta assaulted into the shell of the building and discovered up to 12 dead foreign fighters. This was the first concrete evidence of foreign fighters travelling to Iraq to assist the fledgling insurgency.

Operation *Row* became Operation *Paradoxical* in late 2003, which granted the British a wide-ranging remit to target anti-Coalition forces and in particular the 'trans-national terrorists' entering Iraq. As the insurgency gained pace, the SAS eventually began to transition from hunting the 'deck of cards' to a much more lethal adversary, al-Qaeda in Iraq (AQI) and its leader, the Jordanian terrorist Musab al-Zarqawi, who was attempting to ignite a civil war between the Sunni and the Shia. By this stage the UKSF rotation was known as Task Force Black. Operation *Paradoxical* became Operation *Crichton* in 2005.

The first operation against al-Qaeda in Iraq was Operation *Marlborough* in 2005. Delta was fully committed to western Iraq along the Syrian border with two squadrons deployed to stem the flow of arms, money and foreign fighters so *Marlborough*, a time-sensitive target packet on an AQI suicide bomber cell in Baghdad, was passed to M Squadron of the SBS, which was on the rotation. The SBS conducted a near-faultless operation, killing the three suicide bombers and retrieving significant intelligence.

The mission almost ended in calamity, however, when a low-flying Puma helicopter carrying SBS snipers was caught in the blast of one of the terrorists detonating his suicide vest as the operators gunned him down. Only luck and the phenomenal flying skills of the RAF pilot saved the helicopter and its passengers.

Marlborough became something of a watershed moment for Task Force Black and it was increasingly viewed by JSOC as an integral resource. By the end of 2005, 22SAS had been assigned Iraq, with the SBS taking responsibility for Afghanistan. Early the following year, authority was finally granted for the SAS to work alongside JSOC, with full access to American intelligence and targets, and the SAS began hitting AQI cells in and around Baghdad.

Along with Syrians, Palestinians, Jordanians, Saudis and Sudanese, the British also encountered Pakistani jihadists, foreshadowing their role in the later insurgency in Iraq. There were also the first signs of Iranian influence with the Shia militias. While the war of 'industrial counter-terrorism' continued in Baghdad, a small detachment of SAS was stationed with British forces in the south of the country, in and around Basra.

Called Operation *Hathor*, it included members of 22SAS' Special Reconnaissance Detachment, a similar organization to Delta's Operational Support Troop, which conducted undercover surveillance. In September 2009, two of the operators found themselves compromised on the streets of Basra, dodging the Iraqi Police, which had been heavily infiltrated by the insurgents, as well as the actual insurgents themselves.

The pair ended up stopped at an Iraqi Police checkpoint and believing the policemen to be at least insurgent sympathizers, ended firing on them to effect their escape. The pair were pursued and eventually captured when their locally procured undercover car ran out of steam. Soon footage of the two captured SAS operators, battered and bruised, was flashing across television screens.

After the British Army laid siege to the police station the operators were being held at, the Iraqis smuggled them out of a side door and into a waiting car. Luckily a British helicopter overhead spotted the two, disguised in Arab dish-dashas, being bundled into the vehicle and followed it to a house in the suburbs. By this stage, members of A Squadron and a platoon from the newly established Special Forces Support Group (SFSG) had arrived in Basra and conducted a hasty assault on the target house. After conducting explosive breaches, the SAS found the two prisoners tied up, alive, but with no sign of their kidnappers.

Although now with access to the full AQI and foreign fighter targeting list, the British were skittish about fully following their JSOC comrades in launching raids based on a single piece of intelligence. Instead, UKSF leadership wanted two to three corroborating sources before it would launch. Delta, under the direction of General Stanley McChrystal, followed a punishing schedule of multiple raids a night with intelligence gathered at one target developing the intelligence picture for the next.

At the same time, Operation *Hathor* was reinforced to become Task Force Spartan and began targeting Iranian agents of influence in the south, particularly aiming to stop the importation of deadly Iranian-manufactured, explosively formed projectile IEDs, which had claimed the lives of hundreds of Coalition forces and civilians.

SAS assaulters from Task Force Black in Iraq, 2006, wearing American ACU and DCU pattern uniforms, and Ranger-green Paraclete RAV plate carriers with chest-mounted holsters for their SIG-Sauer P226 pistols. Night vision devices mounted on their MICH helmets are worn here flipped up out of the way. The carbine of the right-hand soldier has the EOTech 551 optic favoured by the Regiment's colleagues of Delta Force, rather than the more usual British-issue ACOG. (Author's Collection)

It was a D Squadron operator from Task Force Spartan who became the second SAS soldier killed in action in Iraq. During a house assault in November 2006 hunting a key foreign fighter facilitator, he was hit with a single round and died at a nearby military trauma unit. The operator had been shot once before only weeks earlier and had just returned to duty when he was killed leading the assault.

Task Force Black was now redesignated Task Force Knight and was instrumental in shutting down an AQI car-bomb network in Baghdad. It had increased the frequency of its raiding and was now on an even par with Delta and the Rangers, striking perhaps as many as five targets a night. It was during one of these operations in early 2007 that a helicopter accident occurred and two SAS soldiers and an RAF aviator were crushed under an overturned Puma. One of the SAS operators survived, although seriously injured, but the other operator and the aviator could not be saved.

In 2007, the SAS received its Australian Bushmaster protected mobility vehicles and was finally able to trade in its worn-out, up-armoured HMMWVs on loan from the US Army. Since 2005, it had been increasingly experiencing small arms and RPG fire, let alone IEDs, on the exfiltration from objectives. 2007 was also the costliest in terms of lives for the Task Force Knight.

In September, an A Squadron operator was shot and killed during an assault in Baghdad, while in November two members perished in another helicopter crash during an operation near Salman Pak south-east of the capital. A Squadron had lost three members; however, it had a significant effect on AQI – in six months its members killed 88 insurgents and captured 335.

2008 was something of an anti-climax for the SAS as the 'Anbar awakening' (see page 23) and their own success in targeting the al-Qaeda networks saw less and less work becoming available for them. Instead they began hitting low-level thugs and gunmen, a waste of a strategic resource, but something which would later come to haunt them again in Afghanistan. With the majority of British forces beginning to leave Iraq in 2008 and a new surge planned for Afghanistan, Task Force Knight was officially dissolved with the end of Operation *Crichton* in May 2009.

Operation *Yukon Boulder/Viking*

Special Operations in Yemen • 2009 to present day

Yemen had been on the radar of America's JSOC since soon after 9/11. A number of undercover Delta Operational Support Troop (later G Squadron) and Intelligence Support Activity (ISA) operators conducted advance force operations to track al-Qaeda elements. Yemen has the questionable distinction

of also being the location of the first Predator UAV (unmanned aerial vehicle) strike outside of a declared war zone like Iraq or Afghanistan, when an al-Qaeda member involved in planning the attack on the USS *Cole* was killed in November 2002.

In 2006, al-Qaeda in the Arabic Peninsula (AQAP) had been formed by a joining of Saudi and Yemeni al-Qaeda members and was considered a key threat not only to Yemen but also to the entire region. Under Operation *Copper Dune*, SEAL Team 6 led US counter-terrorist efforts in Yemen supported by a detachment from Delta's Echo Squadron flying deniable Mi-17s painted in Yemeni markings; this detachment often transported Yemeni operators from the Counter Terrorism Unit (CTU), trained by US Army Special Forces and the British SAS.

Britain deployed an element from the Special Reconnaissance Regiment (SRR) seconded to the Secret Intelligence Service (SIS or MI6), to train Yemeni forces in counter-terrorism in 2006. SRR and SAS teams were operating alongside JSOC in Yemen from 2009 until the collapse of the Hadi regime in 2015 when all US and Coalition special operations personnel were

US Navy SEALs, seen here in Afghanistan, have been heavily employed in the covert war in Yemen. (US Navy, Mass Communication Specialist 1st Class Martin Cuaron)

officially withdrawn. A presence has since been established, although most US SOF missions have been launched from converted special operations Navy ships.

The SEALs conducted a successful hostage rescue mission in November 2014 with a Yemeni partner force from the CTU. They were hunting a kidnapped American but he had been moved by his captors by the time the assault was carried out on a cave in Hagar al-Saiaar. Eight other hostages were safely recovered and their AQAP hostage takers killed.

The following month, the SEALs again had intelligence on the location of the kidnapped American citizen and launched another hostage rescue operation in Dafaar alongside members of the CTU. The operation ended in failure as both the American hostage and a South African hostage were shot before the SEALs could complete their breach.

Both wounded hostages were stabilized on the objective after the SEALs killed all six terrorists. MV-22 Osprey aircraft were called in to exfiltrate the team and the hostages with an attached team from JSOC's Joint Medical Augmentation Unit fighting to save their lives. Sadly one hostage died on the flight while the other passed away on the operating table of a waiting US Navy warship.

In January 2017, one member of SEAL Team 6 was killed during a partnered operation with United Arab Emirates special operators targeting AQAP elements, including the possible presence of the leader of AQAP, in the tiny village of Yakla in southern Yemen. According to a JSOC after-action review, the operation was conducted to exploit 'captured enemy material', probably planning documentation for AQAP external operations.

The mission saw the operators take fire 'from over a dozen compounds in every cardinal direction' from 'barricaded male & female fighters'. The SEALs suffered three wounded and one operator killed in action as they eliminated an emplaced ZU-23 23mm anti-aircraft gun. Some 35 AQAP and between six and 15 civilians were also killed during the operation, with at least some of the civilian deaths caused by aerial gunfire from Marine AH-1W attack helicopters.

According to media reports, US special operators maintain a forward operating location near Yemen's port of Mukalla. This is probably where missions such as the January 2017 raid into Yakla were launched. There is also a nearby Emirati base, which supports their SOF. The US effort, probably including a contingent of SEAL Team 6 operators assigned to Task Force 27.2, is principally involved in counter-AQAP operations.

Both US Air Force Special Operations Command (AFSOC) and JSOC aircraft regularly transit to and from Mukalla Riyan Airport. In addition, unidentified French special operators were confirmed to be operating in Yemen in 2018, also working alongside SOF from the United Arab Emirates.

ACRONYMS

ACE	Army Compartmented Element (USA)
ACOG	advanced combat optical gunsight
ADIV	Algemene Dienst Inlichtingen en Veiligheid (Belgium)
AFEAU	Agrupación de Fuerzas Especiales Antiterroristas Urbanas (Colombia)
AFO	advanced force operations
AFP	Armed Forces of the Philippines
AFPSOCOM	Armed Forces of the Philippines Special Operations Command
AFSOC	Air Force Special Operations Command (US)
AGMS	Armoured Ground Mobility System
AirTEP	Airborne Tactical Extraction Platform
AKS	Politiets Aktionsstyrke (Denmark)
ALP	Afghan Local Police
AMAN	Agaf HaModi'in (Israel)
AMF	Afghan Militia Forces
AMISOM	African Union Mission in Somalia
ANASF	Afghan National Army Special Forces
ANASOC	Afghan National Army Special Operations Command
ANDSF	Afghan National Defense Security Forces
ANP	Afghan National Police
ANSOF	Afghan National Special Operations Force
AOR	area of responsibility
APC	armoured personnel carrier
APKWS	Advanced Precision Kill Weapon System
AQAP	al-Qaeda in the Arabic Peninsula

AQI	al-Qaeda in Iraq
AQIM	al-Qaeda in the Islamic Maghreb
ARAS	Anti-terrorist Operations Unit (Lithuania)
ARV	Armed Response Vehicle (UK)
ARW	Army Ranger Wing (Ireland)
ASG	Abu Sayyaf Group (Philippines)
ASM	anti-structure munition
ASR	Advanced Sniper Rifle
ATGM	anti-tank guided missile
ATMP	All Terrain Mobile Platform
ATO	Ammunition Technical Officers (UK)
ATV	all-terrain vehicle
AVI	aerial vehicle interdiction
AW	arctic warfare
AWM	Arctic Warfare Magnum
BA	Brigada Aviación (Colombia)
BAT	Brigada Antiteroristă (Romania)
BBE-M	Bijzondere Bijstandseenheid Mariniers (Netherlands)
BOA	Biuro Operacji Antyterrorystycznych (Poland)
BOPE	Batalhão de Operações Policiais Especiais (Brazil)
BRI	Brigade de Recherche et d'Intervention (Algeria)
BRI	Brigade de Recherche et d'Intervention (France)
BRI-BAC	Brigade de Recherche et d'Intervention – Brigade Anticommando (France)

BSB	Brigade Speciale Beveiligingsopdrachten (Netherlands)
CAD	combat assault dog
CAG	Combat Applications Group (USA)
CANSOFCOM	Canadian Armed Forces Special Operations Forces Command
CBRN	chemical, biological, radiological and nuclear
CCA	Combatant Craft Assault
CCFLIR	combatant craft forward-looking infrared
CCOES	Commando Conjunto de Operaciones Especiales (Colombia)
CCT	combat controller
CIA	Central Intelligence Agency (USA)
CIF	Commanders In-Extremis Force (USA)
CII	Counter Iranian Influence
CJIRU	Canadian Joint Incident Response Unit
CJSOTF	Combined Joint Special Operations Task Force (USA)
CJSOTF-AP	Combined Joint Special Operations Task Force – Arabian Peninsula (USA)
CN	counter-narcotics
COFS	Comando Interforze per le Operazioni delle Forze Speciali (Italy)
COIN	counter-insurgency
COMSUBIN	Comando Raggrupamento Subacquei e Incursori (Italy)
COPES	Commando de Operaciones Especiales (Colombia)
COS	Commandement des Opérations Spéciales (France)
CP	counter-proliferation
CPA	Commando Parachutiste de l'Air (France)
CQB	close quarter battle
CQB-R	Close Quarter Battle Receiver
CROWS	Common Remotely Operated Weapon Station
CRRC	Combat Rubber Raiding Craft
CRU	Crisis Response Unit (Afghanistan)
CSAR	combat search and rescue
CSASS	Compact Semi-Automatic Sniper System
CSO	critical skills operator
CSOR	Canadian Special Operations Regiment
CSOTC	Canadian Special Operations Training Centre
CTG	Counter Terrorism Group (Kurdish)
CTPT	Counter Terrorist Pursuit Team (Afghanistan)
CTR	close target reconnaissance
CTS	Counter Terrorist Service (Iraq)
CTSFO	Counter Terrorist Specialist Firearms Officer (UK)
CTT	Counter-Terrorist Team (New Zealand)
CTTAG	Counter Terrorist Tactical Assault Group (New Zealand))
CTU	Counter Terrorism Unit (Yemen)
CWIED	command wire detonated IED
CWST	Coalition Warfare Support Team (US)
DA	deliberate action
DA	direct action
DAE	Destacamento de Acoes Especials (Portugal)
DAGOR	Deployable Advanced Ground Off-Road
DAP	direct action penetrator
DCU	Desert Camouflage Uniform
DDMA	defence, diplomacy and military assistance
DEA	Drug Enforcement Administration (USA)
DGSE	Direction Générale de la Sécurité Extérieure (France)
DGSN	Direction Générale de Sûreté Nationale (Algeria)
DIA	Defense Intelligence Agency (USA)
DIAS	Detaşamentul de Intervenţii şi Acţiuni Speciale (Romania)
DMV	desert mobility vehicle
DO	Directorate of Operations (USA)
DPD	diver propulsion device
DPM	Disruptive Pattern Material
DPV	desert patrol vehicle
DRS	Département du Renseignement et de la Sécurité (Algeria)
DSI	Détachement Spécial d'Intervention (Algeria)
DSI	Dienst Speciale Interventies (Netherlands)
DSK	Division Schnelle Kräfte (Germany)
DSU	Directorate of Special Units (Belgium)

EBR	Enhanced Battle Rifle
EDD	explosives detection dog
EEC	Comando Especial del Ejército (Colombia)
EFP IED	explosively formed projectile IED
EKO	Einsatzkommando (Austria)
EMOE	explosive method of entry
EOD	explosive ordnance disposal
ERA	explosive reactive armour
ERU	Emergency Response Unit (Ireland)
ESI	Escadron Spécial d'Intervention (Belgium)
ETF	Expeditionary Targeting Force (USA)
ET-MP	enhanced tactical multi-purpose (grenade)
FAO	Force Appui Opérationnel (France)
FARC	Revolutionary Armed Forces of Colombia – People's Army
FAST	Fleet Anti-terrorism Security Team (USA)
FAST	Foreign-Deployed Advisory and Support Team (USA)
FBI	Federal Bureau of Investigation (USA)
FER	Fuerza Especial de Reacción (Mexico)
FES	Fuerzas Especiales (Mexico)
FESCENT	Fuerzas Especiales del Centro (Mexico)
FESGO	Fuerzas Especiales del Golfo (Mexico)
FESPA	Fuerzas Especiales del Pacifico (Mexico)
FI	Force Intervention (France)
FID	foreign internal defence
FJS IK	Fallskärmsjägarskolans Insatskompani (Sweden)
FKP	Frømandskorpset (Denmark)
FLIR	forward-looking infrared
FOE	Força de Operações Especiais (Portugal)
FOG	Field Operations Group, also known as the Foreign Operating Group (USA)
FOR	Force Observation/Recherche (France)
FORFUSCO	Force Maritime des Fusiliers Marins et Commandos (France)
FRE	Former Regime Elements (in Iraq)
FRISC	Fast Raiding Interception Special Forces Craft
FSB	Federal'naya sluzhba bezopasnosti (Russia)
FSK	Forsvarets Spesialkommando (Norway)
FUDRA	La Fuerza de Despliegue Rápido (Colombia)
GAULA	Grupos de Acción Unificada Libertad Personal (Colombia)
GCPSU	General Command of Police Special Units (Afghanistan)
GEI	Grup Especial d'Intervenció (Spain)
GEK	Gendarmerieeinsatzkommando (Austria)
GEO	Grupos de Operaciones Especiales (Spain)
GEOS	Grupos Operativos Especiales de Seguridad (Spain)
GIA	Groupe Islamique Armé (Algeria)
GIGN	Groupe d'Intervention de la Gendarmerie nationale (France)
GIPN	Groupes d'Intervention de la Police Nationale (France)
GIR	Groupe d'Intervention et de Recherche (Algeria)
GIS	Groupement d'Intervention Spécialise (Algeria)
GIS	Gruppo Intervento Speciale (Italy)
GMV	ground mobility vehicle
GOE	Grupo de Operações Especiais (Portugal)
GOI	Gruppo Operativo Incursori (Italy)
GOPES	Grupo de Operaciones Especiales (Mexico)
GOS	Gruppo Operativo Subacqueo (Italy)
GOSP	Groupement des Opérations Spéciales de la Police (Algeria)
GPNVGs	Ground Panoramic Night Vision Goggles
GROM	Grupa Reagowania Operacyjno Manewrowego (Poland)
GRS	Global Response Staff (USA)
GRU	Glavnoje Razvedyvatel'noje Upravlenije (Russia)
GRUMEC	Grupamento de Mergulhadores da Marinha do Brasil
GSG9	Grenzschutzgruppe 9 (Germany)
GSPC	Groupe Salafiste pour la Prédication et le Combat (Algeria)
GSU	General Service Unit (Kenya)
HAHO	high altitude high opening
HALO	high altitude low opening
HARAS	Height Adjustable Rescue Assault System
HJK	Hærens Jegerkommando (Norway)

HMMWV	high mobility multi-purpose wheeled vehicle
HMT	High Mobility Transporter
HRT	Hostage Rescue Team (USA)
HUMINT	human intelligence
IA	immediate action
ICDC	Iraqi Civil Defense Corps
ICTF	Iraqi Counter Terrorism Force
ICU	Islamic Courts Union
ICV	infantry carrier vehicle
IDF	Israeli Defence Force
IED	improvised explosive device
INTERFET	International Force East Timor (United Nations)
IRF	Immediate Reaction Force
IRGC	Islamic Revolutionary Guard Corps (Iran)
ISA	Intelligence Support Activity (USA)
ISAF	International Security Assistance Force (NATO)
IS-GS	Islamic State – Greater Sahara
ISIL	Islamic State
ISIS	Islamic State
ISIS-K	Islamic State – Khorasan
ISOF	Iraqi Special Operations Forces
ISR	intelligence, surveillance and reconnaissance
ISTAR	intelligence, surveillance, targeting and reconnaissance
JGK	Jægerkorpset (Denmark)
JGSDF	Japanese Ground Self Defence Force
JI	Jemaah Islamiyah (Indonesia)
JOAK	Special Public Security Command (Turkey)
JOH	Special Operations Battalions (Turkey)
JORSOCOM	Jordanian Special Operations Command
JSFG	Japanese Special Forces Group
JSOA	Joint Special Operations Area
JSOC	Joint Special Operations Command (USA and other)
JSOTF	Joint Special Operations Task Force (USA and other)
JSOTF-N	Joint Special Operations Task Force – North (USA)
JSOTF-P	Joint Special Operations Task Force – Philippines (USA)
JTAC	joint terminal attack controller
JTF2	Joint Task Force 2 (Canada)
KCT	Korps Commandotroepen (Netherlands)
KDF	Kenyan Defence Force
KNT	Kovinių narų tarnyba (Lithuania)
KSBU	Kenyan Special Boat Unit
KSK	Kommando Spezialkräfte (Germany)
KSM	Kommando Spezialkräfte Marine (Germany)
KSSO	Komandovanie sil spetsial'nalnykh operatsii (Russia)
LAW	light anti-armour weapon
LITHSOF	Lithuanian Special Operations Forces
LMV	light multi-role vehicle
LRPV	long range patrol vehicle
LRS	Long Range Surveillance unit (Kenya)
LRSW	Long Range Sniper Weapon
LTATV	light tactical all-terrain vehicle
LVAW	low visibility assault weapon
LZ	landing zone
MACOS	Military Airlift Command Operating Staff (USA)
MACV-SOG	Military Assistance Command Vietnam – Studies & Observations Group (USA)
MARCOS	Marine Commandos (India)
MARPAT	Marine Pattern
MARSOC	Marine Special Operations Command (USA)
MARSOF	Maritime Special Operations Forces (Netherlands)
M-ATV	mine resistant ambush protected all-terrain vehicle
MCS	Modular Combat System
MCT	maritime counter-terrorist
MEK	Mobile Einsatzkommando (Austria)
MEK	Mobile Einsatzkommando (Germany)
MFF	military free-fall
MINUSMA	Multidimensional Integrated Stabilization Mission in Mali (United Nations)
MJK	Marinejegerkommandoen (Norway)
MND	Ministry of National Defence (Algeria)
MOD	Ministry of Defence (UK)

MOE	method of entry	OGPK	Objective Gunner Protection Kit
MPC	multi-purpose canine	OMON	Otryad Mobil'nyy Osobogo Naznacheniya (Russia)
MPS	Metropolitan Police Service (UK)		
MRAP	mine resistant ambush protected (vehicle)	OMS	Office of Military Support (USA)
MSFV	Mobile Strike Force Vehicle brigade (Afghanistan)	OTC	Operator Training Course
		PAP	People's Armed Police (China)
MSOAG	Marine Special Operations Advisor Group (USA)	PDF	Panamanian Defense Force
		PDW	personal defence weapon
MSOB	Marine Special Operations Battalion (USA)	PGC	Presidential Guard Command (United Arab Emirates)
MSOC	Marine Special Operations Company (USA)		
MSOT	Marine Special Operations Team (USA)	PI2G	Pelotons d'intervention interrégionaux de la Gendarmerie (France)
MSR	Modular Sniper Rifle		
MTFA	marauding terrorist firearms attack	PIFWC	Persons Indicted For War Crimes
MWD	military working dog	PIRA	Provisional Irish Republican Army
MWMIK	Mobility Weapon Mounted Installation Kit	PJ	pararescue jumper
NAFCOS	Numbered Air Force Combat Operations Staff (USA)	PKK	Kurdistan Workers' Party
		PLA	People's Liberation Army (China)
NAO	named area of interest	PNP-SAF	Philippine National Police Special Action Force
NCO	non-commissioned officer		
NDS	National Directorate of Security (Afghanistan)	POH	Police Special Operations (Turkey)
		PPIED	pressure plate IED
NEDSA	Niruye Daryai Sepah-e Iran	PRC	Provincial Response Company (Afghanistan)
NEST	Nuclear Emergency Search Team (USA)		
NGO	non-governmental organization	PRU	Provincial Response Unit (Afghanistan)
NI	Nationella Insatsstyrkan (Sweden)	PRV	Protected Response Vehicle
NLD SOCOM	Netherlands Special Operations Command	PSR	precision sniper rifle
NMU	National Mission Unit (Afghanistan)	QRF	Quick Reaction Force
NOCS	Nucleo Operativo Centrale di Sicurezza (Italy)	RAF	Royal Air Force (UK)
		RAID	Recherche, Assistance, Intervention, Dissuasion (France)
NOD	night observation device		
NOPO	Counter-terrorism Special Force (Iran)	RAR	Royal Australian Regiment
NORSOF	Norwegian Special Operations Forces	RCIED	remote controlled IED
NSCV	non-standard commercial vehicle	RDP	Régiment de Dragons Parachutistes (France)
NSG	National Security Guard (India)		
NSTV	non-standard tactical vehicle	RESPFOR	Response Force (multi-national)
NSWDG	Naval Special Warfare Development Group (USA)	RHFS	Régiment d'Hélicoptères des Forces Spéciales (France)
NTC	National Transitional Council (Libya)	RIB	rigid inflatable boat
NVGs	night vision goggles	RIDER	Rapid Intervention Droppable Equipment for Raiders
NZSAS	New Zealand Special Air Service Regiment		
ODA	Operational Detachment Alpha	RPG	rocket-propelled grenade
OEF	Operation *Enduring Freedom*	RPIMa	Régiment de Parachutistes d'Infanterie de Marine (France)
OEF-A	Operation *Enduring Freedom – Afghanistan*		

RPO	rocket-propelled flamethrower
RRC	Regimental Reconnaissance Company (USA)
RRT	Rapid Response Team (Netherlands)
RRTF	Reinforced Regional Task Force (Sweden)
RSOV	Ranger special operations vehicle
RSTB	Ranger Special Troops Battalion (USA)
RTF	Reconstruction Task Force (Australia)
SAA	Syrian Arab Army
SAD	Special Activities Division (USA)
SADM	special atomic demolition munition
SAF	Singaporean Armed Forces
SAG	Special Action Group (India)
SAPI	Small Arms Protective Insert
SARC	Special Amphibious Reconnaissance Corpsman (USA)
SAS	Special Air Service (22SAS = UK)
SAS	Sualtı (Turkey)
SASR	SAS Regiment (Australian)
SASS	Semi-Automatic Sniper System
SAT	Detasemen Khusus (Indonesia)
SAT	Su Altı Taarruz (Turkey)
SBS	Special Boat Service (UK)
SBU	Ukrainian Security Service
SCAAT	Service Central Algérien pour Antiterroriste
SCAR	Special Operations Forces Combat Assault Rifle
SCO19	Specialist Firearms Command (Specialist Crime & Operations 19) (UK)
SCORAT	Service de Coordination Opérationnelle et de Renseignement Antiterroriste (Algeria)
SD	Schalldämpfer
SDF	Syrian Democratic Forces
SDV	swimmer delivery vehicle
SEAL	Sea-Air-And-Land (USA)
SEG	Sondereinsatzgruppe (Austria)
SEK	Spezial Einsatzkommando (Germany)
SFA	security force assistance
SFC	Special Forces Command (Turkey)
SFG	Special Forces Group
SFIW	Special Forces Individual Weapon
SFOD	Special Forces Operational Detachment (USA and others)
SFR	Special Forces Regiment (Slovakia)
SFSG	Special Forces Support Group (UK)
SFTG	Special Forces Task Group (Australia)
SFW	Special Forces Weapon
SIG	Särskilda Inhämtningsgruppen (Sweden)
SIIAS	Independent Special Interventions and Actions Service (Romania)
SIS	Secret Intelligence Service (MI6) (UK)
SMW	Special Mission Wing (Afghanistan)
SOAG	Special Operations Advisory Group (international)
SOAR	Special Operations Aviation Regiment (USA)
SOAS	Special Operations Aviation Squadron (Canada)
SOAT	Special Operations Advisory Team (Slovakia)
SOC	Special Operations Command (United Arab Emirates)
SOC FWD	Special Operations Command, Forward
SOCOM	Special Operations Command (US and other)
SOCOMD	Special Operations Command (Australia)
SOER	Special Operations Engineer Regiment (Australia)
SOF	Special Operations Force (Singapore)
SOF	special operations forces
SOFA	Status of Force Agreement (governed the deployment of US forces in Iraq)
SOG	Särskilda Operationsgruppen (Sweden)
SOG	Special Operations Group (Czech Republic)
SOK	Special Operations Kandak (Afghanistan)
SOKOM	Specialoperationskommandoen (Denmark)
SOP	Lietuvos Specialiųjų Operacijų Pajėgos (Lithuania)
SOPMOD	Special Operations Peculiar Modifications
SOR	Special Operations Regiment (Kenya)
SOTF	Special Operations Task Force (Singapore)
SOTG	Special Operations Task Group (Australia)
SOTU	Special Operations Task Unit (Hungary)
SOTV	Special Operations Tactical Vehicle
SOV	special operations vehicle
SOV-Cdo	Special Operations Vehicle – Commando

SOV-MH	Special Operations Vehicle – Mobility Heavy
SPAP	Samodzielny Pododdział Antyterrorystyczny Policji (Poland)
SpR Det	Specialist Reconnaissance Detachment (UK)
SR	special reconnaissance
SRG	Special Ranger Group (India)
SRI	Serviciul Român de Informaţii (Romania)
SRR	Special Reconnaissance Regiment (UK)
SRV	surveillance and reconnaissance vehicle
SSE	sensitive site exploitation
SSF	Special Security Forces (Saudi Arabia)
SSG	Särskilda Skyddsgruppen (Sweden)
SSG	Special Service Group (Pakistan)
SSGN	Special Service Group (Navy) (Pakistan)
SSO	sily spetsial'nykh operatsii (Russia)
SST	Search and Rescue Security Team
ST	SEAL Team (USA)
STAR	Special Tactics and Rescue (Singapore)
STRATCOM	Strategic Command (USA)
STS	Special Tactics Squadron (USA)
SURG	Suppressed Upper Receiver Group
SUV	sport utility vehicle
SVR	Sluzhba vneshney razvedki Rossiyskoy Federatsii (Russia)
SWAT	Special Weapons and Tactics
SWCS	Shallow Water Combat Submersible
TAR	tactical augmented reality
TEK	Terrorelhárítási Központ (Hungary)
THU	Tactical Helicopter Unit (USA)
TIGRES	Tropa de Inteligencia y Grupos de Respuesta Especial de Seguridad (Honduras)

TTP	Tehreek-e-Taliban Pakistan
UAE	United Arab Emirates
UAV	unmanned aerial vehicle
UDT	Underwater Demolition Team (USA)
UEI	Unidad Especial de Intervención (Spain)
UGV	unmanned ground vehicle
UI	Unit Interventie (Netherlands)
UIK	Underbelly Improvement Kit
UIM	Unit Interventie Mariniers (Netherlands)
UKSF	UK Special Forces
ULCV	Ultra-Light Combat Vehicle
UNOPES	Unidad de Operaciones Especiales (Mexico)
UOE	Unidad de Operaciones Especiales (Spain)
UOU	Unit of Special Assignment (Slovakia)
URNA	Útvar rychlého nasazení (Czech Republic)
USMC	US Marine Corps
USP	universal self-loading pistol
USV	unmanned surface vehicle
UUV	unmanned undersea vehicle
UW	unconventional warfare
VBIED	vehicle-borne IED
VBSS	visit-board-search-seizure
VI	vehicle interdiction
WMD	weapons of mass destruction
WMIK	Weapon Mounted Installation Kit
YAT	Yekîneyên Antî Teror (Kurdish/Syrian)
YPG	Yekîneyên Parastina Gel (Kurdish)
YPJ	Yekîneyên Parastina Jin (Kurdish)
ZJ	Zasahova Jednotka (Czech Republic)

INDEX